POLICY ANALYSIS
FOR PUBLIC DECISIONS

THE DUXBURY PRESS SERIES ON PUBLIC POLICY
Charles O. Jones, University of Pittsburgh
General Editor

An Introduction to the Study of Public Policy, 2nd edition
Charles O. Jones

The Domestic Presidency: Decision-Making in the White House
John H. Kessel (Ohio State University)

Public Policy and Politics in America
James E. Anderson, David W. Brady (University of Houston) and Charles L. Bullock, III (University of Georgia)

Understanding Intergovernmental Relations
Deil Wright (University of North Carolina)

Introduction to Budgeting
John Wanat (University of Kentucky)

Bureaucracy and Public Policy
Kenneth Meier (University of Oklahoma)

Policy Analysis for Public Decisions
Duncan MacRae, Jr. and James Wilde (University of North Carolina)

OF RELATED INTEREST

A Logic of Public Policy: Aspects of Political Economy
L. L. Wade (University of California, Davis) and Robert L. Curry, Jr. (California State University, Sacramento)

Democracy in America: A Public Choice Perspective
L. L. Wade (University of California, Davis) and R. L. Meek (Colorado State University)

Politics, Change, and the Urban Crisis
Bryan Downes (University of Oregon)

Duxbury Press
North Scituate
Massachusetts

Policy Analysis for Public Decisions

DUNCAN MacRAE, JR. and JAMES A. WILDE
University of North Carolina
at Chapel Hill

Duxbury Press
A Division of Wadsworth, Inc.

Policy Analysis for Public Decisions was edited and prepared for
composition by Jill O'Hagan. Interior design was provided
by Cindy Daniels. The cover was designed by Oliver Kline.

Library of Congress Cataloging in Publication Data
MacRae, Duncan, Jr.
Policy analysis for public decisions.

Bibliography: p.
Includes index.
1. Policy sciences. I. Wilde, James A.,
joint author. II. Title.
H61.M4178   300'.1'8   78–26053
ISBN 0–87872–207–6

Printed in the United States of America
1 2 3 4 5 6 7 8 9 — 83 82 81 80 79

To EDITH and MELINDA

CONTENTS

CHAPTER **4**

ALTERNATIVES, MODELS, AND DECISIONS

CHAPTER **5**

PERFECT MARKETS, IMPERFECT MARKETS, AND POLICY CORRECTIONS

It is commonplace for us to think of elected decision makers or corporate giants, union leaders, scientists, bureaucrats, and judges when discussing or writing about public policy. Perhaps this fact itself tells us something significant about the state of democracy. There was a time when students of democratic politics might have thought first about the citizen as the vital actor in public policy making.

In *Policy Analysis for Public Decisions*, Duncan MacRae, Jr., and James Wilde assume an important role for citizens and offer instruction for realizing that responsibility. In what surely demands to be a popular approach, MacRae and Wilde specify the ethical basis for all public policy decisions and encourage students as citizens to become involved. This emphasis is not new to the thinking of Duncan MacRae. He has incorporated it into his teaching at the University of North Carolina at Chapel Hill, with the able cooperation of James Wilde, an economist, and he has expressed it eloquently in his important book *The Social Function of Social Science* (New Haven: Yale University Press, 1976):

> The field of policy analysis has a natural affinity with interdisciplinary ethical discourse. It needs this discourse so that its practitioners can intelligently define both their own ends and the relation of their speciality to democratic political responsibility. Wide-ranging ethical discourse will be facilitated by the education of undergraduates, whose responsibilities as citizens may enlarge their view relative to the occupational concerns, career channels, and employment constituencies of applied graduate schools. [P. 291]

These views place the authors squarely in the tradition of classical democratic citizenship, for example, as expressed by John Dewey in *The Public and Its Problems* (New York: Holt, 1927). The responsibilities of Dewey's citizen in the "Great Community" are very demanding, for they require attentiveness to and action on precisely the matters emphasized by MacRae and Wilde.

> The essential need, in other words, is the improvement of the methods and conditions of debate, discussion and persuasion. That is the [author's emphasis] problem of the public. We have asserted that this improvement depends essentially upon freeing and perfecting the processes of inquiry and of dissemination of their conclusions. [P. 208]

Creating a politically aware, active, and mature public remains a significant challenge in modern society. Dewey's skepticism about the wisdom and benevolence of "the policies of the experts" is even more cogent today. *Policy Analysis for Public Decisions* is, therefore, more than a book for the students. It also seeks to persuade teachers that it is right and proper to direct students into the ways of interdisciplinary policy analysis. The practical and theoretical learning available in these pages derives from the authors' integrated view of democratic society. That feature is what makes this work particularly compelling and therefore, hopefully, attractive to teachers of public policy.

Charles O. Jones
University of Pittsburgh

This is an introductory textbook in the developing field of policy analysis. Its purpose is to draw together topics that are now treated in the teaching of separate disciplines and professions and to show that these topics belong together in a new framework. In providing such a framework we aim not only at the education of students but also at gradual structural change in colleges and universities through the formation of groups of teachers who combine their skills in this new field.

The field of policy analysis is a recent development in undergraduate instruction. A number of programs exist that combine these topics, but they are typically regarded as "interdisciplinary," that is, based mainly on knowledge located in existing disciplines. We believe, however, that policy analysis constitutes a field that should be defined by its own internal logic. For this reason courses and materials developed for existing disciplines do not fit together optimally for instruction in policy analysis.

Eventually, separate introductory and advanced texts based on this internal logic will become available. Our intention in this text has been to write not simply for college students beginning in this field but also for teachers of policy analysis at all levels. This intention implies that portions of the text may be skipped by beginning students and may be more appropriate for undergraduates who have learned the relevant prerequisite technical concepts in other courses, especially in economics. The section "Statistical Models" in chapter 4 may require previous work in statistics; and chapter 5, work in economics. We include numerous end-of-chapter notes so that teachers and students trained in one discipline can enlarge their reading in others.

The chapters of this book correspond roughly to subfields of policy analysis that are now taught separately, for the most part, in individual college or university departments. The definition of problems (chapter 2) is dealt with in sociology, political science, and history. General ethical criteria for choice (chapter 3) are dealt with in philosophy and economics as well as in political theory. Models that may be used to connect policies with their effects (chapters 4 and 5) are treated in all the natural and social sciences. Such models may be used in decisions among alternative policies. Decisions themselves are treated in general terms in statistics, if decision theory is stressed, as well as in operations research, systems analysis, and systems engineering. Political feasibility (chapter 6) is treated in political science, sociology, anthropology, and public administration; "personal feasibility" may be dealt with in courses in ethics and religion. The cyclical features of program evaluation (chapter 7) are taught in professional schools as well as in applied social science. In an undergraduate program in policy analysis, more specialized "core" courses might be developed about topics indicated by our chapters.

The title *Policy Analysis for Public Decisions* can be interpreted in several ways. By analogy with Lincoln's phrase, government policies can involve government *of* the public, *by* the public, and *for* the public. The first of these meanings is most general as all government policies affect the public or govern it. The second, however, will be a special concern of this book as we are concerned with government *by* the public or by the informed citizen who can analyze policies. The third meaning is also especially important for this book as we are concerned with government policies aimed at benefiting the public, that is, furthering the public interest or the general welfare. Throughout the book we join the second and third meanings in referring to analysis *by* citizens who seek policies *for* the public, in this sense. Analysis as we describe it can also be used by government officials and employees, acting as representatives rather than as citizens and seeking policies that further the public interest.

Our stress on policy analysis by the public and for the public is thus directed at the reader as an *informed citizen*. It is intended to place *systematic ethics* at the center of the field—that is, principles of right action stated clearly and organized logically. Only in the role of citizen is a person free (in a free society) to choose his or her own general system of ethics, or notion of the general welfare, and then to participate with others in policy choice in terms of such a system. An individual may also make personal choices in ethical terms, such as choices concerning occupation or disposition of personal resources, for example. But in the role of an employee the individual is limited by the employment contract to serve the employer's goals; a consultant or adviser must serve the client; a manager must serve stockholders and customers; and even an elected public official is constrained to serve the public or a constituency. In the role of an employee a person may introduce a concern for ethics or for the general welfare. This concern is clearest and most distinct from narrower interests, however, in the role of the citizen.

Graduate schools of policy analysis typically teach their students "economic ethics," a system of general criteria for choice related to welfare economics and cost-benefit analysis, which sometimes appears to be not ethics but merely economic science. This economic system of choice, which has the advantage of generality and systematic treatment, will be considered here as one among various ethical systems that may constitute bases for policy choice.

Graduate schools in policy analysis have combined elements such as those we present here, for the training of advisers and professionals who are expected to analyze government choices. But it is also important that citizens have access to systematic instruction in policy analysis. Even if active citizens are not trained as professional analysts or engaged as advisers, they may nevertheless play important parts in the making of public decisions, and the quality of their participation influences the eventual quality of the decisions. They thus need every resource that is available to professional analysts and staff advisers —and more.

Professional schools in fields such as law, medicine, and engineering prepare their graduates for particular roles in society, making use of special skills but not encompassing the full range of policy choice. Citizens, however, must learn to cope with a wider range of choice, and of course the professional must also be a citizen. At present, undergraduate education constitutes the major locus of possible development of the competent citizen-analyst. Eventually, adult education and general graduate education, conducted inside or outside the classroom, may furnish other possibilities for advanced work in this field for persons who are not making it a career.

Case studies are an essential ingredient in the teaching of policy analysis. We present only relatively short cases in this text. Teachers who use it are encouraged to make use of supplementary detailed cases that are timely and relevant to their students' interests. Such case studies can serve as approximations of the actual experience of working with others on problems of policy choice. A good case study can be used to weave together the various aspects of policy choice that we discuss. It can illustrate others as well: the irrelevant information that we must separate from the relevant; the important personal characteristics of key individuals and the peculiarities of organizations involved in decisions; the short-run histories and life histories that connect yesterday's commitments, promises, alliances, and enmities with today's and tomorrow's possibilities; and a sense of the often unspoken cultural and time-dependent assumptions that constrain the perspectives of persons involved in decisions.

The most helpful case studies for policy analysis are those that combine the following elements:

1. A problem or an opportunity, together with the perceptions of it by various relevant persons or groups. The case, as presented prior to the student's analysis, should leave some uncertainty in the student's mind as to the right course of action.

2. Alternative feasible policies that may reasonably be considered by decision makers, with the possibility that the student cannot only evaluate alternatives that were considered but also invent new alternatives of his or her own.

3. The possibility of applying ethical criteria (and not merely criteria of the analyst's personal preferences or of political feasibility) to the choice among alternatives. At least some of these ethical principles should require evaluation of anticipated consequences of policy alternatives.

4. The presentation of information relevant to these ethical criteria. Unlike many legal cases in which acts must be fitted to legal prescriptions, a case in policy analysis involves predicting the consequences of policies and relating them to general ethical principles.

5. A consideration of political possibilities: allies, commitments, mobilization of support, decision procedures and action-channels, resources, opponents, persons threatened, and organizational goals.

In addition to possessing these elements, the case studies used with this text should be broadly distributed over subject-matter areas to demonstrate the generality of the field and the insights that may be gained by comparing analyses across areas. In teaching the course on which this book is based, we have used cases in the areas of economic regulation, income redistribution, health, education, and foreign policy. Other areas are suggested by the examples in the text.

Few of the cases we have found include full detail on all the elements above. We hope, however, that in the near future more and better cases will be available in print or portrayed on film or videotape. Cases that are being developed in the graduate schools of public policy may be particularly useful.

Exercises are provided at the end of each chapter for review of the principles presented, and suggested answers are given after the text. Those marked "Advanced Exercises" require either reading ahead in the book, possession of special skills such as facility in calculus, or study of policy questions not discussed in the text. These exercises may be used optionally by students in a basic course who wish to pursue the topics of the chapters further, or they may be used when the text is employed in a more advanced course.

This text can also be used as parallel reading in a more advanced course in which each student chooses his or her own policy problem and works on it through a semester. The senior author has taught such a course for several years, guiding students in their choice of problems and requiring reports on an aspect of the analysis every two weeks. The interchange among students about their reports on projects provides vivid illustrations of the principles in the text.

Readers are encouraged to send us suggestions for revision of this book.

We would like to express our appreciation to the following people who reviewed the manuscript and made several valuable suggestions: Dr. Charles O. Jones, the University of Pittsburgh; Ernest Engelbert, the University of California, Los Angeles; Richard Winters, Dartmouth College; and Louis Weschler, the University of Southern California.

We appreciate the assistance of Gert Rippy, who typed several earlier versions of this book; Betty Ann Dickerson, who typed the final version; Dietrich Schroeer and Charles Hafter, each of whom gave detailed suggestions on several chapters; Robley Winfrey, who gave useful criticisms of Case 4–A; the students who have given us their reactions to previous versions; Jill O'Hagan, who edited the manuscript with care; and the efficient staff of Duxbury Press. The responsibility for errors is of course ours.

1
What Is Policy Analysis?

You are a member of various political communities—a citizen of a nation, state, county, and city or town, and probably a member of nongovernmental groups as well. In each of these communities you have opportunities to influence its choices by voting, working in organized groups, talking or writing to people, or publicizing your position on issues.

The types of choices made by these communities are very diverse. The national community makes choices about taxation, spending, regulation; and about health, education, poverty, social security, the environment, and foreign and military policy. States, counties, localities, and special districts are concerned with many of these same problems, though less with foreign policy and more with primary and secondary education, transportation, police and fire protection, waste disposal, and local recreation. Residential groups, neighborhood associations, clubs, and students' associations also often make decisions affecting their members or try to influence the decisions of larger communities.

You cannot become expert or influential on every issue that all these communities must decide; but some people become more involved than others, and all of us become involved in at least some such choices. The field of policy analysis provides a body of concepts and principles aimed at helping you make choices intelligently, ethically, and effectively.

A chosen course of action significantly affecting large numbers of people is a *policy*. If chosen by government, it is a *public policy*. If chosen by a private organization or an influential private individual, it can still affect large numbers of people, and if the policy is judged in terms of the general welfare or general rightness, it may be analyzed in the ways that we shall discuss. A policy typically involves more than the administrative application of an existing rule to a single case. The decision of a college to admit one applicant is not a policy, but its decision as to what documents to ask all applicants to submit or what weights to place on various sorts of information about applicants is a policy. If the college is publicly supported, public policy is involved.

A policy usually involves a rule, or settled course of action that is to be followed in numerous cases. We shall also include as a "policy choice" any single large choice among possible policies that is analyzable in systematic terms such as the choice President Kennedy faced in the Cuban missile crisis of 1962. A distinguishing feature of a "policy choice," as we define it, is that the choice is expected to make enough difference to warrant our devoting effort and resources to systematic analysis of its expected consequences.[1]

Choices of this magnitude may be made at various stages in the process that connects ideas with outcomes: for example, when plans are proposed, criticisms examined, or presumed causal relations analyzed. Further, these choices may include the passage of laws, the rendering of judicial decisions, or the making of administrative decisions in public or private organizations. Whatever the circumstances under which a policy proposal is made, the proposal must be stated explicitly if it is to be analyzed. A "policy statement" that is merely a verbal indication of a general desired direction of action, even if it is influential, cannot ordinarily be analyzed precisely in the terms we shall consider here. Such a policy statement might be a declaration of a "war on poverty," but this war is not a ready subject of analysis until it is specified as a job training program or a reform of the welfare system.

As we define it, policy analysis is *the use of reason and evidence to choose the best policy among a number of alternatives*. There are two other definitions currently held. The first distinguishes policy analysis from policy-related research, stating that policy analysis "does not include the gathering of information." For us, however, it does. The second definition restricts the term to "*explaining* the causes and consequences of various policies" and excludes from policy analysis consideration of "what governments *ought* to do, or bringing about changes in what they do." [2] We, on the other hand, *are* concerned with the choice of policies that governments ought to follow and with bringing them about.

POLICY ANALYSIS
AND THE INFORMED CITIZEN

The material we shall present in this book has much in common with analyses made for business decisions or for staff reports to governmental officials. It differs, however, in that we expect you as a citizen to make up your own mind as to what goals are to be sought and to define these goals in terms of notions of general rightness, the general welfare, or the public interest. We ask, first, that your goals be general ones and not the goals of profit, advantage, or power of particular groups. Secondly, we ask that your goals be your own, and not those of an employer. Even the ethics of a professional group or of a political association may sometimes support the advantage of special groups rather than society as a whole.

We here imply a notion of the citizen's role that is different from one that many political scientists and economists describe. For them a citizen is a person who is rational in seeking his self-interest or the interest of his group Thus, they ask only whether a citizen can perceive the difference in positions among candidates or parties, as these positions might affect *him*. We ask, on the other hand, that you analyze the effects of possible policies on *all* citizens and perhaps noncitizens as well. We imply a notion of democracy as a collective quest for the *general* welfare rather than as simply a resultant of numerous selfish pressures from interest groups. The role we propose may be difficult for all citizens to fulfill, but we believe that as many should try to do so as possible. It is you as citizen-analyst that we address in this book.

A further aspect of the citizen-analyst role may also be difficult for all to fulfill: the carrying out of detailed analysis itself. Citizens typically have far less time and resources for analysis than do experts. Yet it is precisely because we need citizens who can check up on experts and criticize their recommendations constructively that we ask that you try. It may be that only a small part of the citizenry will be able to carry out policy analyses. If so, we need to be sure that these citizens have notions of the general welfare that represent the welfare of the other citizens who do not carry out analyses. The citizen-analysts may assure this representation by explaining their analyses to their fellow citizens; by being dispersed among various social groups, rather than being associated with only a few interests; and by being recruited from diverse social origins. The mere fact that they are only a small part of the citizenry does not mean that their judgments must be biased, narrow, or elitist in an undesirable sense. And we favor the extension of analytic competence among as many citizens as possible. A body of citizens who are policy analysts would seek not their own private interests but the general welfare through their analyses. They may sometimes choose to forego these calculations or analyses of the general welfare and to vote simply in terms of their personal or group interests. But ideally they should do so only if they have been convinced by analysis that voting in these terms will further the general welfare.

RELATIONS OF POLICY ANALYSIS TO OTHER FIELDS

We may show the relation of policy analysis to other fields with the help of our definition: Policy analysis is the use of *reason and evidence* to make the best policy choice. We must look at the evidence and check one source against others if we can, before we choose a preferred policy alternative. We must also look for logical relations between evidence and choice and ask whether a piece of evidence really relates the values we are seeking to the alternatives we wish to consider. The use of reason and evidence is characteristic of all the basic and applied sciences taught in colleges and universities.

The systematic analysis of policy choices often draws on generalizations from the sciences. If the consequences of a policy alternative flow largely from technology, their evaluation involves applied natural science. The comparison of one technology with another is known as "technology assessment." If the consequences depend on human interactions, their prediction can involve applied social science. Over and above the assessment of expected consequences of policies, we must also ask how problems arise and how proposed policies are put into effect; these aspects of our analysis are particularly related to the social sciences.

Although science is involved in many policy choices, these choices cannot be made on the basis of science alone. They involve ethical or philosophical considerations. Intuitive, or nonscientific, knowledge is also involved in policy choices, since all real problems ramify into realms where science can tell us little. The very fitting of a scientific model to a real problem involves judgments that certain variables can be neglected and that others correspond to certain observations.

Reason is used to trace causal relations between policies and their expected effects. It is also used in relating values to the effects of policies, and values to one another. If our policies are to be consistent, we should relate them to general principles of valuation: ethical principles. In an example treated in case 4–A we consider the choice of an optimum speed limit. People who are concerned with the values of conserving energy or reducing accidents may take these values as reasons for reducing the speeds of vehicles. But we must also consider the value of reducing the time required to reach our destinations, a value favoring faster rather than slower speeds. Conflicting values such as these have to be reconciled, or tradeoffs between them have to be made, if we are to choose policies that reflect as many of our values as possible. Such tradeoffs may often be made by relating each particular value to a larger value system such as that of cost-benefit analysis. You need not use this particular value system for your policy choices. But the advantage of relating particular values to a larger value system is that it permits more consistent choice of policies. Thus, reason is involved in valuative questions as well as factual ones.

As policy analysis aims at choosing the *best* policy among a number of alternatives, it requires you to select your own values or ethical principles and relate them to the expected consequences of various possible policies. The values that guide policy analysis are also studied in philosophy and to some extent in economics. "Expected" consequences must be considered so as to include not only the value of a policy, if put into effect, but also the chance that it can be put into effect.

Policy analysis especially draws on the social sciences. But the knowledge useful for policy analysis is not identical with that of any particular social science. It involves variables over which we may exercise influence, rather than historical processes that we cannot affect. It draws its problems from the realm of action, rather than from the questions asked by particular disciplines.[3] For this reason it typically combines various disciplines and their methods, rather than being restricted to a single scientific discipline.[4] The disciplines on which we shall draw include sociology, philosophy, economics, statistics, and political science as well as other fields.

In some of its features policy analysis tends more to regard our fellow human beings as free—and as partners in dialogue with ourselves—than does social science. In predicting the consequences of policies for persons we make use of deterministic models of their behavior. But in the assessment of political feasibility we consider interactions with other persons whom we persuade and to whom we make promises. In these actions we do not simply observe or manipulate them, but treat them as we expect to be treated ourselves.

Imagination and practicality are also necessary in policy analysis. Imagination is required because the best alternative may be one that has not been tried before or one that has been tried in another city, state, or nation than our own. Practicality is required because we often operate under political constraints and limitations of time. We should not waste our effort analyzing possibilities that are unacceptable in the existing political situation or that cannot be implemented in time.

Policy analysis differs from the concerns of the professions, although it overlaps with them. Various professions face policy choices in education, journalism, health, foreign affairs, welfare, population, law enforcement, and public administration. Professional schools often deal with problems of policy choice. Policy analysis, however, draws together common elements in many of these more specific training programs, such as those shared by health policy and educational policy. It asks whether goals such as health and education can be furthered by means other than the services of the medical or educational professions and whether crime can be reduced by means other than police and correctional services. We believe that the expert knowledge that professionals have about policy choices should be shared with the informed citizen, who acts not through professional roles but through political parties, voluntary associations, voting, and intelligent private discussion.

THE ELEMENTS OF POLICY ANALYSIS

Each analysis of a policy choice involves a set of common elements. The later chapters in this book set out these elements in detail. We shall now summarize them briefly, and in this summary we shall point out further relations between policy analysis and other fields.

1. *Definition of the problem* (chapter 2). In defining the problem you have two tasks: to understand how others see it and to redefine it more clearly for your analysis. Others' definitions of the problem provide initial clues as to what values they hold and what policies they will support. Sometimes, however, their definitions are vague or deal with only parts of a larger problem.

When you decide just what problem you wish to analyze, you are excluding some questions and including others. If, for example, you are concerned with a fuel shortage, you can enlarge the problem to the scope of the nation or the world and include alternative ways of organizing international trade and production, regulating fuel-producing industries, or deciding how self-sufficient our economy should be. You can also limit your definition of the problem to the local level and consider local policies for dealing with the shortage, such as local rationing, car pools, or energy savings in homes and factories. Between these large and small views of the problem you might also consider whether the national market for fuel and energy is functioning as a competitive market should, and if not, whether remedies are available.

As you choose among various definitions of the problem, you will also explicitly or implicitly choose the length of time required for the analysis and the ease or difficulty of getting your recommendations accepted. If your definition of the problem is the same as that held by the persons who can influence the adoption of solutions, your task in implementing a solution will be less difficult than if you have to persuade them to accept your definition.

Several of the social sciences treat the ways in which problems come to be defined. Sociology considers definition of problems in its subfield that treats "social problems"; political science, in the discussion of how issues and political symbols develop and change; history, in the consideration of the ways in which the interpretation of past events constrains and defines later situations. In addition, we must consider the ways in which we ourselves can and should intervene to try to influence others' definition of the problem.

2. *Criteria for choice* (chapter 3). Systematic analysis of policies requires clear and consistent statement of the criteria by which policies are to be judged. These criteria are the subject matter of philosophy or ethics but are also considered within the social sciences, especially in economics and political science.

One criterion widely used for policy choice is reflected in the working of a free market: the satisfaction of individual preferences. Some interpretations of democratic choice see that choice as based on the satisfaction of citizens' preferences. However, there is a difference between voting in terms of selfish preferences—voting for one's own welfare—and voting in terms of maximizing the combined satisfaction of everyone's preferences—voting in terms of the general welfare. Even if we should believe that the good life consists in the satisfaction of preferences, we would still ask that the policy analyst be concerned, not with the satisfaction of personal preferences, but with some combination of the preferences of all.

There are also numerous other bases for ethical systems that can be used in making policy choices. These include justice or equity among individuals; the development or perfection of the individual; and the individual's subjective "quality of life," which is sometimes different from the satisfaction of personal demands or preferences.

It is especially important for you to consider the ethical or philosophic bases of policy choice. In our jobs we are given criteria for choice by the organizations that employ us. If we are elected representatives, we are urged to follow the wishes of our constituents. If we are judges, we are expected to interpret the law rather than to make new laws. But the citizen in a democracy is the equivalent of the "prince" or ruler.[5] No one can tell the citizen what his basic values should be, and he must formulate them for himself.

Even if you place the interests of some political community above your own personal interests, your criteria of choice may still be narrow. You may decide in terms of benefits or costs to your particular political unit at the expense of outsiders. You may, therefore, vote to exclude outsiders from your town when it is faced with congestion. When taxpayers outside your community provide federal funds for grants to your community, you may neglect to count these payments as costs of community projects, or you may disregard the benefits those projects produce for outsiders. You may neglect to count the fees of your profession as a social cost when a proposed policy requires the use of professional services. Thus, as a member of a community or a profession you may use unduly narrow criteria for policy choice. As a citizen of a nation you may choose in terms of the national interest rather than that of a region or town, but even then you may be neglecting the interests of foreigners.

We are concerned with choice between policies that are better or worse, right or wrong, for the public or for humanity generally. Although standards of rightness cannot be proved scientifically, a political community can discuss them rationally. Whatever differences may exist among the standards of various individuals or groups, a standard that is narrow relative to that community cannot command wide consensus. Thus, we shall not consider choices aimed only at the happiness of one person, the profits of one firm, or the power of a single political organization. Some of these more narrowly based choices can affect large numbers of people and can be analyzed by means of reason and evidence; an example is the use of research to promote the efficiency of a firm. But we are here concerned only with policies chosen in terms of systematic ethical standards such as the general welfare or the public interest.

3. *Alternatives, models, and decisions* (chapter 4). To formulate policies, we need to generate a range of alternatives or possibilities that will cope with the problem, minimize harmful side effects, circumvent political objections, and produce information that will aid further choices. One of the alternatives we always consider is to do nothing, or not to intervene in the course of events. Our calculations of benefits and costs are often made in relation to what would have happened if we had done nothing. Alternatives can sometimes be derived from generalizations of the sciences, but creativity is required to find them.

Our expectation that a policy will deal with a problem or influence a value typically derives from some general *model* of a causal process. A model for policy analysis relates policy alternatives to specified criteria or values, as figure 1–1 shows. For one type of value such as efficiency, equity, human development, or subjective well-being we need to know whether one policy will cause more of that value than another. Causal relations of this kind correspond to the horizontal solid arrow in figure 1–1. For another type of value or criterion such as moral or constitutional prohibition we consider the policy itself rather than its consequences, as indicated by the dashed arrow. The model must also take account of variables, other than those altered by the policy, that affect the outcomes we are considering; these are indicated by the diagonal solid arrow. The arrows contain by implication the probability or strength of causation, related to feasibility, which is thus not treated as a valuative criterion. Models may involve theories of natural science, such as the laws of mechanics, or generalizations of medical science, such as the expected relation between administration of a drug and alleviation of symptoms. They may also be more complex simulations of natural, social, or man-machine systems.

Policy choice usually requires the gathering of information about the expected consequences of alternative policies. The first source of information that you should seek lies in previous studies of similar problems or choices. A

Figure 1–1.
How a Model Relates Alternatives to Criteria.

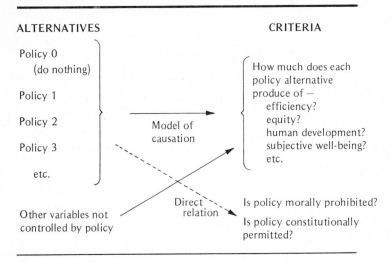

second source lies in available scientific generalizations or research. When these do not suffice, you may have to consider gathering new information. This process may range from inquiry about how the potentially affected persons value various costs and benefits, to statistical studies of outcomes, to the type of research used to test and refine scientific hypotheses. Many of the methods needed for such new data gathering have been developed in the social sciences.

One model of special importance in policy analysis in the United States is the economic model of the free, competitive market (chapter 5). In using this model we begin with the finding that a perfect market would efficiently satisfy the preferences of the persons participating in it. If the problem we are dealing with concerns goods or services that might be sold in a market, we then ask how closely that market would resemble a perfect market. If the resemblance is close, we have little reason for correcting the market on grounds of efficiency. The main grounds for advocating government action would then be that the efficiency of the market did not bring with it the degree of equity, or fairness, that we favored or that efficiency in the satisfaction of preferences was not the goal that we sought. If the market for these goods or services departs significantly from the conditions for a perfect market, then we would have additional reasons for favoring government intervention—taxation, subsidy, regulation, or government production or sale of goods—if these policies would increase efficiency.

4. *Political feasibility* (chapter 6). Choosing a course of action that will help to put your proposed policy into effect is usually the most difficult part of policy analysis. It requires personal skill, detailed knowledge of political institutions and personalities, and often luck as well. Even the best policy

imaginable, as judged in ethical terms, may be impossible to put into effect because of the resistance of persons who will be harmed by it or consider it undesirable or the inaction of persons who give it low priority. You must therefore estimate the chances of enactment and implementation of various policies that you may propose, including the effect that you can have on these chances. Such estimates usually involve judgment about what persons or organizations are likely to favor or oppose particular policies and what modified policies are likely to obtain greater support if it is needed. Political scientists and sociologists study the relations among organizations in general terms. To translate these generalizations into diagnoses and recommendations in particular situations requires more specific information, as well as the recognition that you yourself as a policy analyst are involved in the situation. In addition, your own personal values may interfere with your pursuit of the general welfare. We may consider it infeasible to propose and support a policy we know is right if it threatens our own interests or draws on scarce political resources. We ourselves often share the narrowness of perspective that we must anticipate in others.

The conditions for maximizing the political feasibility of a given policy vary over time and among persons. For example, a proposal for a new tax mechanism may be made by an academic economist, a representative of an interest group, or a congressional representative, and even though each proponent may intend to enact the same law, each may possibly make the greatest contribution to the feasibility of enacting that law by expressing the proposal in different terms.

In assessing feasibility you must make intuitive judgments that cannot easily be expressed in scientific terms. Nearly all policy recommendations that have any hope of being effective are transmitted through interpersonal or organizational channels. Conceivably, a policy analyst might merely compare alternatives scientifically and publish an impersonal report on his or her findings. But this approach is usually ineffective by itself. If you are to be effective as an analyst, you must learn who is to act on your recommendations, what motivates and concerns these individuals, and how your recommendations must be presented. You must also be aware of your own roles in relation to individuals whom you may influence—in defining your problem, in consulting others as your analysis proceeds, in anticipating their reactions, and in translating your findings into terms that are intelligible and acceptable to your audiences. These requirements extend beyond the rigorous aspects of social science. In addition to being aware of the conditions for political feasibility, you must also act on your analysis by communicating your reasoning, persuading others, analyzing and influencing political relations, and being aware of your own biases and limitations.

5. *The cycle of policy analysis* (chapter 7). The series of steps listed above are often repeated once an initial policy is put into effect. After that policy assumes a particular form—a program, a set of programs, or possibly an experiment—we may reconsider our policy options in view of information

gained from its operation. This second cycle of policy analysis may require that we design the implementation of the initial policy to generate useful data concerning how well it worked. Analysis in the second cycle may become more specific because of the embodiment of the policy in a particular program. The development of new policies related to existing programs typically involves evaluation of these programs—a specific type of policy analysis. In this evaluation the values of those who are carrying out the existing program and the political stakes of those committed to it influence the definition of the problem, the possibility of gathering information, the development of criteria, and the generality of the questions asked. The mere decision to evaluate a particular program constitutes an important part of the definition of the problem.

Although we shall discuss these five elements of policy analysis separately, in practice they are closely interrelated. We have seen in figure 1–1 how criteria, alternatives, and models relate to one another. Definitions of the problem by those involved aid us in assessment of feasibility. A policy we propose may be a response to one group's definition of the problem but not to another's, and the latter group may oppose it. In addition, valuative criteria are involved throughout the process of analysis. Definitions of the problem are typically made in terms of values that are threatened or attainable. Valuative criteria are the end-variables in our models, and the assessment of feasibility again relates to the values that various participants hold.

We have now defined the field of policy analysis and summarized the elements of the field, which will be discussed in the remainder of the book. We proceed in the following chapters to consider these elements in greater detail. After you have finished the book you should be able to analyze policy choices such as we present, not merely proceeding in the sequence of the chapters but understanding how the chapters are interrelated.

GLOSSARY

Alternative: one of several possible policies.

Policy: a chosen course of action significantly affecting large numbers of people.

Policy analysis: the use of reason and evidence to choose the best policy among a number of alternatives.

Policy choice: a choice among two or more possible policies (alternatives).

Political community: any set of persons who regularly make collective decisions.

Political feasibility of a policy: the degree of possibility that the policy can be enacted and carried out.

Public policy: a policy made by government.

Valuative criterion (pl., criteria): a principle according to which (a) acts with known consequences may be judged better or worse, or (b) acts with known characteristics may be judged right or wrong. Examples: (a) One act is better than another if it satisfies preferences more fully. (b) An act involving murder is wrong.

EXERCISES

1. Give examples of acts or courses of action that are policies, and others that are not.

2. Distinguish between two notions of democracy that differ as regards the citizen's goals or the citizen's criteria for support of policies.

3. Why does this book stress policy analysis by the *citizen*?

4. Read case 3–B on controlling city growth. Are citizens of communities that wish to restrict growth considering the general welfare? The public interest?

5. In figure 1–1 what is the difference between the solid arrows and the dashed arrow?

NOTES

1. James W. Vaupel, in "Muddling Through Analytically," in Willis D. Hawley and David Rogers, eds., *Improving the Quality of Urban Management* (Beverly Hills, Calif.: Sage Publications, 1974), summarizes the condition justifying analysis in the formula $pd > c$, where p is the probability that analysis will make a difference, d is the expected difference that analysis will make if it succeeds, and c is the expected cost of analysis. We shall return to this condition in chapter 4.

2. The first of these definitions is from Walter Williams, *Social Policy Research and Analysis* (New York: American Elsevier, 1971), pp. 13–14; the second is from

Thomas R. Dye, *Understanding Public Policy* (Englewood Cliffs, N.J.: Prentice-Hall, 1972), pp. 5–6.

3. See James S. Coleman, *Policy Research in the Social Sciences* (Morristown, N.J.: General Learning Press, 1972).

4. See Gary D. Brewer and Ronald D. Brunner, eds., *Political Development and Change: A Policy Approach* (New York: Free Press, 1975), pp. 13–16.

5. This parallel is stressed in William D. Coplin and Michael K. O'Leary, *Everyman's Prince: A Guide to Understanding Political Problems*, 2d ed. (North Scituate, Mass.: Duxbury Press, 1976), especially as regards calculations of political feasibility.

2
The Definition of Problems

Policy analysis begins with a clear statement of the problem you propose to analyze. Often the problem will seem to be defined clearly in advance, but it will still be useful to stand back and consider other ways of defining it. By considering other definitions you may both improve your analysis and anticipate some of the problems of political feasibility that result from people's differing views of the problem. This chapter will present some ways of understanding other people's definitions of problems, tell you how to relate their definitions to the definition you yourself choose, and suggest ways in which you can participate in the discussion and communication by which your problem may be redefined.

THE PROBLEM SITUATION AND THE ANALYST'S PROBLEM

The alternative policies among which we choose center ordinarily about some particular problem or widely sensed deficiency in a situation. They may also derive from a new opportunity for action, such as that produced by the availability of new technology or a change in control of some major governmental office. Making a policy choice often starts by considering alternatives related to such a widely perceived situation calling for action, both for economy of search and because of the support we may expect when we propose solutions to a recognized problem. But you as an analyst must consider redefining the problem by either generalizing it, making it more specific, or proposing new alternatives. You must consider redefinition either because the values involved in various problem areas are interrelated, because policies in one area influence values or problems in other areas, or because the need for support requires reformulations that are more acceptable to potential supporters.

Let us call the problem (or opportunity) as it is presented to us the *problem situation;* it may consist of a set of definitions of the problem held by various participants—those who may influence policy choices or are affected by them. Sociologists are concerned with problem situations when they consider the sources of "social problems," states of affairs that have arisen in particular societies or social groups. Problem situations change over time, and our possibilities for analysis or intervention change correspondingly, depending on when we become involved in this process of change.

In contrast to the problem situation, we designate the aspect of the situation that you choose to work on as *the analyst's problem.* You may generalize the problem situation or select a part of it, relate the situation to more general or more precisely stated values, try to reconcile the various views of persons affected or persons who make decisions, or choose the viewpoint of one group of participants over another.[1] Your modification of the problem situation may depend on your own values, the time and resources you have for analysis, your interaction with those affected, your eventual findings, or the positions of the persons or groups on whom you depend for putting your recommendations into effect.

We thus begin by looking at *people's concerns* as well as at the substantive matters they are concerned with. Our analysis will deal with these substantive matters. But what we decide to consider in our analysis influences its ultimate success or failure of acceptance and is largely affected by people's concerns with these substantive matters. These concerns may prove to be unfounded, and we may eventually have to persuade people to abandon them if we can.[2] They may be directed to a symptom of a deeper and more lasting problem of which people are unaware. Our analysis of the substance may direct us to that problem, and we may have to persuade people of its significance. Or people potentially affected may be unaware of a problem we regard as important. But before we begin our substantive analysis, if we wish to gain support in the short run, we must examine the context of values, expectations, and concerns among persons affected and among those who may shape the decision. Description of the problem situation is thus a description of people's concerns. Formulation of the analyst's problem is statement of a substantive problem involving policy alternatives and their consequences.

One way in which we may redefine a problem situation is by seeking to formulate general values that underlie it. Rather than being concerned with the problem of poverty in our own country, for example, we might extend our view to poverty throughout the world, and then to the problem of the world's material resources, population, and nonmonetary as well as monetary means of dealing with problems caused by poverty. There is much to be said for extending our view in this way; and even though it sometimes seems impractical, it can also often save us from a blind concern with narrow and immediate goals and means. A still more general way to search for alternatives is to start with a system of values and look for possible policies or problem situations that relate to it.

A search for important problems, though apparently a rational procedure, is difficult, just as it is difficult to canvass all conceivable alternative policies that might deal with a given problem and to analyze their consequences. Moreover, if we spend all our effort on this search for wider classes of alternatives, we may also sacrifice immediate accomplishment and support. If we wish, while choosing among policies, to earn a living and the respect of our fellow men as well as to contribute to the accomplishment of values in the shorter run, we may often narrow our scope. We do so not because a more comprehensive view is impossible, but because it requires the investment of time and effort for persuasion and organization and the generation of information on a wider scale.[3] We often narrow our scope, therefore, not because doing so is a virtue, but because it is a necessity. In addition, the experience we gain in dealing with smaller problems may later serve us as we face larger ones.

The problem situation that we encounter initially may be either general or specific. Very often the goals as initially defined have to be enlarged so that alternative policies considered for one problem situation can be related to the values involved in other problems, through tradeoffs. For example, in the deposit-bottles case (case 5–A) we may begin with a view by citizens of a problem as involving pollution or litter but then find that remedies for this social problem may impair a productive process that also serves citizens as consumers. The analyst's problem may then be enlarged to that of seeking a policy that maximizes the overall degree of preference satisfaction.

In other cases, however, especially when we need to be more specific in our analysis, we must narrow the range of alternatives. A broad initial view is desirable, but limitations of time and resources usually require us to concentrate on a few alternatives for intensive analysis. The persons we encounter may be concerned with either the specific or the general aspects of problems. In working with them we may wish to change our own definitions toward theirs as well as to persuade them of the advantages of ours.

Figure 2–1 shows some examples of problems of various degrees of generality. Each of the general problems listed combines two or more intermediate-level problems. But some of the specific problems shown relate to more than one intermediate problem. For example, the problem of day care relates not only to economic equality for women, but also to a developing view of the family as a collection of individuals more than a group and thus as less organized by social norms.

The problems listed in figure 2–1 are not identical with policy alternatives. Although we often see "the problem" as that of enacting or implementing a particular policy, when we do so, we have already either completed the analysis phase or skipped it. The values threatened are not necessarily identical with general systems of valuative criteria, even for the most general statements of the problems. Each value is a partial one, not fully representative of a notion of the general welfare. Thus, an ethic aimed only at maximizing equality (ignoring efficiency) or one aimed only at reducing disorganization would not necessarily guide us toward a social order that we would approve. Finally, although the values implied in these problems are widespread today, they should not be taken as the authors' values. We have included two apparently contradictory values—that of equality and that of excellence (implying *in*equality)—in order to indicate that the choice of values for policy analysis is up to you. We ask that you formulate your values consistently and precisely to make analysis possible, but we do not ask that you subscribe to any single "official" value system.

The definition of a problem situation often implies that certain goals or values are to be sought. Thus, if the existence of an organization is threatened, persons in the organization may take its survival to be the goal of analysis. Yet the survival of that particular organization may not be in the public interest, and policies that aid the organization may impose costs on nonmembers. The citizen is properly concerned with broader values for the public in general or all persons. These values include preference satisfaction, security, material welfare, self-realization, and justice, within constraints such as those set by law and

Figure 2–1.

Specific and General Problems.

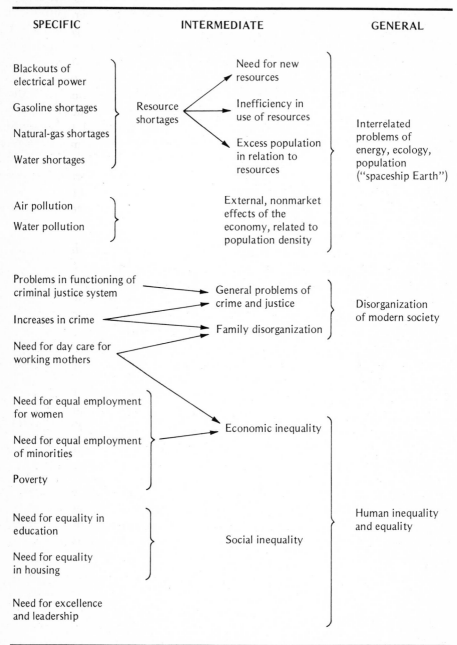

SPECIFIC	INTERMEDIATE	GENERAL

Blackouts of electrical power

Gasoline shortages

Natural-gas shortages

Water shortages

Resource shortages

Need for new resources

Inefficiency in use of resources

Excess population in relation to resources

Air pollution

Water pollution

External, nonmarket effects of the economy, related to population density

Interrelated problems of energy, ecology, population ("spaceship Earth")

Problems in functioning of criminal justice system

Increases in crime

Need for day care for working mothers

General problems of crime and justice

Family disorganization

Disorganization of modern society

Need for equal employment for women

Need for equal employment of minorities

Poverty

Economic inequality

Need for equality in education

Need for equality in housing

Need for excellence and leadership

Social inequality

Human inequality and equality

obligation. Values such as specific organizational goals, which are vital only to members of particular organizations, need to be related to ends defined more by general values if they are to carry weight for citizens in general.[4]

Our ability to look beyond particular organizational goals to larger values that these organizations may serve has an analogy in international policy. For example, in the Cuban missile crisis of 1962, the goal that most United States policy makers sought was the removal of the Soviet missiles from Cuba. This goal was seen as a means of achieving national security, but the ultimate human goals affected by national security or by the threat of nuclear war were considered so obvious by the participants in Washington that they were not discussed in detail.[5] In the Vietnam war, however, the goal of military victory was eventually reconsidered in relation to other values.

The competing claims of general and specific views of problems permeate both the theory and the practice of policy analysis. Amitai Etzioni has proposed to reconcile them by alternating between them. He illustrates this alternation as it occurs in chess.

> A chess player cannot study all the strategies at each move. Better players . . . quickly review several strategies and then explore a sub-set of them in greater detail and an even smaller sub-set in still more detail. They reject all strategies of the first sub-set but one on the basis of some obvious disadvantages which make them undeserving of detailed examination. Were they able to examine all strategies in detail, they might discover that an alternative that had been rejected in this first round would have been the optimal one. But they cannot optimize. Still, we expect them to do better with this sequential combination of different kinds of scanning, going from vague but encompassing to detailed but exclusive examination, than players who only "increment" on the strategy with which they began or which [they] have used successfully in the past.[6]

In this proposed alternation, which he calls "mixed-scanning," one can take a broader view at certain times and at other times work within a set of constraints that are temporarily taken for granted. From the broader view the problem and the goal values can be seen in more general terms; and the range of policy alternatives that are feasible—perhaps in the longer run—may be enlarged.

THE PROBLEM OF CHANGING POLITICAL DECISION STRUCTURES

In a very broad view we might consider changing the structure of decision systems rather than making individual decisions within those systems.

We are especially likely to take this view if we have found it difficult to enact or implement particular policies within an existing structure, and if we believe there is a chance of changing the structure to make enactment or implementation easier. Political leaders, heads of organizations, and others with a long-range perspective are most likely to consider structural change of this sort.

An example of this sort of change took place in the House of Representatives in the 1960s and 1970s. Before this change, the Rules Committee had had a generally conservative influence by preventing numerous pieces of liberal legislation from reaching the House floor. The frustration of liberals with the committee's action led them first to seek the appointment of more liberal members to the committee and then to change the committee's powers. Eventually, under the Nixon administration, the entire committee system was reformed so as to decrease the power of senior members. In this way a change in a general decision structure occurred, affecting many pieces of legislation. Whether you consider this a desirable change depends, of course, on the criteria of judgment you bring to bear on it and your more detailed examination of its consequences.

Similarly, organizational structures may be changed when existing organizations seem ineffective in carrying out desired policies. President Carter believed that by creating a new Department of Energy he could facilitate the conservation of scarce energy resources. Local police forces have been merged with fire services in departments of "public safety" with the aim of increasing their overall efficiency. In many instances of national legislation, a new law has created a new agency to regulate an industry or administer a program. Conceivably, the job could have been given to an existing organization, but the proponents of the law believed that a new agency would do the job better.

The most fundamental change in decision structures would be a change in the Constitution itself. The American Constitution assumes the separation of powers among legislative, executive, and judicial branches of government—an arrangement that does not exist in all nations. It has also been interpreted to assume the existence of private property and free markets. In this text we take that structure for granted and deal only with lesser problems such as how decisions should be made by an existing governmental structure or whether particular functions should be exercised by government. In choosing the problems with which we are concerned in this book, we thus omit problems that would call for governmental reorganization and constitutional change. These are important policy problems, which are studied in political science and public administration. But they are not easy to analyze in precise terms, and larger problems of this kind are not often accessible to citizens for choice.

Our choice between the broader and narrower views depends on the degree of confidence that we have in the combination of parts in the whole system. It also depends on our diagnosis of possibilities and on the resources we can devote to analysis and action. As revolutionaries point out, some problems cannot be solved incrementally, that is, by a gradual succession of small steps. Small steps may sometimes lead to blind alleys as well as to cumulative successes. Our decision to deal only with smaller problems in this book reflects in part their appropriateness at the introductory level and in part a confidence that larger problems can be dealt with elsewhere.

HOW PROBLEM SITUATIONS ARISE

In order to understand other people's definitions of problems, we must understand the general social processes that lead people to become concerned about their situations. If members of a decision-making group agree that a problem exists, the analyst who has access to this group need not begin by convincing them of the need for action but can proceed to study policy alternatives. If a group's shared expectations are disturbed and its values threatened—by a challenge from another group, a disaster, an economic change, the spread of a disease, or the malfunctioning of an organization—then their attention, and ours, is focused on means to alleviate this difficulty.[7]

Thus, a social problem has been defined by Robert K. Merton as a "significant and unwanted discrepancy" between the standards of a collectivity and actual conditions.[8] A current text gives a similar definition: "an alleged situation which is incompatible with the values of a significant number of people who agree that action is necessary to alter the situation." It gives as examples "war, pollution, traffic jams, and crimes."[9] In each of these examples there is not only an objective state of affairs, such as the prevalence of war, but also an expectation that it should be otherwise. These expectations are not universal, however. In earlier historical periods war was considered inevitable or a normal part of human existence. In more recent periods factory smoke was considered a sign of prosperity more than a source of atmospheric pollution. Our expectations have changed over time; they can change again, and our notions as to what problems are important can change with them.

The above definitions of social problems avoid the question of whether the people involved are *right* about either the desirability of the change they want (it may hurt someone else), the possibility of change, or the effectiveness of the means they may propose. Our task is to propose policies that are both right and effective and to use our scarce resources on problems that are important and that offer genuine hope for remedies.

To understand the diverse perspectives on a problem we must look for the sources of people's expectations as well as of the objective state of affairs. These expectations are often related to people's position in the social structure. Members of different social classes or ethnic groups may have different expectations concerning what is a satisfactory state of health, level of unemployment, or type of education available. The values that people feel are threatened, such as freedom, privacy, or governmental authority, may be embodied in major political institutions, but attitudes toward these institutions may change and may differ among groups. Categories such as "international aggression," "serious unemployment," or "serious inflation" often derive from interpretation of the situation in relation to previous ones.

When the categories of action or of problems are associated with particular organizations, these categories may be embodied in the operating procedures of these organizations. In the Cuban missile crisis of 1962, one particular bundle of actions was proposed by the Air Force as a "surgical air strike." [10] This alternative (and the corresponding definition of the problem) was understood quite differently by President Kennedy than by the armed services. Kennedy expected that an air strike would remove the Soviet missiles from Cuba but would not attack other installations. The armed services, however, had a different plan for an "air strike."

> *The Services had prepared and coordinated a contingency plan for military action against Castro—in case an opportunity should arise. That plan deeply reflected the lesson that these organizations had learned from the Bay of Pigs: the Kennedy administration could not be trusted to do what was required in the heat of military action. When these leaders wanted military action, they would have to sign on to a plan that called for massive military force.* [11]

For Kennedy the problem was the removal of the missiles. For the Air Force the Kennedy administration itself was part of the problem.

To characterize the problem situation we must describe the values or expectations that various persons and groups feel to be challenged. We as analysts need to know these diverse definitions, even if we cannot reconcile them, in order to assess the feasibility of various policies. We may find ourselves allied with one party to a conflict if we can justify the policy that that party favors in general ethical terms. But when there is conflict as to what the relevant values are, we cannot say that the problem situation consists of a single view of the problem.

One source of problem situations is social change—gradual change in the conditions of social life. This may be economic and demographic change, moving jobs and power from one section of a nation to another. The growth of the West and more recently that of the "Sunbelt" have created regional problems from the time of the Missouri Compromise to the present. Population movements have also influenced the concentration of people in cities and the ethnic composition of these cities. The "baby boom" of the 1950s led to the rise and subsequent decline of certain age groups in the population. Declining death rates have increased the proportion of elderly persons. We cannot easily influence such changes, even though much effort has been devoted to population policy analysis. But to some extent we can anticipate and react to them.

Technological change is also an important source of problem situations. [12] The rise of the automobile has influenced the growth of suburbs and shopping centers and the deterioration of inner-city areas. The technology of production with its requirement of higher skills in jobs has led to a closer connection between training and job opportunities. The technology of birth control has influenced our sexual mores. These and many other examples suggest that human societies need time to adjust their norms to new technology and that, in the interim, problem situations are likely.

Some of these processes are exemplified in the city-growth case (case 3–B). In that case residents of a number of smaller cities, such as Petaluma, California, and Ramapo, New York, have sought policies for limiting their rate of population growth by restricting in-migration. We may better understand the causes of their concern, as well as the problems of those who seek to move into such cities, by considering the demographic sources of the problem situation. With the general growth and urbanization of the United States population there has come an enlargement and expansion of major metropolitan areas. The political boundaries of older cities have included only a limited part of this population growth, much of which has taken place in suburban communities. At the same time, the central cities have come to include a larger part of the working-class and black population, while the outlying cities and towns have gained in well-to-do white population.

The voters in the outlying towns have often moved there in order to enjoy a higher standard of living and more pleasant surroundings. To do so, however, they have often felt it necessary to protect that standard of living against possible threats from the in-migration of more people (creating congestion) and, although they do not always say so explicitly, from in-migration of poorer neighbors. For the same reasons, they have resisted efforts to include their cities in larger metropolitan governments. The result is a conflict of interest and of ethical criteria or notions of the "general welfare" between residents of some of these cities and outsiders who wish to move in.

Changes in the power relations among groups can also create problem situations that ramify beyond these power relations themselves. European nations that formerly controlled colonies on other continents have responded to the stress of decolonization with defensive assertions of national dignity. The rise of the Nazi movement in Germany after her defeat in World War I was attributed in part to that loss of national prestige. A related interpretation has been offered for the rise of Senator Joseph McCarthy after World War II when America, though victorious, faced new responsibilities in world affairs. McCarthy's concern with the danger of communist infiltration was shared widely during that period.[13]

Social change may affect both the substantive state of affairs (as in the case of migration to the cities or their suburbs) and people's attitudes about problems (as in the effect of America's world involvement on McCarthy's support). In the former case, projections of migration will be part of our substantive analysis; in the latter, study of the sources of political support may be part of our analysis of the conditions under which policies are feasible. We must not, however, allow the study of sources of support to blind us to the merits of a policy. McCarthyism as well as opposition to fluoridation of drinking water and advocacy of the alleged anticancer substance laetrile have been associated with a political tendency known as the "radical right," which has been analyzed extensively by sociologists. The social source of a policy position, however, is not a logical guarantee of its rightness or wrongness. Outsiders, neurotics, and "extremists" may occasionally produce policy proposals worthy of attention, even though the social conventions of academic research tend to screen them out.[14]

The motives and anxieties resulting from social change have often been considered as bases for mobilizing support. From our viewpoint as policy analysts and participants, knowledge of these potential bases of mobilization may aid us in persuasion. In a political campaign, a survey of voters may reveal discontent concentrated in a particular social group, to which a candidate may then appeal. A candidate may thus conduct market research for political ideas that he or she wishes to propagate, much as the seller of a product plans an advertising and sales campaign.

But the first task of the policy analyst is reasoned analysis of the problem presented, rather than persuasion related to the social situations of other persons. After we have analyzed a problem, we may wish to increase the feasibility of our recommended policy by persuasion. Such persuasion may, of course, simply involve presentation of our findings and our reasoning to a qualified audience. For audiences with less training, we may simplify our reasoning. If we were professional politicians, we might present arguments for our proposed policy selectively in ways calculated to appeal to particular persons whose support we needed.[15] If we were campaign managers, we might consider a range of appeals from the rational to the emotional. But if policy analysis is to be influential by processes other than the manipulation of symbols by elites, it must face the test of reasoned public discussion in view of evidence and notions of the general welfare, neither of which should rest on mere appeal to our listeners' social situation.

THE USE OF STATISTICS
TO DEFINE PROBLEMS

People's expectations depend in part on what they have experienced in the past. As we have noted, their judgments as to a normal rate of inflation or unemployment depend on the rates they have known previously. This comparison between past and present can be made not only in terms of one's own experience in looking for jobs or in buying goods but also in terms of publicly available statistics. Once government agencies begin publishing periodic reports on rates of inflation and unemployment, people will begin to interpret their own experiences as typical or atypical in relation to these general statistics.

Table 2–1.

Military Expenditures by the United States and the Soviet Union, 1936–1948

| | Military Expenditures | |
| | US | USSR |
Year	(billion dollars)	(billion rubles) [a]
1936	0.91	14.8
1937	0.94	20.1
1938	1.03	27.0
1939	1.08	41.0 [b]
1940	1.50 [b]	57.1
1941	6.04	70.9
1942	23.94	108.4
1943	63.16	124.7
1944	76.70	137.9
1945	81.22	128.2
1946	43.18	72.2
1947	14.39 [b]	68.5 [b]
1948	11.77	66.0

Source:
Ole R. Holsti "The Baseline Problem in Statistics: Examples from the Study of American Policy," *Journal of Politics* 37(1975): 190. Reprinted by permission of *The Journal of Politics,* © 1975.

[a] Old rubles (officially valued at $.20).
[b] Figures selected by Kolko and Kolko to depict trends.

Similarly, time series of crime rates are likely to affect people's judgments as to whether crime is a serious problem. Indices of this kind, which measure trends in the state of the economy or the society, are known as *economic* or *social indicators.*[16]

An example of the use of time series in defining problems is the comparison of military expenditures between the United States and the Soviet Union, as shown in table 2–1. Here we compare not only two time series but also two countries. The time series presented in this table for the period 1936–1948 were used in discussion of whether the United States was spending more than it should on its armed forces. One book on the subject had contended that the Russians were unable to mount a military threat to the United States in the years following World War II, pointing out that "Soviet military expenditures in 1947 were at about the same level as in 1939, whereas the United States outlays were about nine times those of 1940." The critic who presented the longer time series shown in table 2–1 pointed out that the USSR was already on a war footing in 1939, but the United States was not in 1940. Since the conclusions we reach depend on the year we choose as baseline, we need to be careful about baseline values chosen to support a particular argument. It is more reliable to look at a long time series and to see whether the particular year chosen for the baseline is representative. If we fail to think carefully about the baseline problem, the baseline presented by somone else can affect the expectations we bring to the problem.

The critic goes on to point out that

> the data for the entire period will support any number of conclusions, not only that of relative Soviet impotence. For example, it would have been no less valid to assert that between 1945 and 1948 American defense spending dropped by 85.5 per cent, whereas during the same interval the Soviet military budget declined by less than 50 per cent."[17]

If we want to analyze military policy carefully, we need to ask other questions as well, including whether the data are valid and what the military needs of a nation are at a particular historical period. But the main point is that the choice of baseline years affects our expectations.

In addition to comparing data over time, we can also compare data between population groups as a way of defining problems. Table 2–2 presents a comparison between whites and nonwhites relative to the incidence of early death (before age 65) from various causes in 1972. For each row in the table, the likelihood of early death was computed for nonwhites and for whites, and the ratio of the two was entered in the table. Nonwhites were found 8.9 times as likely to die early from homicide as were whites. For tuberculosis the ratio was 5.4 and so on till the last and lowest ratio in the table, 0.57 for suicide.

All but one of the ratios shown are greater than unity, indicating that for all but one of the causes listed nonwhites were more likely than whites to die early. We are also tempted to define the problem as more urgent when the ratio is higher, in view of the tacit expectation that whites and nonwhites should have similar life-chances in the United States—an expectation that runs counter to the data in the table. But the urgency of the analyst's problem and the desirability of making public policy may not be reflected exactly by these ratios. We can more easily seek to provide equal health services to deal with tuberculosis than we can alter homicide rates in different groups. Moreover, it is possible that analysis will show that the actual numbers of deaths vary considerably among the rows in the table, and that we can obtain more improvement by working on a lower row containing greater actual numbers than on a higher

Table 2–2.

The Ratio of Nonwhite to White Early Death Rates for Various Causes of Death in 1972

Cause of Death	Likelihood of Early Death from This Cause for Nonwhites As a Multiple of the Likelihood for Whites at 1972 Mortality Rates
Homicide	8.9
Tuberculosis	5.4
Nephritis and Nephrosis	4.8
Diabetes Mellitus	3.1
Influenza and Pneumonia	2.5
Appendicitis	2.4
Hernia and Intestinal Obstruction	2.0
Infant Mortality	2.0
Cirrhosis of Liver	1.9
Accidents, other than Motor Vehicle	1.8
Cardiovascular Disease	1.7
Peptic Ulcer	1.7
Malignant Neoplasms (Cancer)	1.3
Motor Vehicle Accidents	1.2
Suicide	0.57

Source:
James W. Vaupel, "Early Death: An American Tragedy," p. 109. Reprinted with permission from a symposium on Valuing Lives appearing in *Law and Contemporary Problems* Volume XL, Number 4, Autumn, 1976, published by the Duke University School of Law, Durham, North Carolina. Copyright 1977 by Duke University.

row (with a higher ratio) that corresponds to a smaller number of actual cases. Thus, intergroup comparisons are relevant for the definition of problems, but our inferences from them depend on how they are presented, and our initial rapid inferences may have to be reconsidered.

A similar use of ratios, in the form of percentages, to define a problem appears in the deposit-bottles case (case 5–A). The report on that case contains the following information:

John R. Quarles, the deputy administrator for the Federal Environmental Protection Agency, said that during the time that beverage consumption had risen 33 per cent, the number of bottles discarded had gone up by 262 per cent—from 15.4 billion in 1959 to 55.7 billion in 1972.

While containers make up only 8 per cent of the solid-waste load, . . . they now account for between 54 and 70 per cent of the volume of highway litter. Containers . . . are the fastest growing segment of the waste load—increasing 8 per cent a year.

The statistics cited by Quarles consist largely of percentages. Like each figure in table 2–2, they compare one percentage or proportion with another. If we wished to construct ratios similar to those in table 2–2 from the Quarles data, we could compute 262%/33% = 7.9, or 54%/8% = 6.75. These percentages and the corresponding ratios tell us that discarded bottles have increased more rapidly than beverage consumption, and the proportion of containers in highway litter has increased more rapidly than their proportion in solid waste during the period chosen for reporting by Quarles. They do not in themselves tell us, however, how important the problem is because ratios of this sort could be produced by very small amounts of litter. The actual figures on numbers of bottles discarded are a more useful measure of the possible social cost from discarded bottles.

The examples we have given show that statistics are an important means for defining problems; that they are often used to make comparisons between an actual situation and another situation on which our expectations might be based; and that they have to be used carefully in defining the analyst's problem.

REDEFINING PROBLEMS

When you have chosen your own definition of the analyst's problem and your analysis then leads you to make recommendations, you will often have to persuade others that your definition is better than theirs. This persuasion may well begin before your analysis is complete. In the process of discussion, you may be persuaded to change your own definition, either for intellectual reasons or to increase the political feasibility of your proposals. In this process of persuasion and discussion, both you and other people may come to redefine a problem as more or less important, as more or less general, or as involving different values from those initially presented.

Even when a problem is defined in advance—by an entire affected group or by parts of it—we can consider redefining it. The United States responded to the Soviets' orbiting of their first satellite Sputnik in 1957 by changes in elementary-school education in the sciences. It responded to problems of race relations in the 1960s by acting on poverty. Radicals used the depression of the 1930s as an occasion to advocate not simply relief for the unemployed but major changes in the economic and political systems. An energy crisis can be attributed to the actions of foreign nations, of our own government officials, of private industry, or of the consuming public. Such redefinitions by ourselves or others may increase or decrease the sense of urgency with which a problem is viewed. Whether they are justified is itself a possible policy question.

If you are to engage in this sort of persuasion, you must understand the types of arguments that people use to support serious consideration of a problem or to dismiss it as unimportant. We shall next describe some of the processes by which people redefine problems so as to discourage action, processes in which you yourself may sometimes engage.

A discrepancy between social standards or values and an actual state of affairs need *not* always lead to a call for action. Whether we call for action depends in part on the socially established explanations that pervade our society. Some states of affairs are regarded as inescapable; thus, the "problem of death" has long been seen as lying in the province of religion rather than medicine. Social expectations may have been changing, however, in that society now devotes more resources to the prolongation of life than before. Another indication of the influence of expectations is that we are more concerned with drug abuse than with automobile accidents, even though the deaths and injuries caused by automobiles are far more numerous.[18] Perhaps we are more accustomed to automobile accidents and consider them less voluntary. Similarly, the American Business Creed long defined unemployment as inevitable, the fault of the individual, and thus "natural." Poverty has also been defined diversely. Certain levels of living in affluent societies may be defined as intolerable and requiring public remedies, although the same levels in poorer societies are seen as "normal."

A problem may be explained away by the argument that behavior is typical of members of a group or of persons in a particular situation. If it is not considered "natural," it may in any event be "cured by the passage of time."[19] But problems are also defined through discussion, and *we* can sometimes affect their definition by participating in that discussion.

In redefining a problem, we often have the possibility of placing blame for the situation on persons or institutions. We can often gain more support for action if it is directed against an object of blame. This action may not always be the most effective way to cope with the problem, however, because it can provoke counterforces that obstruct our efforts. When one group places blame on another, it also influences the second group's definition of *its* problem. A group that acts to cope with a problem that *it* perceives may then be seen by others as parts of *their* problem. This sort of reaction developed against supporters of Joseph McCarthy in the 1950s, when the senator made widespread accusations of communist penetration in government, and against student protestors of the late 1960s, who saw the Vietnam war and the involvement of universities with power in society as problems. Both groups were themselves seen as a threat to order and security.

The diverse views of problems with which participants start can thus be accentuated and polarized through an escalation of counteraccusations. Community conflicts can develop in this way, with members increasingly choosing sides and developing negative views of the other side, and each side developing a progressively more generalized partisan view of the problem.[20] Such conflict may be inescapable in dealing with certain problems, but it usually closes the door to analysis. Dispassionate analysis of problems may not arouse people to action as successfully as blame and conflict, but it may find new solutions if undertaken before conflict develops. It can be undertaken for a party on one side of a conflict, and its recommendations may themselves generate conflict. But pressure for analysis to conform to a predetermined partisan position limits the options of analysis.

Persons in certain social roles have more opportunity than others to propose definitions that will be accepted: government officials, intellectuals, religious leaders, business leaders. The problem situation that we encounter may thus be that of a dominant or influential group. But efforts have been made by "outsider" groups to gain attention and redefine problems by introducing new terms to call attention to their definitions. The terms "black," "native American," and "chairperson" instead of "Negro," "Indian," and "chairman" are evidence of these efforts at redefinition. Similarly, the extension of preexisting terms to new meanings reflects efforts to heighten concern with problems: the meanings of "genocide" and "aggression" have been extended in this way, and "obscene" has been used for this purpose to refer to violence as well as sex.

If you have an opportunity to present new data or devise new social indicators for measuring the state of affairs, you may be able to influence people's definition of problems. In the fluoridation case (case 6–A) the Newton, Massachusetts, Health Department conducted a study of dental decay among school children. The findings were reported in front-page stories by the three local newspapers.

You may also be in a position to develop support for a particular definition of a problem through organizational work such as recruiting members, persuading them, and assigning and monitoring tasks in a campaign of persuasion (see case 6–A). The mobilization of support may result in part from impersonal social processes, but it is also due in part to the activity of organizers who control resources.[21] The redefinitions that result from organizational work are important to an analyst in two ways. First, you must learn about others' efforts at persuasion as they have influenced the present problem situation, since this situation may importantly limit the types of proposals we can consider.[22] Secondly, you can consider whether you can try to redefine the problem yourself.

Your opportunities to change others' definitions of problems depend on the roles you occupy and on events that increase people's receptiveness to new definitions. If you have access to newspapers or television or if your activities are considered newsworthy, you may be able to phrase or depict a problem in a way that appeals to others. At various stages in the development of public issues, you may have opportunities to affect the public agenda—the "listing of items for action." [23] Events that permit a new definition of the problem include acts by important groups, the development of new technology, and changes in the personnel occupying important positions.[24] When a new president takes office, for example, his staff are usually called on for the development of new policies and new issues. Some of these issues may also have been introduced during his campaign for office.

You may also be able to affect the "refashioning" of social problems [25] by involving people in gathering information. A "self-study," or a participatory form of research by members of a community, can often lead them to see problems they had not considered before. Extended participation and consultation are especially necessary when the "client" is a group with diverse views that need to be reconciled. The process of participation, together with its possible consequences in involvement, problem definition, and consensus also relates to the problems of political feasibility discussed in chapter 6.

THE ANALYST'S CHOICE
OF DEFINITIONS

The citizen-analyst may consider all the means of redefinition that we have just described. But if you recall our initial definition of policy analysis as involving "reason and evidence," you will see that we expect public discussion based on analysis to be somewhat more rational than public discourse has often been. Some means of redefinition will therefore be less available to you if you want to engage in rational persuasion. You may also have to distinguish between permissible and less permissible means of persuasion. We shall return to these distinctions in chapter 6.

The initial definition of a problem is often related to its apparent causes. The analyst's redefinition must sometimes move away from these causes to find policies that can deal with the problem. Sometimes a problem can be alleviated by means unrelated to its apparent causes. For example, sickle-cell anemia, though considered to be caused genetically, can also be treated by use of the chemical urea. Events caused by unalterable natural processes (rain, snow, earthquakes) may still be dealt with by adjustment to them, either by mitigating their effects (umbrellas, snow plows, design of buildings) or giving advance notice (weather reports, earthquake forecasting). And if such events are repetitive, an individual "problem" (one flood) may be generalized into a longer-run problem concerned with this *type* of event and with prevention (building dams).

Similarly, the natural occurrence of a drought can have a large impact on agricultural production and on the prices of basic farm products through the normal behavior of markets. Although irrigation techniques may alleviate such a situation somewhat, there could be a tendency to despair of solving this problem. However, considerable attention has been given to proposals for stockpiles or buffer stocks of farm products, the existence of which could cushion the swings in agricultural consumption and prices. Clearly, technological advances in food preservation contribute to the lessened feelings of the inevitability of "feast or famine."

Our intervention to change social definitions of problems may have many goals. In this book we first consider the typical definitions of problems that increase interest in action to solve them. But people who are less interested in action or innovation may also be interested in analysis to show that action is undesirable. Their analysis may be just as rational as that of those who wish action; indeed, analysis may reveal that a proposed policy is worse than inaction. Thus, the analysis conducted by people who wish to defend the existing situation must be considered seriously.

We ask a citizen-analyst to take a broad perspective and consider how policies affect all concerned. This approach may lead you to consider the viewpoints of people other than those with whom you first discuss a problem. For example, in the deposit-bottles case (case 5–A), you might begin by thinking only of the problem of roadside litter. But the convenience of consumers who use discardable containers can also be considered as an aspect of the general welfare or public interest. And the inconvenience of the workers who must change jobs if there is regulation of discardable containers is also a social cost, even though a temporary one. By considering a wide range of consequences and interests in your definition of the problem, you may judge among policies in a way that more validly reflects the public interest. But at the same time you may find that you are not in complete agreement with any of the particular groups involved.

If you take this broad perspective, you may even encounter problems as to which political unit commands your allegiance as a citizen. In the city-growth case (case 3–B) you may begin with the perspective of a citizen of a community that is trying to preserve its natural beauty and standard of living by limiting in-migration. But if you then take the viewpoint of a citizen of state or nation and include the interests of outsiders, you may find yourself in disagreement with many fellow citizens of your community. Similarly, in the Texas oil case (case 5–B) you may begin with a concern for the loss of revenues by the state of Texas or the loss of jobs that resulted from a sudden decrease in the price of oil in 1931. But if you include the possible advantages to consumers outside Texas from cheaper oil, you may find yourself at odds with your fellow state citizens.

The clarity of problem definition that you seek as an analyst may sometimes conflict with your search for support and consensus. In order to bring people together, you may seek problem definitions that many can share. But a difficulty in the necessary process of forming inclusive problem definitions is that sometimes a large coalition can be formed only at the expense of clarity and consistency of the policy proposed. The gathering of disparate clienteles beneath ambiguous symbols is well known in political campaigns. The same difficulty can arise for legislation, as is illustrated by the various meanings of "welfare reform" held by supporters of President Nixon's Family Assistance Plan proposed in 1969.[26]

When we participate in discussion to redefine problems, we may be aiming to increase not only the general welfare but also the political feasibility of our proposals. It is important to conduct this discussion in ways that promote the reasoned comparison of alternatives, rather than mere manipulation of our fellow participants. Moreover, to engage in policy analysis implies that choice is possible. We should not attempt analysis of problems when we know that there is no hope of choosing policies to deal with them. The comparison of an existing situation with a completely unattainable ideal may give rise to a sense of problem, but it is not part of policy analysis.

SUMMARY

Policy analysis begins with a definition of the problem you wish to analyze. Your choice of this definition is often of vital importance. If you hastily or unthinkingly accept someone else's definition of the problem, you may omit important alternatives or neglect the perspectives of major participants. We thus ask you to distinguish between the problem situation, as you find it, and the *analyst's problem*, the view of the problem that you choose.

Even though it is important that you reformulate the problem for yourself, you should also understand in detail the views of the problem that others hold. Some of their views may be general, and others specific. If so, you may wish to combine them through mixed-scanning. You may wish to reformulate the problem to include tradeoffs among the interests of various groups. You may need to enlarge others' definition of the problem to cope with it in more general terms, or you may have to narrow it in order to deal with it in a situation of limited time or resources. If you have considerable resources and time, you may sometimes wish to enlarge the problem to include possible changes in the political structure through which numerous decisions are made.

To understand others' definitions of problems, you should learn the general ways in which problem situations arise. When people feel that a particular situation constitutes a problem, they are contrasting the actual state of affairs with the expectations and values that they bring to it and that define for them what the situation should be. These expectations may arise from their social class or group memberships, or the organizations in which they work. Disparities between people's expectations and their situations may arise from changes in their social conditions, including those that result from migration or from the introduction of new technology. The mere fact that we can sometimes explain people's expectations in this way, however, does not mean that their judgments are necessarily wrong or that we should ignore their arguments.

Descriptive statistics provide an important source of problem definition. They express social conditions in quantitative form and permit comparison between the present situation and people's expectations of it. These expectations may themselves be influenced by statistical presentation, as they are related to statistics that describe previous time periods or that compare the situation of one group with that of another. An analyst need not, however, agree with the problem definition that others reach on the basis of the statistics presented to them.

When you choose your own problem definition, you may then have to try to persuade others of its rightness. For this purpose you need to know the types of arguments that people make for and against taking problems seriously. You need also to know how one apparent problem can be related to another concerning which action can be taken, how the use of language and data affects these changes, how support can be obtained for your definition of the problem, and how others can be involved with you in developing a shared definition.

The problem definition that you choose may not be the one that would most easily occur to people involved in the situation. By broadening the definition of the problem, you may find new alternatives. If you take a broad view of the public interest, you may find yourself in disagreement with members of particular affected groups and even with the majority of citizens in your community or state. A precise definition, suitable for analysis, may not be the one on which a majority can agree. You thus face important and difficult choices in defining your problem.

Having defined the analyst's problem, or the general territory in which our analysis takes place, we shall next move to the more specific elements of analysis. In chapter 3 we consider the criteria of choice, the values or disvalues that we shall use to test whether one policy alternative is better than another. Many of these values are expressed or implied in our definition of the problem (e.g., litter, unemployment, a threat to national security). But these implied values are often vaguely stated or are so specific as not to be comparable with one another. You must therefore take another step toward clarifying the values you seek—a redefinition of values similar to your redefinition of the problem.

Analyst's problem: the more precise definition of the problem that you choose as a basis for your further analysis.

Mixed-scanning: alternation between general and specific views of a problem.

Problem situation: the problem or opportunity as it is presented to you. It may consist of a set of definitions held by various participants.

Self-study: a study of problem conditions by a group of people who are themselves involved.

Social change: gradual change in the conditions of social life.

Social indicator: an index measuring social conditions, published in regular time series.

EXERCISES

1. Use figure 2–1 to show several different ways of defining the problem of water shortage; of defining problems related to crime.

2. How do sociologists define a social problem? In what ways can the analyst's problem differ from this?

3. If we are able to trace aspects of the problem situation to social change, how does this information affect our activities as analysts?

4. What types of arguments do people make when they want to avoid action or decrease concern with an alleged problem? When they want to increase concern? What other means are available for increasing understanding and concern?

5. How do economic and social indicators contribute to the definition of problems?

6. Presented here is a discussion of President Nixon's Family Assistance Plan. Four related questions follow the discussion.

    Early in 1969 newly elected President Nixon conceived the idea of proposing legislation to cope with the "welfare problem" associated with increasing payments of aid to families with dependent children (AFDC). He eventually proposed to Congress the Family Assistance Plan, which was intended to systematize the welfare provisions in the various states and at the same time to provide a work incentive by a "negative income tax," which would allow welfare recipients to keep a portion of the money they earned for themselves.

One of Nixon's principal advisers in this policy area, Daniel P. Moynihan, has written detailed accounts of the politics involved.[27] In a sense Moynihan was a policy analyst. But the initial idea of a negative income tax had been proposed much earlier by Milton Friedman and other economists. (Some analysts do use other people's ideas, of course. And some analysts may be ahead of their time, studying problems that are not widely recognized.) A detailed experiment on the work incentive aspect of a negative income tax was being performed in New Jersey, and its final results were not available at the time when the legislation was introduced. (Analysis *is* often too late. Timing is important.) Moynihan examined data prior to this experiment, and, most important, he studied the conditions for the feasibility of enactment of the bill. The problem situation he encountered was quite complex. Moynihan writes:

> In 1963, the United States Department of Labor created a policy-planning staff, which I headed as an Assistant Secretary. Any such organization . . . searches for problems that do not seem well in hand and are not the "property" of some parallel organization. Welfare dependency was an obvious choice. It was clear that the bureaucracy at Health, Education, and Welfare was avoiding the subject. . . . Moreover, Labor had a certain claim to concern for dependent children." [28]

In looking for the causes of welfare dependency, he studied the relation between the number of new AFDC cases opened per year and the unemployment rate. There was initially a close relation but later this changed. He was led first to consider family allowances as a remedy—regular and unconditional payments to all families—but changed to advocacy of a negative income tax, partly because of the strength of other support for it.

Nixon's election called for new proposals on the part of the Republicans—proposals that would gain uncommitted votes after his close margin of victory, would still be consistent with Republican principles, and would break with the practices of previous Democratic administrations. Professionals and government employees who had carried out previous Democratic programs would be bypassed by a program that gave money, rather than services or hopes of political power, to welfare recipients. A proposal for a negative income tax, which was sometimes considered to provide a "guaranteed income," was thus incorporated in Nixon's Family Assistance Plan legislation. As this legislation was debated in the House of Representatives and the Senate, it was referred to by its proponents as "welfare reform" and "workfare." It was opposed on the grounds of its insufficiency by the National Welfare Rights Organization and also opposed in the Senate Finance Committee as not constituting genuine welfare reform.

a. What demographic factors may have contributed to the rise of this problem situation?

b. List at least five perspectives that were involved in the problem situation at the time the legislation reached Congress.

c. How was Moynihan's choice of the "welfare dependency" problem in 1963, as well as his eventual advocacy of a negative income tax, influenced by the resources available to him?

d. What opportunities for redefining the problem were created by Nixon's election in 1968?

7. Read case 6–A, the fluoridation case. Note especially that during the early phases of the campaign, the Newton Health Department conducted a study of tooth decay among local school children. The results of this study, emphasizing the problems of tooth decay, were reported in front-page stories by local newspapers.

At a subsequent meeting, "it was agreed that questions from the floor would be restricted to Newton residents." The case goes on to note that "it was discovered that every week anti-fluoridation material was included as part of a regular radio broadcast on a major Boston station. Through contacts with the radio station and certain advertisers, it was possible to secure the removal of this highly biased material from the series of programs."

a. Were the means used for redefining the problem situation justified in this case? What circumstances affect whether they would be justified?

b. When a new opportunity exists for carrying out a policy and no strong sense of need exists, what options are open to persons who wish to alert fellow citizens to this opportunity?

ADVANCED EXERCISES

8. Read case 5–A, the deposit-bottles case. Imagine that you are an analyst. You see the effect of litter on viewers who did not bargain for it as indicating an imperfection in the market. You propose that the problem be analyzed from the standpoint of overall efficiency, in an effort to consider the values of both clean roadsides and convenience in use of containers.

a. What was the technological source of this problem situation?

b. Describe the two major perspectives on nonreturnable containers that entered into the problem situation confronted by the analyst.

c. How does the analyst's redefinition of the problem differ from the definitions of the situation by the participants in part b? What valuative criterion does the analyst choose, and how does it differ from those of the participants? Are there values or interests in the case that the concept of efficiency neglects, which you think should be included?

9. Read case 5–B, the Texas oil case. Imagine that a policy analyst had been called in by Governor Sterling from outside the state and asked how best to

regulate production. Imagine further that the policy analyst, after a little figuring on the back of an envelope, had decided that regulation of Texas oil was not in the public interest, since consumers outside Texas were benefitting from the reduced price of petroleum products, and that the analyst had thus declined to take on the job.

a. Describe three major perspectives on regulation that entered into the problem situation encountered by the analyst.

b. How does the hypothetical analyst's definition of the problem differ from those of the participants in part a? What value-criterion does the analyst choose, and how does it differ from those of the participants? Are there values or interests in the case that the analyst neglects, which you think should be included?

NOTES

1. If your choice involves envisaging "a cluster of interlocked problems . . . as one problem," you are considering what David Braybrooke and Charles E. Lindblom, in *A Strategy of Decision* (New York: Free Press, 1963), have called a "synthetic problem."

2. See Peter Uhlenberg, "Changing Structure of the Older Population of the USA During the Twentieth Century," *The Gerontologist* 17(1977):197–202, which shows that some concerns about a continually increasing elderly population in the United States have been exaggerated.

3. This more comprehensive view is known also as a "synoptic" view; see Braybrooke and Lindblom, *A Strategy of Decision*, ch. 3.

4. See Duncan MacRae, Jr., "Professions and Social Sciences as Sources of Public Values," *Soundings* 60(1977):3–21. The broader values listed here are discussed further in chapter 3 of the text.

5. Graham T. Allison, *Essence of Decision* (Boston: Little, Brown, 1971).

6. Amitai Etzioni, *The Active Society* (New York: Free Press, 1968), p. 285. Exercises distinguishing short-run and long-run perspectives are given in William D. Coplin, "Introduction to the Analysis of Public Policy from a Problem Solving Perspective," Learning Packages in the Policy Sciences PS6 (Syracuse, N.Y.: Syracuse University, International Relations Program, 1975).

7. On disasters see Allen H. Barton, *Communities in Disaster* (Garden City, N.Y.: Doubleday, 1969).

8. Erwin O. Smigel, ed., *Handbook on the Study of Social Problems* (Chicago: Rand McNally, 1971), p. 293.

9. Earl Rubington and Martin S. Weinberg, eds., *The Study of Social Problems*, 2d ed. (New York: Oxford University Press, 1977), pp. 3, 4.

10. Allison, *Essence of Decision*, pp. 59–60.

11. Ibid., p. 125.

12. A classic statement was that of William F. Ogburn in *Social Change* (New York: B. W. Huebsch, 1922), p. 202.

13. See Talcott Parsons, "Social Strains in America—1955," in Daniel Bell, ed., *The Radical Right* (Garden City, N.Y.: Doubleday, 1963), p. 175.

14. Dean S. Dorn and Gary L. Long, in "Sociology and the Radical Right," *American Sociologist* 7(1972):8–9, have contended that the arguments of the "radical right" should be considered on their merits, rather than in terms of their social and psychological sources. Allan Mazur, in "Disputes between Experts," *Minerva* 11(1973):243–262, notes that dissenting views by experts have been treated differently in the cases of fluoridation and nuclear fallout.

15. See Morton H. Halperin, *Bureaucratic Politics and Foreign Policy* (Washington, D.C.: Brookings, 1974), pp. 158–168.

16. See Judith I. de Neufville, *Social Indicators and Public Policy* (New York: American Elsevier, 1974). Indicators not only affect people's feelings about problems but also allow us to monitor changes in the substantive aspects of problems; see William D. Coplin, "Introduction to the Analysis of Public Policy from a Problem Solving Perspective," pp. 17–19.

17. This discussion is taken from Ole R. Holsti, "The Baseline Problem in Statistics: Examples from the Study of American Public Policy," *Journal of Politics* 37(1975): 187–201. The first quotation in the text (cited in Holsti, p. 189) is from Joyce Kolko and Gabriel Kolko, *The Limits of Power* (New York: Harper & Row, 1972), p. 54; the second is from Holsti, p. 191. Later in his article Holsti criticizes another writer for selecting a baseline so as to create the impression that America was spending too *little* on defense.

18. See Amitai Etzioni, *Social Problems* (Englewood Cliffs, N.J.: Prentice-Hall, 1976), p. 1.

19. See John P. Hewitt and Peter M. Hall, "Social Problems, Problematic Situations, and Quasi-Theories," *American Sociological Review* 38(1973):368.

20. See James S. Coleman, *Community Conflict* (New York: Free Press, 1956).

21. See John D. McCarthy and Mayer N. Zald, *The Trend of Social Movements in America* (Morristown, N.J.: General Learning Press, 1973).

22. Edgar E. Schattschneider, *The Semi-Sovereign People* (New York: Holt, Rinehart, and Winston, 1960).

23. See Charles O. Jones, *An Introduction to the Study of Public Policy*, 2d ed. (North Scituate, Mass.: Duxbury Press, 1977), pp. 39–43.

24. Halperin, *Bureaucratic Politics and Foreign Policy*, pp. 101–104.

25. Smigel, *Handbook on the Study of Social Problems*, p. xiii.

26. Daniel P. Moynihan, *The Politics of a Guaranteed Income* (New York: Random House, 1973).

27. Ibid.; and Daniel P. Moynihan, "Income by Right." *The New Yorker* 48(1973): I, 13 Jan., 34–57; II, 20 Jan., 60–79; III, 27 Jan., 57–81.

28. Moynihan, "Income by Right," *The New Yorker* 48(1973): I, 13 Jan., p. 39. © 1973 by Daniel P. Moynihan.

3

Criteria for Choice

In order to choose the best policy from among a set of alternatives, we need to be clear about the meaning of "best." You will have to choose this meaning for yourself, just as you chose the definition of the problem. Choosing a clear meaning for "best" will enable you to gather relevant data and compare the expected results of policies to see which is best.

In this chapter we suggest guidelines you can use for stating and systemizing your *criteria* for policy choice—the principles in terms of which you choose the best policy. You can try to organize these principles and express them in a way that is clear, consistent, and general. You can distinguish the desirability of a policy from its political feasibility, while taking both into account. You can also distinguish between ethical criteria that apply to consequences of policies and criteria that apply directly to policy alternatives themselves.

Although value criteria derive from many sources, one important source of the criteria used in policy analysis is the discipline of economics. Economics begins with the preferences of consumers and others and seeks means for satisfying them. Criteria resulting from this approach, which we shall discuss later in the chapter, include the Pareto criterion and cost-benefit analysis. But, in addition, equity or fairness and various other criteria can be important for policy analysis.

Different people are likely to choose somewhat different meanings of "best," even if they are all seeking the public interest or the general welfare. Some may wish to maximize the gross national product (GNP), judging one policy to be better than another if it leads to a larger GNP. For these people, we say that the criterion for choice is maximization of the GNP. Others may wish to minimize poverty, to maximize happiness, or to develop human potentialities fully. Criteria of this sort can be used in policy analysis if they can be measured quantitatively. Some people may wish to apply several criteria at the same time. Usually we qualify our choice of policies by requiring that the chosen policy be morally permissible (e.g., that it not involve assassination). We do not, however, include purely selfish criteria, such as maximization of one's own income or maximization of the welfare of one racial group regardless of others. We are seeking *ethical* criteria.

THE FORM OF ETHICAL CRITERIA

In formulating our criteria, as in redefining a problem, we often begin with a collection of specific values and disvalues, which we then try to systematize. They constitute a first approximation to the criteria that we will later use. In the deposit-bottles case (case 5–A) for example, the initial values included those of clean streets, employment for workers in the container and beverage industries (who would be threatened by regulation), and the convenience of purchasers of beverages who wished to discard containers rather than return them. In analyzing this case you may wish to add other values to the list or to omit some. If we consider the values listed, we then may ask whether we can formulate any overarching value criterion that includes them all and allows us to make tradeoffs among them. In chapter 5 we suggest that one such criterion is efficiency, though we shall have to define "efficiency" more precisely in order to use the term in our analysis.

In chapter 4 we consider the question whether a medical screening test should be performed on an entire population. The initial values include that of health and prolonged life (as contrasted with the suffering and mortality from colon cancer), the cost (a negative value) of the screening test, the cost of a later confirmatory test, and the cost of surgery. We try to combine these in the overarching criterion of cost-benefit analysis, including the controversial question whether we can properly place a monetary value on human life.

In case 4–A we ask what the optimum speed limit on American highways should be. The initial values considered include those of energy economy and reduction of traffic accidents. We later add the value of arriving at one's destination quickly. Again, to make tradeoffs among these values, we use cost-benefit analysis.

In chapter 7 we consider the values involved in evaluation of public programs. The principal question that people raise in such evaluation is whether a program is accomplishing its stated goals. Is it delivering a sufficient volume of health services, providing day care for children, getting money to the poor? Yet further consideration of a program may reveal that it is producing other, perhaps unplanned, values or disvalues. We need to include these in the balance of assessment as well. Equally important is the question whether the resources we use on this program might be spent better on something else. For this reason we should ideally know whether the services provided are worth, for example, the money spent, or whether a certain amount of health services is worth a corresponding amount of day care. These sorts of comparisons are not always easy to make; but if we can make them, we will broaden the range of alternatives that we can compare.

You should thus try to make your ethical criteria *clear*, so that they can be used in quantitative analysis; *consistent*, so that you can reconcile various values and disvalues with one another; and *general*, so that they will allow you to compare a wide range of policy alternatives.[1] These are requirements about the *form* of your criteria. They do not tell you what your criteria should be, but they may help you to develop a set of criteria that can be used over and over in a series of analyses that you can then relate to one another.

The problem of making your criteria clear can be illustrated with some examples of unclear criteria. We have mentioned the "general welfare" and the "public interest" as terms that refer to types of criteria that are ethical in meaning. But neither of these terms by itself has the clarity necessary for analysis. Each actually can be given a multiplicity of meanings such as we listed at the beginning of this chapter. A similar problem exists for the term "the greatest good." To say without further detail that this was your criterion would not enable you to carry out an analysis because the term is vague. To clarify this criterion, you would probably have to specify its meaning not only in words but in terms of a procedure for assigning quantitative values to "good," a problem that we consider later.

Another example of an unclear set of criteria is what David Braybrooke and Charles E. Lindblom call the "naive priorities method." This method involves listing in order of priority a set of terms that apply to abstract values, but providing insufficient detail to tell just when to turn from one value to the next. As they point out,

> It may put "freedom" ahead of "economic growth" and "economic growth" ahead of "equality"; or "combatting unemployment" ahead of "combatting inflation" and both of them ahead of "restoring competition."
>
> Declarations of this kind no doubt supply some information about the evaluator's general attitudes—but how much use are they in settling on specific policies? [2]

Such a list of words in order of priority is unclear both because the individual words need to be defined precisely and because we need also to tell exactly what "ahead of" means. At what level of "freedom" do we stop working on freedom and start working on "economic growth"? These matters can be made clear, but to do so requires much work, and the process may also reveal disagreements among persons who had initially agreed on the vague verbal formulation.

The test of consistency in your criteria can be illustrated by a criterion attributed to Jeremy Bentham: "That policy is best which produces the greatest good for the greatest number." Let us assume at this point that we have defined "good" precisely and thus satisfied the condition of clarity. Assume further that "good" is an aggregate quantity, summed over the entire population being considered. Given these meanings, a problem of consistency remains: We cannot always both provide the greatest total good and distribute that good among the greatest number of people. One possible policy might produce a large total of "good" but provide it only to a few, and another might produce small increments of "good" for a much greater number. The two words "greatest" in the criterion are thus inconsistent with one another for some possible sets of alternatives.

The test of generality is illustrated by criteria that are not general, but apply only to a particular limited set of alternatives. An example is the criterion "For policy choices involving air pollution, that policy is best that produces the least concentration of sulfur dioxide in the air." This criterion is less general than some others because it does not help in policy choices that do not involve air pollution. Similarly, the criterion "Educational institutions should not spend their resources on care for their students' health" does not help in choices that do not involve such expenditures.

The criterion we shall consider that comes nearest to being clear, consistent, and general is that of net benefit, in cost-benefit analysis. A substantial literature exists specifying procedures for estimating costs and benefits, even though some ambiguities remain. The use of one single overarching criterion (net benefit and nothing else) makes the system consistent. The criterion is applicable to all policy choices that permit monetary estimates of benefits and costs and is therefore quite general. It may not, however, agree with all our particular moral values; a challenge thus remains to formulate other criteria that rival that of cost-benefit analysis in its attractive formal properties but conform better to our substantive moral judgments.

Although general criteria have the advantage of permitting comparison of wide ranges of alternatives, analysts do sometimes make use of criteria that apply only to the limited set of alternatives in which they are interested. These specific criteria are sometimes easier to construct and use than general ethical principles. One way to compare a specific set of alternatives for policy choice is to list their possible consequences and ask a decision-making group to assign quantitative weights to them as from 1 to 10. A procedure of this kind has been used to rate the degrees of adverse environmental impact of various aspects of possible highway locations.[3] Such ratings can be used to compare various highway plans, all of which have the same cost. They cannot be used to tell whether any one of the plans is worth the cost or to compare spending on highways with spending on social services, police protection, or public television, for example.

It is desirable to begin with criteria of choice and then make use of them (together with relevant facts) to seek out the best policies. Unfortunately, much actual argument in support of policies goes in the opposite direction: People choose their policies first and then find arguments to support them. Such arguments may occasionally be correct and well reasoned, but more often they risk being merely an embellishment of choices that have been made on other grounds. To make correct decisions we must be prepared to admit that our convictions in favor of certain policies may be in error, if evidence shows that these policies do not in fact do what they were intended to do. We may also have to admit that these policies violate values to which we subscribe.

People often come to favor or oppose policies because their friends favor the policies, because they dislike the proponents of the policies, or because the policies have attractive-sounding titles. But policy analysts should be prepared to devote time and effort to seeing for themselves whether a policy will really promote the general values they hold, even if it is sponsored by a stranger or an opponent. When President Nixon proposed the Family Assistance Plan, a welfare reform bill that would have helped many poor Southern families, many liberal Democrats could not bring themselves to believe that a president whom they had long known as "tricky Dick" could propose a policy having such benefits. Their opposition contributed to the failure of the bill. Similarly, the policy of court-ordered busing for school desegregation came to be supported by black groups pressing for equal education and opposed by groups favoring inequality and privilege to such an extent that some of the unintended consequences of this policy were deliberately ignored. The observation by some social scientists of a connection between desegregation orders and "white flight" from the desegregated schools was seen by others as a manifestation of racism, not as a genuine result of policy analysis.[4] It is sometimes said that it is a misfortune not to be granted our wishes, but an even greater misfortune to be granted them and to discover that the results are not what we wanted. The chances of this latter misfortune may perhaps be reduced if we carry out analysis based on general goals and values.

DESIRABILITY AND POLITICAL FEASIBILITY

The meaning of "best" that we ask you to choose has to do with the *desirability* of policies—whether they relate to the general welfare or to general standards of morality. We ask you to distinguish desirability from *political feasibility*—the degree of possibility that a policy can be enacted and carried out. The two concepts are closely related, and we need to understand these relations as well as the distinction between them.

The eventual value that is produced by a policy depends both on how beneficial it would be if carried out—its desirability—and whether it is actually carried out. Thus, we might be tempted to say that its expected value is the product of its desirability and the probability that it will be carried out. We cannot make use of such a probability, however, if we are trying to persuade a decision maker whose own actions are part of that probability. We cannot go to the decision maker and say that the value of a policy must be modified by the probability that he himself will favor it. We want to tell him what its value will be *if* he favors it, in order for our persuasion to be effective.

The value that a policy produces also depends on how much of your own effort and resources you use in support of it. In this respect you are like the decision maker in the preceding paragraph. You would like to estimate how much value the policy would provide if you worked hard for it and if it were put into effect. You do not want to consider your own activities as governed by given "probabilities" as your own activities involve choice and effort. However, you may be willing to regard other people's activities as characterized by probabilities. In that case you might estimate the probability that the policy would be implemented without any effort on your part, with moderate effort, and with maximum effort.

In these terms you might make your own *personal* analysis of benefits and costs (*not* the same as cost-benefit analysis) to see whether the social value produced would be worth the cost to you personally. Such systematic analyses can indeed be used to guide personal decisions.[5] They cannot, however, be used in public forums to guide informed decision by the citizenry because your personal costs are of less concern to others than they are to you. Your loss of sleep, of leisure, and of career possibilities and your promises and commitments made to persuade others to favor the policy are of less public concern than personal concern. Public officials do often balance public gains against personal costs. But these are private decisions, not the ethical decisions necessary for informed public debate.

Political feasibility is not, therefore, an objective number that can be discovered by research. It involves your own efforts and those of the people whom you wish to persuade. When we engage in this persuasion, we tell people how desirable a policy would be if it *were* implemented. They may respond that others are unlikely to implement the policy. We may later wish to go to those others and persuade them. Our assessments of feasibility thus relate to the actions of the persons with whom we are talking and are not easily made the subject of quantitative analysis. For these reasons we separate our relatively precise analyses of desirability from our less precise analyses of feasibility, which vary with our conversation partners.

If we engage in public discussion of analyses based on desirability of policies, we set aside temporarily some of the subjectivity, or interindividual variation, in arguments about feasibility. There may still remain differences among citizens in their basic ethical criteria. Even these differences may be the subject of public debate. And although basic values are difficult to change, the process of systematizing them may increase somewhat the long-run possibility of agreement on the resulting value systems.[6]

Any systematic analysis of policy choices must of course be concerned with what is feasible as well as with what would be desirable. A totally infeasible policy is not a good one. But even though policy analysis, like diplomacy, is "the art of the possible," we shall first consider the relative worth of policies and only afterward ask what is possible. We ignore from the start those alternatives that are totally infeasible, such as those that demand resources totally beyond our control or those that would threaten the existence of organizations through which we must work. Only later, however, do we consider the detailed conditions and chances for enactment and implementation of policies. Thus, we do not begin by asking who will support each alternative policy, whose career it threatens, or whether it can be carried out. Nor in a democracy do we begin by asking whether public opinion favors one policy or another. Our aim as citizens is to decide on what grounds the other members of the relevant public should choose and to try to persuade them on those grounds.

An important condition for feasibility of policies is usually the agreement of various people to support the policies. The form in which we ask you to express your criteria—including clarity, consistency, and generality—may nevertheless interfere with getting agreement on particular policies that you advocate. People can often agree on specific policies even when they favor them for different reasons. If you ask them to agree first on a clear, consistent, and general ethical system, you may postpone agreement. Braybrooke and Lindblom point out that such an approach requires not only agreement on policies but also "a more ambitious agreement . . . on the deductive system in which these agreements would be incorporated." [7]

Such a deductive system is cost-benefit analysis, which tries to compare diverse consequences of policies in monetary terms. If we wanted to obtain agreement on cost-benefit analysis as an ethical criterion, we would have to spend much time and effort specifying how the costs of cancer could be compared with those of inadequate education or estimating in monetary terms the benefits from "self-reliance, freedom from fear, the joys of outdoor recreation, the pleasures of clean air, and so forth." [8] Such estimates are not out of the question, but if we want to agree on particular policies, it is easier to use more specific criteria that do not extend to all possible policy choices.

We nevertheless ask that you learn to analyze policy choices in terms of general ethical criteria. We do so because clarity of thought is an important aspect of general education about public problems. We hope that in the long run more of the people you encounter in working on policy problems will think in these terms. Many professional analysts already use cost-benefit analysis. You will therefore find it useful to understand reasoning based on this value system, even if you choose to disagree with some of its assumptions. In addition, the analysis of public problems in terms of general ethical systems can give rise to a research literature with well-defined standards of excellence, which can serve as a useful resource for citizen-analysts.

We next outline some of the criteria that are commonly used in policy analysis. In choosing your own criteria, you may wish to select one of these types or to tell how it differs from yours.

ETHICS: GOALS AND IMPERATIVES

Analysts ordinarily use two different types of ethical criteria for choosing policies. One type, known as *teleological* (from the Greek *telos* or "end"), is concerned with ends or goals beyond the act itself—consequences of an act or policy in terms of which we judge its rightness. These are the criteria for which science is more relevant, as they require knowledge of causes and effects for our estimation of consequences. Examples of teleological criteria are the survival of a group or species, the satisfaction of preferences, the maximization of the gross national product, happiness, and self-realization, all of which are ends to which our policies may be causally connected.

We also make many choices in terms of criteria that are independent of consequences, or *nonteleological*.[9] Examples of nonteleological criteria are the prohibitions from breaking one's promise or committing murder, no matter how beneficial the consequences might be. Nonteleological criteria are typically imperative in nature, as they tell us not to adopt a certain type of policy, "no matter what." Nonteleological criteria, although used by analysts, do not play a great part in policy analysis itself because they apply directly to the policy alternative and do not require detailed analysis of its consequences.

Many of the nonteleological criteria that we use derive from political obligations. An example is the elimination of an alternative on the ground that it is illegal or unconstitutional. In the long run laws and constitutions may be changed. But in the short run they often cannot, and we feel obligated to obey them.

In the city-growth case (case 3–B) the second section, "Conflicting Court Actions," indicates the way in which court interpretations of the law provide the limits within which policies are considered. Communities that are considering new regulations watch court decisions with care. They are concerned, of course, with what will be feasible in view of the actions of courts that follow the precedents of earlier cases. But when a firm interpretation has been established, people may come to regard it as an obligation, not merely as a limitation on what is feasible. Similarly, the decisions of the Supreme Court on school desegregation and busing have come to be regarded as the law of the land, even though a different interpretation prevailed several decades earlier.

In a democratic society, if we participate in an election and our side loses, we generally feel obligated to acknowledge the winners' occupancy of their offices, at least until the next election. Analogously, we sometimes feel that if we enter a preexisting group, we are obligated to respect its values and its definition of its problems. In this connection some policy analysts judge their first task to be to discover the values of the group that they enter so as to formulate policy proposals in terms of the group's values. But it seems an excessive limitation to accept the group's values without qualification. Analysts, especially if they are citizens, can sometimes choose whether to enter a group. They can also try to persuade the group that it is concerned with the wrong problem or using the wrong values. Such a possibility can be difficult, but we must not ignore it.

The promises and contracts we enter into in social roles other than that of citizen can also lead to obligations that impose nonteleological criteria on our choices as citizens. Once we have entered an agreement, we feel an obligation not to break it, even if we could accomplish a greater public benefit by breaking it. Similarly, if an organization is created with a given purpose, both those who work in it and outsiders may feel that it should not be used for other purposes. Thus, parents as well as teachers may acknowledge that preventive dental care could be included among a school's activities; yet this activity may be defined as outside the school's function.[10]

The teleological and nonteleological criteria we have discussed differ in an important way. A teleological criterion ordinarily *compares* alternative policies with respect to whether they produce some specified result or whether one produces more of some value than another.[11] Thus, a revolutionary's criterion might be to judge all policies relative to whether or not they bring about the downfall of a regime. A more common teleological criterion in our discussion will be whether one policy produces a greater net benefit in monetary terms than another.

A nonteleological criterion ordinarily asks whether a given policy is right or wrong in *absolute* rather than comparative terms: Does an act involve breaking a promise, breaking the law, or departing from the given purposes of an organization? Such a criterion can thus be applied to a single policy under consideration without comparing that policy with alternatives. Our stress on comparing alternatives, or on "best" policies, suggests that policy analysis is at least to some degree concerned with teleological criteria.

The nonteleological commitments that we make are sometimes chosen and at other times taken for granted. Policy choices often consist of a sequence of decisions in which we alternate between the small and the large view, between obeying laws and remaking them, and between factoring problems into manageable parts and reconsidering the larger perspective that relates the parts to one another. Etzioni's mixed-scanning approach is a way of carrying out this alternation.[12] Thus, in taking jobs and entering into social contracts we restrict our later alternatives. But we can at least try to be aware of that restriction when we make a choice. The consultant in systems analysis or operations research often takes as a given constraint the "charter" of the organization for which he works. For a consultant to the Department of Defense, "Defense of the nation, economical use of resources, destruction of the enemy, safety to friendly operating personnel, and desirability of heroism are typical matters that the charter makes statements about." [13] A distinctive feature of our particular approach to policy analysis is that it includes systematic reflection on the desirability of serving the goals of an organization or system prior to agreeing or contracting to do so.

The employer is of course also a party to the agreement. If policy analysts carry through their recommendations to the point of creating or changing an organization, they may themselves become employers or administrators. They are then under obligation to honor employment contracts and to treat employees fairly. Such agreements may limit their opportunities to reshape the organization later in view of new information.

For any policy choice we ordinarily act within certain defined social roles (citizen, official, employer, etc.), and it makes a great deal of difference what role we occupy. We might regard all roles related to a problem as facing a common set of right and wrong choices but each role as ruling out certain choices in terms of its associated conditions of political feasibility. But if we were to look only at political feasibility, we would be considering our roles only as practical conditions of action and ignoring the binding obligations they involve. For both these reasons it may be proper for a legislator to make choices that a judge or an administrator cannot, or for a citizen of one country to consider alternatives that a citizen of another cannot easily contemplate. We can consider changing norms and rules, but only at personal cost and at costs to society in predictability and precedents.

We may also feel certain means to be morally prohibited, even if the ends they serve seem desirable. The use of falsehood in persuasion, the corruption or bribery of officials, the imprisonment of the innocent, or the deliberate fostering of distrust between groups may seem undesirable in themselves. But the norms that we would violate if we did these things may also be seen as having value in terms of their consequences. If the norms of a society allow its members to expect honesty in private and official transactions, the existence of such norms may affect other values. In that case what appeared to be a nonteleological criterion would be justifiable in teleological terms. A policy furthered by dishonest means may thus have costs—difficult though they are to estimate—deriving from its effects on the normative arrangements of society.

One way to combine teleological and nonteleological criteria into a single decision criterion relates to the *form* that they usually assume. When teleological criteria are made clear and operational, they are often quantitative and vary continuously with the alternatives. Therefore, we may consider maximizing them through quantitative tradeoffs between alternatives. Welfare, preference satisfaction, net monetary benefit, and degrees of equality have this feature. In contrast, nonteleological criteria are usually *discrete*. They simply specify one class of acts that are forbidden and another class that are not. One way to consider the two types of principles together in a consistent system of calculation is to maximize the teleological criterion only within the range allowed by the nonteleological constraint.[14] We can stay within that range by eliminating from our analysis all alternatives that are prohibited by that constraint, just as we do for totally infeasible alternatives. For moral prohibitions we often do this automatically.

An example of maximization within such a constraint is the choice of the policy alternative having the best consequences in view of a legal restriction. The law may have specified, for example, that the racial composition of schools in a city not vary by more than a specified amount. We may then specify other educational goals such as amount learned, degree of social equality, and the relations of these variables to costs. Conceivably, our optimum policy in view of these other variables will fall within the requirement of racial composition. But if it does not, then our choice of alternatives will be constrained by the law and will lie somewhere on the boundary of the region of permissible policies as set by the law.[15]

Another example is the problem of maximizing the nutritive value of a diet within the constraint that the budget not exceed a given amount.[16] The setting of a budget is, in a sense, an example of a moral rule established by legislative or administrative action. A program or policy might well yield much more in benefits if it could be allowed to exceed the budgetary limit. Nevertheless, budgetary procedures do not usually permit such arguments to be used for overrunning the amount allowed.

There are, however, criteria that take the form of discrete limits or constraints but do not arise from moral or social rules. In discussion of environmental policy we often set forth specific limits of concentrations of substances in air or water. From an economic point of view we should regard these threshold concentrations as possibly alterable as the prices of resources change and the value-tradeoffs between production and environmental harm are altered. As energy becomes scarce, for example, we reconsider the use of coal in spite of the environmental hazards associated with its use. But in the short run, as long as such an environmental limitation is in effect, we may have to consider it as a nonteleological constraint when we formulate other policies.

Another type of criterion that appears to be discrete and nonteleological is the guarantee of a minimum level of education or health care for all citizens. In the discussion of such guarantees we often refer to them as "rights," implying that they are to be granted regardless of their consequences. But from time to time we may also reconsider such a rule in terms of its costs or benefits. An increase or decrease in available resources might increase or decrease the minimum level that is considered a "right."

When we consider policies toward crime, we encounter both teleological and nonteleological criteria. Many citizens regard punishment for criminal acts as appropriate regardless of its consequences. But Gary S. Becker, following an economic approach, proposes to analyze policies toward crime simply by maximizing welfare or minimizing loss to society.[17] In these terms incarceration not only removes possible sources of crime but also prevents people from producing and earning. Incarceration of the very productive (those who earn high salaries) detracts considerably from the GNP. Becker thus proposes fines as a type of penalty that would allow convicted persons to return to productive activity, assuming that their production would benefit the rest of society. This approach treats crime from a purely teleological point of view. It ignores, for example, any principle that retribution is proper regardless of its consequences.

Finally, the distinction between teleological and nonteleological criteria may sometimes be a matter of degree. Some consequences of a policy may flow from it so simply and directly that they are nearly synonymous with the policy itself. The two cases presented at the end of this chapter are borderline cases of this kind.

The laetrile case (case 3–A) involves the choice between continuing to ban the sale of laetrile, a substance believed by some to cure cancer, and legalizing its sale. To simplify the case, we assume that laetrile has no ascertainable effects on health. The criterion that James J. Kilpatrick uses in the case in support of legalizing laetrile is the satisfaction of preferences. The criteria advanced by Daniel S. Martin include health (as determined by medical scientists), possible costs to patients, and the desirability of truthful presentation of facts. There is a direct relationship between each policy alternative and the corresponding criteria. Each of these criteria can be involved in more complex models connecting it with other policies, but no elaborate models are needed here.

The city-growth case (case 3–B) was also chosen as involving a difference between possible criteria but requiring no elaborate models to connect policies with criteria. The two policies in question are, first, to limit migration into several (mostly suburban) cities and, second, to allow freer in-migration. The first policy is favored by residents who define the "general welfare" in terms of "the people who are already there—not those who may want to come there." The second policy would be more likely to be favored by a definition of the general welfare that included outsiders. Although the general welfare is a teleological criterion, each policy is so directly related to one definition of the general welfare that no elaborate models connecting policies to their consequences are needed.

A similar situation can also arise if we choose as criteria not the ultimate human values that philosophers would consider, but short-run or intermediate goals such as increasing the budget of an organization, delivering a certain amount of a service, or obtaining a certain racial mixture in a city school-system. The policies that lead to goals of this sort are connected relatively simply and directly with the short-run goals themselves.

SOURCES OF ETHICAL CRITERIA

As a citizen you are free to choose you own values or criteria in terms of which to compare prospective policies. At the same time, however, you are engaging in a collective choice with fellow members of a political community, and if you want to have your policy choices enacted you may wish either to draw values from that community or to persuade your fellow citizens to choose in terms of values that you propose. You are therefore making your choice of values not in isolation from your fellow citizens, but in interaction with them.

A society contains numerous groups that stand for values or value systems. Religious bodies and the legal system assert some of these values—for example, the values implied in the Judeo-Christian ethic or the Bill of Rights. The political culture of a nation also embodies informal understandings about what acts or values are proper. We learn from our families and communities about such values as political and economic freedom, material welfare, human equality, and human excellence. The values that different groups learn in a pluralistic society are not all alike, but they contain many common ingredients. A major task in formulating values for policy analysis is to understand and, where possible, synthesize values shared by participants, and to translate these values into precise and measurable form.

There are also more specific institutions and groups that assert values or stand for them. Various professions, such as medicine, law, and social work, may stand for values such as the furtherance of health, justice, and well-being. These values may be expressed in particular terms as a result of discussion in the profession. For example, the measurement of delivery of health services, such as the number of patients seen by doctors, may be a presumed substitute for the measurement of improvement in health itself.

Members of academic disciplines also sometimes advocate values that are related to the concepts of their disciplines. Biologists and ecologists have referred to survival as a criterion for public policy. Physicists and engineers have been concerned with the conservation of scarce energy resources. Social scientists also more often express concern for values related to the concepts of their fields: Psychologists sometimes mention personality development as a criterion for public policy, and economists often use the satisfaction of consumer and producer preferences as a criterion.

When social scientists and professionals try to assess the merits of competing policies, they proceed most often by asking whether the consequences of these policies make individuals better or worse off. In doing so they tacitly or explicitly develop teleological ethical criteria that supply definitions of the terms "better off" and "worse off." They may, for example, ask whether people are more or less satisfied with their jobs, their communities, or their family life. They may ask whether people are healthier or whether disease rates are likely to increase as a result of one policy or another. They may ask whether people are richer or poorer. Or they may try to ascertain whether people's preferences are likely to be more or less satisfied as a result of various policies. It is sometimes considered that citizens' preferences will be better satisfied if there is greater public access to policymaking.[18] Similar reasoning has been used to support the decentralization of decisions through revenue sharing.

The criteria that are used in the assessment of policies or programs are often specific indicators rather than general valuative variables because specific indicators can be measured more easily. Thus, we sometimes measure passenger-miles of transportation rather than the values that are realized by transportation, access to educational institutions rather than learning, test scores at graduation from school rather than the capacity to produce and earn or to be an informed citizen, or the delivery of health services rather than health. Even if we have to use indicators of this kind as substitutes for general values, we should keep in mind the fact that changes in such indicators are not necessarily good or bad in themselves.

In judging whether a policy makes people better off social scientists in different disciplines tend to take different approaches. These approaches relate both to the characteristic methods of the disciplines and to the valuative notions implicit in these disciplines of what it means to be "better off" or to enjoy greater welfare or well-being. The most systematic comparison of policies has been carried out by economists, who use abstract models of the market economy or estimate benefits and costs in monetary terms. Researchers in sociology and other social sciences, relying on sample surveys, have more often asked people questions intended to measure the effects of past policies on them and have not put these questions in monetary terms. Political scientists have more often asked questions about respondents' *opinions* concerning the desirability of alternative policies. But questions of this kind call for respondents' judgments about *other* people's welfare as well as their own.

The basic criterion of economics relative to whether people are better off is the satisfaction of the preferences of the relevant participants, be they consumers, workers, or investors. If a person prefers one bundle of goods to another, he is deemed to be better off if he has the one he prefers rather than the other. If an investor prefers one portfolio of assets to another, once again, his own system of values is accepted in ascertaining the portfolio with which he is better off. Similar statements can be made about a person making choices between work and leisure. If two persons engage in a voluntary exchange of goods, bonds, or labor services, then presumably both prefer the situation after exchange, and therefore both are better off as a result.[19] The underlying ethic is that of maximizing preference satisfaction.

We speak of an "ethic of preference satisfaction" because the satisfaction of a person's preferences corresponds to one notion, but not the only possible notion, of what is good for humanity. An observer may judge that what a person prefers is not good for him, as when he smokes cigarettes, eats tasty but unhealthful food, or buys laetrile (case 3–A). The observer may also judge that a person prefers lower forms of entertainment or culture when he might learn to appreciate higher forms. There are thus other notions of the good life than that of preference satisfaction, and these other notions correspond to other ethics that you may choose for policy analysis.

The ethic of preference satisfaction is also only one among various ethics because it recognizes that in actual markets an individual's opportunities to have his perferences expressed are usually limited by his economic resources. Rather than being allowed to express abstract wants or desires, the person indicates his willingness to engage in exchange (to part with his income or past savings) and thus shows what economists often call an "effective demand" for bread, leisure, or shares of IBM stock. For example, although most of us might admire the Rolls Royce as a means of transportation, we would no doubt believe that the economic system was probably following consumers' preferences in producing few of this automobile because few drivers are willing to give up sufficient resources to meet the high Rolls price-tag. Thus, the opportunity to express our preferences in an economic system is limited by our share of the total available resources or purchasing power. In this way the ethic of preference satisfaction in economics must be related to the ethical aspects of the distribution of economic power. We shall turn to these distributional aspects in greater detail later.

It should be clear that in relying on individuals to decide what is best for themselves rather than to have others choose for them, the ethic of preference satisfaction involves an esteem for decentralized decision making. A pricing system that transmits information back and forth among exchange participants to facilitate the production and distribution of goods and services is the explicit indication of that respect for individual choice. However, this very respect for individual choice creates complications in the search for criteria for judging public policies. In order to establish methods for selecting the best policy, an approach must be found that can take account of the preferences of a large number of individuals. Utilitarian approaches that use phrases such as "the greatest good for the greatest number" have been advanced for this purpose. But as we have seen, such criteria need to be made clear and consistent. It fell to an area of inquiry called "welfare economics" to establish a consistent and closely reasoned set of criteria to account for the preferences of a large number of individuals.

The basic standard of welfare economics takes its name from its formulator, Vilfredo Pareto, who searched for a rule to establish the circumstances under which one situation could be unambiguously judged to be superior to another. According to the *Pareto criterion* situation A is better than situation B if at least one person prefers A to B and no one prefers B to A. This criterion relies on individuals to utilize their own preference orderings in determining whether or not they are better off. It is more specific than the utilitarian notion mentioned earlier in that "the greatest number" is identified to be everyone in the sense that no one can be harmed if the Pareto criterion is used. When this criterion is extended to encompass all possible changes from some given starting point, we describe a situation as being "Pareto optimal" if it is impossible to make any change without harming at least one person.

To see how the Pareto criterion operates, consider a hypothetical community including three members faced with four policy choices: do nothing, build a new park, create a new day-care center, or pave one of the streets. Assume that the three persons in question will bear all the burdens (such as taxes) and reap all the benefits of the policy choice, that is, only they are affected. We begin with their rank-order preferences among the four policies, as shown in table 3–1. Person 1 prefers the park to the three other alternatives and has least preference for inaction (doing nothing). Person 2 prefers to do nothing rather than enact any of the other policies, and his or her lowest preference is for paving the street. Person 3 most prefers the day-care center and has least preference for the park. The table says nothing about how intensely people prefer one alternative to another but limits our information to

Table 3–1.
Preference Rankings of Four Policies by Three Persons

	Person		
	1	**2**	**3**
Most preferred	Park	Nothing	Day care
	Day care	Day care	Nothing
	Street	Park	Street
Least preferred	Nothing	Street	Park

rank orders of preference, which is all the information needed to apply the Pareto criterion.

Let us first ask whether any of the policy alternatives is preferred to doing nothing by the Pareto criterion. Since person 2 most prefers to do nothing, any other policy will make him worse off in terms of his preference ranking. Therefore, regardless of the preferences of persons 1 and 3, there is no policy better than doing nothing according to the Pareto criterion. Since no change can be made from the do-nothing policy without harming person 2, the do-nothing policy is Pareto optimal. For similar reasons the park and day-care policies are also Pareto optimal if taken as starting points. If the group enacted them and then moved away from them, these moves would harm persons 1 and 3 respectively.

The only policy that is not Pareto optimal as a starting point in table 3–1 is that of paving the street. A change from the street policy to the day-care policy would lead all three persons to be better off in the sense of moving to a more preferred policy. We cannot, however, say that a change from paving the street to building a park would be a Pareto improvement, as it would leave person 3 lower on his or her preference ranking.

The Pareto criterion is difficult to dispute; yet it has struck many analysts as overly conservative and status quo oriented. Many (if not most) situations on which public policy attention has been focused cannot be changed without imposing harm on at least one person. It is precisely the difficulty of comparing one person's loss (based on the individual's evaluation) with another person's gain (based on the individual's own preferences) that prompted Pareto to set up his criterion as he did. How can we say whether the rain that washed out your tennis match but also watered my crops was on balance beneficial or harmful to the two of us taken together? If we cannot therefore judge whether cloud seeding would be a good policy, the Pareto criterion reveals itself as lacking in generality. There are many policy choices for which it is not helpful.

The very prevalence of cases in which policies would be simultaneously beneficial to some and harmful to others led welfare economists to try to develop a framework for extending the Pareto criterion. This extension involves comparing the gains and losses of different individuals. One result was the "Kaldor criterion," according to which a given change would be considered an improvement if those who are better off calculate their gain to be large enough to compensate the losers for their loss. Such a compensation scheme is most workable if the participants accept a common standard of value. This most often involves the use—as a measurement of preference satisfaction—of a monetary unit that is already accepted as the means of exchange in market transactions. Under the Kaldor criterion it is not necessary for actual compensation of losers to be made, only that the total gains exceed total losses so that compensation is possible. This new standard allows policy makers to consider a wider range of policies for improving the welfare of the society, as defined by the preferences of each of its members. But only if the ethic of preference satisfaction is joined by a further ethic that objects to the existence of losers would actual compensation of losers be required. In such a case we would essentially be back with the Pareto criterion.

ANALYSIS OF BENEFITS AND COSTS

The Kaldor criterion begins with a ranking of each person's preferences and then asks that the losers' losses be comparable in monetary terms with the gains of at least some of the gainers. It is only a short step from the somewhat abstract Kaldor criterion to the practical real-world criterion of cost-benefit analysis, which requires that we measure *all* gains and losses in monetary terms. Cost-benefit analysis also attempts to outline when society is better off as a result of a particular policy or change. The gains involved in the construction of a new dam would be counted as benefits in the form of increased irrigation opportunities and the accompanying agricultural opportunities, reduction in expected flood damage, and potential for expanded sailing and swimming activities. On the other hand, losses would appear as costs in the form of reduced wildlife and agricultural acreage or of fewer opportunities for hiking and white-water canoeing. A policy is considered an improvement in cost-benefit analysis if the benefits exceed the costs.

Construction of lodging and eating facilities around the lake associated with the dam, however, might not be a net social benefit if it took resources from elsewhere.[20] A basic assumption of cost-benefit analysis is that two equilibrium states of a market are being compared. The overall social benefit of a policy must then be calculated as the difference between the gains in earnings and production where they increase, and the losses in earnings and production where they decrease. If lodging or eating facilities were only moved from elsewhere to the lake, these gains and losses would tend to cancel out.

A similar problem of counting costs and benefits arises in the deposit-bottles case (case 5–A). A major complaint of managers and workers in the disposable container and beverage industries was that if deposit bottles were required, jobs would be lost in their industries. A cost-benefit analyst would ask, however, whether there would be offsetting gains of jobs elsewhere. If so, the loss of jobs in these industries would not be counted as a net cost. If the economy were in a state of full employment and the workers laid off were needed for equally well paying jobs, a cost-benefit analyst might not count the loss of jobs as a cost at all. By calculating in this way, however, he or she would be considering only the long-run or equilibrium effects of the policy of requiring deposit bottles and might be ignoring the inconvenience and costs of retraining for the displaced workers.[21]

The costs and benefits of a proposed policy are usually assessed relative to the alternative policy of taking no action. We thus *define* the net benefit or the net cost of doing nothing as zero. This reference to the status quo does not mean that no changes will occur in the future. The policy of not building a new dam, for example, would entail continued expectation of possible future flooding, even though no clouds are presently in the sky. Thus, the continuation of existing trends constitutes the zero or reference point from which to estimate the costs and benefits of proposed changes or policies. Future trends may indeed leave people worse off than at present and increase their sense that a problem exists. But in cost-benefit analysis changes that result from following a policy of doing nothing are not referred to as costs.

When a proposed policy entails the expenditure of funds, the associated cost clearly must be included in cost-benefit analysis. The similarity of this calculation to the gain-loss analysis of the Kaldor criterion is apparent if we include in our analysis the concept of "opportunity cost." To the economist opportunity cost is the value forgone by the selection of an alternative. The opportunity cost of putting money in the cookie jar is the interest earnings that could have been made by depositing the same funds in a savings account. An opportunity cost of attending college is the income that could have been earned if the student had instead taken a job during those four years. The opportunity cost of an afternoon on the golf course could be the commissions that might otherwise have been earned as an insurance agent. The construction of a new dam entails the use of concrete, labor services, and machinery, all of which could have been used in alternative projects. It is usually presumed that in obtaining the use of these resources the project director of the dam must bid them away from other uses, thus making the price paid for them (costs) a reflection of their value elsewhere. By including in costs the market price of resources, we are acknowledging our loss in the form of the value of projects forgone due to the dam construction. The opportunity cost includes the value of projects that could have been undertaken in the private sector of the economy—values that would have been realized by a do-nothing public policy. But they do not (conventionally) include the values of other possible public policies.

Cost-benefit analysis has been used extensively in government decision making. Although the ability to employ a common monetary standard of measurement is one of the prime attributes of this analytic technique, attempts at application frequently encounter types of costs and benefits that clearly are poorly suited to monetary evaluation. One of the alleged costs of building a dam on the New River in North Carolina and Virginia is the destruction of possible archeological treasures. Although we might be able to make estimates of the value of artifacts that have already been discovered since there is a type of market for them among museums and other collectors, the uncertainty as to what might yet be discovered if the dam is not built makes the estimation of this opportunity cost very difficult. Moreover the evaluation of the benefits of waterskiing in the lake behind the new dam is likely to be haphazard since there usually is no price charged for such recreational activity. Furthermore, when projects are expected to have an extended life, the extent of future costs and benefits becomes less certain and it is necessary to adjust for the time element in making overall cost-benefit calculations. Economists have devised a technique called "discounting," which adjusts costs or benefits for the time in which they occur (under the rationale that you will have to promise me more than one dollar twelve months from now to make it the equivalent of one dollar now). But there is little present agreement about what the appropriate discount rate should be.[22]

We have thus far indicated that an improvement over the status quo has taken place if the net benefits of an action (or total benefits minus total costs) are positive. But, just as in the case of the Pareto criterion, policy analysis goes beyond the mere identification of good policies (those with net benefits) and searches for best policies. This entails the acknowledgment of possible constraints on decision making such as a limited amount of funds available. Where such constraints exist, they may prevent decision makers from adopting some good policies during a given period. Two possible reactions to such constraints would be making programs smaller than optimal or phasing in new programs gradually.

It is also important to take account of the scale of a project, thus placing the net-benefits data in a proper perspective. Suppose project A had expected costs of $2 million and benefits of $2.3 million and project B entailed costs of $100,000 and benefits of $125,000. On the basis of the size of net benefits alone, A would be the clear preference. However, if there were twenty projects that had the same costs and benefits as B, those twenty taken as a group would provide greater net benefits than A. Policy analysts will often adjust for these scale situations by ranking all possible actions according to the *ratio* of total benefits to total costs, thus computing a type of rate of return for the various alternatives. If we have a fixed budget or if projects can be varied in scale, the ranking of projects based on their benefit-cost ratios can permit us to choose the best projects more accurately than rankings based solely on the size of net benefits.

The benefit-cost ratio has an analogue in cases in which we cannot measure benefits in monetary terms, but can provide some other quantitative measure of them. If our outcome or benefit measure is expressed in terms of the number of persons employed, reduction in cases of illness, or number of new therapeutic drugs found by a testing procedure, we can compute a *cost-effectiveness ratio*—the number of beneficial outcomes per dollar spent. Such a ratio can be used to compare several policies that can be varied in scale but that all produce the same type of result, as measured by the same indicator of effectiveness. Such ratios are useful, but as ethical criteria they are lacking in generality. They are not helpful in comparing projects of fixed scale because the amounts of effect and of cost are not commensurable. Nor are they helpful for comparing projects that produce types of outputs that are not measurable by the same effectiveness index (e.g., persons employed and drugs found).

A benefit-cost ratio or a cost-effectiveness ratio can serve as a test of *efficiency*, a criterion that is sometimes used in policy choice. Efficiency, in this sense, means getting the greatest amount of desirable results per unit cost or getting a given amount of results at the least cost ("productive efficiency"), either of which would be consistent with maximizing one of the above ratios. In our further discussion of efficiency in chapter 5 we shall judge efficiency in terms of preference satisfaction and then make use of the related test of net benefit—the excess of benefits over costs. We shall treat the perfect market as efficient in this sense and, in some examples, as efficient in the sense of producing Pareto optimal results.

Cost-benefit analysis shares with the Pareto criterion a blindness to the identity of gainers or losers and to the distribution of costs and benefits among individuals. All costs and benefits, as measured by the monetary preferences of the people involved, are typically given equal weight in the calculations, in spite of the possibility that such estimates may be affected by the economic circumstances of the people in question. For instance, a poor person might be willing to pay a smaller amount (his or her estimated benefits) for access to a kidney dialysis machine than a wealthy individual receiving the same treatment. Attempts have been made to adjust for these circumstances by the application of different weighting factors for the cost and benefit estimates of different segments of the population. Analyses of this type have become controversial because they involve a more obvious ethical criterion—equity, or fairness—as to whose interests are to be of more and less concern to society in choices of public policy. This is not to imply that the cost-benefit analyses based on equal weightings are devoid of ethical assumptions, but only that those judgments are hidden behind the mask of uniform weights. In either case the ethic of preference satisfaction once again is linked to considerations of fairness. We shall now turn our attention to equity as an important public policy criterion.[23]

THE CRITERION OF EQUITY

The criteria of Pareto optimality and cost-benefit analysis have customarily emphasized what economists refer to as "efficiency," through minimizing costs, or maximizing net benefits, in terms of preference satisfaction. It is important to recognize, however, that concerns for justice may often play a major role in public policy studies. This is extensively discussed in Arthur Okun's *Equality and Efficiency: The Big Tradeoff*. The title itself emphasizes the critical dilemma that analysis often reveals, namely, that equity and efficiency are frequently inconsistent criteria that lead to incompatible optimal solutions.

Okun provides an imaginary experiment by which you can estimate how important equity in income is to you.

> *A proposal is made to levy an added tax averaging $4,000 . . . on the income of the affluent families [the top five percent] in an effort to aid the low-income families. Since the low-income group*

. . . has four times as many families as the affluent group, that should, in principle, finance a $1,000 grant for the average low-income family. However, . . . the money must be carried from the rich to the poor in a leaky bucket. Some of it will simply disappear in transit, so that the poor will not receive all the money that is taken from the rich.[24]

Okun then asks the reader to decide how much leakage he or she would accept and still support such a transfer. Your answer is an indication of the importance you attach to equity between income groups.

The term "equity," though widely used by economists, does not have nearly the clarity of "efficiency" as an ethical criterion. There is nevertheless some value in trying to set up a framework in which different views of equity, or fairness, can be compared. One such attempt is the drawing of a distinction between "horizontal equity" and "vertical equity." Horizontal equity has been defined as "the equal treatment of equals." Although this may seem to be a rather indisputable concept, it has little meaning until the circumstances under which people are considered equals, as well as what constitutes equal treatment, can be specified. In the realm of politics horizontal equity could mean granting one vote to each person over the age of eighteen. In the labor market it might mean equal pay for equal work. In education it might entail equal education for all children, though the phrase "equal education" may receive various interpretations—for example, equality of facilities or of outcomes and equality within communities or among them. If there is to be busing to achieve racial integration, horizontal equity might call for whites and blacks to do an equal amount of bus riding. Horizontal equity as applied to public finance can be interpreted as calling for equal taxation of all those with the same income levels, although this is frequently qualified further by reference to age, size of family, and other characteristics.

In contrast, vertical equity has been defined as "the unequal treatment of people in unequal circumstances"—usually to make them more nearly equal. Some of the more frequent applications of vertical equity standards are to matters of income distribution and taxation. Legislatures are continuously faced with the opportunity of applying vertical equity standards in decisions concerning the relative burdens of taxes. Lyndon Johnson's War on Poverty was waged (at least partially) in accordance with the rationale that the market's distribution of income was unjust.

There may also be situations in which the notion of vertical equity becomes irrelevant. Such would be the case if we were to argue that there should be no such thing as unequals where opportunities to vote are concerned. The judicial system in this country has devoted considerable attention in recent years to the "equal protection of the laws" provision of the Fourteenth Amendment and to identifying situations or characteristics that warrant differential treatment.

We shall often find that standards of vertical equity are more difficult to apply than those of horizontal equity. Not only do we have to identify reasons for treating people unequally, but we must also decide how unequally they should be treated. Although it might be easy to achieve agreement that the rich should pay more taxes than the poor, it would be more difficult to reach a consensus on how progressive the tax structure ought to be. Vertical equity may therefore require a deeper look into our system of values.

The role of equity considerations becomes especially crucial in the analysis of government transfer payments. If the nonpoor are unwilling to contribute voluntarily to the relief of poverty, the Pareto criterion will prohibit any transfers from rich to poor. Cost-benefit analysis would traditionally count the dollars extracted from the rich as a cost, find an equal amount of benefits in the form of payments to the poor (assuming no administrative costs of such a program), and reject the transfer program because of zero net benefits. It is therefore left to vertical equity criteria to justify governmental policies of redistribution, although, as we indicated earlier, these criteria may be interwoven with cost-benefit analysis in the form of higher weights for the gains of the poor than for the losses of the rich.

Another interpretation of equity, that people should receive what they deserve in terms of efforts, ability, or even inheritance, may lead us into a discussion of the desirability of private property or meritocracy. These considerations necessarily enter into policy analysis, but they call for disciplined thought about how to frame such criteria consistently. In such discussions we must also be careful to distinguish between equity and efficiency criteria.

An additional aspect of equity concerns policies that change people's situations relative to what they have expected. If property owners have invested in land that is to be taken by government for a highway or a dam, they are compensated. On the other hand, investors in roadside facilities, the value of which decreases when a competing road is built, may protest and their loss may be a cost to them (even if not counted as a social cost), but having no legal right, they are not ordinarily compensated as a matter of right. Policies to mitigate the effects of economic fluctuations or unemployment also tacitly consider the values or disvalues of sudden changes in people's situations. The problem of dealing justly with persons harmed by legal changes has been referred to as that of "transitional equity." [25]

These various aspects of equity may be illustrated by cases presented at the end of this and later chapters.

The criterion of horizontal equity would seem to apply whenever a law is made that affects equally all persons in a given category. Thus, legalization of laetrile (case 3–A) would affect all laetrile purchasers equally; controls on city growth (case 3–B) would affect equally all who wished to move in; the provision of free medical screening tests for colon cancer (chapter 4) would equally affect all persons in a given age category to whom the tests were provided; a fixed speed limit (case 4–A) treats all drivers equally; and the fluoridation of a city water supply (case 6–A) would affect all residents of the city equally.

Some persons affected by these policies, however, might claim that they were *not* "equal" to others and were thus being treated unfairly. When the sale of laetrile was prohibited, some potential purchasers might have complained that they were being singled out for control, that they were being prevented from purchasing a harmless product while cigarette smokers were not being so controlled. They would thus have been redefining the category of "equals" to include cigarette purchasers as well as themselves. When a city considered the fluoridation of its water supply, those citizens who required kidney dialysis treatment might have claimed that the policy imposed an unfair hardship on them because the fluorides had to be removed from the water used in their treatment. They would thus have been claiming that they were not simply "equals" as residents of the city but should be treated as "unequals." The criterion of horizontal equity therefore requires considerable clarification if it is to be used as a precise guide to policy. Some of this clarification is carried out by the courts.

In the city-growth case it was claimed that zoning regulations aimed at slowing growth were economically discriminatory—that they excluded housing for middle- and low-income people. Literally, this was a claim that the policy treated unequals unequally. But the claim was that it made unequals *more* unequal rather than less. In legal terms the claim implied that people of different income groups should be treated as *equals* for purposes of moving into a community. The concept of "discrimination" here implies unequal treatment of persons who should be treated equally.

A small degree of vertical equity is involved in the equal provision of medical screening tests or fluoridation because the costs of these policies are probably not equally apportioned over the population. Insofar as the rich pay more taxes for these services than the poor, the provision of these services involves a transfer of resources from the rich to the poor and thus an element of vertical equity. In the case of fluoridation the poor tend to have more tooth decay and thus to benefit more from the policy in terms of reduction of children's tooth decay.

An element of horizontal *in*equity also arises from taxing all citizens for a good or service from which only certain citizens benefit. Since fluoridation is primarily beneficial to children with developing teeth, there is an inequity in taxing elderly childless couples for this purpose. For some policies this inequity can be alleviated by charging users for the good or service, but the cost of fluoridation is so small and the administrative cost of charging for it would be so great that this small inequity is ignored by policy analysts.

Transitional equity is involved in the deposit-bottles case (case 5–A) if a policy is adopted of banning or taxing discardable beverage containers. The need for workers to change jobs and for management to reallocate resources may lead policy makers to phase in the new policy gradually or to provide for retraining of workers. These modifications of the policy may be motivated by concern for transitional equity, that is, concern for making amends for depriving people of conditions to which they claimed a right. But these modifications might also be justified by the possibly greater hardship that workers would experience from rapid than from slower adjustment; or they might be motivated by concern for political feasibility and for lessening the opposition of managers and workers to the enactment of the policy.

All these aspects of equity relate to the systems of norms, or of legitimate expectations, that exist in a given society. The rights and duties associated with particular social roles, such as that of property ownership, lead to the expectation that when laws are changed, people will be compensated for resulting damages. The social and legal definition of people as equal in a given respect leads to the expectation that they will be treated equally. People who are socially defined as in different situations may be treated differently according to norms such as those of merit or deservingness.

Our possible policy choices may, however, extend to the change of these norms themselves. We may argue, as John Rawls has done, that to reward persons in terms of their merits is inconsistent with principles of justice.[26] The women's liberation movement has argued that some of the social categories according to which women have been regarded as different from men should be altered so that the sexes are treated alike. The Equal Rights Amendment expresses this argument. Thus, the social categories defining similarity and difference cannot always be taken as given, but themselves are sometimes subjects for policy analysis.

One conceivable way to make the criterion of vertical equity more clear would be to define some new measure of welfare for individuals that would in effect treat them more equally than do costs and benefits. If we wished to include equity or distributional features in cost-benefit analysis, we might consider weighting the costs and benefits to individuals by some function of their income by assuming that the welfare value of income increased at a decreasing rate as income increased. For a given change in income, the presumed welfare change would then be greater for the poor than for the rich. Progressive taxation is sometimes justified on this basis. One such function is the logarithm of income. An analyst could also repeat his analyses for several such functions and present the results to others to judge which they considered most equitable.

The judgment among alternative policies in terms of weighted costs and benefits, like judgment in terms of costs and benefits themselves, is an example of using as a criterion a "social welfare function." Such a function is a number that corresponds to the expected results of each policy alternative and purports to measure the welfare to society that that alternative would bring. For cost-benefit analysis that function is the total income of all concerned, discounted for the future. For the modification of cost-benefit analysis suggested above, it would be a total of values of a certain function of income, such as a logarithm, over all units receiving income. Both these functions are simply sums over individuals to obtain a presumed social welfare.

Advocates of happiness as a criterion might wish that the social welfare function be a total of happiness, assuming that it could be measured. They would not then be concerned with its distribution. They would, of course, have to decide (or agree with others) on conventions for making interpersonal comparisons of happiness. These comparisons cannot be made on scientific grounds alone but require agreement on "yardsticks," or presumed bases of comparison —goods, circumstances, or reported situations—that might be supposed to correspond to equal happiness (satisfaction, utility) for various persons.[27] An extensive body of research using interview surveys has been developed for the measurement of happiness and satisfaction, but these measurements may not yet have the precision desirable for measurement of a criterion in policy analysis.[28]

In the absence of quantitative information, classification of those affected into *categories* is also often used. Even when a quantitative measure is available (such as scores on a test of educational achievement), it may be transformed into categories such as "high," "medium," and "low." Income is also often transformed in this way (in terms of a poverty line), and health status can be treated in categories.[29] If the category that is stressed consists of a small part of the population that is worst off—the poor, the least educated, or the sick—then the use of such a classification will tend to stress vertical equity.

The criteria we have considered have been described in terms of individuals and relations among them. They may thus appear to deal with relatively minor changes in policies within a given system such as that of representative government or a capitalistic free economy. But the logic of policy analysis also extends to major alternatives such as the choices among forms of government or among economic systems. A basic "policy" alternative that logically precedes others is the choice of systems of law and government. The framers of the United States Constitution, for example, were guided by the experience of other regimes as well as by considerations of feasibility of ratification. The ethical criteria invoked in the Declaration of Independence included nonteleological notions of rights, and the Preamble to the Constitution specified several teleological criteria including the promotion of the general welfare.

SUMMARY

To choose the best policy among alternatives, you need to formulate a clear criterion, or principle of choice, which specifies the meaning of "best" that you wish to use. This criterion should express ethical values rather than selfish or private values. Ideally, it should be not only clear but also self-consistent and general in application. It should express the desirability of various policy alternatives, as distinguished from their political feasibility.

Two major types of ethical criteria are commonly used: teleological criteria, such as satisfaction, survival, or material welfare, which are attained in various degrees as *consequences* of policies; and nonteleological criteria, such as the prohibition from committing murder, which are features of the policy itself. These can be used in combination with one another.

The ethical criteria that we use originate in the values of our society or of groups within it. The discipline of economics, together with its subfield of welfare economics, is the source of one closely reasoned approach, which is the basis of cost-benefit analysis. This approach begins with the assumption that the satisfaction of preferences is the criterion for policy choice. It first develops the Pareto criterion, according to which a new policy is considered an improvement on a preexisting state of affairs if some of the affected persons prefer the new policy and no one prefers the existing situation. The approach then moves to the Kaldor criterion, according to which a new policy is an improvement if those who prefer the existing situation (the losers) could hypothetically be fully compensated by the gainers. One further step takes us to cost-benefit analysis in which all gains and losses are estimated in monetary terms. In this procedure the benefits and costs of proposed projects constitute the basis for policy choice.

A further set of criteria that modify cost-benefit analysis, though they are less precise, are those of equity. They concern primarily the equal treatment of equals (horizontal equity) and the unequal treatment of unequals so as to make them more equal (vertical equity). The application of the criterion of vertical equity requires consideration either of individuals' income or of other categories in which respondents are placed by society. In the next chapter we shall consider the models of causation that connect our policy alternatives with the criteria we have chosen.

GLOSSARY

Benefit: a monetary gain realized (actually or potentially) as a result of a public policy, in comparison with the monetary amount that would have been realized if no new policy had been undertaken.

Benefit-cost ratio: the ratio of the benefit of a policy to its cost; used to rank policies or programs when costs are drawn from a fixed sum, such as a budget, or when programs may be varied in scale.

Clarity: the property of a criterion that allows policies to be ranked in unambiguous order if their properties and consequences are known.

Consistency: a set of criteria is consistent if it does not lead to contradictory rankings of policy alternatives.

Cost: a monetary loss incurred, in comparison with the situation if no new policy had been undertaken.

Cost-benefit analysis: a criterion for policy choice that judges policies better and worse in terms of their net monetary benefits to the economy.

Cost-effectiveness ratio: the ratio of a measure of effectiveness of a program (in nonmonetary terms) to its monetary cost.

Criterion (pl., criteria): a principle or standard against which policies may be judged (see also value criterion in Glossary to chapter 1).

Deservingness: an aspect of equity according to which persons are favored or disfavored by policies according to positive or negative qualities they are judged to have shown in the past. Examples of frequently considered favorable qualities are previous military service, previous contribution to Social Security funds, and widowhood; of negative qualities, alleged immorality.

Efficiency: the state of making the best use of resources. Productive efficiency is achieved when least-cost methods or combinations of inputs are used in production; allocative efficiency is achieved when resources are divided among industries so as to reflect all relevant costs and benefits.

Equity: fairness or justice (see also horizontal equity; vertical equity).

Ethic of preference satisfaction: the criterion according to which policies are judged better or worse according to the extent to which they satisfy people's expressed preferences.

Ethical: concerned with the general welfare, the public interest, or general moral principles or rules, as distinguished from the interests of particular individuals, groups, or organizations.

Ethical system: an interrelated set of ethical criteria.

Generality: the property of a criterion that makes it applicable to a wide range of policy alternatives.

Horizontal equity: the equal treatment of equals.

Kaldor criterion: a criterion according to which a change from one situation to another is desirable if, after the change, those who are better off can compensate all losers for their losses. Actual compensation of losers does not have to be made.

Net benefit: benefit minus cost.

Nonteleological criterion: a criterion that judges a policy right or wrong without considering its consequences.

Opportunity cost: that cost of a policy alternative which is incurred by the use of resources that could otherwise have been put to other use.

Pareto criterion: a criterion for choice between situations or states of affairs, based on individuals' preferences among them. According to this criterion situation A is better than situation B if at least one person prefers A to B and no one prefers B to A.

Role: one of a set of positions defined by a society, with a corresponding set of rights and duties—for example, citizen, employee, student, husband, mother.

Social welfare function: a numerical function of policy alternatives that is claimed to represent, as an ethical criterion, the total welfare of society.

Teleological criterion: a criterion that judges policies better and worse according to their consequences.

Transitional equity: a criterion used to justify compensating people for changes in their situations, especially losses they have incurred due to governmental action.

Vertical equity: the unequal treatment of persons unequally situated, so as to make their situations more nearly equal.

Welfare economics: the branch of economics that is concerned with criteria for policy choice and their application. Includes development of the Pareto criterion, the Kaldor criterion, and the basis of cost-benefit analysis.

EXERCISES

1. An analyst proposed as a criterion "the greatest benefit at the least cost." Criticize this criterion from the standpoint of its consistency.

2. Show that there is an extensive class of policy choices for which the Pareto criterion does not say which alternative is better. Then show that if we regard the Pareto criterion as indifferent between two such choices (A = B), we can have A = B and B = C, but A ≠ C.

3. A number of American communities have considered policies that would restrict the amount of migration into them (see case 3–B). What criteria can be used for evaluating these policies from the standpoints of (a) the welfare of present residents versus the welfare of outsiders? (b) legality? (c) equity as regards the right to realize the benefits of one's plans and investments? (d) vertical equity? Would our criteria be different if we were considering migration between nations rather than communities?

4. In the city-growth and Texas cases (cases 3–B and 5–B) a governmental unit was making policy decisions that affected not only citizens of the unit itself but also outsiders who were not represented in those decisions. What possible remedies exist for this lack of representation?

5. In international policy a criterion frequently used is that of maximizing

the security of the United States. Does this criterion relate to the welfare of persons who are not citizens or residents of the United States? In what ways does it take their welfare or security into consideration? Are there other criteria for international policy that would incorporate the welfare of noncitizens differently?

6. When policies are considered for regulating the production of nonreturnable beverage containers, the manufacturers of containers contend that they will lose business and their employees complain that they will lose jobs (see case 5–A). Would these losses be counted as costs in cost-benefit analysis? According to your own ethical criteria (specify), would you count them as net social costs?

7. Classify the following ethical criteria as teleological or nonteleological:

   a. No illegal policy will be chosen.

   b. Policies involving murder are prohibited.

   c. That policy is right that produces the greatest realization of human potentialities.

   d. The best policy is one that maximizes the chances of survival of the human race.

   e. Among policies to deal with poverty any policy that fails to bring people above the poverty line is ruled out.

8. Laetrile, a substance made from apricot pits, is believed by some to be a remedy for cancer, but its sale is disapproved by federal authorities on the ground that there is no scientific evidence of its effectiveness (see case 3–A). Assume that it has no scientifically ascertainable effects, favorable or unfavorable, on the patient. Would its sale be favored or not by an ethic of preference satisfaction? What other ethical standards might be invoked against its sale?

9. In "The Bases for Collective Action," James M. Buchanan points out that a policy favored by a minority may be superior to that favored by a majority, if the minority members are affected to a large extent by the difference between policies and majority members are each affected to only a small extent. What two competing criteria are illustrated by this example?

10. In view of the rising homicide rate in cities it has been proposed to tax guns. Suppose that the tax is $5.00 per gun and that homicide is more prevalent in lower-income areas of cities than in upper-income areas. Does this differential prevalence affect the likely success of the policy? Why or why not? Can the policy be criticized on the ground of equity? If so, in what way?

11. Prisoners are granted the opportunity to be released on parole in view of various criteria, including the nature of their crime and their behavior in prison. Suppose that social research has shown that the likelihood of a parolee's committing another crime while on parole is statistically related to his socioeconomic status. Would it be justifiable to include socioeconomic status as one of the bases for granting parole? Would the criteria of efficiency and equity differ in their application to this policy choice?

12. In order to assess whether people are good credit risks, major credit-card firms consider many types of information. These include "home ownership, length of employment, credit history, [and] where someone lives." Statistically, knowledge of place of residence helps these firms to predict whether a person should be given or refused credit. The possibility of using information about place of residence for this purpose results from a provision of the Equal Credit Opportunity Act. But this provision is under criticism from those who wish "both to eliminate geographic location as a basis for denial of credit and to restore the principle that credit worthiness must be determined on the basis of individual merits." It has also been argued that a provision of this kind will lead people to move out of certain neighborhoods, and that the provision may imply racial discrimination.[30] List the criteria that have been brought to bear on the question whether this law should be amended. State the criteria in sufficiently general terms that they can be applied to other policy choices as well.

ADVANCED EXERCISES

13. In the field of health policy several criteria are often proposed as quantities to be maximized: (a) quality of health services; (b) availability of health services; (c) equity in availability of health services; and (d) health itself. In what respects are these criteria possibly consistent with one another, and in what respects do they lead to policies that are distinct from one another? Which of these criteria is likely to encounter the greatest difficulty because it cannot easily be measured?

14. In the field of population policy a question often discussed is that of estimating the optimum population of a given area in terms of specified ethical standards. Can the following two standards be used for this purpose: (a) maximizing the quality of life; and (b) maximizing preference satisfaction? Indicate possible uses and difficulties.

15. In the field of peace research a criterion often considered is that of conflict resolution. This criterion often leads to compromise or mediation. For dealing with conflicts in general terms what disadvantages does it have?

16. Social surveys may be used as guides to policy choice in several ways: (a) In advance of a policy choice, citizens may be asked their opinions as to what policy should be chosen; (b) In advance of a policy choice, citizens

may be asked how they think it would affect them personally; (c) After a program has been in effect, citizens may be asked in what ways they think it should be changed; (d) After a policy has been in effect, those affected may be asked how it has affected them. What ethical criteria are implied by these four approaches? What notions of democracy are implied?

17. When we consider transfers of income from the nonpoor to the poor, several criteria may be used: (a) vertical equity; (b) maximization of welfare, utility, or happiness; (c) cost-benefit analysis; (d) Pareto optimality, taking into consideration that the nonpoor may prefer to transfer some of their income to the poor. Which of these criteria is likely to lead to the most precise conclusions about how much income should be transferred? Which is likely to imply the greatest transfer of income?

18. When a factory produces smoke that leads to costs for nearby residents, R. H. Coase has proposed that the "external effect" may be taken into account so as to set an efficient level of production, by *either* a compensatory payment from the factory owners to the residents *or* a payment by the residents to the factory to induce the factory to produce less smoke.[31] Assume that either of these methods will lead to the same eventual level of production and smoke. What other criterion might be invoked to justify our choice of one of these policies as against the other?

19. In consideration of health policy and policy concerning automobile accidents cost-benefit analysts have developed standards for the evaluation of additional years of human life. One such standard values a span of life in terms of the person's expected earnings, discounted so as to weight future earnings less than present earnings. Criticize this standard from an ethical point of view. Can you propose an alternative standard for quantitative evaluation of years of life?

20. In cost-benefit analysis it is customary to discount future benefits and costs because of our opportunity to invest resources at prevailing interest rates. Consider, in contrast, the case of a Robinson Crusoe, marooned alone on an island, without such opportunities. Would his effective discount rate vary depending on whether he were young or old? If Crusoe had certain knowledge that after his departure from the island a second young man was to be shipwrecked there, would Crusoe be justified in discounting the value of the benefits that that second person might obtain from facilities that Crusoe built and left for the second person?

1. Duncan MacRae, Jr., *The Social Function of Social Science* (New Haven, Conn.: Yale University Press, 1976), ch. 4; John Rawls, *A Theory of Justice* (Cambridge, Mass.: Harvard University Press, 1971), pp. 20–21.

2. David Braybrooke and Charles E. Lindblom, *A Strategy of Decision* (New York: Free Press, 1963), p. 7.

3. See Marlan Blissett, ed., *Environmental Impact Assessment* (New York: Engineering Foundation, 1976), pp. 167ff.

4. On Nixon's Family Assistance Plan, see Daniel P. Moynihan, "Income by Right," *New Yorker* 48(1973): I, 13 Jan., 34–57; II, 20 Jan., 60–79; III, 27 Jan., 57–81. On busing see James S. Coleman, Sara D. Kelly, and John A. Moore, *Trends in School Segregation, 1968–73* (Washington, D.C.: Urban Institute, 1975).

5. See James W. Vaupel, "Muddling Through Analytically," in Willis D. Hawley and David Rogers, eds., *Improving the Quality of Urban Management* (Beverly Hills, Calif.: Sage Publications, 1974), for the example of a hypothetical mayor who combines the interest of the community with consideration of her own reelection chances. See also Morton H. Halperin, *Bureaucratic Politics and Foreign Policy* (Washington, D.C.: Brookings, 1974), p. 84.

6. MacRae, *The Social Function of Social Science*, ch. 4.

7. Braybrooke and Lindblom, *A Strategy of Decision*, p. 33.

8. Alice M. Rivlin, *Systematic Thinking for Social Action* (Washington, D.C.: Brookings, 1971), pp. 51, 57.

9. See the appendix to this volume.

10. Braybrooke and Lindblom, *A Strategy of Decision*, p. 156.

11. Ibid., pp. 150–51, 256–57. These authors actually define a slightly different classification of moral rules as "meliorative" and "peremptory" in terms of whether alternatives are compared or not.

12. Regarding the mixed-scanning approach see Amitai Etzioni, *The Active Society* (New York: Free Press, 1968), pp. 282–309.

13. G. O. Wright, *A General Procedure for Systems Study*, Wright-Patterson Air Force Base, Ohio, 1960, reference from Stanford L. Optner, ed., *Systems Analysis* (Harmondsworth, Middlesex, England: Penguin, 1973), p. 98.

14. This procedure is known as "constrained maximization." Rawls, *A Theory of Justice*, p. viii, suggests that this approach is roughly what is done in the practical application of utilitarianism: "Most likely we finally settle upon a variant of the utility principle circumscribed and restricted in certain ad hoc ways by intuitionistic constraints."

15. One mathematical procedure for solving problems of constrained maximization is linear programming; see for example John G. Kemeny, J. Laurie Snell, and Gerald L. Thompson, *Introduction to Finite Mathematics* (Englewood Cliffs, N.J.: Prentice-Hall, 1957), ch. 6.

16. Ibid., pp. 263–64.

17. Gary S. Becker, "Crime and Punishment: An Economic Approach," *Journal of Political Economy* 76(1968):169–217.

18. See Philip F. Beach, *Public Access to Policymaking in the United States* (Morristown, N.J.: General Learning Press, 1974).

19. James M. Buchanan, *The Bases for Collective Action* (Morristown, N.J.: General Learning Press, 1971), p. 5.

20. Robert H. Haveman and Burton A. Weisbrod, "Defining Benefits of Public Programs: Some Guidance for Policy Analysts," *Policy Analysis* 1(1975):181.

21. We refer to such problems of transition as "dynamic problems" in chapter 5.

22. One value of the discount rate that has been used for public projects is the rate of interest available in the money market, on the ground that investment in public projects forgoes the opportunity to invest privately at that rate. Some critics have argued, however, that the future benefits of public projects should be valued more highly. See Richard A. Musgrave and Peggy B. Musgrave, *Public Finance in Theory and Practice* (New York: McGraw-Hill, 1973), pp. 170–76.

23. Further examples of calculation of benefits and costs will be given in chapter 4 and case 4–A.

24. Arthur M. Okun, *Equality and Efficiency: The Big Tradeoff* (Washington, D.C.: Brookings, 1975), p. 91.

25. Harold M. Hochman, "Rule Change and Transitional Equity," in Harold M. Hochman and George E. Peterson, eds., *Redistribution Through Public Choice* (New York: Columbia University Press, 1974).

26. Rawls, *A Theory of Justice*, pp. 106–07.

27. See Julian L. Simon, "Interpersonal Welfare Comparisons Can Be Made—and Used for Redistribution Decisions," *Kyklos* 27(1974):63–98.

28. See Angus Campbell, Philip E. Converse, and Willard L. Rodgers, *The Quality of American Life* (New York: Russell Sage Foundation, 1976).

29. Braybrooke and Lindblom, *A Strategy of Decision*, pp. 179ff.

30. This problem is reported in Sylvia Porter, "Maybe Zip Code Kept You from Getting a Loan," Raleigh, N.C., *News and Observer*, 22 Sept. 1977.

31. R. H. Coase, "The Problem of Social Cost," *Journal of Law and Economics* 3(1960):1–44.

The Laetrile Controversy

This case is chosen because contrasting policy proposals depend primarily on the criteria used. An argument for regulation of laetrile is given by Daniel S. Martin. An opposing argument for free consumer choice is given by James J. Kilpatrick.

LAETRILE: A 'FRAUD' [1]

State governments are being manipulated to legalize the quack cancer nostrum laetrile. Their action is a negation of knowledge by the political process.

For a state to sanction the sale of this worthless product, overriding the Federal Government's finding that laetrile is an unproved drug, is a dangerous deception. It lends respectability to the illusion that laetrile does indeed have anticancer activity. Then the public will reason: Why should an anticancer drug be reserved only for the terminally ill? Wouldn't it "work" better on early cancer? And better yet, as a preventive, before one gets cancer?

This line of reasoning is precisely the propaganda being propagated by laetrile's promoters. Thus, legalizing this apricot-pit extract will lure people to take laterile in preference to proved medical treatment. The harm in taking laetrile is the time lost while cancer advances to the point where no cure is possible.

A strong motivation for legalizing laetrile has been compassion for the terminally-ill cancer patient. This accession to a dying person's wish would have virtue if it were harmless overall.

But beyond individual concern, and above it, lies the higher moral imperative of promoting the general welfare.

But even as an act of individual grace, such compassion is ridiculous on its face. For any placebo effect of this inert drug to be perceived by the patient, he or she and all those around the patient—especially the physician—must make believe that laetrile actually has an anticancer effect. To state clearly to the patient that a drug has only psychological placebo benefits is to remove them. Legalization propagates this make-believe, to the detriment of the individual and of society.

One need not be a cancer specialist to perceive that laetrile is a fraud, as a common-sense review of the following facts makes clear:

> 1. Every anticancer drug ever shown to work in humans was first proved to have an effect on some animal cancer—but not laetrile. Numerous case histories put forward by laetrile boosters to prove its clinical benefit have proved to be hearsay or subjective testimonials, without objective evidence of an actual anticancer effect.

2. Laetrile's promoters claim it is freely available in 23 countries. Why then are the cancer statistics of those countries no better, and often worse, than figures in the United States, where laetrile has been banned?

3. Mexico, Mecca of American cancer victims seeking laetrile, last year canceled its approval of the substance because, the Mexican Government stated, "no positive results were obtained in clinical research carried out at Mexican Center General Hospital."

4. The laetrilists spread the vicious canard that the American medical "cancer establishment" opposes laetrile because of its vested economic greed. How does this jibe with the fact that the Soviet Union, where there is no private enterprise or profit motive, and where cancer research is at a high level, has declared laetrile ineffective?

5. All drug manufacturers must meet lawfully defined standards that assure efficacy before they are allowed to sell their medicines. Why should an exception be made for laetrile? Is the laetrilists' "freedom-of-choice" claim really a red herring to evade standards they are unable to meet?

6. "Freedom of choice in cancer therapy" is the battle cry of the pro-laetrile forces. Does it make sense? In medical matters, the public has meaningful freedom of choice. One chooses a personal physician, knowing that the "M.D." means a license from the state proving competence to practice medicine. So, too, in cancer therapy, a patient is free to choose (through his or her physician) any of 38 proved anticancer drugs, licensed by the Food and Drug Administration as being of proved efficacy. In these circumstances, is not the laetrilists' "freedom-of-choice" demand really a request for license to defraud?

The laetrile controversy is not a medical matter, but a political and consumer-protection issue. Does American society want the uninformed, the naive, the innocent, the cultists, the gullibles, the fanatics, the poor, the very young, and the desperately sick to be left defenseless, buying a fraud thinking it a "treatment," with neither laws nor regulatory agencies to protect them? Should state legislatures protect the seller's efforts to make money by allowing misrepresentation of facts?

Caveat emptor—"let the buyer beware"—seems an immoral, unethical and particularly reprehensible doctrine in the medical marketplace, where human life is at stake.

DOCTORS NEED
A SHOT OF HUMILITY [2]

A gentleman by the name of Stephen Barrett, M.D., chairman of the board of the Lehigh Valley (Pa.) Committee Against Health Fraud has filed a formal complaint against me with the National News Council. Other doctors, elsewhere in the land, have been unloading remarkably stuffy letters.

Dr. Barrett says I am paranoid. Others charge that I am irresponsible, even "criminal." Thirty-five years in the news business have given me a hide of pure asbestos, but these birds are producing a slow burn. I feel a brawl coming on, and by George, it is a grand and glorious feeling.

These various spokesmen for the medical establishment are outraged by several columns I have lately composed about the Great Apricot Kernel Gang. For those who have come late to the free-for-all, it should be said that the gang is composed of organic food nuts, non-conforming doctors, assorted eccentrics and other freeborn citizens. They are convinced that a substance known as Laetrile may be useful in treating some forms of cancer.

The government and the medical establishment regard Laetrile as a sham, a hoax, and a fraud. The substance, derived from apricot pits and other natural foods, has been known for generations as amygdalin. No scientifically acceptable tests ever have demonstrated its worth in cancer therapy. The government has declared it unlawful for any person to import, sell, or distribute the stuff, and the government has not hesitated to seek criminal indictments against the alleged conspirators.

Very well. So far as I know, as I have said repeatedly, the medical experts are right. When it comes to treating cancer, taking Laetrile is probably as useful as chewing Juicy Fruit gum. Cancer victims who spend their money on Laetrile capsules almost certainly are throwing their money away. A patient would be a fool to pin his hopes on this stuff before every medically accepted remedy has been tried.

But. Let us move back the chairs and tables and clear a space on the barroom floor. The arrogance of the medical establishment, in my own view, is uglier by far than the "quackery" of the Great Apricot Kernel Gang. Dr. Barrett and his swell-headed colleagues are doubtless sincere, high-minded, dedicated, informed, and reputable fellows, but they never ran for God in an August primary and no one ever elected them the Possessors of All Wisdom.

What has become of humility? What has become of professional modesty? What has happened to personal freedom in a free society? These are the issues here. It is immaterial whether amygdalin is or is not a "vitamin." It is beside the point that the stuff may be dangerous in certain chemical situations. Vitamins are matters of wild disagreement, and almost everything under the sun may be dangerous in some situations.

What matters is freedom. What is at stake is the right of a free citizen to fritter away his money—and his life—if he wants to. The medical establishment is howling that the promoters of Laetrile make money on their worthless product. Some of the fees that might be paid to reputable physicians are going to "quacks" instead. The reputable doctors can't stand it.

Says Dr. Barrett: "People who use Laetrile instead of orthodox treatment will lose their lives." Astounding! More than 300,000 cancer victims every year use orthodox treatment instead of Laetrile and they also lose their lives. Eventually everybody loses his life. The proponents of amygdalin insist that many apparently terminal patients have benefited from the stuff, and at least one federal judge, Luther Bohannon of Oklahoma City, accepts their evidence. Maybe the patients are hallucinating or maybe they're suffering from illusions. So what? More things are wrought by faith than this world dreams of.

Over the years I doubt that any columnist has been more friendly to the medical profession than I have been. In season and out, I have fought the doctors' battle against overweening government. But it seems to me time for some of the high-and-mighty ones, the know-it-all ones, to put hubris aside and to acknowledge the vastness of their ignorance of the human being. It is the sickness of freedom that troubles me. I wish it troubled my lordly antagonists.

Notes

1. Daniel S. Martin, *The New York Times*, 3 June 1977. © 1977 by The New York Times Company. Reprinted by permission.

2. James J. Kilpatrick, Washington Star Syndicate, 1 April 1976. Reprinted by permission of the Washington Star Syndicate, Inc. © 1976.

CASE 3–B

Controlling City Growth

This case is chosen because policy positions depend in large measure on contrasting conceptions of the general welfare as criteria for choice. The case consists of two articles, both by Gladwin Hill.

NATION'S CITIES FIGHTING TO STEM GROWTH [1]

On March 21, the city of St. Petersburg, Fla., adopted an ordinance requiring the last 25,000 people who had settled there to move out.

This extraordinary edict was rescinded only a fortnight later as manifestly unconstitutional and impractical.

But the incident epitomizes rapidly changing attitudes toward community growth: Countless communities around the country, far from welcoming growth in the traditional bigger-is-better vein, now fear they are being overwhelmed by it and are moving hastily to stop it.

Limitations on growth, ranging from population ceilings to moratoriums on building permits, are proliferating by the day. Each place has its own reasons. Water supply and sewage treatment are overloaded. Open space or other environmental values are threatened. Taxpayers are outraged at the prospect of big new capital investments needed to provide community services for some populations.

But whatever the reasons for growth controls, however logical they may seem on a local basis, collectively they are confronting the nation with a difficult tangle of questions, questions perplexing to the real estate and construction industries, the legal world, civil rights advocates, demographers, planners, politicians and millions of people simply looking for homes. For example:

> Upward of 50 million people are going to augment the nation's population in the next 25 years. If growth-limitation becomes general, where are these people going to live?

> Does a community have a right to "pull up the gangplank" and shunt future population elsewhere?

> Granting that many communities have real growth problems, who is to decide which ones should be allowed to adopt limits?

> If states undertook to apportion growth equitably among communities, who would then decide on equitable apportionment of population among the states?

> How can community constraints on expansion be reconciled with people's right under the Constitution to travel freely and to settle wherever they please?

In sum, growth controls are aggravating this country's traditional philosophical tension between private initiative and public regulations.

And in practical terms, in the view of some observers, they are tending to price a large portion of middle-income people out of the housing market.

The first rumblings of what land use experts are calling the growth-control "explosion" came as far back as the 1960s, when the Pennsylvania courts began getting suits from subdividers whose projects had been rejected by communities on the ground that they just didn't want more people.

By 1970, District of Columbia suburbs in Maryland and Virginia were becoming so overbuilt in relation to sewage treatment facilities that state and county officials were impelled to impose moratoriums on building permits and sewer connections—measures that have continued and been extended ever since.

In 1971 the City of Boulder, Colo., made headlines when its 70,000 residents voted on whether to adopt a population ceiling of 100,000. The proposal was narrowly defeated. But a year later, residents of the plush resort community of Boca Raton, Fla., did take substantially the same step by adopting a zoning plan with a limit of 40,000 residential units—a measure that is still in litigation.

Meanwhile, growth controls have erupted elsewhere at a rate that has reached epidemic proportions. Marin County in California invoked growth controls on the ground that its water supply could not serve many more people.

Palo Alto, Calif., zoned 10 square miles of undeveloped land into 10-acre parcels to thwart building.

Southampton, Long Island, with a population of 39,000, adopted a zoning plan with an ultimate limit of 127,000.

Keyed to Pupil Space

San Jose, Calif., last year voted a two-year freeze on any new residential zoning that would reduce pupil-space in schools.

Orange County, Calif., with 1,500,000 people, has cut back its population ceiling for the year 2020 from 4 million to 2.9 million.

Only a few days ago, Loudoun County, Virginia, a Washington suburban area, refused to approve a $112-million, 4,200-unit "new town," even though the developer promised to reimburse the county for installing the necessary public services.

By last year, according to the Environmental Protection Agency, sewer-hookup moratoriums were in effect in 160 cities and in 40 communities in Florida.

As of Mid-April this year, 30 of the 112 communities in New Jersey's Passaic basin had building moratoriums of one sort or another.

All told, according to the latest survey by the Department of Housing and Urban Development, some 226 cities have imposed moratoriums on building permits, water or sewer connections, rezoning (to permit development), subdividing, or other essentials of growth.

In some cases growth-control measures have been only temporary, pending construction of facilities to serve new residents. But in many if not most cases, communities' avowed reason for growth controls has been to curb unending influxes of new residents.

Population Density Down

Virtually never has the demonstrable cause of such moves been actual exhaustion of physical space.

Contrary to a widespread impression, urban population density in the United States has been steadily declining for half a century, from 6,580 people per square mile in 1920 to 4,230 now—a reflection of "urban sprawl."

Dr. Kenneth E. F. Watt, University of California ecologist, has calculated that the 25,000 people now typically spread over 10 square miles in tract housing could be comfortably accommodated in six 13-story apartment towers covering only 1/50th of a square mile—1/500th of the tract space—with even more pleasures of "the great outdoors" provided immediately at hand. While perhaps only a minority want to live in apartments, the huge space differential in Dr. Watt's figures is considered to reflect spatial economies possible in communities generally.

Studies of relative population pressures on many cities, according to Dr. Judith Blake, University of California demographer, indicate that in many cases growth controls are simply a reactionary "pull up the gangplank" syndrome on the part of established communities resistant to any change in accustomed amenities.

This outlook was typified in a housewife's exhortation at a public hearing in Orion, Mich.: "Don't change Orion or it will become just like so many of the cities we've moved away from. We paid dearly to come out here."

In many other cases, however, growth controls are conceded to be a natural response to inadequate community planning and to belated realization that additional population does not always pay its own way.

While some surveys sponsored by real estate people have indicated that big new developments can be an economic plus, many communities have made contradictory findings, and either blocked developments or concocted heavy surcharges on developers to defray costs of facilities such as streets, water, sewer, and electric lines, schools and parks.

A 1972 Denver study indicated that each new residence would cost taxpayers $21,000 for community services. A Stanford University study at Half Moon Bay, near San Francisco, indicated that a 1,262-unit subdivision would cost the community $400,000 a year by 1982 in indirect subsidies for public services.

Palo Alto's zoning came after a study indicating that a $17,000 surcharge would have to be imposed on a $45,000 home, in addition to regular taxes, if it were to pay its share for the additional public services it occasioned.

Beyond moratoriums, the repertoire of growth controls includes a variety of zoning practices—sequestration of open land, from which development is excluded; large-lot zoning, making home sites too expensive for anyone but the wealthy; and restrictions on commercial development and apartments or other multiple housing.

Another set of devices is special levies for large-scale developers—high permit fees, extra charges of schools, and the other community services a new development entails; requirements that developers deed a sizable portion of their land to community facilities such as parks; imposts to pay for parks in other parts of a community; or simply fees levied in the name of helping out with community overhead—that go into a city's general treasury.

Controls as Scarcity

Blending these measures in various combinations are "phased-growth" plans, which in effect ration building permits and other development over a period of years.

Last January Fairfax County, Va., a major Washington suburb, adopted a 20-year program banning all building that did not qualify under a point system covering its need and feasibility from the standpoint of costs to the community.

Growth controls so far have not taken the form of uniformed officers heading off newcomers at city limits. Even in communities with building moratoriums there is a turnover in population. There are always residences to be had—at a price.

Instead, controls have taken the subtler form of making buildable land and residences scarcer, automatically pushing prices steadily upward.

The Advance Mortgage Corporation of Detroit estimated that growth constraints deprived the country of at least 50,000 housing units last year.

The National Association of Home Builders says that the median price of a home has jumped in just two years from $25,000 to $35,000—more than can be attributed to normal price components—and that home construction is dropping 40 percent, from 2.4 million units in 1973 to a projected 1.4 million this year.

In Petaluma, Calif., scene of a major growth-control controversy, there have been as many as 1,600 applications for the annual "ration" of 500 building permits.

The Home Builders Association of Westchester County, N.Y., estimates that a home in the area of Purchase [Westchester County] that could have been bought for $40,000 five years ago would be priced at around $70,000 today.

Since sewer-connection moratoriums became widespread in the Washington suburbs of Montgomery and Prince Georges counties in Maryland, home building has dropped between one-third and one-half, building industry spokesmen say.

'Overriding Obstacle'

"While the crucial questions of financing, energy conservation and land and labor costs continue to plague the building industry," Ray Lehmkuhl, president of the Pacific Coast Builders Conference said a few days ago, "the overriding obstacle to providing adequate shelter for our citizens continues to be restrictive land use policies by municipalities."

The effects of growth controls have been pronounced enough to convince many responsible people that they constitute an infringement on citizens' legal rights of mobility.

The right to travel among the states and settle where one pleases is not mentioned in the Constitution. But it was set forth in the Articles of Confederation, precursor of the Constitution, so explicitly that the United States Supreme Court has held repeatedly that it is an inferential part of the Constitution.

"Individually these attempts to protect the cultural and physical environment are for the most part desirable," comments Dr. Arnold W. Reitze, Jr., a law professor at George Washington University. "But in totality they threaten to leave the majority of Americans with no chance for home ownership. The poor and the elderly who do not have access to an automobile have already been blocked from most suburban housing. Now much of the middle class is being added to the group priced out of the housing market."

An Unusual Alliance

Opposition to "exclusionary" land use measures has created an odd alliance between the development industry, which on occasion has been accused of discriminatory practices itself, and civil rights organizations.

The National Association of Home Builders, while eschewing litigation itself, has established a $200,000 fund for legal assistance to its regional and local affiliates, which have been plaintiffs in many key lawsuits challenging certain kinds of zoning and other practices aimed at growth control.

In some cases courts have agreed with them: in others not. Over-all, the basic issue of constitutional validity, like many other aspects of the growth-control movement, remains undecided.

Nevertheless, says James Rouse, mastermind of the celebrated "new town" of Columbia, Md.:

"It's very clear that we are in the midst of probably the most radical change in our concept of private property rights that we have ever seen in this country.

"The notion that a developer has a right to develop because he owns a piece of land, and that the public must let him, is rapidly changing."

CONFLICTING COURT ACTIONS
PERPLEX TOWNS
SEEKING TO CURB GROWTH [2]

Not many residents of typical American communities are aware of it, but in the last few years they have become campers in a fast-growing legal jungle.

The community growth-control movement across the country has precipitated a series of conflicting court decisions that becloud any community's options in shaping its future.

From coast to coast, environmental, economic and social pressures have impelled hundreds of cities and towns to adopt limitations on the size and character of their populations.

These constraints range from zoning restrictions to elaborate programs of "rationing" development over the years ahead. They restrict additional population not by barring people at a community's outskirts but by making housing scarcer. As logical as such moves may seem, they are posing an array of perplexing problems.

On the one hand, no community can be expected to go on expanding indefinitely: It faces eventual limits on space, on the public services it can supply, and on residential density.

On the other hand, under Supreme Court interpretations of the Constitution, people have a right to move freely among the states and settle where they please.

What Limits Are Legal?

Hence the focal question arises: What restrictions can a community reasonably and legally impose on its growth?

That is a question the courts have not come anywhere near resolving. For the time being, a community beset by growth problems and wanting to do something about it must steer a course among legal guidelines and precedents as tortuously as a steel sphere bouncing off the obstacles in a pinball machine.

The issue of how far a community can go in regulating its form goes back more than half a century. A legal landmark is the 1926 United States Supreme Court decisions that upheld zoning as a valid exercise of a community's "police power," or authority to act for the general welfare.

But how far zoning—and, by extension, community planning generally —can go without infringing on someone's rights has been a matter of argument ever since.

A major legal problem is the fact that no two communities' problems, or proposed remedies for them, are ever identical, and rarely come before the same court. So, unlike other areas of law where precedents become guidelines, community-planning rulings often do not apply beyond the original cases.

An early salvo in the current legal battle came in 1970, after Concord Township in Pennsylvania tried to block a projected subdivision on population grounds. In a decision that dismayed many community planners, the Pennsylvania Supreme Court said:

"If Concord Township is successful in unnaturally limiting its population growth through the use of exclusive zoning regulations, the people who would normally live there will inevitably have to live in another community, and the requirement that they do is not a decision that Concord Township should alone be able to make."

Two Key Decisions

But the legal ball soon bounced the other way.

The month of November, 1972, brought two court decisions that made planners jubilant. The United States Court of Appeals for the First Circuit—in a ruling that has not been appealed higher—upheld the right of Sanbornton, N.H., to zone half its area for three- and six-acre lots, thereby effectively putting a sharp brake on population growth.

The second action was the United States Supreme Court's refusal—for asserted lack of a "substantial Federal question"—to review a decision of New York's highest court upholding a growth-control plan of the township of Ramapo in Rockland County, 30 miles northwest of New York City.

"Ramapo" is a landmark case on which volumes have been written, cherished by planners and anathema to the development and construction industries, which have been the leading plaintiffs in growth control cases.

"Ramapo" loomed large because it involved a sort of model delayed-growth plan, extending over 18 years, with a point-score system under which applicants for annually rationed building permits must show their projects won't unduly burden municipal services.

"Far from being exclusionary," the New York Court of Appeals held, "the present amendments [to the local zoning code] merely seek, by the implementation of sequential development and timed growth, to provide a balanced, cohesive community. . . .

"Ramapo asks not that it be left alone, but only that it be allowed to prevent the kind of deterioration that has transformed well-ordered and thriving residential communities into blighted ghettos. . . ."

The Petaluma Ruling

"Ramapo" stood as a guiding beacon for other control-minded communities for a year. But then last January—to the elation of the development industry—the United States District Court in San Francisco went the other way. It held that a similar phased-growth plan adopted by the exurb of Petaluma was unwarranted and unconstitutional.

Citing the Pennsylvania court's sentiments about communities arbitrarily shunting population elsewhere, Judge Lloyd H. Burke enjoined Petaluma from implementing any policy "which may have the effect, the intent, directly or indirectly, of placing any numerical limitation, whether definite or approximate, upon the number of persons permitted to enter the city of Petaluma in order to establish residence."

Waving away the argument that requiring Petaluma to enlarge its water and sewerage facilities would be tantamount to telling citizens how to vote on the necessary bond issues, Judge Burke said:

"Neither Petaluma city officials nor the local electorate may use their

Figure 3B–1.
Location of Ramapo, N.Y., and Petaluma, Calif.

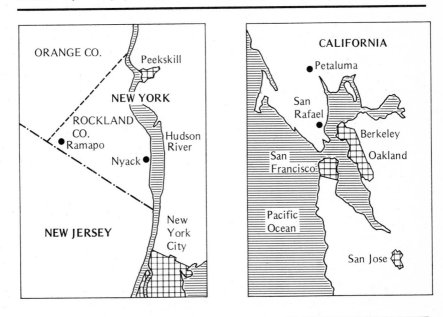

power to disapprove bonds at the polls as a weapon to define or destroy fundamental constitutional rights."

But hardly were Judge Burke's views—which are being appealed—on
record before the United States Supreme Court on April 1 handed down a
decision that was stunning alike to the development fraternity and its frequent

Figure 3B–2.
*Water Consumption and Availability
in Petaluma, Calif., 1965–1975.*

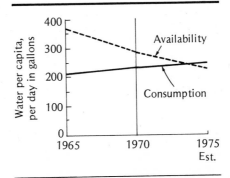

co-plaintiffs, civil rights groups fighting zoning "exclusionary" toward lower-income groups.

This decision, written by Associate Justice William O. Douglas, upheld the "anti-commune" ordinance of the village of Belle Terre on Long Island.

The ordinance not only limited land use in the community to single-family dwellings, but specified that a "family" could not include more than two persons "not related by blood, adoption or marriage."

Emphasis on Serenity

The ruling, while not involving population restriction directly, placed great emphasis on serenity and other environmental values, and appeared to give communities close to a maximum degree of discretion in shaping their destinies.

Still immersed in litigation is the case of Boca Raton, Fla., a community of 45,000 persons, which made history in November, 1972, by adopting what amounted to an explicit numerical ceiling on its population.

Boca Raton now has about 18,000 homes, and citizens approved a zoning program that would limit ultimate development to 40,000 dwellings.

There have been many decisions by courts high and low dealing with special aspects of growth control, such as the validity of special municipal charges on big developments, and the validity of particular moratoriums on building permits and sewer connections.

The cumulative product, Dr. Arnold W. Reitze Jr. of the George Washington University Law School commented recently, is "a legal labyrinth."

A major unresolved question is the extent to which communities can go in zoning plans that tend to exclude housing for middle- and low-income people—an issue that civil rights organizations have been doggedly fighting in New York, New Jersey and elsewhere.

The suburban Action Institute, based in White Plains, N.Y., is suing five New Jersey communities—Livingston, East Brunswick, Wayne, Holmdel and Franklin Lakes—on the ground that their zoning regulations are economically discriminatory.

Seven Practices Challenged

The suits challenge seven practices—certain bans on apartment houses and trailer homes; limitations on land zoned for apartments; limits on rooms, bedrooms and floor space in apartments; and building design requirements.

The suits were dismissed by the New Jersey Superior Court in March, but appeals are pending. Mayor Thomas Pawelko of Franklin Lakes commented: "We will fight any appeal because we believe home rule is one of our very basics."

While there is precedent for requiring developers to include housing for the less affluent, there have also been contrary rulings.

The Virginia Supreme Court last year rejected a Fairfax County requirement that 51 percent of all new subdivisions be middle- and low-income on the ground that it amounted to inverse exclusion and invalid "socio-economic zoning" exceeding the county's authority.

Because the basic impact of community growth controls is economic—through making reasonably priced housing scarcer—some lawyers see the courts as being pushed into a judgmental area as imponderable as obscenity.

This is the "fair share" issue—the question of how much of a region's industry, commerce and population a community can be expected to accommodate, and what the economic stratification of a given community's residents should be.

A Realist's Growth Plan

Herbert M. Franklin is a Washington lawyer and a consultant on land use and community planning. Without speculating about legal prospects, he has suggested that a community growth regulation plan, to be satisfactory in social terms, should include these features:

Some commitment for public investment to assimilate growth.

A zoning scheme that is farsighted enough to obviate drastic future alterations.

Recognition of present and expectable requirements of regional housing and employment.

Inclusion of commercial and industrial development as well as residential development.

A premise of local "tax effort" (ratio of total tax payments to household income) in line with that of surrounding communities.

From the "labyrinth" of court opinions, some lawyers have drawn these tentative inferences on the legality of community plans:

A community that adopts growth controls simply to preserve the status quo, with no demonstrable social or economic pressures, may well have difficulties in court.

A growth-control plan that is patently exclusionary of lower-income groups is legally vulnerable.

Temporary growth controls, such as moratoriums on building permits and sewerage construction, if their need can be demonstrated, have a good chance of standing up in court.

A well-thought-out, long-range, phased-growth plan has at least an even chance of being sustained.

Before the Petaluma ruling, many thought that community refusal to enlarge water and sewerage facilities was a fairly impregnable device for stopping growth, because courts could hardly force citizens to underwrite bond issues. But now, like so many other aspects of growth controls, this question is up in the air.

No one has any idea when it will be possible to weave the proliferating threads of court rulings into a usable legal blanket.

"Somehow," one lawyer commented, "we have to get over an essential contradiction in this situation: a community's police power supposedly is related to the general welfare of the community. And 'general welfare' by definition involves the people who are already there—not those who may want to come there."

Notes

1. Gladwin Hill, *The New York Times,* 28 July 1974. © 1974 by The New York Times Company. Reprinted by permission.

2. Gladwin Hill, *The New York Times,* 29 July 1974. © 1974 by The New York Times Company. Reprinted by permission.

4

Alternatives, Models, and Decisions

After we choose our criteria for analysis, we must proceed to relate them to possible alternative policies so as to choose among those policies. This relation of alternatives to criteria is the subject of this chapter. We must first state our policy alternatives clearly and then estimate the extent to which various alternatives will produce the values (positive or negative) corresponding to our criteria. This connection of policies with their valued or disvalued consequences involves the formulation of models of causation, which can make use of a wide range of findings and procedures of natural and social science. A particularly important aspect of the use of these models is the measurement of indices of the value criteria.

We conclude this chapter by illustrating a procedure that is useful for choosing among several policies when we know the probabilities and values of various possible outcomes—the decision tree. We apply this procedure to the decision whether to conduct a medical screening test. In case 4–A, which follows, we present another example of model construction and decision, the choice of an optimum speed limit.

POLICY ALTERNATIVES

Policy analysis involves the comparison of precisely stated alternative policies in terms of specified criteria. But as we have seen, the problem situation does not always take the form of precise, analyzable alternatives or of well-defined criteria. One of the analyst's tasks is to redefine the problem.

The problem situation—others' definition of the problem—may take the form of concern about vague, verbally expressed values. In this case you may wish to express those values more precisely and consistently and then to seek policies that will further them. Or the problem situation may be defined by others in terms of one particular remedy, in which case you may wish to enlarge the range of policies by considering others as well. In either case you will be setting forth a list of *alternative policies* to be analyzed.

When we consider alternative public policies, we begin by designating them by names. But to analyze policy alternatives, we need to specify them in much more detail. In the laetrile controversy (case 3–A) a policy might be "legalize laetrile" and might consist in repealing a previous regulation. The inverse policy, "prohibit laetrile," would require specifying the substance being prohibited, the types of container labels that would define it, the penalties for violation of the law, and the agency charged with enforcement. In the city-growth case (case 3–B) one policy might be called "restrictive zoning," but for a particular city this would require specification of just what types of land use were allowed in specific areas of the city. Repealing or prohibiting a particular zoning law would be a policy that was simple to specify, but establishing such a law would be more complex. A court that had to judge whether such a law was constitutional might simply rule favorably or unfavorably. But in giving the reasons for its ruling the court might have to draw distinctions between types of cases and so create precedents that would affect zoning laws elsewhere.

A policy alternative often takes the form of a bill prepared for submission to a legislature. The role of an analyst may include suggesting the contents of such bills or predicting their consequences if enacted. The provisions of such a bill can be numerous and detailed, and you may wish to analyze one part at a time. For example, a bill to reform the welfare system of the United States could involve amendments to several existing laws; provisions for various classes of people, such as the poor, the sick, and the dependent; provisions about who will be eligible for aid and how eligibility will be determined; and assignment of the responsibility for carrying out these provisions to certain government agencies. This variety of provisions illustrates not only the complexity of some policies but also the possibility that the results of enacting the bill may depend on what the implementing agency does. Assigning a task to the Social Security Administration may produce different results from assigning it to the Internal Revenue Service.

In analyzing the consequences of a proposed bill we may specify the policy that it represents in two ways. First, we may assume hypothetically that the activities specified in the bill will be carried out faithfully and promptly and examine what the consequences will be. Second, we may include an assumption that these activities will be carried out only to some degree, depending on the willingness and efficiency of the agency to which the tasks are assigned. The second procedure is more realistic and must be considered in actual policy choices. But an analyst within government cannot easily say publicly that a particular government agency is unlikely to carry out a policy faithfully. It is more customary in government analyses, therefore, to consider the consequences of the policy *as though* it were fully implemented and to treat the difficulties of implementation separately—privately or in personal communication.

A citizen-analyst or an investigative reporter who does not mind antagonizing an agency may analyze the probability of implementation publicly. Those who do so may risk setting the agency's sights too low. If a major group supporting a policy states publicly that it expects only sixty percent likelihood of implementation, it risks telling the agency that it need not work hard putting the policy into effect. Thus, even for an analyst outside government there are difficulties in public analysis of probabilities of implementation.

This variation in the likelihood of implementation is illustrated by the difference in meaning between a "policy" and a "plan." A policy closely resembles a plan except that the latter usually involves a lesser assurance that what is contemplated will actually be carried out. A plan can be entertained as a piece of advice and can exist without being enacted formally. Even when officially approved, it can be subject to later change. Thus, it seems more problematical that a plan will be carried out after approval than that a policy will be carried out once enacted. In either case full enactment may depend on a succession of later decisions; a city plan may depend on later municipal ordinances, some of which may modify it, and a federal program may depend on annual appropriations for its continuation.[1] In spite of variations in the certainty of implementation, our analysis will deal first with the values and disvalues associated with the state of affairs expected if a policy *is* implemented.

Among the policy alternatives we consider, one is usually to do nothing, that is, to take no new governmental action and allow the existing situation to continue. We have discussed this alternative in chapter 3 as a baseline for cost-benefit analysis. Other alternatives explored are typically those that are expected to lead to better results, in terms of the values in question, than doing nothing.

It is important in your initial consideration of alternatives to be imaginative and creative. A wide variety of alternatives dealing with larger and smaller aspects of the problem need to be considered. In this way you will be less likely to ignore important options, and you will later have more options for compromise and negotiation to increase the political feasibility of your policy recommendations.

One source of alternatives, which we shall consider in chapter 5, is the operation of the market. In seeking alternatives for a medical screening test, which we shall discuss later in this chapter, we may consider whether people should simply be allowed to purchase diagnostic tests themselves—a do-nothing option for public policy. But by examining possible defects of this policy, we may be led to better policies and to fuller understanding of the reasons for those policies. Another direction in which market notions lead us is that of "quasi-market policies" that promote individual choice and incentives. Examples of such policies are voucher systems for schools, by which parents make use of public funds to choose the school that they think will be best for their children, and performance contracting, by which organizations compete to provide school instruction and are rewarded in terms of how much the students learn. We discuss the evaluation of some quasi-market policies in chapter 7.

Another source of alternatives is the experience of other cities, states, or nations. In the fluoridation case (case 6–A) citizens of Newton, Massachusetts, learned of the fluoridation alternative from discussions in nearby cities. At present, citizens interested in reducing children's tooth decay can look to the experience of European countries that have introduced fluoride into milk. Parole systems that have been tried in one state can be evaluated on the basis of that state's experience before being tried in another; so can the policy of releasing mental patients for community treatment. The prior use of policies elsewhere provides us not only with alternatives but also with information about their effects.

An additional source of alternatives is our knowledge of science and technology. Initially, the possibility of fluoridation resulted from scientific research concerning the conditions affecting tooth decay. The possibility of a negative income tax was proposed by economist Milton Friedman on the basis of economic theory. Municipal systems for reporting crimes rapidly to patrol cars draw on possibilities of efficiently using telephone switchboards together with human organization.

Once you have set forth a wide range of alternatives, you will then wish to reduce this list to manageable form by rapid scanning. You may eliminate those alternatives that appear to have very little technical or political feasibility. You may retain some alternatives that are known to work if enacted, even though they are very infeasible to enact, since they require little effort for further analysis. You may include alternatives that have support from important organizations or groups, as you may have to argue that other alternatives are better than these, or choose among these, or compromise by including some of their features. Practical considerations of this kind will affect your choice of those alternatives on which you spend time and effort in analysis.

PERSONAL ALTERNATIVES

Your choice of alternatives to analyze is actually part of a larger set of *personal* alternatives within which your analytic alternatives are embedded. One of your first personal choices is whether to devote your effort to analyzing the problem in question—whether to take on that job or assignment, if you are a member of a voluntary association, or to devote your own time and resources to it as a citizen. Next, you may have to decide at what level to define the problem, for example, whether to work on a particular substantive aspect of it, to analyze it in depth, or to generalize the definition by working on possible changes in a larger decision-making system.

You also face a choice whether to move directly toward a recommendation in view of the information available to you or to take time to gather more detailed information. This choice may range from action with no analysis to analysis that takes so long as to be irrelevant for action. Intermediate between the two possibilities, you will often need to make a rapid, approximate analysis in order either to decide whether to become involved further or to meet the time requirements of action. This rapid analysis may take the form of a back-of-the-envelope calculation, an analysis with a one-week deadline, or the use of a similar analysis made by someone else.[2] If this approximate analysis leads you to judge that further analysis is needed and if you have time and resources to do it, you may proceed to a more prolonged study.

Even when you have chosen a policy (or a set of acceptable policies), you will still face a number of personal alternatives concerning how to present it and to whom. You may wish to gain the attention or commitment of public officials or group leaders; to gain public attention through the press, the broadcast media, or professional publications; or to try to create organizations such as committees, commissions, or coalitions of existing associations.[3] In general, you have a choice whether to present your recommendation with little further action; to work for enactment of your policy; or, if it is enacted, to work for its implementation as well. Each type of personal choice can involve a different degree of commitment on your part and a different expected value in terms of your ethical criteria.

In a complex social system where numerous participants are concerned with the same problem, it is possible that if you did not intervene, others would. The net effect of your own intervention might thus be less than it appeared. You could of course assess the difference between the results if *no one* intervened and those if *someone* intervened in a given way, and this assessment might be a useful contribution to public discussion. But just as in an economic system where the employment of persons in one industry may be accompanied by unemployment elsewhere, so too our own intervention to cope with a problem may substitute for someone else's.

MODELS

To choose among alternative policies in terms of their consequences we need to predict those consequences. We thus need to be able to relate the choice of policies, as a cause, to its effects. Our formulation of the causal relations that connect policies with effects is known as a *model* of those relations. The expression of a model may range from a simple and highly approximate verbal statement (e.g., "deficit spending causes inflation") to a set of mathematical equations or an elaborate computer program. A model may also be expressed as a physical structure (e.g., a small-scale model of a bridge that may be subjected to stresses). Each of these is an approximate representation of a relation that is believed to exist between policies and their consequences.

Our initial notion that a proposed policy will produce better results than doing nothing implies an expected connection of cause and effect, which constitutes a preliminary model of an aspect of the world. It is a first approximation, often based on intuitive or commonsense notions of causation. Such notions lie behind our initial consideration of alternatives. In our more systematic analysis of consequences of alternatives we test such models, improve their formulation, and in the process revise our list of preferred alternatives.

Models vary in their degree of rigor and in the degree of confidence we can place in them. Some, as we have indicated, are based merely on common sense, rather than on scientific generalizations or research. Others are based on repeated tests of policies or devices in situations similar to those for which a policy is proposed. Still others embody verified scientific theories and laws. More reliable knowledge of causal relations is available for some policy problems than for others. Designers of new aircraft can draw on the mathematical theories of aerodynamics, but designers of new organizational structures have no such precise and verified laws to use. Nevertheless, prototypes of new aircraft require experimental testing and sometimes malfunction, since the details of their fuctioning cannot all be represented by the drawings, plans, or equations used in their design.

The degree of confidence we can place in our models depends not only on the type of knowledge involved (e.g., natural versus social science) but also on the time and resources we have for analysis. Policy decisions are made at times that the analyst cannot usually control. Analysis of a pending or urgent problem is thus limited by deadlines for which we have to muster whatever information we can. For urgent decisions common sense can still be valuable. If we have more time for analysis, we may benefit from the review of our analyses by scientific or technical groups and thus make a greater claim to expert knowledge.

A policy-relevant model ordinarily includes a set of causal statements linked together. The relatively simple model for fluoridation of a city's water supply takes for granted that fluoride can be placed in the water, dissolved, and sent to homes. The central part of the model concerns the effects of this water on those who drink or use it: changes in children's teeth, possible changes in elderly people's bones, and possible effects on persons who use it for kidney dialysis. We may be more confident in our knowledge of these effects if they are related to general theories of dental development or physiology.

A model of the effects of changing speed limits (case 4–A) may involve many individual statements about the functioning of automobile engines, the causes of accidents, and the consequences of getting people and merchandise to their destinations on time. Other policy-relevant models can be still more complex; examples are models of a national economy, a weapons delivery system, an urban traffic system, or a watershed in terms of water quality, hydro-electric power, and probabilities of floods.

A great variety of policy-related models have been proposed, making use of findings of the natural and social sciences. One specific source of such models is in the fields of operations research, systems analysis, and management science. These fields, which are largely concerned with optimization decisions by business for increased productive efficiency, are also relevant to public policy. Among the problems that they analyze are the optimum sequencing of steps in manufacturing processes, the optimum combination of factors of production given a fixed budget, and the optimum size of inventories to be stored in view of the costs of storage and the risk of exhaustion of the inventory. Other such models derive from engineering and the professions.

Examples of individual statements from such models are:

1. Increasing the coefficient of friction on a road, or decreasing the velocity of a vehicle, will decrease skidding.

2. The use of a particular drug will reduce the incidence of a disease.

3. An increase in the interest rate by the Board of Governors of the Federal Reserve System will slow the growth of the economy.

4.   School integration will increase the test scores of pupils from minority groups.

5.   Competition among government bureaucracies will reduce spending.

6.   Plurality elections, in contrast to proportional representation, will eventually decrease the number of political parties.[4]

The models of causation used in policy analysis must always connect some possible choice of acts to valued or disvalued outcomes—benefits or costs in relation to specified ethical criteria.[5] In policy analysis as we define it the valuative outcome variable should be related to a general ethical system.

The dependent variables in the six statements we have listed are not—with the possible exception of disease and health—usually regarded as ultimate human values or disvalues. A systematic ethical approach, however, leads us continually to question whether changes in such variables are worthwhile and to relate these variables to one another in larger logical systems, specifying the tradeoffs between them. Statements 1 and 2 might be related to one another in terms of the value of human life, since skidding affects the loss of life through accidents, and disease likewise threatens life. The economic criterion of productivity might relate statements 3 and 4, since the growth of the economy can be expressed in terms of production, and one consequence of learning in school (as measured by test scores) is the capacity to produce more. The criterion of efficiency, which economists use to relate production to costs, would connect productivity (in statements 3 and 4) with cost or spending (in statement 5). Statement 6 is hardest to connect with the others in this way because the effects of political competition on human life, productivity, and efficiency are indirect and hard to estimate. Moreover, even the general valuative variables we have suggested—years of life, production, and efficiency—require connection in a more general ethical system if we are to choose among policies that affect these three different values.

The causal relations listed in the six statements deal with the relations between valued outcomes and policy variables that may be changed by human decisions. But our models also include relations between those outcomes and nonpolicy variables that are either unalterable or unrelated to the policies we are considering. For example: rain also affects the chance of skidding; the introduction of germs affects the incidence of disease; a rise in the price of foreign oil affects the growth of the economy; and family background affects pupils' test scores. We need to know the effects of these nonpolicy variables as well in order to single out those effects that are due to policy variables.

The importance of considering nonpolicy variables can be illustrated by models of causation of crime. Presumably crime rates can be affected by public policies such as changes in law enforcement by the police, but also by social characteristics of potential criminals (the aged are unlikely to engage in mugging), activities of potential victims (home protection), and characteristics of communities (some are more law-abiding or more likely to encourage reporting of crime to the police). Though most of these variables can ultimately be affected by public policy, let us assume that in the short run we are analyzing the effects of police activities and that the other variables are not policy variables.

One way to formulate a model of the effects of law enforcement on crime is to compare data on police activities and crime rates for various cities or other areas at a given time (a "cross-sectional" study). The results of such a comparison can be invalid, however, if cities also differ in other ways that affect their crime rates and police activities. We cannot make valid inferences about the effects of police activity unless we set aside the effects of these other nonpolicy variables.

Another way to estimate the effects of police activities on crime, however, is to study changes over time in the crime rate in a particular city when a change in police activity is introduced (a "longitudinal" study). Such a comparison over time is not affected by the characteristics of the city, which we usually assume do not change in the time period under study. By combining time-series studies with comparisons between cities we may be able to estimate the effects of policies more accurately.

Models useful for policy analysis may be either general or specific. They may be general in applying to a variety of apparently different situations and providing insights that may be transferred from one field to another. Thus, the properties of certain statistical distributions, such as the normal distribution, apply to numerous types of data, and the mathematics that describes the motion of fluids resembles that which describes electric fields. On the other hand, for evaluation of a particular program it may be preferable to use a model pertaining only to that program, rather than to expend a great deal of effort seeking a more general model.

Models may also range from simple to complex, depending both on the nature of the systems we are describing and on the time and resources we have to describe them. If we have little time for analysis we may approximate a complex system, such as an organization, by a simple model. We then recognize the approximate character of the model by modifying our inferences from it in view of experience.

The functioning of a complex system may sometimes be described by a set of relatively independent, simpler models that describe its subsystems or parts. In case 4–A, for example, we break down the effects of automobile speed into three parts that concern effects on travel time, costs of operation, and accidents. We may also alternate between simple and complex models as we shift between smaller and larger perspectives in the mixed-scanning approach.[6] In terms of organizational choices our alternatives may range from decisions within existing structures in which given persons hold office, to the replacement of persons within these existing structures, to the alteration of the structures themselves. Thus, if we were dealing with Congress, we might try to get a bill passed, to elect new members, or to change the committee structure or legislative procedures. In a still larger perspective we might consider the alteration of regimes, societies, or cultures.[7]

We may alternate between simple and complex perspectives not only in time but also by dividing the labor of analysis between persons who study short-run practical problems and long-run theoretical problems. These two types of analysis must be connected, however, if the long-run analyses are to be useful.

In practical application the depth of analysis we conduct depends not only on the importance of the decision but also on the time and resources available. James S. Coleman has stressed that policy-related research has to be delivered when it is needed.[8] President Kennedy's decision in the Cuban missile crisis was constrained by time and by the lack of much important information.[9] In other decisions relevant resources may include information, scientific generalizations, analytic skills, and the cooperation of persons with access to these resources. Our initial models of the effects of policy alternatives may be based on estimates made in advance of systematic analysis. Given time and resources, we can test and improve them through research.

The choice between simpler and more complex perspectives may be illustrated by our selection of policy variables. When we seek alternatives to deal with a problem, we often look first for remedies for conditions that have led to the problem. Thus, we may try to reduce disease by reducing the dissemination of germs or to reduce the number of defects in a manufactured product by improving workers' performance. But we may also consider changing the system within which the germs or workers function: We may try to increase the body's resistance to disease or change the materials that the workers use. We can also sometimes deal more effectively with symptoms than with deeper-lying causes of problems, and for some purposes this may be adequate. The general principle is that we look wherever we can for alternative policies and not seek merely to remedy the immediate and apparent cause of a problem. Our models of causation should make us aware of the range of choices open to us, their relative efficacy and cost, and the aspects of the situation that are beyond our control.

UNCERTAINTY IN MODELS

The models we use vary not only in their complexity but also in the degree of certainty with which they predict outcomes. Models involving the natural sciences often make predictions with a very low amount of uncertainty or statistical variation. Those of the social sciences usually involve an explicit recognition that random error may be present, and their predictions are thus statistical in character. Some social-science models are qualitative and merely state that a change in a policy variable is expected to be associated with an increase (or decrease) in an outcome variable. The examples we gave above of six statements from policy-related models illustrate this variety. Statements about the motion of automobiles, for example, are likely to be more precise than those about the effects of electoral systems.

When uncertainty is present in the systems we are analyzing, we may nevertheless analyze them if we can attach numerical probabilities to uncertain events. We sometimes estimate probabilities as relative frequencies with which these events are expected to occur, based on samples drawn from larger populations. Thus, the probability that a person will have a given disease, if that person is a randomly chosen member of a specified age group, can be estimated on the basis of a sample of that age group. We shall use probabilities of this sort later in this chapter in connection with analysis of a medical screening test.

For some models, however, there are still more difficult problems in estimating probabilities. A model stated in purely qualitative terms might be used to tell us whether one policy is better than another. But without quantitative expression it cannot tell us how much better or whether the improvement is worth the cost. Some analysts make use of quantitative estimates that are expressions of personal or subjective expectations. Although this is necessary in the absence of more systematic study, it does not provide for reasoned criticism to the extent that scientific observation does.

There are many important policy choices for which objective estimates of probability are unavailable. For example, the choice whether to develop nuclear energy depends in part on the probability of accidents or sabotage, leading to danger from explosions or radioactivity; decisions concerning recombinant DNA may relate to the probability that new and dangerous microorganisms will be produced. In each of these cases there seems little agreement about what the relevant probability is or even about means of estimating it. For problems of this sort policy analysis can be of only limited value.

Our choices among large political, economic, or social systems also have consequences to which it is difficult to attach numerical probabilities in an objective fashion. Political scientists are concerned with the choice among democratic, totalitarian, authoritarian, and aristocratic regimes—a subject worthy of serious consideration but one rarely considered in quantitative terms. Even their more specific concerns with the effects of electoral laws, constituency boundaries, voting rules, and legislative procedures are difficult to express in quantitative models. Economists have been concerned with the merits of a free and competitive market as compared with other means of allocating resources and distributing goods and services. The model of the free market, in fact, is so central to policy analysis in economies such as our own that we shall devote the next chapter to it. But the argument for a free market system is usually based on abstract reasoning, rather than on observed probabilities that certain results will flow from it.

A related type of policy choice is that between alternative decision processes within a given system. We may wish to decide not simply how to educate children but how to allow parents to choose among schools. Or we may wish not simply to allocate resources to certain sports but to create a system of competition in which all who have the ability may compete for sports resources. Even for smaller choices of this kind it seems impractical to estimate probabilities of particular results in objective terms, since it is difficult to observe a large number of such systems that are sufficiently alike.

Our estimates of probabilities also sometimes become less valid over time. Research done in one historical situation may become less valid when conditions change. An example is the generalization made in the 1950s that black children's self-esteem will be less if they are educated in segregated schools. Since that time, movements have developed for voluntary racial separation, and the existence of these movements may have changed some of the conditions for self-esteem.

A further type of model in which it is difficult to make quantitative estimates of probability is that of policy implementation. Our own involvement and the effort we may exert make it hard to consider objective probabilities of success. If, however, we set aside our own involvement and that of persons we are trying to persuade, we may try to make such estimates. Suppose, for example, that we wish to establish an organization for the delivery of services; we can learn something of the types of organizational structure, recruitment, and training that make service delivery most effective.

If we can vary the internal functioning of such an organization systematically, we may make models of the effects of this variation. We need not then rely solely on intuition, personal experience, and particular examples to anticipate the conditions under which a policy will be carried out. The models of organizational effectiveness that we then make will involve variables such as budget, structure, planning, internal monitoring, and enforcement, as these variables affect outcomes. Thus, if we have systematic knowledge of the effects of these variables, their alteration may be considered part of our policy choice. If our knowledge of these variables is limited to intuition and personal contacts, we are more likely to limit our formal analysis to a model of the effects of the "policy" that would correspond to perfect implementation.

STATISTICAL MODELS *

When there is uncertainty in the system we are studying but that uncertainty can be expressed quantitatively in terms of probabilities, we can statistically analyze the causal relations involved.[10] This type of reasoning is illustrated in its simplest form by our decision whether to carry an umbrella on a certain day. Our criterion for this decision (not a policy decision if we are

* The student who has not had a prior course in statistics may skip this section.

making it only once for one person) will be the equivalent monetary benefit or cost to ourselves. Assume that the monetary equivalent of the cost to us of the inconvenience of carrying the umbrella, relative to not carrying it on a dry day, is $1; the cost of getting wet (including discomfort, inconvenience, chance of catching a cold, and damage to garments) is estimated at $10; and the probability of rain that day is 30 percent. We then calculate the *expected value* (i.e., expected amount) of the cost or loss associated with either of our alternatives, which is found by weighting the number associated with each outcome by its probability. If we carry the umbrella, there is a loss of $1 with a probability of 1.0, that is, certainty. If we do not carry the umbrella, we lose nothing with a probability of .7 and we lose $10 with a probability of .3. The expected monetary loss (EML) from not carrying the umbrella is then given by

$$\text{EML} = (\$0 \times .7) + (\$10 \times .3) = \$3$$

As this loss is greater than $1, we decide to carry the umbrella that day.

In making the decision in this way we in effect consider the costs that would be incurred if we faced this decision many times and made this choice repeatedly. Not to carry the umbrella on days of this kind would cause a loss of $0 in 70 percent of the cases and a loss of $10 in 30 percent. The long-run average of the results would be equivalent to a loss of $3 on each occasion. As this is greater than the certain loss of $1 from carrying the umbrella each time, we decide to carry it.

Our model here involved the causal relation between carrying or not carrying the umbrella and various results—discomfort, inconvenience, chance of a cold, and damage to clothes. We summarized the disvalue to us of the results in expected monetary terms. The incidence of these results was also affected by the weather—another causal variable in our model, though not one affected by our choice.

If our policy choice can vary not simply between discrete alternatives (such as carrying or not carrying an umbrella) but in a continuous fashion, other types of models are appropriate. We may then want to decide *how much* of some activity a government should carry out, such as how much regulation, taxation, or production of a service it should provide. In such cases we wish to estimate the expected value of the outcome for each possible amount of the policy variable. One type of statistical model widely used for this purpose, especially in the social sciences, is a *linear* model based on a straight-line relation between policy and effect. Such models may be used either because we have reason to believe that the underlying relation is genuinely linear or as approximations chosen because of simplicity or convenience.

In such a model a dependent variable Y is considered to be caused by an independent variable X, and this relation is expressed by the equation

$$Y = a + bX + e \tag{1}$$

where a and b are the intercept and slope of a straight line and e is an "error" or residual term corresponding to departures of the actual value of Y from this straight-line prediction. The error term is usually assumed to be random, that is, not systematically associated with X or Y. If we are able to estimate the constants a and b, the expected value of Y for a given value of X is given by

$$\hat{Y} = a + bX \qquad (2)$$

The value $\hat{Y}$ is also known as the predicted value of Y. The difference $(Y - \hat{Y})$ between the actual and predicted values is e, the residual.

If equation (1) specifies the causal relation between X and Y accurately, then we may expect that when we change X by variations in policy, the corresponding change in Y will, on the average, be b times as great. But if some other variable is really the cause of both X and Y or if X is associated with some other variable that also causes changes in Y, then b can no longer be expected to measure the effect of X on Y. Thus, if X is expenditure on schools and Y is pupil achievement but both are related to the social and economic composition of the school district, b as ordinarily estimated will not tell us the effect of increasing the budget.

A simple example of the use of a linear model for policy analysis is provided by statistics cited in the *Swann* v. *Charlotte-Mecklenburg Board of Education* lawsuit.[11] Judge James B. McMillan, in justifying a busing plan to correct previous patterns of educational segregation, cited test results for four junior high schools. On a spelling achievement test (SP) the average scores shown in table 4–1 were reported (in grade equivalents) for the eighth grade in 1968–69.[12] The score of 64 for Williams school, for example, indicates performance at about the sixth grade level. These scores show that the pupils at Randolph Road and Eastway were performing at about the level expected nationwide for the eighth grade, while those at Williams and Northwest were performing at about the sixth and seventh grade levels respectively. The judge claimed that these and other data illustrated "the effects of unequal education."

Table 4–1.
Average Spelling Achievement Scores for Eighth-Grade Students in Four Schools in the Charlotte-Mecklenburg (N.C.) System, 1968–1969

School	Percent Black	W × 100 Percent White	SP Average Score
Williams	100	0	64
Northwest	100	0	71
Randolph Road	28	72	82
Eastway	4	96	86

Source:
Swann v. Charlotte-Mecklenburg Board of Education, Supplementary Opinion and Order, 1 Dec. 1969, 306 F. Supp. 1299 (1969), p. 1309.

He also observed, on the basis of these data and tests on other subjects, that "Randolph Road, 72% white and 28% Negro, has eighth grade performance results approximately comparable to Eastway, which is 96% white, and Randolph results are approximately two years ahead of all-black Williams and Northwest."[13] In this statement he seems to have been expressing a causal model connecting racial desegregation (in Randolph Road) with test scores. But there is another causal process that may be contributing to Randolph Road's higher average score than Williams and Northwest; it contained a higher percentage of white students. Conceivably, mere mixing of students with different scores, without any effect of desegregation on their scores, would have produced some of the observed difference.

In this instance a policy of desegregation was being considered, and the previous mixture of students by race at Randolph Road, in comparison with the other schools, was taken as an example of desegregation. The judge wished to assess the results of such a policy. There are, however, two ways in which the policy can affect the average scores of students: by changing scores and by simply averaging unchanged scores. We could separate these effects most clearly if we had separate scores for the two racial groups, but the judge apparently did not have this information.

We shall use a linear model to examine the effect of simply averaging students' unchanged test scores. This effect must be set aside if we are to see how much difference in average scores might be due to the change in scores produced by desegregation. If we could assume that the pupil populations of the schools were drawn from larger homogeneous populations of blacks and whites, we might try to estimate the coefficients in the equation

$$SP = a + bW + e \tag{3}$$

where SP = spelling score and W = proportion of white students in a school. We shall treat the average of the spelling scores for Williams and Northwest, 67.5, as an estimate of the average score of black students in all-black schools. The difference of seven points between the scores for these two schools allows us to make a rough estimate of the possible uncertainty or variability in the data.

We shall use the linear model in (3) not as an indication of the effects of desegregation policies, but as an indication of what the effect of racial composition on test scores would be if there were *no* change in performance when pupils changed from segregated to desegregated schools. Judge McMillan's statement seems to imply that desegregation at Randolph Road led to a higher set of achievement scores than would have been observed otherwise. To see what might have been observed otherwise, we may estimate a and b in (3) from the data given for all-black and nearly all-white schools and see how much SP for Randolph Road differs from the predicted value.

Let us estimate the coefficients a and b in (3) by substituting two known data points (SP, W): (67.5, 0) for Williams-Northwest and (86, 0.96) for Eastway. With only two points to fit, we assume e to be zero and solve the two simultaneous equations obtained by substituting these two points in (3).[14] The results are $a = 67.5$, $b = 19.27$. Substituting in (3), ignoring e, we obtain for Randolph Road the expected spelling score of $67.5 + 19.27(.72) = 81.37$. The actual score is 82 and the residual $+.63$. The positive sign of the residual is in the direction corresponding to increased scores due to desegregation, but it seems small compared to the possible random variation among schools; the average scores for Williams and Northwest differed by seven points. If these were the only data we had, they would not provide strong support for desegregation.[15]

If we had more than two data points, we could not in general expect them all to lie exactly on a straight line. We might then wish again to estimate values of a and b corresponding to a straight line such that the expected or predicted value of $\hat{Y}$ for a given X was given by (2). In this case we could estimate a and b for a set of observed values of X and Y by the principle of least squares, which determines a and b in such a way that the sum of all the values of $(Y - \hat{Y})^2$ is a minimum. We call this sum, $\Sigma(Y - \hat{Y})^2$, the *residual variation* in Y. The formulas for computing a and b, derived from the principle of least squares, are given in introductory statistics textbooks. The resulting equation (2) is then known as a *regression* equation.

In using a regression equation we may wish to express the degree to which the equation successfully estimates the observed values of Y. Had we not used the prediction from X at all, our best prediction would have been $\hat{Y} = \bar{Y}$ (the mean of Y) for every observed value of Y, and the variation of the actual Y's about $\bar{Y}$ would have been the *total variation* $\Sigma(Y - \bar{Y})^2$. We can then express our success in predicting Y from the regression equation as

$$r^2 = 1 - \frac{\Sigma(Y - \hat{Y})^2}{\Sigma(Y - \bar{Y})^2} \tag{4}$$

where r is known as the correlation coefficient between X and Y. The expression for r^2 achieves its maximum value of 1.0 when the regression equation perfectly predicts all the observed values of Y so that $\hat{Y} = Y$ for every observed point and the numerator of the fraction in (4) is zero. If our prediction is completely unsuccessful, $r^2 = 0$.

This reasoning may be extended to the problem of *multiple regression*, which involves finding the best linear combination of predictor variables (X_i) to estimate a dependent variable Y. The coefficients in the equation

$$Y = a + b_1X_1 + b_2X_2 + b_3X_3 + e \tag{5}$$

for example, can also be estimated according to the principle of least squares. If we can be sure that X_1, X_2, and X_3 are all distinct direct causes of variation in

Y, we can estimate their effects by means of the corresponding b's. These *partial* b's are then estimates of the effects of the independent variables X_i taken one at a time, with the others "statistically controlled." A coefficient R^2, the multiple correlation coefficient, expresses our degree of success in prediction as in (4), with $\hat{Y}$ now denoting the estimated value of Y in (5) without the error term e.

The partial b's in (5) are genuine estimates of causal effects only if (5) specifies the causal relations accurately. In order for this to be true, X_1, X_2, and X_3 must have separate causal connections to Y, rather than one working through another. They may be associated with one another. But as in (1), they may not have causes that are also causes of Y.

Linear causal models such as (1) and (5) have typically been used with data collected for a single time only and containing observations on a number of similar units (cross-sectional data) to infer causal relations that would presumably obtain if we intervened in a system. They may also be used with time-series data that are not based on deliberate policy intervention. For example, we might study the past relation between the gross national product (GNP) and government expenditures.[16] But we would have more confidence that government expenditures caused changes in the GNP, rather than the reverse, if the expenditures were changed by deliberate policy intervention. We would have still more confidence that government expenditures caused changes in the GNP if it were possible to intervene according to an experimental design insuring that the intervention was not affected by other variables such as economic conditions.

An important piece of policy-related research that made use of regression models was *Equality of Educational Opportunity* by Coleman et al. In this study data were gathered on pupils and schools throughout the United States. The data included test scores, characteristics of the pupils' families, pupils' attitudes, and characteristics of the schools. Test scores were predicted by means of multiple regression equations, and the additional contribution made by school characteristics, over and above family characteristics, was expressed by the corresponding increase in R^2 when school characteristics were added to the equation. The report led to pessimistic conclusions about the efficacy of school characteristics in reducing inequality, except for the effects on minority students of their schoolmates' educational background and aspirations. This last finding was widely interpreted as favorable to school desegregation.[17]

A central concern of this report was to analyze the productivity of schools as they affect equality. The effects of school composition that the report showed relate to one of the inputs to school productivity, even though these effects do not work through the conventional organizational channels of teaching and facilities. The report also suggested that "the effect of good teachers is greatest upon the children who suffer most educational disadvantage in their background."[18] Additional studies of the productivity of public organizations—hospitals, schools, police forces—have been made since this report and promise to be useful for policy analysis.

INDICES OF VALUED OUTCOMES

The criteria and models we have discussed so far have been described by words and concepts more than by measurement. In the natural sciences these two sorts of description correspond closely, but in the social sciences they are more distinguishable. In the social sciences we can more easily imagine an operation or measurement that provides only a partly valid measure of a given concept. Thus, we must consider the problems that arise when we translate models into measurement, especially for our valuative dependent variables.

If we hope to estimate the value of alternative policies in quantitative terms, we must first choose a valid index, related to our valuative criteria, to measure the value of policy outcomes. In the decisions of an individual or a firm such an index might be the expected monetary value of the outcome, with various possible outcomes weighted by their probabilities.[19] In decisions intended to improve the well-being of large numbers of persons, an index corresponding to aggregate monetary value is the gross national product—often used for national economic decisions, but also criticized for its possible biases. An analogous index for a particular project is the expected net monetary benefit, or benefit minus cost. If we wish to measure the value of a policy per unit spent, then a benefit-cost ratio may be used.

Indices of the monetary value of policies may also be obtained by conducting surveys that ask those affected how much money various consequences would be worth to them. Julian L. Simon reports a study in which faculty members were asked to place monetary values on specific degrees of availability of books when a university was considering policies for the storage of some of its library books.[20] From such individual judgments, if we could be sure they were honestly given, we might estimate the aggregate benefits of various policies.

It is conceivable that analyses of benefits and costs of policies could be made in terms other than monetary units, but techniques of doing so require much development before they can be used practically. If our ethical criterion for policy choice included special consideration for the poor, we might apply weighting factors to count benefits to the poor more heavily than benefits to the nonpoor. We should then have to apply these same weighting factors to the costs of policies. This would require estimation of the incidence of taxes on various income groups in order to provide a correspondingly weighted figure for costs.

We might also take as a criterion the direct value of life experience resulting from various policies, without relating this value to income or money. Milton D. Weinstein and William B. Stason have proposed that benefits of health and medical policies be measured by questions to those affected, such as asking them what fraction of a year of life they would be willing to give up in order to be completely healthy for the rest of the year.[21] But it seems impracticable to measure the number of quality-adjusted life-years sacrificed by the taxpayers who pay for health policies. For this reason this approach leads to the measurement of benefits in years and costs in dollars and prevents us from measuring the net benefit (benefit minus cost) of the policies in question.

If outcomes cannot be evaluated in monetary terms and thus cannot be measured in the same units as costs, we may then try to construct indices of effectiveness and relate them to costs. Other examples of measures of effectiveness of policies are test scores related to education, measures of health status, and amount of services delivered. The effectiveness of a policy, of course, like any measure of its value, is not identical with a measure of the state of affairs after the policy has been carried out. We must examine *changes* in index values attributable to the policy, if we are really to measure "effectiveness."

A ratio of effectiveness to cost, such as clinical successes per thousand tests in drug screening, can be used to measure the value of a policy that may be carried out on a larger or smaller scale.[22] Such a ratio can then be used to compare various policies that contribute to the type of effectiveness that it measures. But the ratio cannot compare various sorts of effectiveness, as among policies for health, education, and national defense.

Economic indicators, such as the unemployment rate or the consumer price index, are used as dependent variables in some models. Similarly, "social indicators" have been developed as measures of social conditions (e.g., health, knowledge, victimization, satisfaction), and these may also be used as dependent variables in models. These indicators are usually based on samples of the general population and provide statistical expression of the condition of a population as a whole. By summarizing that condition, a social indicator can alert us to the existence of a problem. But if our purpose is to test and refine a model or to see whether a particular policy has succeeded, we will more often wish to measure the same variable for the part of the population that the policy is aimed to affect (the "target population"). We may also wish to incorporate the measurement into a well-designed experiment, making sure that the measurement on the target population is also made on a comparable control group.[23] Studies of social indicators for the entire population, however, can reveal unintended consequences for persons outside the target population.

If we measure a dependent variable and use the measure or index repeatedly for decisions, persons affected by its use may change its meaning. If repeated use of this index is known to persons potentially affected by the decisions based on the index, then they may seek to influence the index rather than the concept or value for which it stands. School entrance examinations may come to measure successful cramming as well as aptitude; counts of units produced by a factory in a nonmarket economy may lead to emphasis by managers and workers on quantity rather than quality. Affected persons may in this way alter the model itself either by changing the meaning of the measured variables in it or by changing the causal relations among variables.[24]

This possibility of adaptation by affected persons poses a special problem for policy-relevant models. Among the ways to reduce this effect are the use of multiple measures of the variable in question and the location of evaluative research in organizations whose budgets do not depend on its results. We may also try to choose indices that lead to desirable types of adaptive behavior and to involve the persons affected in the process of choice of indices.

TESTING AND IMPROVING MODELS

If the causal relations with which we are concerned are persistent, a model devised at one time can retain its validity and usefulness later, and we may spend time testing and refining it. We thus can look to the broader perspective of universities or research institutions as a supplement to the citizen's judgment or the practitioner's experience, a recourse analogous to the choice of a broader perspective in "mixed-scanning." Published discussion and criticism of scientific research can contribute much to the refinement and generalization of policy analyses in the long run. These general results will of course have to be interpreted in concrete terms in order to be relevant to specific policy choices.

Our initial formulation of a model, especially if we are under the pressure of time, may be based on rough estimates and available data. Published data and administrative records are often cheaper than new data gathered by research procedures such as survey interviews.[25] But if analysis of available data is to be useful, it is important that records of good quality be kept. Useful data may exist in the files of hospitals, police departments, schools, and other organizations. If we have access to such data, however, we must examine their quality carefully before analyzing them.

For the development and verification of models over the long term, the perspective of university-based policy research is especially relevant. This perspective is not, however, identical with that of the basic scientific disciplines. The motives for research in basic science are not always the same as those that lead to effective policy application. Basic research seeks general factual statements about the world but does not require results in time for decisions or stress manipulable variables. Even in the long run, models that are relevant to policy analysis may differ from those of the basic disciplines because they involve valuative outcomes. And for policy choice we may also be interested in relations between concepts from different disciplines, such as the connection between industrial concentration and politics or between a competitive economic system and personality development.

We may test a model either to see whether it includes the correct variables or to estimate the effects of given variables more accurately. If the model is general, and not limited in scope to statements about a specific program, we may deduce implications from it and compare these deductions with observation. Even implications unrelated to policy choice can still be tests of the adequacy of the model. For example, a model of epidemics devised by Maurice S. Bartlett could be tested by its predictions of the relation of the frequency of epidemics to city size.[26] Even though city size is not a variable that we can easily alter by policy, the confirmation of this deduction and others from the model increases our confidence in the model. Such a model may be used to account for nonpolicy influences on illness rates so that when we see the rate decrease, we can better judge whether the decrease was due to our policies or to events that would have occurred in any case.

For policy analysis we need not only to improve our models but to judge their adequacy for our purposes to see whether they need improvement. We thus test the *sensitivity* of our results to changes of variables or parameters in the model. Policy analysis must often use rough estimates of data, and we need at least to know how serious the consequences of these approximations will be.

Policy-related models require testing in practice, not merely under controlled or "laboratory" conditions. Engineers know that new electronic or mechanical devices need extensive practical tests to supplement the theoretical considerations of their design. The same caution is appropriate for the design of social institutions or social policies. But the difficulty of instituting a full-blown social program and knowing its consequences requires that we find ways to conduct smaller-scale experiments. Ideally, our policies should themselves be designed as experiments so that their effects can be measured efficiently.[27]

The choice among policies is not necessarily a once-and-for-all choice making use of a given model. Rather, it can involve gathering information to test a relevant model, revising policies, and putting them into effect in ways that permit systematic evaluation of their effects. A repeated feedback cycle of this kind may allow successive approximation to a workable and beneficial policy choice. At the same time, successive approximations may permit judgment about the political feasibility of a given approach,[28] although this is distinct from judgment about desirability.

The cycle between analysis and action can be carried out to serve various goals. It may be directed at ongoing improvement of organizational functioning or at reconsideration of the status of the organization itself.[29] But it may also be aimed at the improvement of general policy-relevant models. Evaluation research can help to develop such models and thus suggest a wider range of possible policies, if comparable variables are measured in a variety of evaluation studies. This advantage will be enhanced to the extent that the various studies are interrelated to maximize the information obtained relative to the model. Similarly, the measurement of valuative social indicators can be related to the development of models if the same variables are measured in indicator and evaluation studies. The ideal result is a model in which evaluation of programs contributes to generalizations that can be used in subsequent policy choice for new types of programs.[30] Such research will yield results more general and lasting than the evaluation of a particular program.

The methods of social research are especially relevant to the testing of policy-relevant models. If we could tell in advance what social and economic conditions would affect the consequences of a negative income tax, we might better estimate the desirability of enacting it. If we could specify the variables that would best predict students' accomplishment in a racially desegregated school system, we might better judge educational policies.[31] An increasing number of carefully designed experiments are being conducted to test whether new social policies will work.

The consequences of adopting a policy are not, however, limited to the immediate effects on persons at whom it is directed. Persons initially affected by a policy may *react* to it and change its effect or incidence. We noted earlier that persons affected may adapt in such a manner as to change the meaning of indices used to measure outcomes. But they may also adapt by leaving the target population. Those who dislike the internal policies of an organization, a state, or even a nation may resign or emigrate.[32] Parents of children in desegregated school districts may send their children to private schools. Manufacturers of taxed products may raise prices, passing the tax on to the purchaser. The regulation of hydrocarbons and carbon monoxide in automobile exhausts has led to redesigns that increased the emission of oxides of nitrogen.[33] Persons (or organizations) affected by a policy may also react so as to facilitate it—for example, some patrons of a new urban transportation system may eventually sell their cars. We may try to incorporate reactions of this kind into the models that we formulate, as in dynamic economic models or the theory of games.

Testing and improving models requires resources for research. These resources may be available to citizens through researchers' publications, through the conduct of open research in which the researcher plays the role of citizen and is concerned with the general welfare, or through the mustering of resources by voluntary "public interest" associations.

DECISION TREES

Policy analysis makes use of models to permit decisions. The alternatives among which we decide may be either discrete (a set of distinct possibilities such as starting a new program or doing nothing) or continuous (choices of amount or scale). For the case of discrete choices a useful diagrammatic approach to decision making is the *decision tree*. An example of continuous alternatives is presented in case 4–A.[34]

The use of a decision tree may be illustrated with the example given earlier concerning the choice whether or not to carry an umbrella, as shown in figure 4–1. The probability of rain is .30 and the monetary losses corresponding to various possible events are shown at the right in the figure. The decision tree in the figure begins at the left and branches out to the right. It contains two types of branches or "forks": a "decision fork" (indicated by a square box) at which we make a choice whether to carry the umbrella or not and a "chance fork" (indicated by a circle) at which one or another event (rain or no rain) occurs with a certain probability. If we choose the upper branch and carry the

Figure 4–1.
Decision Tree for Carrying an Umbrella.

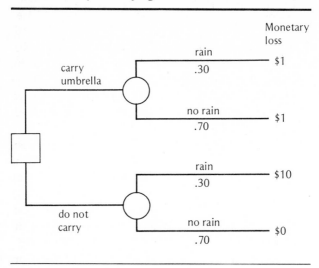

umbrella, we receive the combined value of the two possibilities at the chance fork (rain and no rain). This combined value is simply the expected value; the certain monetary loss of $1 is equivalent to the expected monetary loss (EML) for carrying the umbrella,

$$\text{EML (carry umbrella)} = .30(\$1) + .70(\$1) = \$1$$

If we choose the lower branch and do not carry the umbrella, the expected monetary loss is

$$\text{EML (do not carry umbrella)} = .30(\$10) + .70(\$0) = \$3$$

We choose the branch with the lower expected monetary loss, which corresponds to carrying the umbrella on a day with a probability of rain of .30. We would actually make this decision as long as the probability of rain exceeded .10.

Figure 4–1 illustrates some general features of decision trees. As we have noted, they allow us to systematize our choices among discrete alternatives, each of which corresponds to a branch from a decision fork. We assume in drawing such a tree that the model of cause and effect is known and that it involves uncertainty. In the upper branch from the decision fork in the figure, there is actually a certain loss of $1. If there were certainty in the lower branch as well, the diagram would be of little use. In assuming that the model is known, we imply that the probabilities for branches at chance forks are known. The various effects that flow from a given choice, together with particular chance events, are summarized in a number at the right-hand end of each final branch.

Our basic operation in the use of decision trees, as we indicated, is the computation of expected values. For this purpose it is essential that we attach numerical values to the outcomes at the right-hand ends of the branches. The numerical values in a given tree may all be increased or decreased by a constant, however, without affecting our choice. It is for this reason that we can conveniently set the gain or loss from one outcome (e.g., not carrying the umbrella when there is no rain) at zero. The numerical values can also be multiplied by a constant without changing our choice. If that constant is −1, converting gains to losses, we need only choose the policy affording the least expected loss, rather than the greatest gain or benefit.

The examples that we give here are simplified as we assume the probabilities to be known. In more advanced types of decision trees we may be less certain of these probabilities, knowing only the characteristics of a sample and wishing to make inferences about the population from which it is drawn. A further complication, involving more than one step in the cycle of action and observation, concerns the possibility of a series of decisions. We make one choice and then observe results that depend in part on our own choice and in part on unknown or random variables beyond our control. We then proceed to make another choice, with the possibilities branching out as in a tree. At later stages the alternatives become more numerous. In a sequence of branching choices of this kind the necessary calculations are more complex.

The steps in the sequence of choices may also involve the gathering of information itself.[35] If new information is costly and if our available information suggests that new information is not worth gathering, we may decide not to gather it. One decision of this type is the initial choice we make when we decide whether analysis of a policy problem is worthwhile.[36] We summarize a decision of this sort in the decision tree of figure 4–2.

Suppose we face the choice whether to analyze a problem or not. We estimate that the analysis will involve a cost c, including not only the expense of gathering and processing data but also intangible costs such as the opportunity cost of possibly delaying a desirable program. The estimated probability that our analysis will make a difference is p. The estimated difference that analysis will make if it is successful is d, taking into account the size of the group affected by our proposed policies, the possibility of transferring the results of our analysis to other areas and problems, and the length of time for which our analysis promises to be valid. If we choose the upper branch at the decision fork, we decide to conduct no analysis, and we designate the benefit of this choice as v. Note that the quantities at the right (v and d) are expressed as benefits in figure 4–2, rather than losses. These symbols stand for quantities that are difficult to estimate. Nevertheless, we shall be able to see an interesting relation among them.

If we choose the lower branch at the decision fork, we have chosen to conduct analysis at cost c, indicated by the barrier across that branch. We then encounter a chance fork, at which the probability of an improved decision is p and that of the same decision $1-p$. The value of an improved decision is

Figure 4–2.

Decision Tree for the Decision Whether to Analyze a Problem.

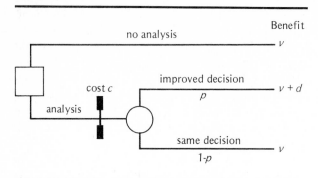

Source: This figure is reprinted from *Improving the Quality of Urban Management,* Urban Affairs Annual Reviews, Volume 8, Willis D. Hawley and David Rogers, Editors. © 1974, p. 203, by permission of the publisher, Sage Publications, Inc. (Beverly Hills/London).

$v + d$ and that of the same decision v. Since we paid c for analysis, the overall benefit from an improved decision is $v + d - c$, and that of the same decision $v - c$. We consider analysis to be desirable if the expected value of benefit for the lower branch at the decision fork exceeds that of the upper branch. Calculating expected values by weighting each possible result at the chance fork by its probability, we find that analysis is desirable if

$$p\,(v + d - c) + (1 - p)(v - c) > v$$

Expanding the inequality,

$$pv + pd - pc + v - c - pv + pc > v$$

The terms containing v cancel, indicating that it makes no difference what value we choose for the value of "no analysis," a baseline from which the values of the other branches are measured. Two terms in pc also cancel, leaving

$$pd - c > 0$$

or

$$pd > c$$

We thus decide to conduct analysis only if the product of p and d—the expected value of the difference that analysis will make—exceeds the cost. This relationship explains why it may be worthwhile to society to employ a staff of analysts to study a problem of persisting national import (high d), whereas a nonrepetitive local problem may be worth only a rapid judgment. It also leads us not to waste analytic resources on alternatives that have little chance of being put into effect, unless they are of very great potential importance.

We have concluded, in effect, that analysis is worthwhile if its expected value pd exceeds its cost c. This conclusion actually applies to any policy. In figure 4–2 we may substitute any policy for "analysis" and draw a similar conclusion. In this perspective d is the benefit that would result if the policy were put into effect and p, the probability that it will be put into effect. The two in combination—desirability and feasibility if we choose the policy—determine whether the policy is better than the do-nothing alternative. It is for this reason that in chapter 1 we defined "better" policies in terms of both desirability and feasibility even though the former is easier to analyze objectively.

We might also enlarge figure 4–2, extending the "improved decision" branch to lead on to the choice whether to work for enactment and implementation or not. This choice might provide both public benefits for the general welfare and personal costs, such as we discuss in chapter 6 under the heading "Personal Feasibility." Analysts and decision makers do have to weigh personal costs against the public good. But for general public discussion of the value of policies, it is important to present analyses based on the public good alone. We next present a numerical example using the public good as a criterion.

A MEDICAL SCREENING PROBLEM

The use of a decision tree may also be illustrated by a problem in medical diagnosis. A problem in large-scale medical screening is that of deciding whether to conduct one or several tests on all members of a population in which a given disease may exist. Using the decision tree shown in figure 4–3, we consider whether to conduct a stool guaiac test for blood in the stool, "a sign of nonsymptomatic (silent) cancer of the colon." [37] Filter paper impregnated with guaiac, a substance obtained from a South American tree, is used to reveal the presence of blood.

For simplicity we shall consider only the decision whether to conduct a single guaiac in the population of persons over the age of forty, but the procedure we present may also be applied to the decision whether to conduct two, three, or more tests in order to find cancers that may have been missed by earlier tests.

The question whether a diagnostic test is desirable is a special case of the more general question whether information is worth gathering in view of its costs and the benefits that might flow from it. In this particular case the value of the test depends on its cost and on the benefits that might flow from diagnosing cancer and treating it. Since the test will have to be performed many times on persons who do not have cancer, its value depends on the incidence of cancer in the population as well as on the reliability of the test. Figure 4–3 expresses the costs and benefits per person examined for two policies: guaiac or no guaiac. Probabilities, dollar costs, and algebraic symbols in figure 4–3 indicate estimates of these quantities, computed from data that we shall assume to be correct as cited in our source. In this tree the quantities symbolized at the right are again costs or losses.

Our criterion in this case will be cost-benefit analysis, including the controversial step of placing monetary values on human lives. At the start we shall ignore differences among individuals, assuming that the only alternatives under consideration involve treating all members of the population equally and basing our choices on average benefits and costs. After demonstrating the use of the decision tree, we shall reexamine some of our assumptions more closely.

There is only one decision fork in figure 4–3, fork 1 at the extreme left. Our decision in figure 4–3 (at fork 1) is whether to conduct the guaiac test. This is followed by various chance forks, depending on which initial decision we make.

Our procedure will be to proceed from right to left—the reverse of the actual sequence of events—branch by branch. This tree involves a sequence of

Figure 4–3.
Decision Tree for Choice Whether to Conduct Guaiac Test.

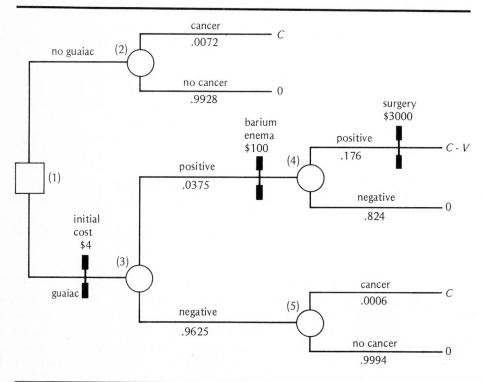

chance forks in some branches. In order to find the expected values (i.e., the expected losses) of the two initial branches at decision fork 1, we shall first calculate the expected value at chance fork 2; then the values at chance forks 5 and 4, which contribute to that at chance fork 3; and finally the value at chance fork 3. We then compare the expected monetary losses at chance forks 2 and 3, taking into account the cost of the guaiac at chance fork 3, and choose the branch with the lesser expected loss.

If we choose no guaiac (the upper branch at decision fork 1), we shall then face chance fork 2 at which the probability of cancer is .0072 and that of no cancer is .9928. We designate the loss from an undetected cancer as C. For this and the losses from other outcomes we use algebraic symbols at the start in order to solve the problem in general terms and show the degree of sensitivity of the results to various numerical assumptions. We assume that these losses can be expressed, at least approximately, in monetary terms. (We shall later see that the value of C is immaterial, as it drops out of the analysis.) We define the loss from the absence of cancer as 0, taking this condition as the base from which losses or costs are calculated. We shall compare alternatives in terms of their expected monetary loss (EML), as in the rain-and-umbrella example. The EML at chance fork 2 for the upper branch from decision fork 1 (the choice of no guaiac) is then given by

$$.0072C + .9928(0) = .0072C$$

We next need to calculate the EML for the lower branch from decision fork 1, corresponding to a decision to employ one guaiac test. The initial cost of conducting one such test is $4 and contributes to the EML if we choose that lower branch. We next encounter chance fork 3, the upper branch of which corresponds to a positive result of the test ($p = .0375$) and the lower to a negative result ($p = .9625$). The fact that .0375 is greater than .0072 implies that some people have positive test results even though they do not have cancer.

If the result is negative (lower branch at chance fork 3), the probability of cancer at chance fork 5 is reduced to .0006 or less than one-tenth its value in the entire population. This remaining probability of cancer corresponds to "false negatives" from the guaiac test. The EML at chance fork 5 when the test is conducted and is negative (lower branch of fork 3) is then .0006C; and its contribution to the EML at chance fork 3 is .0006$C \times$ .9625 = .0006C also, to this degree of accuracy.

The most important and most complex branch corresponds to a positive result from the guaiac (upper branch at fork 3). The guaiac test is not a certain indicator of cancer, as it merely indicates blood in the stool. Some of these positive indications may be "false positives." Before surgery is indicated, a second diagnostic test, a barium enema, must be conducted. This test costs an additional $100, as indicated just before fork 4. After chance fork 4, the probability is .176 that this will be positive if the guaiac was positive (known as "true positives" from the guaiac if we consider the barium enema to have no error), and .824 that it will be negative ("false positives" from the guaiac). In the event of a positive test surgery is indicated at an estimated cost of $3000 and with a net loss thereafter of $C - V$. A loss of $C - V$ is the same as a gain relative to untreated or undetected cancer of V, the expected monetary value added to the patient's remaining life span by surgery.[38]

We proceed to compute the EML of the state of affairs after the barium enema has been conducted. For the possibility that the enema is positive, the contribution of the upper branch of chance fork 4 is .176 $(3000 + C - V)$. For the possibility that this test is negative, the contribution of the lower branch of chance fork 4 is .824 $(0) = 0$. Thus, the EML of the upper branch at fork 3, including payment for the barium enema, is

$$100 + .176(3000 + C - V) + .824(0)$$

This expression consists of three parts: the $100 cost of the barium enema; the expected loss if the enema is positive, $.176(3000 + C - V)$; and the expected loss if the enema is negative, $.824(0)$, which is of course zero. The entire expression gives the expected loss at chance fork 4 plus the cost of the barium enema.

This entire set of events, corresponding to a positive guaiac test, will occur with a probability of .0375; thus, the overall EML at chance fork 3, after the decision to conduct the guaiac, is

$$.0375[100 + .176(3000 + C - V)] + .9625(.0006C)$$

and the overall EML of the lower branch at fork 1 will include the additional cost of $4. The guaiac is worth conducting if the EML of the lower branch at fork 1 is less than that of the upper, or if

$$4 + .0375[100 + 528 + .176(C - V)] + .9625(.0006C) < .0072C$$

Simplifying the left-hand side, we get

$$4 + 23.6 + .0066C - .0066V + .0006C < .0072C$$

The terms in C cancel as they are equal on both sides of the inequality. This follows from the fact that the overall probability of cancer is the same for the patient population regardless of whether the guaiac is conducted. The inequality thus simplifies further to

$$27.6 < .0066V$$

or

$$4200 < V$$

In other words, if we are willing to place a monetary value on the expected gain in life for the average patient and if this value is greater than $4200, then we should consider the guaiac test desirable. Since $4200 is small compared to estimates that have been made, our decision is not very *sensitive* to variation in the estimated value V of treatment. We might even consider studying the value of further guaiacs for that part of the population for which negative test results were observed on the first guaiac.

In order to make a decision in this case, we must place a monetary value on human life, if only approximately. D. Neuhauser and A. M. Lewicki avoid this question by asking, "Given a fixed budget for health services, how can we spend it to maximize life expectancy of constant quality?" [39] But in a more general perspective public funds spent on health services might be spent on other types of policy or retained by taxpayers. A rational comparison of these uses of resources requires us to compare their benefits.

Neuhauser and Lewicki later note, however, that the amounts spent on hysterectomies suggest that the cost per year of life saved is approximately $15,000 and that "early detection [of cancer] will prolong life by an average of 4 years." [40] This would seem to lead to an estimate of V of $60,000, far greater than required for the decision to conduct the guaiac.

To place an unconditional monetary value on human life, however, would be highly controversial. Human lives are not bought and sold in the market. If such a standard were used without qualification, it might lead to decisions that most people would consider morally abhorrent, for example, the decision that certain individual lives were not worth saving or that certain individuals should be sacrificed for a presumably greater social good. A society based on notions of human rights shrinks from such judgments. Occasionally, comparisons of the value of life among particular individuals are required, as in the case of a crowded lifeboat or scarce kidney dialysis facilities, but even in these cases it is unlikely that we would make quantitative calculations. Nor would a physician make such calculations in deciding whether a patient should receive costly treatment at the expense of taxpayers or an insurance company. Nonteleological rules in our society seem to restrict this sort of calculation to the setting of general, impersonal policies that have no reference to particular individuals, and even this degree of calculation regarding human life is sometimes challenged.

In addition to this basic ethical problem the particular costs and probabilities we have used may also be debated. But certain basic issues concerning policy choice are raised by the example. One such issue concerns who should pay for such tests. Even if we accept cost-benefit analysis as a criterion, should persons under forty pay for tests on those older? Similar questions are being raised about the Social Security program. Even though the young can expect to become older, they may wish to wait until they are older to pay the rates then in effect. For a relatively small expense such as the guaiac test, the administrative cost of charging a separate fee might be too great. But the issue remains. Even among older persons, some might not wish to have the test, and we might ask whether they should have to share the cost. By arguments of this kind we gradually move back to the question whether such tests should be paid for by the individuals who receive them, rather than by the taxpayers generally.

The choice in question might be made not only by a public health official or a legislator considering general policies. It might be made by a private patient or by a physician. The general line of reasoning would presumably be the same as shown in our decision tree; yet the decision might not. Individual patients might place special value on their own lives—more, perhaps, than outsiders considering general health screening policies. Their relatives and associates might judge likewise. Patients might also make subjective assessments of the probabilities that they had cancer in view of symptoms they themselves had observed. For these and other reasons an individual patient might judge that the test was desirable for *him* even it if was not desirable for an entire population from which he was drawn. Or conversely, he might judge himself to be in excellent health and not wish to pay the initial $4.

Questions of vertical equity also arise if we consider that rich people might place higher values than poor people on their lives and might be better able to afford the tests. Realizing this, we might consider the government's provision of free tests to be a justifiable form of income transfer. But this argument alone might lead us to advocate transfer of money rather than provision of guaiac tests, allowing the recipients to spend the money on things they most demanded. Only if we believe in equity *and* in making policies that take precedence over consumer preference—such as preventive measures that protect people's health more than they want to protect it themselves—would we require such a test for all or even provide it on a free but optional basis. These issues of individual versus collective choice will be discussed further in chapter 5.

The source of payment will also influence the decision actually made. If payment is available through health insurance so that the patient does not have to bear the expense for this particular test directly, then he may judge that the cost to *him* is smaller and that the test would be justified even if our calculations had indicated otherwise. A physician who knows that his patient is covered by insurance might similarly conduct the test, thinking it his duty to the patient to give him the best possible care. Such a decision process would ignore the cost to others who paid insurance premiums (or taxes) and the possible eventual changes in insurance rates if large numbers of tests were conducted on the basis of this sort of individual calculation.

This example of decision analysis is intended, therefore, to provide an elementary introduction to a complex field and to a procedure that is being used increasingly in policy analysis.

SUMMARY

Policy analysis, in its more precise aspects, begins with clearly expressed policy alternatives that often require considerable detail in statement. We perform this more precise analysis on policies as if they were enacted and implemented, and we treat enactment and implementation separately and less precisely. Another separate and less formal aspect of analysis will concern our personal alternatives, including the efforts we make and their personal costs.

A central element of the more precise part of analysis is a model of the effects that policy alternatives are expected to have. These effects are judged in terms of the values they produce, and our models must therefore relate to our valuative criteria. In a model these values may be affected not only by policy variables but also by nonpolicy variables. We need to distinguish the two effects clearly. Models vary from simple to complex and from relatively certain to uncertain and qualitative.

When the uncertainty in a model can be expressed in terms of probabilities, causal relations can be studied in statistical terms. Choices among alternatives may be based on statistical expected values; this principle of choice may be applied to continuous as well as discrete alternatives. A frequently used model for continuous alternatives is of a linear type, which can be extended to include several causal variables acting at once. A model of this kind has been used in analysis of the degree of equality of opportunity provided by American schools.

Quantitative policy analysis depends on quantitative indices of the valued outcomes that policies may produce. Benefits, costs, quality of life, and effectiveness are among the variables used for this purpose. But when quantitative indices are used repeatedly for policy purposes, the persons affected may adapt to their use and thus change the meaning of the indices. We should also recognize that one type of reaction to a policy is the departure of people from the affected population.

Models may be tested and improved by all the procedures that the sciences provide. But because policy analysis often proceeds under limitations of resources and time, we need to make use of available data such as administrative records, if they are of good enough quality. Social experiments with new policies, as well as evaluation of existing programs, may add to our knowledge about models.

A useful technique for the analysis of discrete policy alternatives is the decision tree. In this diagrammatic approach we compute the expected values for various branches, corresponding to our policy alternatives and the events that may follow them, and thus decompose a problem into simpler parts. The decision-tree approach may be applied to personal decisions, to the decision whether to carry out analysis, and to public policy problems such as whether to conduct a national medical screening test.

In the next chapter we consider a model particularly important for policy analysis—that of a free market.

Correlation coefficient: a coefficient r measuring the degree of success of prediction in a regression equation; equal to zero for completely unsuccessful prediction and attaining the value such that $r^2 = 1$ for a perfectly successful prediction.

Decision tree: a branching diagram depicting discrete alternatives (at decision forks) and discrete events (at chance forks); used for systematizing decisions.

Dependent variable: the effect or outcome variable in a model; in policy analysis, such a variable must relate to your valuative criteria.

Error (in a model): the departure of individual observations from their predicted values; assumed, for some purposes of estimation, to be random.

Expected monetary loss (EML): the expected value of the monetary loss associated with two or more alternative events whose probabilities sum to unity.

Expected value: a probability-weighted combination of numbers associated with two or more alternative events (the probabilities should sum to unity).

Independent variable: a policy or nonpolicy variable that affects the dependent variable(s).

Model: a statement of the causal relations that connect alternative policies with their effects.

Personal alternatives: the choices you face concerning allocation of your limited personal resources in policy analysis.

Quasi-market policy: a policy that sets up monetary or competitive incentives for performance analogous to those of the market.

Regression equation: a linear statistical model predicting a dependent variable from one or more independent variables.

Sensitivity of a model or a decision: the degree to which decisions based on a model depend on the values of particular parameters in the model.

Statistical model: a model involving uncertainty and probabilities that must be explicitly considered.

1. When we are evaluating a recently instituted program, we are usually expected to consider the possibility of abolishing the program (as well as continuing, expanding, or modifying it). We are less likely to consider abolishment of a long-established program. Why is this alternative especially likely to be considered for recently established programs?

2. What are the dependent variables in the following statements (which might be parts of policy-related models), and what more general values (criteria) might they be the means to increasing or reducing?

   a. Fluoridation of water supplies is likely to reduce the incidence of dental decay and to reduce the amount paid for dentists' bills.

   b. The establishment of a negative income tax will provide greater incentives for welfare recipients to work than will payments that are provided only up to a specified income threshold and not given to people whose income exceeds that amount.

   c. Postcard registration of voters is likely to increase registration by the poor but also to provide possibilities for fraud.

   d. Providing scholarships for medical students with the requirement that they practice for several years after graduation in rural or inner-city areas will increase the access of rural and inner-city residents to medical services.

   e. A system of fixed sentences for convicted criminals, in place of discretion on the part of parole boards, is likely to decrease recidivism (the likelihood that a released prisoner will commit another crime).

3. A number of American communities have faced shortages of electricity (as evidenced by blackouts or brownouts) or of water. For each of these problems, list as many alternative policies as you can that might alleviate the problem.

4. In Judge McMillan's decision in *Swann* v. *Charlotte-Mecklenburg Board of Education* (discussed in the text), the entire table of junior-high-school achievement test data for 1968–69 was as follows:

	PM	SP	LANG	ACM	ACN	AAPP	SS	SC*
Randolph Road (28% black)	60	82	79	62	79	76	79	81
Williams (100% black)	52	64	52	49	61	55	56	56

	PM	SP	LANG	ACM	ACN	AAPP	SS	SC *
Northwest (100% black)	58	71	56	50	61	58	57	58
Eastway (96% white)	82	86	81	67	82	75	82	87

* Key:

PM—paragraph meaning
LANG—language
ACN—arithmetic concepts
SS—social studies

SP—spelling
ACM—arithmetic computation
AAPP—arithmetic application
SC—science

Interpret the table shown in this exercise, using the straight-line model suggested in the text. What overall recommendations do the results suggest, if any?

5. A newspaper article on the problem of highway litter (case 5–A) provides the following facts. Which are most relevant, and which least relevant, to measuring the disvalued consequences of alternative policies?

a. Between 1959 and 1972 the number of bottles discarded increased by 262 percent, from 15.4 billion in 1959 to 55.7 billion in 1972.

b. Containers make up only 8 percent of the solid-waste load, but they account for between 54 and 70 percent of the volume of highway litter.

c. Containers are the fastest-growing segment of the waste load, increasing 8 percent a year.

d. The cost of 1000 nonreturnable soft-drink bottles is estimated at $42.33, compared with $83.43 for the same size of returnable bottles. But studies in Oregon have shown that returnables make at least 10 trips.

e. If New York City passed a deposit-bottle law, it might force the Schaefer brewery out of the city.

6. Suppose that you are deciding among policies for school desegregation and that your criterion for choice is the degree of numerical desegregation in the schools (in the Charlotte-Mecklenburg case, this would mean obtaining an approximate 70–30 ratio of white to black pupils in each school). Which one or more of the following models would be most relevant and why? (Assume that the models are true.)

a. Numerical desegregation (in contrast to segregation) causes higher test scores for minority students.

b. Numerical desegregation causes greater equality in income for school graduates.

c. Numerical desegregation causes a higher quality of informed citizenship.

d. Choice of school district boundaries causes differences in numerical desegregation.

7. In the medical screening problem discussed in this chapter, suppose we were dealing with a population in which the expected incidence of colon cancer was considerably less, for example, .001. Such a proportion might be estimated for a young population. In what way, if at all, would this difference in incidence affect our decision whether to administer the guaiac test routinely?

Suppose the cost of surgery were only $1000 rather than $3000. In what way, if at all, would this difference in cost affect our decision whether to administer the guaiac test routinely?

ADVANCED EXERCISE

8. How can the $pd > c$ rule be used to interpret the relative value of basic and applied research for policy decisions?

NOTES

1. Another example of a projection of expenditures, which limits future policy options but does not determine them completely, is the procedure of the British Public Expenditure Survey Committee; see Aaron Wildavsky, *Budgeting: A Comparative Theory of Budgetary Processes* (Boston: Little, Brown, 1975), ch. 19.

2. Back-of-the-envelope decision analyses are stressed in James W. Vaupel, "Muddling through Analytically," in Willis D. Hawley and David Rogers, eds., *Improving the Quality of Urban Management* (Beverly Hills, Calif.: Sage Publications, 1974). An example of a one-week exercise at the Berkeley, Calif., Graduate School of Public Policy is Carl V. Patton, "A Seven-Day Project," *Policy Analysis* 1(1975):731–753.

3. These activities, related to the feasibility of a policy, are considered in more detail in chapter 6.

4. Further examples are given in E. S. Quade, *Analysis for Public Decisions* (New York: American Elsevier, 1975), ch. 10.

5. Charles L. Schultze refers to these models as "social production functions"; see Schultze, *The Politics and Economics of Public Spending* (Washington, D.C.: Brookings, 1968), pp. 57–64. Kenneth C. Land, in "Social Indicator Models: An Overview," in Kenneth C. Land and Seymour Spilerman, eds., *Social Indicator Models* (New York: Russell Sage Foundation, 1974), calls them "social policy models."

6. Amitai Etzioni, *The Active Society*, (New York: Free Press, 1968), pp. 282–309.

7. The largest choices can be difficult to analyze systematically, however; see David Braybrooke and Charles E. Lindblom, *A Strategy of Decision* (New York: Free Press, 1963), pp. 78–79.

8. James S. Coleman, *Policy Research in the Social Sciences* (Morristown, N.J.: General Learning Press, 1972).

9. Graham T. Allison, *Essence of Decision* (Boston: Little, Brown, 1971).

10. The statistical models most directly relevant to policy analysis are causal models; see Arthur S. Goldberger and Otis Dudley Duncan, eds., *Structural Equation Models in the Social Sciences* (New York: Seminar Press, 1973).

11. Swann v. Charlotte-Mecklenburg Board of Education, Supplementary Opinion and Order, 1 Dec. 1969, 306 F. Supp. 1299 (1969), p. 1309.

12. Data on other tests for these four schools are presented in an exercise at the end of this chapter.

13. Swann v. Charlotte-Mecklenburg Board of Education, Supplementary Opinion and Order.

14. A simpler procedure may also be followed for these data. If E is the score for Eastway and A the average score for Williams-Northwest, the expected score for Randolph Road is $.75E + .25A$.

15. Statisticians often find that their rigorous requirements for inference prevent them from recommending policies that command wide sympathy; see B. W. Brown, Jr., "Statistics, Scientific Method, and Smoking," in Judith M. Tanur et al., eds., *Statistics: A Guide to the Unknown* (San Francisco: Holden-Day, 1972), p. 47.

16. See Leonall C. Andersen, "Statistics for Public Financial Policy," in Tanur et al., eds., *Statistics: A Guide to the Unknown*.

17. A detailed review of this report is Frederick Mosteller and Daniel P. Moynihan, eds., *On Equality of Educational Opportunity* (New York: Vintage, 1972).

18. James S. Coleman, Ernest Q. Campbell, Carol J. Hobson, James McPartland, Alexander M. Mood, Frederic D. Weinfeld, and Robert L. York, *Equality of Educational Opportunity* (Washington, D.C.: U.S. Govt. Print. Off., 1966), p. 317.

19. Howard Raiffa, *Decision Analysis* (Reading, Mass.: Addison-Wesley, 1968).

20. Julian L. Simon, "Some Principles of Practical Welfare Economics," *Management Science* 13(1967):B-621–B-630.

21. Milton D. Weinstein and William B. Stason, "Foundations of Cost-Effectiveness Analysis for Health and Medical Practices," *New England Journal of Medicine* 296(1977):716–721.

22. Concerning ratio of effectiveness to cost in drug screening see Charles W. Dunnett, "Drug Screening," in Tanur et al., eds., *Statistics: A Guide to the Unknown*.

23. Henry W. Riecken and Robert F. Boruch, eds., *Social Experimentation* (New York: Academic Press, 1974). See also chapter 7 of the text.

24. Richard L. Henshel and Leslie W. Kennedy, "Self-altering Prophecies: Consequences for the Feasibility of Social Prediction," *General Systems* 18(1973):119–126.

25. An extensive study using hospital records is Lincoln E. Moses and Frederick Mosteller, "Safety of Anesthetics," in Tanur et al., eds., *Statistics: A Guide to the Unknown*. We consider administrative records further in chapter 7.

26. Maurice S. Bartlett, "Epidemics," in Tanur et al., eds., *Statistics: A Guide to the Unknown*.

27. Donald T. Campbell, "Reforms as Experiments," *American Psychologist* 24(1969): 409–429.

28. Braybrooke and Lindblom, *A Strategy of Decision*. See also chapter 7 of the text.

29. Michael Scriven, in "The Methodology of Evaluation," in Ralph W. Tyler, Robert M. Gagne, and Michael Scriven, eds., *Perspectives of Curriculum Evaluation* (Chicago: Rand McNally, 1967), refers to these two goals as those of "formative" and "summative" evaluation respectively.

30. Martin Landau, "On the Concept of a Self-Correcting Organization," *Public Administration Review* 33(1973):533–542.

31. Glen G. Cain, ed., *Symposium on the Graduated Work Incentive Experiment, Journal of Human Resources* 9(1974):156–278, 504–555; Coleman, et al., eds., *Equality of Educational Opportunity*.

32. Albert O. Hirschman, *Exit, Voice and Loyalty* (Cambridge, Mass.: Harvard University Press, 1970).

33. Murray Gell-Mann, "How Scientists Can Really Help," *Physics Today* 24(1971): 23–25, cited in Quade, *Analysis for Public Decisions*, p. 2.

34. Decision trees are treated in Raiffa, *Decision Analysis*. The criterion variable here is continuous for both discrete and continuous alternatives; we are not concerned in this chapter with the discrete criterion variables mentioned in chapter 3 for nonteleological criteria.

35. When we incorporate information gathering as one of the decisions we face, our sequence of decisions resembles that of the research scientist who is concerned with both improving his model and applying it; we must then balance the claims of the two types of activity in terms of the values that we expect them to produce. Such a perspective on research can lead us to modify our standards for acceptance of a hypothesis, depending on the relative benefits and costs of various types of "errors."

36. The following derivation is adapted from Vaupel, "Muddling Through Analytically," in Hawley and Rogers, eds., *Improving the Quality of Urban Management*, pp. 202–204.

37. D. Neuhauser and A. M. Lewicki, "National Health Insurance and the Sixth Stool Guaiac," *Policy Analysis* 2(1976):176.

38. Later in this section we discuss the ethical problems of placing a monetary value on human life.

39. Neuhauser and Lewicki, "National Health Insurance and the Sixth Stool Guaiac," p. 186.

40. Ibid., pp. 187–188, 185. We consider the monetary valuation of life in further detail in case 4–A in connection with automobile accidents.

The Optimum Speed Limit

Early in 1974 a general national speed limit of 55 miles per hour (mph) was introduced in the United States. Introduction of the limit followed a gasoline shortage and a presidential request for such a limit to the states. This was one of a number of responses to the fuel shortage, but it has persisted longer than some responses (e.g., arrangements for access to gasoline stations on even and odd days in relation to license plate numbers), and seems to have been more effective than others (e.g., advocacy of car pools). In this case study we ask whether analysis can lead us to a choice of an optimum speed limit. Our aim is to illustrate procedures in cost-benefit analysis and model construction as well as other aspects of policy analysis. This is an example of a continuously variable policy, in contrast to the discrete alternatives considered in the decision trees of chapter 4.

By analyzing this relatively simple problem, we shall show the complexity of the information that needs to be taken into account; the numerous simplifying assumptions that have to be made; and the uncertainty of the results, which should be reported in order to reveal the implications of uncertainty in the model and the data.

Problem, Alternatives, and Criteria

Although a few scientists had periodically warned of an energy shortage, the problem was brought home to the American public in October 1973 when the Organization of Petroleum Exporting Countries (OPEC) imposed an oil embargo limiting the flow of oil to the United States.[1] This measure coincided with fighting between Arab countries and Israel. President Nixon, facing Watergate accusations, asked Congress in November for emergency energy legislation and requested that all states move toward a lowered speed limit of 55 mph.

Fuel costs rose, and in response to this and the reduced speed limit truckers protested in December by blocking key highways in several states. A fuel shortage was anticipated for the winter, and energy chief William Simon outlined a plan of priorities for fuel allocation. At the end of December, Arab oil ministers decided to increase the flow of oil to most countries, excluding the United States and the Netherlands, which would remain under embargo. They also doubled the price of Persian Gulf crude oil. In January 1974 major oil companies showed a sharp rise in earnings in the fourth quarter of 1973 during the Arab oil embargo. Congress had adjourned without passing emergency energy legislation but in January passed a law denying federal transportation funds to states with speed limits over 55 mph.

By February 1974 the gasoline shortage had grown in many states. By February 15 seven states and the District of Columbia had implemented a form of rationing based on odd and even numbered license plates. For the first four months of the year, "gasless" Sundays were widely observed. By early March 1974 a 55-mph limit was in effect in all fifty states.

On March 18 the Arab oil embargo was lifted and some of the energy restrictions were removed. Prices were not rolled back, however. The immediate crisis of gasoline shortage was reduced, though discussion continued about what longer-range measures should be taken. The national speed limit of 55 mph continued, though enforced to different degrees in various states, and has been continued since that time.

The immediate problem situation with which drivers were concerned resulted from the shortage of gasoline and the increased price for it. Some people were also concerned with the longer-run prospect of an energy shortage. As we noted in chapter 1, the problem of energy shortages may be interpreted in various ways. It can involve international considerations, multiple sources of energy, and intervention at many stages in the production and consumption of energy. We shall consider only the use of gasoline by automobiles and only a limited range of alternatives for dealing with it.

We also introduce a modified criterion for choice in moving from the problem situation to the analyst's problem. Citizens' definition of the problem has often been concerned with energy conservation and safety, and much discussion seems to assume that these are the only two criteria that matter. But if we take such criteria literally, then for safety we should presumably reduce speeds to zero and for energy efficiency we should reduce them to the most efficient speed, about 35 mph.[2] Once we realize that these preliminary criteria may lead us to "unreasonable" conclusions, we begin to introduce a neglected criterion, the value of travel time, and try to deal with tradeoffs between this criterion and the others. We are thus led to cost-benefit analysis as a more inclusive criterion.

In choosing to analyze only speed limits we set aside numerous other policy alternatives. A great many policy options are available for improving transportation conditions and highway safety, as well as for conserving energy. The development of public transit systems has often been proposed as a means for energy saving, even though particular transit systems are sometimes less effective than their advocates expect.[3] Car pools and the use of bicycles may also be considered. Highway safety can be furthered by improving road surfaces, visibility, driver behavior, car design, car inspection, or car safety features. The likelihood of accidents can also be influenced by the construction of four-lane rather than two-lane roads, the avoidance of sharp curves, and the redesign of intersections. Restrictions on speeding or reckless driving can be selective as well as uniform. And one of the most effective ways of reducing speed would be to place mechanical speed governors on cars.

We define the analyst's problem in terms of speed limits because of its value in teaching, even though this narrowing of the problem runs counter to our advice in chapter 2 to consider a wide range of problem definitions. By focusing on alternatives concerning speed limits we avoid the engineering detail that might be involved in automobile engine design (for energy savings) or highway design (for safety). We have also chosen a problem that involves few considerations of vertical equity—drivers from all income groups are to be treated alike—and one that involves little consideration of discounting of benefits and costs (except in the evaluation of human life).

Most of our analysis will be devoted to estimation of the optimum average speed for vehicles on a given type of road. For such an estimation we might proceed to choose a speed limit, perhaps somewhat above the optimum average speed. The relation between the desired average speed and the speed limit will be relegated to the category of "feasibility" or "implementation." But as we shall see, feasibility is one of the most important parts of the analysis and some might wish to consider it first. In one expert opinion: "The consensus of traffic engineers in the United States is that motorists usually adjust their speeds according to conditions on the road and not necessarily to posted speed limits." [4]

We begin by expressing benefits and costs in terms of the *average* speed of vehicles, even though we shall later see that the *distribution* of speeds is also of great importance. We make this initial simplification in order to clarify the analysis and to illustrate that the construction of models usually proceeds by approximations.

The analyst's problem must be specified so that it will yield determinate results as far as possible. Optimum speeds depend on many local and individual conditions, including type of road, driving conditions, grade or curvature, intersections, condition of car, and characteristics of the driver. We shall choose those conditions under which an upper national speed limit would presumably make the most difference: driving in the daytime on straight stretches of divided highways with no grade. We shall refer below to these conditions as high-speed conditions. We shall consider only passenger vehicles for most of the analysis, but we shall then introduce possible corrections that would be necessary for trucks. We shall consider conditions of low traffic volume because, as we shall show, costs are approximately proportional to traffic volume, and high volume depresses the average speed over and above the effect of the speed limit.[5] To standardize for changing costs due to inflation, we have converted costs to 1976 dollar equivalents.

Even if we have restricted the policy alternatives greatly in this case study, the alternatives we consider are of interest because the problem is likely to recur. Because of the continuing interest of the problem, d in the expression $pd > c$ is larger than it would be for a problem of only temporary importance.

Models

The citizen seeking information relevant to the choice of speed limits may take advantage of extensive applied research done by governmental and private agencies. Most of this research deals with parts of the problem, however, rather than with the speed-limit problem itself. To know where to look for appropriate research, we may benefit from constructing a model that breaks the problem down into parts (the root meaning of "analysis"). We begin by considering the valued and disvalued effects of changing the speed distribution of vehicles. But we must remember that speed distribution is a possible result of policies, not a policy itself.

We shall consider three principal values or disvalues that may be affected by a speed limit.

1. The value of time for drivers and passengers and for freight transportation;

2. Expenditures for operation of cars;

3. The costs of accidents.[6]

In our model we wish to state how each of these components of cost depends on speed. Eventually, we must estimate how much the speed of automobiles is affected by a change in the speed limit. We ignore the costs from pollution because they are difficult to estimate and because many of the roads on which the overall maximum speed limit has an effect are located in the less congested parts of the country.

During the initial part of the analysis we also ignore expenditures for law enforcement or publicity aimed at compliance with the speed limit. Later, when we consider the feasibility of implementing a desired average speed, they will be of greater importance, though data on the effects of enforcement expenditures are less precise.[7]

If the choice of speed involved consequences only to the driver who also paid for the operation of the car, then conceivably the calculation of costs and benefits could be carried out by each driver individually without regulation by government. As observers or government officials, we might nevertheless consider that such calculations were inadequately informed and intervene by supplying information. Or we might judge that in spite of all information some drivers would decide wrongly, and for those cases we might resort to a speed limit.

There are four respects, however, in which the choice of speed affects persons other than the driver. First, it may affect the likelihood of accidents involving others (just as our choice of our own health care may affect others if the disease we may have is contagious). Second, the likelihood of two-car accidents is affected by the *relative* speed of cars (as we shall see). For this reason the speed that we might choose as a recommendation to an individual, with the speed of other cars given, will not necessarily be what we would recommend as a speed limit to be enforced for all cars on the road. In addition, we may conclude that *minimum* speed limits should be set. Third, even if only the driver and his car are directly affected, his probability of accidents affects others through their insurance premiums. A fourth such effect is the possibility that excessive use of energy in the present will deprive future generations of it. In this connection we might judge that for policy analysis the value of gasoline should be set higher than the actual sale price. All these considerations are reasons for government intervention and are analogous to conditions for government regulation of the market (externalities) that we shall consider in chapter 5.

A First Model

We begin model construction with a highly simplified first approximation. Inspection of the results from this approximation will give us a sense of what variables and relations need to be studied in greatest detail.

Let us assume that the total cost of operating a given vehicle under the conditions specified is a sum of three terms:

$$\text{Cost} = (\text{cost of time spent}) + (\text{cost of operating vehicle}) + (\text{cost of accidents})$$

or

$$C = C_t + C_o + C_a$$

As a first approximation we shall try to express these components of cost in terms of the average speed v of vehicles on the road. We shall then try to find that value of v for which the total cost is a minimum. But in order to estimate total cost, we have to know what proportion of the vehicles on the road were traveling outside of the urban areas where lower speed limits were in force. We can bypass the estimation of this proportion if we simply seek the optimum average speed for those vehicles traveling on roads of the type we have specified, where speeds are highest. If costs are proportional to vehicle-miles traveled, then we can express each component of cost as a cost per vehicle-mile.

Consider first the cost of time. If all vehicles were traveling at the average speed v and if the value of time was the same for all passengers in them, then we could write for C_t, the time cost per vehicle-mile,

$$C_t = \frac{a}{v}$$

where the constant a represented the product of the value of time per person and the average number of persons in a vehicle. We shall go on to consider refinements of this approach.

For an initial estimate of the value of time to vehicle occupants, we can make use of a standard established by others. The American Association of State

Table 4A–1.

Estimated Costs per Vehicle-Mile by Average Speed *

Average Speed (mph) (v)	Cost of Time ($C_t = \$3.00/v$)	Cost of Operation ** (C_o)	Cost of Accidents ($C_a = \$.000508v$)	Total Cost (C)
35	.086	.055	.018	.159
40	.075	.055	.020	.150
45	.067	.056	.023	.146
50	.060	.058	.025	.143
55	.055	.059	.028	.142
60	.050	.062	.030	.142
65	.046	.066	.033	.145
70	.043	.070	.036	.149

* Data in table pertain to cost for an average passenger car traveling at uniform speed on a level road.

**Data recalculated from Robley Winfrey, *Economic Analysis for Highways* (Scranton, Pa.: International Textbook Company, 1969), p. 680; total running cost has been multiplied by 162.5/103.25 to adjust for increase in cost of private transportation; see *Statistical Abstract of the United States: 1976*, p. 440, for Consumer Price Index figures (162.5/103.25) used in recalculation.

Highway Officials used a figure of $1.55 per vehicle-hour in 1960. Using this figure allows us to postpone estimating the number of people in an average vehicle. But since we are seeking results for 1976, we must at least take inflation into account. Using the Consumer Price Index for this purpose, we get $a = \$1.55 \times (169.2/87.3) = \$3.00/\text{hour}$.[8] The cost of time for a vehicle going at 30 mph would then be $3.00/30 or $.10 per mile; at 60 mph it would be only $.05 per mile. Figures for other speeds are given in table 4A–1.

The dependence of operating cost on speed must be expressed in tabular or graphical terms, as it does not correspond to any simple explicit function. A set of estimates for operating cost based on tests with individual cars, expressed in 1976 dollars, is given in table 4A–1. Again we make the simplifying assumption that average operating cost is the same as if all cars were traveling at the speed v. Approximate cost of accidents and total cost are also included in table 4A–1 for later reference.

Estimating the increase in accident cost per unit increase in average speed involves still further assumptions. We shall examine these assumptions further, but as a first approximation we simply assume that cost of accidents is proportional to v.

We then need to estimate the expected cost of accidents for the average vehicle on the road. Figures are available on total costs during a given year, and for 1975 this total was estimated at $35,972 million.[9]

The first two components of cost (time and operation) have been expressed as costs per vehicle-mile, and a similar measure seems appropriate for accidents. If national accident costs per vehicle-mile are proportional to v, we can obtain the constant of proportionality by dividing the total costs by the total vehicle-miles and then by v. Total vehicle travel in the United States in 1975 is estimated as 1,332 billion vehicle-miles. The cost of accidents per vehicle-mile is thus $35,972 \times 10^6/1.332 \times 10^{12}$ or $2.701 \times 10^{-2} = \$.02701$ per vehicle-mile. In 1976 dollars, $\$.02701 \times (169.2/161.2) = \$.02835$. If the average speed in 1975 was 55.8 mph, then the constant of proportionality measuring increase in cost per mph is $\$.02835/55.8 = \$.000508$ per vehicle-mile per mph.[10]

We have estimated costs of accidents by a very crude model in order to see whether they are appreciable in comparison with the other components of cost. We can now see that these crude assumptions are not quite acceptable for the relation of accident costs to speed because accident costs (as regards the effect of speed on them) cannot be neglected in comparison with vehicle operating costs. The variation of all three components of cost and of total cost with speed, based on this approximate model, is shown in figure 4A–1. From this figure or from table 4A–1 we estimate the optimum value of v as between 55 and 60 mph. For these speeds the total cost assumes its lowest value of $.142 per vehicle-mile. We do not attempt to express the optimum v more precisely because (as we shall see) the data and assumptions do not warrant it. Even for these data the minimum is very flat.

After obtaining an order-of-magnitude estimate of the optimum v, we might proceed to study the problems of enforcement effectiveness and costs. It is good general practice for an analyst to survey all aspects of his problem rapidly before possibly wasting time on an aspect that proves not to be crucial. However, the value of v we have found exceeds the present national speed limit of 55 mph. If we allowed for the fact that speed limits are conventionally set somewhat higher than v, we might find that our chosen policy would involve little new enforcement activity and might even involve an increase in the 55-mph limit. We therefore proceed to more detailed examination of the three component costs as they depend on v, both to illustrate some problems of cost-benefit analysis and to see whether the apparently high value of v obtained has resulted from some of our assumptions.

The Value of Time

Our choice of $3.00 per vehicle-hour as the value of time (a) actually conceals a number of possible sources of variation in this figure. The cost of time spent traveling, to the extent that we can express it in monetary terms, varies with the comfort and aesthetic circumstances of the trip, with the purpose

Figure 4A–1.
*Estimated Costs per Vehicle-Mile, by Average Speed.**

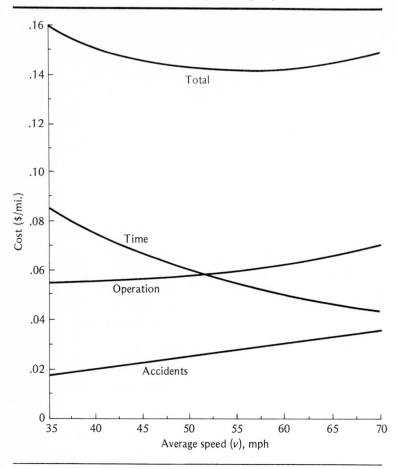

* Plotted from data in table 4A–1.

of the trip (work or leisure), and with the wage rate of the traveler, among other things.

The difficulty of reducing such considerations to a monetary value is illustrated by Robert Frost's poem "Stopping by Woods on a Snowy Evening." Writing of an earlier day, traveling in a horse and buggy, the narrator stops to watch the snow falling in the woods. There was some value to him of reducing his speed of travel to zero. He ends by recalling, "But I have promises to keep / And miles to go before I sleep," because even then he lived in a society that required us to reach our destinations.

It is conventional to relate the value of time to the wage rate, a relation we shall explore shortly. But the picture of automobiles rushing about in order to save time usable for earnings is not necessarily an attractive one. Even if the earnings are then to be used for intrinsically valuable things or if the travel is aimed at activities that the driver and passengers deliberately choose *instead* of earnings, the picture of calculation is one that some will question. Additional questions may be raised about the equity of valuing the time of high earners more than that of low earners.

We proceed nevertheless to ask how much automobile drivers and passengers would be willing to pay to arrive at their destinations sooner. Some economists have asserted that if people in the labor force could freely exchange work time for other uses of time, they would make this exchange in such a manner as to value time at their wage rate. Others, after studying the actual tradeoffs that people make in choosing among routes with their associated road tolls, have concluded that motorists' actual valuation of time is considerably lower. One review of the literature tentatively concludes that "the value of time with respect to nonwork travel is between one-fourth and one-half of the wage rate." [11] Values for commuting and for work travel are somewhat higher.

The estimates obtained from studies of drivers' valuation of time thus vary. Two 1962 studies use values of time per vehicle-hour as disparate as $1.48 and $2.80. Robley Winfrey estimates that values of time "lie within the range of $1.00 and $4.00 per car-hour." [12] In view of this possible variation we must examine the sensitivity of our estimate of the optimum v to possible variation in the value of time. The value we have used, $1.55 per vehicle-hour in 1960, is near the lower end of these ranges. If we considered time to be more valuable, we should increase the steepness of the curve of time cost in figure 4A–1 and move the minimum v to the right, to a still higher speed. Viewing the problem in another way, we might consider that those persons traveling fastest were valuing time at a higher dollar rate, either because they were traveling as part of their work or because they were highly productive persons earning a high hourly rate. Enforcement of a national speed limit would presumably bear most heavily on them. Note that in analyzing the sensitivity of the minimum to the value of time, we consider only the *slopes* of the curves in figure 4A–1, not their absolute heights.

A further argument in favor of high valuation of time derives from the use of time for commercial transportation. Winfrey gives estimates of dollar value of travel time for commercial vehicles (1965), ranging from $3.65 to $8.29 per hour.[13] These values are high for large trucks and would also be high for perishable goods. The fact that these values are generally higher than our assumed value of time again implies a higher value of the optimum v in terms of the cost of time alone (neglecting the effect of the trucks' speed on accidents and operating costs). Thus, truckers were first to object to the reduction of speed limits in 1974. In this case, as in many others, economic conditions help to explain the formation and action of political pressure groups.

We have continued to neglect the effect on time-cost of the variation in speed among vehicles. For one vehicle (i) traveling at speed v_i we might write

$$C_{ti} = \frac{a}{v_i}$$

Because this relation is nonlinear, the average cost would be higher than a/v, as the cost to the slower vehicles would weigh more heavily. But the drivers of these slower vehicles may be choosing to go slowly for other reasons and may not be incurring the costs we attribute to them (in place of a we might substitute various values of a_i. Furthermore, the speed of these slow vehicles may not be influenced as much by a general reduction in speed as the speed of the faster vehicles. We shall see that this is what happened when the pattern of vehicle speed changed from 1973 to 1974. These intangible factors must be borne in mind—as in most cost-benefit analyses—when we try to interpret the results for policy choice.

The Cost of Operation

Our estimate of the cost of operation of motor vehicles, although it seems less controversial than the cost of time, also involves assumptions that need to be explored. Perhaps most significant in a time of rising gasoline prices and energy shortage is the effect on the speed limit of a higher price of gasoline and oil. The data we have used to estimate operating costs were based on the 1968 price of gasoline, exclusive of taxes: $.23 per gallon ($.39 in 1976 when adjusted for change in the Consumer Price Index component for gasoline). The tax was not counted because it was not considered a genuine social cost of operating vehicles.[14] Gasoline taxes are often used for new highway construction and are thus considered unrelated to the costs of driving on existing roads.

If the price of fuel continues to increase or if we conclude that this price fails to reflect the actual cost to society of depleting scarce resources, we may ask how our optimum v would be affected by such an increase. It would lead to a steeper rise in operating costs relative to v in figure 4A–1 and would move the minimum of total cost to the left, to a lower average speed. We may make a rough estimate of the effect of a large increase in the price of gasoline—to about $2.00 a gallon—by assuming that gasoline is the major variable item in costs of operation and multiplying the C_o column in table 4A–1 by 5. In this case the optimum v would be reduced to between 40 and 45 mph.

We should also note that available sources differ somewhat in their estimation of costs of operation. One detailed study still cited in recent publications was based on pre-1950 automobiles and assumed the 1959 price of gasoline to be $.32 a gallon.[15] Technical changes since that time have made cars more efficient at higher speeds. Not only price information but also data on technical performance characteristics of automobiles need to be continually updated if studies of this sort are to be accurate.

The Cost of Accidents

The most difficult aspect of our problem to formulate precisely, and one that requires the most careful consideration of the model involved, is the estimation of accident costs as they depend on speed limits. We shall see, however, that these difficulties are compensated by the fact that our previous estimate of the rate of change of accident costs relative to speed may be an *overestimate* in some respects.

We may check our previous estimate in several ways. First, using the same time series on costs of accidents as we used before, we may try to check the assumption that costs vary in proportion to v by examining the effect on accident costs when drivers reduced their speed between 1973 and 1974. There was a decline in median speed (nearly identical to v) between those years from 60 to 55 mph. Costs of accidents increased from $30,407 to $30,415 million between 1973 and 1974, a considerably lower increase than occurred in any other one-year period between 1970 and 1975. But total vehicle-miles traveled decreased from 1308.5 to 1289.6 billion in this same period, leading us to conclude that dollar costs per vehicle-mile had increased. The Consumer Price Index increased from 133.1 to 147.7 in the same period.[16] From these figures we may infer that in constant dollars the costs of accidents per vehicle-mile decreased by 8.5 percent. The median speed of vehicles decreased by 8.3 percent; thus, the changes were nearly proportional, and our assumption of a proportional relation seems justified. More data are needed to confirm this inference, however.

Our reasoning in the preceding paragraph concerned that part of our model relating average speed to accident costs. We set aside the nonpolicy variable, total vehicle-miles traveled, which affected accident costs but which we do not judge to be affected by a change in speed limit. We also set aside effects of changes in consumer prices, since we wish to measure the real cost of accidents, rather than simply their dollar cost.

A second type of check on our estimate of the dependence of accident costs on speed is to seek additional overall estimates of accident costs per vehicle-mile. The figures used so far for total accident cost are from the Insurance Information Institute and are in agreement with figures from the National Highway Traffic Safety Administration. In contrast, Winfrey cites a 1958 Chicago study, with prices corrected to 1966, giving costs of accidents per 10^8 vehicle-miles for various types of streets or highways, ranging from about $160,000 (full expressway section of Congress Expressway) to $1,000,000 (signalized areas of Congress Expressway in central business district).[17] These correspond to costs per vehicle-mile of $.0016 to $.01, as contrasted with the figure of $.027 estimated earlier. The difference may relate to speed, type of road (costs are less with fewer intersections), inflation, or differences in the basic assumptions involved in estimation. If these lower estimates of accident costs were used, we would arrive at a still higher value of the optimum v.

The third way to check the estimate of accident costs is to examine systematically the set of assumptions on which the estimates are based. Our previous methods of estimation have been shortcuts aimed at getting a general perspective on the problem, but we cannot be certain that they are right. For example, all may involve a common assumption that we do not, in the end, wish to make.

The most controversial estimate in assessing accident costs is that of the monetary value of human life. We have already encountered this question in connection with the decision problem concerning the medical screening test in chapter 4, where we found that the decision was not highly sensitive to the estimated value of the added years of life. But before returning to this question, we should ask which of several types of accidents—those involving only property damage, those involving nonfatal injuries, or those involving fatalities—makes the largest contribution to estimated costs. In two studies that made such estimates the dominant category was that of nonfatal injuries, with fatal accidents contributing less than one-half to less than one-tenth as much.[18] It seems that our results concerning the optimum v will not be highly sensitive to our estimates of the value of human life, even though the probability that accidents will be fatal does increase sharply with speed.

Nevertheless, we may indicate several ways in which estimates of the value of human life are made. The value of income minus consumption has been used extensively but appears more relevant for insurance purposes, measuring the benefits furnished by the individual to others, than for estimating the benefit of years of life to society as a whole, including benefits to the victims themselves.[19] This estimate, like several others, is customarily "discounted" so that future net earnings are counted at a lower rate than present earnings.

A modified procedure is to estimate the discounted value of future income without subtracting consumption. This approach treats the individual's income stream as a contribution to the national income but still counts the future as less valuable than the present. This seems to be the approach most widely used in assessing the "livelihood" component of the cost of traffic fatalities and is the one on which the estimates used here were based.

Other estimates of the value of life have been based on the individual's (or his associates') willingness to pay for a given increase in the probability of his remaining alive or living a specified number of additional years. This method is a more direct expression of the ethic of preference satisfaction.[20] These estimates are made by asking the individual about an entire sequence of years so that no additional explicit discounting is needed. This method has been criticized, however, on the ground that responses to questionnaires may furnish less reliable evidence than actual behavior relative to choice in a market situation.

Individuals may also be asked to judge the value of years of life, given various conditions, by telling what fraction of a life-year they would be willing to forgo in order to enjoy the remainder in perfect health. By extension, we might ask people what probability of extended life they would be willing to forgo in order to arrive at their destination an hour sooner. This last approach, corresponding to "quality-adjusted life-years," does not provide monetary measures unless some conversion is made.[21] It does circumvent some of the problems of inequity among income groups that result from monetary measures. It also circumvents problems of inequity between the sexes from income-related measures.

A more accurate estimate of the dependence of accident costs on speed might begin with the distribution of accident types (property damage only, non-fatal injury, fatal) for each of various speeds and then apply cost figures for the various types of accidents to these distributions. However, approximate results may be used as a general indication of the direction that policies might take.

We have also left unchecked our assumption that the cost of accidents is proportional to traffic volume—that is, that in dividing by vehicle-miles we have not ignored a nonproportional source of variation that should be included among our initial conditions together with type of road, time of day, and so forth. But it has in fact been shown that on a given segment of road numbers of accidents are roughly proportionate to average daily traffic up to more than 10,000 cars per day.[22]

We have assumed and roughly confirmed that the cost of accidents is approximately proportional to the average speed v. Yet it is also known that as the speed v_i of individual vehicles decreases, the number of accidents per vehicle-mile increases. J. C. Oppenlander, in what was apparently one of the earliest cost-benefit analyses of speed regulation, made use of a generally observed negative relation between speed of individual vehicles and rates of accident involvement (fewer accidents and lower cost per mile for cars going faster).[23]

It makes no sense, however, to infer that a general reduction in speed of all vehicles would increase the rate of accident involvement. We must therefore look more closely at the data. The high rate of accident involvement at low speeds is apparently largely due to collisions between these slower-moving cars and others traveling at higher speeds. The importance of *differences* in speed as a source of rear-end collisions has also been noted by David Solomon.[24] As he points out, this effect might lead us to try to decrease the variation in speeds among vehicles, for example, by setting minimum speed limits on certain roads.

The overall effect of the speed limit on accident costs is thus clearly different from the effect of choices of speed by individual drivers, given the speeds of others. We therefore require an accident-cost function, such as the proportional relation we have used, that increases with increasing speed limit or average speed of the traffic stream. Some light can be thrown on the detailed effects of changes in the speed limit by an evaluation of the 55-mph limit imposed in 1974.[25]

Evaluation of the 55-mph Limit

In choosing among speed-limit policies we now have the valuable experience of several years under a 55-mph speed limit, enforced to various degrees in various states and years. More detailed studies might take advantage of the differences in implementation. In August 1977, for example, North Carolina introduced a new administrative policy of rigorous enforcement of the 55-mph limit. Conceivably, close study of the effects of such an administrative change could also throw light on our problem.[26]

We restrict our attention to national changes occurring from one year to another. From 1973 to 1974 and succeeding years there were changes not only in speeds (our policy-related variable) but also in nonpolicy variables. Gasoline became less available, at least temporarily, and its price rose. Citizens' and motorists' views of the seriousness of the energy crisis may have changed. In 1974, as compared with 1973, the median speed of vehicles on main rural highways decreased from 60 mph to 55 mph. Total travel decreased, as we have seen, but by less than one percent. This decrease seems more pronounced if we compare it with regular annual increases in previous years.[27] The total estimated dollar cost of traffic accidents remained nearly constant. In constant dollars it declined by 8.5 percent. Deaths from highway accidents dropped between 1973 and 1974; and, unlike the costs of accidents, they remained low in 1975.[28]

What really happened in this period? Although we shall need further information to be sure, we shall see that speeds did *not* simply decrease proportionately over the entire range of speed. Rather, decreases were greater at high speeds so that the variation of speed among vehicles decreased.[29] We may show this effect most clearly in the form of a graph, as shown in figure 4A–2. To

Table 4A–2.
Percentage Distributions of Speeds of Motor Vehicles in 1973 and 1974

Percent of vehicles in speed category:	Distribution 1973	Distribution 1974	Percent of vehicles at or below:	Cumulative Distribution 1973	Cumulative Distribution 1974
40 or below	2	2	40 mph	2	2
40.01–45	4	5	45	6	7
45.01–50	10	14	50	16	21
50.01–55	14	28	55	30	49
55.01–60	20	30	60	50	79
60.01–65	19	15	65	69	94
65.01–70	17	4	70	86	98
over 70	14	2	infinity	100	100
Total	100	100			

Source:
Statistical Abstract of the United States: 1976, p. 599.

clarify that graph we first present the data in tabular form. Table 4A–2 shows in the two left-hand columns the percentage distributions of speeds on main rural roads during off-peak hours (which we assume to correspond to high-speed conditions) in 1973 and 1974. The two right-hand columns give the corresponding *cumulative* percentage distributions, showing what percent of vehicles were traveling at or below each indicated speed. For each of the two years the two distributions tell us the same information in different ways. Each of the cumulative distributions is formed from the ordinary percentage distribution by adding up the entries from the top down. For example, in 1973, 50 percent of vehicles were traveling at or below 60 mph. This value may be obtained by adding 2 + 4 + 10 + 14 + 20 at the top of the ordinary distribution for 1973.

In order to see more clearly how the distribution changed from 1973 to 1974 we plot the two cumulative distributions on a special type of graph with a distorted horizontal axis. This distortion of the axis transforms the

Figure 4A–2.
Speed Distributions for 1973 and 1974, on Normal Probability Scale. *

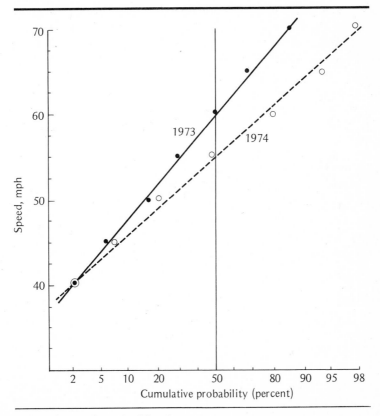

* Plotted from data in table 4A–2.

S-shaped curve that would have been obtained by plotting cumulative percentage (horizontally) against speed (vertically) into a straight line, if the speeds are distributed in the form of a normal distribution (a statistical model to which many actual distributions conform). The points for each of the two years fall approximately on a straight line, and we show such a straight line for each year. The upper line, for 1973, shows that the 50 percent point (median) is about 60 mph. The lower line intersects a vertical line from 50 percent at a median value of about 55 mph.

If the effect of the change in speed limit (or of other factors) had been simply to move the entire speed distribution to a lower value, the two lines would have been parallel. This could not literally have happened, however, without moving the speed of stationary vehicles to negative values, an unreasonable change. If the changes in speed had been proportional—a constant percentage decrease in speed at all speeds—then the two lines would have approached one another at lower speeds and intersected at zero speed. What actually seems to have occurred, however, is that speed reductions took place entirely for speeds of over 40 mph. Thus, there was a decrease in the variation of speeds due to a decrease in higher speeds. Relative speeds of vehicles with respect to one another were decreased, and this contributed to a decreased frequency of accidents. The number of vehicles at high speeds also decreased, decreasing the cost per accident for that group of vehicles.

To devise a better model of accident costs as they depend on the speed limit would require taking all these complications into account. Not merely the average speed but the variations in speed among vehicles and the probable results of accidents would have to be considered. For our present purposes, however, a rough approximation suffices.

Average Speed and Speed Limit

So far we have dealt only with the optimum average speed, v. Now, we must ask how the speed limit should be chosen to bring the actual average speed close to the desired v.

Two quite different notions may be put forward about the relation between the desired v and the posted speed limit. One is an engineering convention that the speed limit be set at the 85th percentile of the actual speed distribution—that is, so that only 15 percent of the vehicles traveling under given conditions will be expected to exceed the posted limit. The other is that even though *most* vehicles under high-speed conditions may be expected to *exceed* the posted speed limit, nevertheless few will exceed it by more than a certain amount, for example, 10 mph if they expect enforcement only at that amount of excess speed. Toward the end of 1974, as concern for gasoline shortage decreased, average speeds rose again to their pre-1974 values. But at the same time, the proportion of vehicles exceeding 65 mph was drastically reduced and remained low even when the average speed had risen again.[30]

Since we have estimated the optimum v as between 55 and 60 mph, we cannot favor a general speed limit as low as 55 mph unless we assume that the majority of vehicles will exceed the posted speed limit. In that case the low speed limit might have a real effect, even though paradoxically most vehicles on main rural roads would be in violation of it. We cannot estimate what the effect of such a disparity between official norms and real norms would be on the respect for law in general. But it is possible that this disparity has existed to some degree for traffic and other laws in any event.

In 1974, when the uniform national speed limit of 55 mph was in effect, the median speed of vehicles on the rural highways studied was 55 mph. Half of the vehicles were exceeding the posted speed limit even in this year of maximum compliance. If we take this behavioral fact as a desirable state of affairs, then we would see little reason for changing the existing 55 mph limit if we desired an average speed of from 55 to 60 mph. But our use of 1974 data as a definition of the desirable relation between regulations and reality bypasses the entire problem of how laws should be formulated and enforced in relation to the desirable distribution of behaviors.

Recommending a Speed Limit

Under the circumstances it is difficult to make a recommendation for changing the existing 55 mph speed limit, even apart from conditions of feasibility. If we had produced our analysis concerning an optimum speed limit for a decision maker with a deadline, we might have asked him to add something of his own intuition to it in deciding. If we had produced it for a citizens group that was reviewing the question of speed limits because of its general interest, we might not have been obligated to make a recommendation. An analyst might be obligated to the group to justify his activity by making a recommendation, if he has made use of the group's resources, and such a group may wish to take a stand to attract members and keep itself in the public eye. But aside from such considerations as these, the analyst can refrain from making a recommendation at this stage if he wishes.

A second major uncertainty concerns the proper "social" price of gasoline, reflecting its long-run value to society. We have indicated that a price of about $2.00 a gallon for gasoline (an arbitrarily chosen figure) would lead to an optimum v of about 45 mph. If we accept this price as the social value of gasoline and take the optimum v as the value at which we set the posted limit, then the limit should be reduced to 45 mph. But we have not done the analysis that would tell us what price truly reflected the social value of gasoline. It would involve not only consideration of how the market reflects the prospective international shortage of energy but also questions concerning national energy independence.

The result is that we leave this exercise in analysis unfinished. In a sense, every analysis must be left unfinished, since we can always expect unanswered questions and controversial assumptions to remain at the time when an analysis must be used. If we were employees, we might take comfort in the ultimate responsibility of our employer for the decision in which our analysis was used. If our citizens group, faced with a need to take a position on a pending state decision, believed that the posted limit should be the same as the desired average speed, and that the 1976 price of gasoline (exclusive of tax) fairly reflected its social cost, then we should favor no reduction of the 55-mph speed limit and possibly a slight increase.

Even though the analysis has not led to a precise recommendation, it has added to our knowledge. The notion that the 55-mph limit may be too low may be surprising. Some variations in our assumptions may even lead us to favor raising it. In addition, we know how our recommendation will be altered by various changes in our assumptions and values.

If we wish to make recommendations that go beyond our analysis, we have every right as citizens to do so. Similarly, as employees or group members we may be asked for our judgments when the rigorous part of the analysis yields ambiguous recommendations. When we make judgments of this kind about the best policy, we should try to separate that part of our reasoning that rests on rigorous analysis from the part that is based more on intuition. If we can set forth the rigorous part clearly and state the additional assumptions we have made, our analysis is most likely to have value for others whose assumptions are different. It is possible that by stressing this separation we can encourage rational public discussion while still making the choices we must make.

Feasibility

We have pursued our analysis backward, first considering desirable speeds and only then investigating how to bring them about. The means we consider for bringing about desirable speeds are speed limits, and we have speculated as to what the relation between speed limit and average speed might be. This relation is indeterminate in part because it depends on law enforcement activity, that is, on implementation.

The problem of feasibility, in this case as we have presented it, centers about implementation rather than enactment. We have said little about the array of interest groups and organizations that might be involved in any effort to reduce the speed limit or increase its enforcement. If we wished to relax a limit that had once been instituted, a choice analogous to termination of an existing program, we might find some of these same groups concerned. Problems of decision points and the relation between state and federal authority might also be involved.

As regards implementation, we have not yet shown that a change in the posted speed limit actually changes the distribution of vehicle speeds in a determinate way. The changes that occurred between 1973 and 1974 included other variables besides a change in the speed limit. Consequently, our evaluation of a change in the limit in 1974, even controlling for vehicle-miles traveled, was not a conclusive demonstration of causation. If we had to make a recommendation, we would have to judge whether this evidence was adequate and act on it. But we should also gather new evidence on the effects of the new change, as part of the continuing cycle of analysis and improvement of models.

We next briefly consider models of implementation. Such models lie in the domain of social or behavioral science and are less precise than those we have considered so far. Implementation, or enforcement of new speed limits, also involves costs, which can be an important element in policies related to crime and justice. In this case we neglect them, assuming that the costs of enforcing a new speed limit will be approximately the same as those for the old.

Unfortunately, the findings concerning effects of changing posted speed limits seem far from clear. A review article summarizing dozens of studies concludes that there are important differences between the United States and Europe.

> Studies of speed in Europe have shown, almost without exception, that the speed of vehicles can be considerably reduced by installing a speed limit. Experience in the United States on urban and rural roads indicates that drivers do not drastically alter their speed pattern with changes in speed limits. One possible explanation is that European experience generally deals with the application of speed limits for the first time; studies of U.S. experience usually deals [sic] with revision of existing speed limits.[31]

One Wisconsin study shows that an increase in enforcement affects the proportion of vehicles exceeding the legal limit, but not average speeds.[32] But the reviewer concludes that "it is clear that drivers respond favorably to reasonable speed limits and disregard those unreasonably high or low." [33] If this is true, we are led to ask what leads drivers to consider a speed reasonable. Possibly the existence of a given speed limit for a long time eventually leads drivers to consider it legitimate. This habituation, rather than the inherent reasonableness of United States speed limits, might account in part for the differences in findings between the United States and Europe.

What, then, might lead drivers to consider a new speed limit "reasonable"? It is not clear that a public information campaign including arguments such as those in our analysis would have such an effect. A sense of urgency related to a gasoline shortage might make a difference, but drivers would also have to be aware of the relation between speed and cost. Conceivably, a continued concern for the energy shortage, if it were supported by continuing evidence of that shortage, would keep the question before the public.[34] But here we are engaged in sheer speculation with little systematic information to help us. The degree of conformity to norms by the public may well depend on the reasons that they can advance in favor of those norms. But this verbal statement does not provide us with a basis for precise analysis.

A further complication of implementation concerns possible systematic efforts to circumvent the law. We noted that truckers were especially opposed to the 55-mph limit and that the value of transportation time to them might well explain their opposition. But since their protest, many truckers have also purchased citizens-band radios and cooperated with one another in warnings of the presence of "Smokey Bear." This effort does not seem to be regarded as seriously by the police as many other forms of organized law violation. Nor can such new developments easily be anticipated by policy analysts. This aspect of implementation then also remains a puzzling problem, especially if we believe that general confidence in the law is weakened by publicized violation.

Consideration of these difficult problems of implementation returns us to a point we raised at the beginning of this case: Speed limits may not have an easily predictable effect on speeds. Perhaps the strategic tasks of the analyst should be to be aware of this problem as rapidly as possible and then to concentrate his or her analysis on it, rather than on finding the optimum v. To the extent that this is true, we have presented a teaching example of cost-benefit analysis and optimization, but not a genuine example of expert policy analysis.

Summary

This case study of choice of an optimum speed limit was selected for its use in teaching analysis of policy choices with continuous alternatives. After outlining the history of the development of the problem situation, we moved to a cost-benefit criterion including the value of time saved. We then developed a model aimed at minimizing the total cost of operating vehicles on those roads where they travel fastest. This model aimed to predict costs of travel time, of operation of vehicles, and of accidents as they depend on speed.

In an initial part of the analysis we worked toward finding an optimum value of v, the average speed of vehicles on the road, that would minimize total cost. In developing an approximate model we made a number of simplifying assumptions, an important one being that v would adequately characterize the results of the speed limit.

From this preliminary model we concluded that the optimum value of v would be between 55 and 60 mph, somewhat above the present limit of 55 mph. We examined the sensitivity of this conclusion to various assumptions, finding that higher valuation of time would lead to higher speed limits, as would lower valuation of the cost of accidents, but that higher values for gasoline would lead to lower optimum values of v.

Additional insight into the model was gained from evaluating the results of the 55-mph limit. We found that between 1973 and 1974 the introduction of this limit had lowered speeds above 40 mph but apparently not below. We were left with numerous uncertainties as to a recommendation. In such a case we should try to distinguish the rigorous inferences from the less rigorous assumptions that enter into our recommendations.

1. Use the data in table 4A–1 to reestimate what the optimum v would be if the cost of operation of cars increased by a factor of five.

2. Calculate the accident cost per vehicle-mile for 1973, and then for 1974 in 1973 dollars. Find the percentage change from 1973 to 1974.

3. Suppose that the cost of enforcement of the speed limit were included in our overall analysis and that this cost increased as the speed limit was lowered. What would be the effect, if any, of this added cost element on our estimate of the optimum v?

4. Studies of vehicle speeds and of routes chosen in relation to costs suggest that drivers place a higher value on working time than on nonworking time. Would this finding lead you to advocate lower speed limits on weekends than during the week? Explain and justify your answer.

5. Do you consider it permissible to evaluate tradeoffs between minutes or hours saved and the probability of loss of years of life through accidents? If so, what methods might be used for estimating the preferences or tradeoffs of persons affected?

6. Specify at least *ten* simplifying assumptions that were made in the formulation of the model in this case.

7. Examine the sensitivity of the estimated optimum v to a change in the relation between accident costs and v. Use the data in table 4A–1 to reestimate the optimum v if accident costs were *halved*.

Advanced Exercise

8. What examples of merit or demerit goods are mentioned in this case? (See chapter 5.)

Notes

1. This account of events makes use of the chronology in the *World Almanac 1975* (New York: Newspaper Enterprise Association, 1974) and of Forrest M. Council, Linda Pitts, Michael Sadof, and Olin K. Dart, *An Examination of the Effects of the 55 mph Speed Limit* (Chapel Hill, N.C.: University of North Carolina, Highway Safety Research Center, 1975), pp. 1–2.

2. See Robley Winfrey, *Economic Analysis for Highways* (Scranton, Pa.: International Textbook Company, 1969) p. 680.

3. Charles A. Lave, "Transportation and Energy: Some Current Myths," *Policy Analysis* 4(1978):297–315.

4. Robert E. Titus, "Speed Regulations and Other Operational Controls," in John E. Baerwald, Matthew J. Huber, and Louise E. Kafer, eds., *Transportation and*

Traffic Engineering Handbook (Englewood Cliffs, N.J.: Prentice-Hall, 1976), p. 854. A similar skepticism about the possibility of modifying human behavior is often expressed in the field of health policy.

5.   The effect of traffic volume on speed was noted in J. C. Oppenlander, "A Theory on Vehicular Speed Regulation," *Highway Research Board Bulletin* 341(1962): 77–91. For a more detailed specification of these conditions we might also have to state whether there was a minimum speed limit and what proportion of the traffic consisted of trucks.

6.   These sources of value were specified in ibid., with the addition of the intangible "travel comfort and convenience." We ignore possible effects of speed on highway maintenance costs.

7.   Tradeoffs between enforcement costs and other costs are treated in general terms in Gary S. Becker, "Crime and Punishment: An Economic Approach," *Journal of Political Economy* 76(1968):169–217.

8.   See Louis J. Pignataro, *Traffic Engineering: Theory and Practice* (Englewood Cliffs, N.J.: Prentice-Hall, 1973), p. 70; he specifies that this figure is the product of $.86 per hour and 1.8 persons per typical passenger vehicle. An alternative estimate, also in 1959 dollars, is $.89 × 1.6 or $1.42; see Winfrey, *Economic Analysis for Highways*, p. 267. Consumer price data are from U.S. Bureau of the Census, *Statistical Abstract of the United States: 1976* (Washington, D.C.: U.S. Govt. Print. Off., 1976), p. 439.

9.   *Statistical Abstract*, p. 600. Here we use cost data for all roads, speed data for rural roads, and 1975 as the year. Similar cost data, with a detailed description of their derivation, are given in Barbara Moyer Faigin, *1975 Societal Costs of Motor Vehicle Accidents* (Washington, D.C.: National Highway Traffic Administration, 1976). Note the assumption that accident costs on rural roads vary in the same way with speed as accident costs on all roads.

10.   The estimate of total travel in the U.S. in 1975 is from W. Johnson Page, Alexander French, and Joseph E. Ullman, "Estimated Highway Fuel Savings in 1975," *Federal Highway Administration Bulletin*, 18 Nov. 1976, p. 3. The average speed in 1975 of 55.8 mph is given in Federal Highway Administration, *Traffic Speed Trends* (Washington, D.C.: U.S. Govt. Print. Off., 1976). In the next section on the cost of accidents, we obtain a similar estimate by a different procedure. Note the simplifying assumption that accident costs per vehicle-mile under high-speed conditions can be estimated as overall national accident costs per vehicle-mile.

11.   Frank J. Cesario, "Value of Time in Recreation Benefit Studies," *Land Economics* 52(1976):37. These studies nevertheless assume that there *is* a value of time, the same for longer and shorter intervals. Their estimates relate to individuals rather than vehicles.

12.   Oppenlander, "A Theory on Vehicular Speed Regulation," p. 89; Herbert Mohring, cited in Leonard Merewitz and Stephen H. Sosnick, *The Budget's New Clothes* (Chicago: Markham, 1971), p. 155; Winfrey, *Economic Analysis for Highways*, p. 269. Some of this variation may be among types of persons. If we

knew the distribution of types of persons on the road (high and low wage rates; business and pleasure drivers) we might arrive at more precise estimates.

13. Winfrey, *Economic Analysis for Highways,* pp. 274–275.

14. For cost of gasoline see *Statistical Abstract,* p. 440. That part of highway taxes used for road repair and maintenance or for replacing old roads with new, however, might properly be charged to drivers; see chapter 5.

15. American Association of State Highway Officials (AASHO), *Road User Benefit Analysis for Highway Improvements* (Washington, D.C.: AASHO, 1960), pp. 112, 129ff. Data reproduced in Pignataro, *Traffic Engineering: Theory and Practice.*

16. *Statistical Abstract,* pp. 439, 592, 599, 600; see also table 4A–2.

17. Winfrey, *Economic Analysis for Highways,* p. 406.

18. These ratios were obtained by multiplying cost per accident by accident frequency in data presented in Rolin F. Barrett, *Crashes and Costs,* (Raleigh, N.C.: North Carolina State University, 1974), p. 2, and ibid., p. 406.

19. This procedure, used by Winfrey, *Economic Analysis for Highways,* pp. 379–380, gives a much lower value of life than does a procedure based on income alone.

20. See Jan Paul Acton, *Evaluating Public Programs to Save Lives: The Case of Heart Attacks* (Santa Monica, Calif.: Rand Corporation, 1973), ch. 6.

21. Regarding "quality-adjusted life-years" see ch. 4 on the medical screening case; and Richard Zeckhauser and Donald Shepard, "Where Now for Saving Lives?" *Law and Contemporary Problems* 40(1976):5–45.

22. Council et al., *An Examination of the Effects of the 55 mph Speed Limit,* p. 61, cite a study in which a logarithmic regression yielded a coefficient of 1.23, rather than unity. Graphs presented in Winfrey, *Economic Analysis for Highways,* also suggest coefficients of this magnitude.

23. Oppenlander, "A Theory on Vehicular Speed Regulation."

24. David Solomon, *Accidents on Main Rural Highways Related to Speed, Driver, and Vehicle,* U.S. Department of Commerce, Bureau of Public Roads (Washington, D.C.: U.S. Govt. Print. Off., 1964), p. 17.

25. For a detailed evaluation in one state from the viewpoint of safety, see Council et al., *An Examination of the Effects of the 55 mph Speed Limit.* We discuss evaluation further in chapter 7.

26. Some of the statistical problems in evaluating local speed-limit changes are discussed in Margaret C. Lewis, "Evaluating Effects of Lower Speed Limits on Safety: A Case Study of Route 2" (Cambridge, Mass.: Harvard University, John F. Kennedy School of Government, 1973).

27. *Statistical Abstract,* p. 592.

28. Ibid., p. 600.

29. See Council et al., *An Examination of the Effects of the 55 mph Speed Limit,* p.

21. A similar conclusion, detailed below, is based on data in *Statistical Abstract*, p. 599.

30. Council et al., *An Examination of the Effects of the 55 mph Speed Limit*, p. 20.

31. Donald E. Cleveland, *Speed and Speed Control*, in revision of *Traffic Control and Roadway Elements in Their Relationship to Highway Safety* (Washington, D.C.: Highway Users Federation for Safety and Mobility, 1970), p. 6. © 1970 by Highway Users Federation for Safety and Mobility.

32. Robert P. Shumate, *Effect of Increased Patrol on Accidents, Diversion, and Speed* (Evanston, Ill.: Northwestern University Traffic Institute, 1958).

33. Cleveland, *Speed and Speed Control*, p. 9.

34. The effect of a new enforcement program can decline after an initial period of public concern, as shown in H. Laurence Ross, Donald T. Campbell, and Gene V. Glass, "Determining the Social Effects of a Legal Reform: The British 'Breathalyzer' Crackdown of 1967," *American Behavioral Scientist* 15(1970):110–113.

5

Perfect Markets, Imperfect Markets, and Policy Corrections

The field of economics has contributed a set of analytic techniques in the form of models of markets, which have played an important role in policy analysis. These models have served two types of valuable functions. The first function is one of descriptive understanding, whereby the models are capable of showing a variety of cause-and-effect relationships and thus improving our ability to predict the outcomes of changes in circumstances or policies. For instance, a market model could be used to understand why an oil embargo by Middle Eastern countries would affect gasoline prices or to predict the impact of a higher minimum wage on employment levels. It could be used to understand the effects of a hypothetical drought in the "wheat belt" of the United States on the incomes of wheat farmers, on the price of bread, on the well-being of consumers, and on the sales of nonagricultural manufacturers. In addition, by setting up and using different models for various types of competitive conditions, economists have been able to compare the ways in which varieties of monopolistic circumstances may affect the ultimate impact of a change in cigarette taxes, for example. In specifying causal relationships between policies and valued or undesired consequences, these various models are quite similar to the noneconomic models discussed in chapter 4.

The economic models of various markets also have a second, prescriptive function. Following the lead of Adam Smith and his reference to the "invisible hand" of the market, economists have been able to identify a particular combination of market conditions that is capable of yielding a "best" result, that is, a result that best satisfies consumer preferences. When all of these conditions exist simultaneously, a so-called "free market" is said to exist. Because the free market is said to yield the desired objective of preference satisfaction, it is important that we understand the ways in which it works. Moreover, by identifying types of market conditions in which free market characteristics do not fully apply, we are able to pinpoint cases of so-called market failure, that is, circumstances in which preference satisfaction is not perfectly achieved. In such cases of market failure we may then explore the possible roles of public policy in correcting for market imperfections.

This chapter presents the basic outlines of economic market models. Because of space constraints, extensive treatment cannot be given to the broad range of possible market structures. Therefore, we shall use the free market model to illustrate the interrelationships between market participants and market forces and we shall outline its role in satisfying consumer preferences. Through the description of free market conditions, we will discuss what happens when ideal conditions do not hold and what might be done to offset the failures of imperfect markets.

The free market model takes as its focus an act of voluntary exchange. In a modern economy that exchange is usually one of a good or service for money rather than the direct barter of good for good. The existence of a generally accepted monetary unit is widely thought of as a prerequisite for an efficient economy precisely because it facilitates desired exchanges. A voluntary exchange may be prompted by one person reading an ad in the newspaper for a used car priced at $500. If a deal is subsequently struck at that price, we may assume that both buyer and seller are better off as a result of their transaction and that the purchase represents a Pareto improvement. In other words, it seems safe to say that the seller is better off for having 500 more dollars and one less car and the buyer is better off with one more car and 500 fewer dollars. The efficiency aspects of this isolated exchange seem clear, but we shall want to develop these ideas later in this chapter in the context of a wider market containing many buyers and sellers.

The free market model, based on the assumption of free exchange, presents an analytic framework that has applicability beyond what might be thought of as the narrow confines of economics. James M. Buchanan has provided an interesting example of this generality in the case of two college roommates.[1] In their dormitory the living conditions are identical for both roommates and therefore a matter for joint decision, unless a decision rule such as that of seniority is somehow imposed. If one person wishes the room temperature to be 75° and the other prefers 65°, one or both will be unhappy with the outcome regardless of the ultimate thermometer reading. Similarly, the two roommates might have different preferred times for turning out the lights at night. In such circumstances it becomes possible for the students to set up a "market" for temperatures and lights-out times and thereby to trade off these two goods according to their relative importance for each person. As Buchanan describes the result,

> By simultaneously considering two variables rather than each variable separately, the possibility of mutual agreement between the two parties is enhanced and there is less need for reliance on arbitrary decision rules. The results are more efficient than under such rules, in that the preferences of the parties are more fully satisfied.[2]

This last phrase of Buchanan's is very significant because it reveals the importance that economists place on the ability of a system to satisfy the preferences of participants. This quality is most clearly evident in economists' use of the term "efficiency." An economic system responsible for deciding which goods and services will be produced will be judged to be more or less "efficient" depending on how closely this allocation of resources corresponds to the preferences of consumers and producers.

Such an economic criterion has an analogy in politics. We are accustomed to evaluating political systems according to how well their outcomes coincide with the wishes of citizens or voters, but in this evaluation all voters count equally. In emphasizing the efficiency, or preference satisfaction, criterion, economists may be paying scant attention to the equity aspects of the free market system. Whereas "one person, one vote" will be the standard of justice for many political scientists, the analogue in the free market becomes "one dollar, one vote." This means that the economy listens with ten times as much attention to the expressed preferences of the person with a $50,000 income as it does to another with an income of $5,000. Whether or not this distribution of economic votes is considered fair depends on one's judgment about the equity of the initial distribution of incomes. Such a judgment will stem from philosophical or moral principles as well as an understanding of the economic bases for an unequal division of income by the market.

Although the free market model can help us to understand why some people are economically rewarded more than others, it does not necessarily involve any ethical judgment about the resulting income distribution. For instance, it is possible that the $500 price established in our used car example resulted to some extent from desperation on the part of the seller needing to buy fuel oil to heat his home. If he had had other resources with which to buy fuel, he might not have been willing to sell the car at all or might have been able to wait for a $600 offer. Moreover, there may have been a third party whose transportation needs could be deemed more important than the actual purchaser's, but who was unable to outbid the purchaser because of lack of funds. Thus, the initial distribution of income and wealth can influence not only which goods go to whom but also the ultimate terms of the transaction.

Society may decide to intervene in order to alter the division of consumer voting power and its associated levels of welfare. This intervention could take a variety of forms. It could entail the setting of income levels by the government rather than by the market, as is implied in the phrase "From each according to his ability, to each according to his needs." The elimination of free labor markets is involved in this strategy along with the likely erosion of incentives to work and produce as we often think of them.

Another possible tactic would call for the institution of a tax system that would alter the division of reward among groups in society in the direction of those considered especially deserving of help. By this means the basic forms of free labor markets could be maintained, as workers would still be rewarded for their contributions to productive activity. However, the government could modify (but not ignore) those reward decisions through tax-based redistribution from rich to poor, young to old, healthy to sick, or working to nonworking.

A third method is similar to the second in not restructuring labor markets or markets for other factors of production. It would have the government provide various public services that were tax-financed to entail a similar kind of reshuffling of rewards. For instance, a country could establish public schools, parks, and free health clinics, all financed out of property tax revenue.

A fourth alternative would involve intervention in free product markets by setting different prices for different consumers. A current example of this type is the proposal to permit lower fares for public transportation for senior citizens.

The possible conflicts between the two criteria of equity and efficiency run through most discussions of economic systems, situations, and problems. The issues involved should become clearer if the working of the free market model is fully understood. The next section outlines that model in order to set the stage for the discussion of governmental intervention.

DEMAND AND SUPPLY AND THE BEST USE OF RESOURCES

Students of introductory economics have been known to say that the subject is all a matter of demand and supply. To a large extent this is true, although the statement clearly overlooks the complexities that may be involved. Even a rudimentary understanding of demand and supply can help us to understand why a system based on price signals sent back and forth among participants produces a desired set of results.

If we consider demand as an element of a consumer good market, we observe the interest of a particular individual, family, or society in a good or service (e.g., bread). The interest is a voluntary one, based on a desire to obtain the most satisfaction (or utility) from a given amount of resources, and indicative of a willingness to part with something (usually money) in order to obtain a certain amount of bread. In expressing this interest demanders should know how many resources are available to them (primarily their income but also their other assets). They should be aware of the various attributes of all available goods and judge whether the goods are appealing. And they should realize what it would cost to purchase each of these products.

A traditional demand curve indicates how much the demanders' willingness to purchase an item is affected by changes in only one influence, namely, the price of the product in question. At each possible price (assumed to be constant regardless of the amount purchased), the demand curve shows the unique amount of the good that the purchaser is willing to buy. Let us illustrate this with the demand curve DD' in figure 5–1, which we will assume is the curve of one person at a particular time. If at a price of $1.00 per loaf the demand curve indicates an apparent interest in buying two loaves of bread, this information suggests that a combination of two loaves of bread and a bundle of other goods is a better use of the person's funds than combinations of one loaf and a bundle of other goods that he could obtain, three loaves and other goods, or any other combination obtainable with his income. In other words, if this person initially had only one loaf of bread and some other goods, he would gladly give up a dollar's worth of other items in order to buy a second loaf. However, the sacrifice of a third dollar's worth of other goods in order to obtain a third loaf would be disadvantageous in the sense of yielding less satisfaction than the two-loaves-plus-others combination. Under this reasoning each point on a person's demand curve is a most preferred (utility-maximizing) point under the circumstances of a given set of preferences, prices, and resources.

Figure 5–1.
Demand and Supply in a Market.

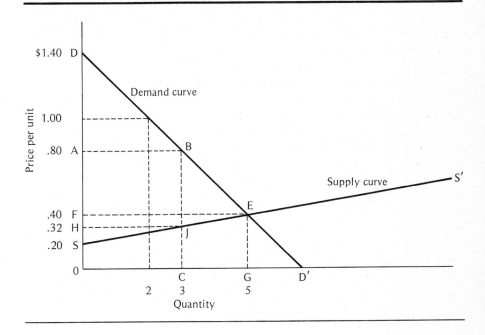

Suppose the same person's demand curve also indicated that at a bread price of $.80 a loaf, he was willing to buy three loaves. Surely, it would be unusual for this individual not to want to buy at least the two loaves that he was interested in at a $1.00 price. If he is willing to buy a third loaf also, it must mean that he prefers to give up $.80 worth of other purchases in order to buy the third loaf. In this sense we can get a general measure of the dollar value of particular products to a given buyer by examining that buyer's demand curve. If 0A in figure 5–1 corresponds to $.80 and 0C to three loaves, then we can say that the third loaf must be "worth" $.80 to the consumer if he will not buy that many loaves until the price gets down to $.80 a loaf. And if the demand curve has the negative slope shown, it should be clear that the second loaf must be worth more than $.80 (in fact $1.00 from the earlier information) and the first loaf still more ($1.20). Thus, the shape of the demand curve corresponds to the usual belief of economists that successive units of most goods are worth ever smaller amounts to a consumer as quantity increases (or diminishing marginal utility).

If the above method of estimating the monetary value to a consumer is accurate, namely, that we can read the value of any given unit of a good by measuring the vertical distance up to the consumer's demand curve, we can compute the total monetary value to the demander of all units desired by adding the values of the individual units: $1.20 + $1.00 + $.80 = $3.00. We can also estimate this total value approximately by finding the area *under* the demand curve out to the given demanded quantity.[3] When this method is used, the value of three loaves of bread (0C in figure 5–1) would be indicated by the trapezoid 0DBC. If this person will not buy three loaves unless the price falls to $.80 (or 0A), then he will be paying only a total of $2.40 (or the area of rectangle 0ABC) to buy those three loaves. Thus, the total amount spent on a product will usually be less than the total value of the purchased items to the buyer (area 0DBC, which is $3.30 if point D corresponds to $1.40).

This stems from the fact that the buyer usually pays the same per unit price for all purchased quantities. The resulting difference between total worth and total purchase payments has been referred to as the "consumer surplus" (or area DAB at price 0A). This "consumer surplus" is an indication of how much better off the buyer is from having engaged in an exchange of money for goods. It measures the net benefit to the buyer. We can also see a graphical proof of the fact that the purchaser prefers lower prices, for the lower price of creates a higher consumer surplus DEF.

The same principles that applied to an individual's demand for a single product show up in the market demand for that good by all interested consumers. The market demand is derived by horizontally adding all the individual demand curves. This geometric construction simply means that for each and every possible price we have aggregated all the quantities that potential consumers would be willing to buy. This method is called for by the private nature, or "rivalness,"as we shall refer to it, of the commodity bread: Any given loaf of bread will be providing satisfaction to only the person (or family) who buys it. Only by adding all the quantities demanded can we be assured that everybody's preferences have been satisfied or taken into account. If the individual demand curves are negatively sloped, the aggregate demand curve will also be negatively sloped. The general principle of diminishing marginal utility for successive units of bread will be reaffirmed in the aggregate curve. We may also assert that each point on the aggregate curve represents the best point at the corresponding price for the entire consuming group, each "member" of which has optimized on his own. Moreover, the consuming group as a whole prefers lower prices since those lower prices increase consumer surplus both individually and in the aggregate.

Let us turn our attention to the supply side of a consumer good market. Assume that the supply curve SS' in figure 5–1 indicates the interest of one producer in selling his goods to consumers. The interest is once again a voluntary one, based on an assumed desire to make the maximum possible profits for the owners of the business. The curve suggests a willingness to exchange the business's products for something else (usually money). In revealing his price-quantity relationship the supplier bases his decision on the available state of technology and know-how, the productivity of the various inputs (factors of production) that may be combined to produce the output, and the prices of those inputs. With this information he can determine the least-cost combination of inputs that is appropriate to each and every possible output level, a type of efficiency calculation that is based largely on engineering principles.[4] We may say that a supplier who is identifying the least-cost method is achieving "productive efficiency."

A traditional supply curve indicates how much the supplier's willingness to sell his product is affected by changes in only one variable, namely, the selling price of the product. At each possible price the supply curve shows the unique quantity that the producer is willing to sell. Let point J in figure 5–1 indicate that at a price of $.32 (or 0H) there is a willingness to supply three loaves of bread (or 0C). The apparent unwillingness to supply a fourth loaf *at that price* suggests that the producer would obtain less profit at an output of four loaves. Since buyers would be paying $.32 for the fourth loaf, the inferior profit position must be due to the fact that the fourth loaf costs more than $.32 to produce (even when production is carried out in the least-cost fashion). In this sense each point on a supply curve is a profit-maximizing point under the circumstances of a given set of technologies, input prices, and output prices.

The supply curve in figure 5–1 indicates that the fourth loaf of bread will be supplied to the market only if the price rises to some level greater than $.32. In fact, we can obtain insights about costs to producers from the supply curve in the same way that we estimated the value to consumers from points on the demand curve. The producer is motivated to supply only those units of bread for which his receipts are at least able to cover costs. We should therefore be able to approximate the costs of producing each unit of output by measuring the vertical distance up to the supply curve. A positively-sloped supply curve is a reflection of a situation in which successive units of output cost ever higher amounts as production expands.

This assumption of rising costs as quantity increases may seem at odds with our knowledge or intuition about how the economy in fact works. This is particularly true when we remember reading about Henry Ford and the cost savings realized by assembly line techniques and mass production. Let us consider both possible cost situations with the aid of figure 5–2. The two cost curves shown, expressing average cost and marginal cost as they depend on the quantity produced, must be carefully defined. Average costs (AC) are calculated by dividing the total costs of production by the relevant number of units of the good produced. Total costs include both the fixed costs such as those associated with purchasing the building and the assembly line equipment (costs incurred even if the assembly line is shut down) and the variable costs such as those for raw materials, energy, and wages that are directly related to the level of production. Marginal costs (MC) are the extra costs incurred to produce an extra unit of output and are thus reflective of only variable costs. That is, the marginal cost at an output level of twenty loaves of bread is equal to the total costs of twenty loaves minus the total costs of nineteen loaves.

Economists frequently assume (on the basis of considerable empirical research) that the typical AC curve has a U-shape as shown in figure 5–2. This suggests that over some initial range of output (here from zero to Q_0), the firm finds that average costs decline as it takes advantage of mass production tech-

Figure 5–2.
Alternative Cost Relationships: Decreasing and Increasing Costs.

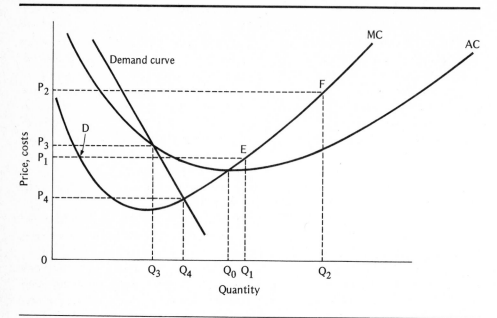

niques and spreads the large fixed costs over an ever-larger output. However, at some point production bottlenecks are encountered and important inputs are more difficult to find (especially at the same quality), the result being a reversal of the average cost reductions. Beyond Q_0 the ever-rising marginal costs become quantitatively more important and cause the AC curve to turn upward.

Let us now confront a profit-maximizing supplier with a price such as P_1, assuming initially that he can sell all he wishes at that price. This price intersects the cost curves at both the downward-sloping and upward-sloping portions. If we remember that price represents revenue to the producer, it should be clear that he would be foolish to halt output along the falling cost range of the MC curve since losses (costs greater than revenues) would be incurred to the left of D, and profits would be made farther to the right. The crucial range for making profits is the DE portion of the MC curve in which each unit of output imposes fewer costs than it generates in revenues. Faced with P_1, the supplier will find his profits are highest at output Q_1. Similarly, at price P_2 profits are maximized at Q_2. In both cases the producer finds it unprofitable to extend output beyond the level where price equals marginal cost. The rising part of the MC curve, traced out by points such as E and F, is thus the same as the supply curve we discussed earlier. This is an important result, which we shall refer to again. Moreover, as long as there is a U-shaped AC curve, a profit-maximizer will seek to operate in the increasing cost range. Only if the market is so small that the supplier is unable to sell all that he wishes will he stop short of the increasing cost range. This will be further discussed later as the natural monopoly case.

If the above method of estimating costs to producers is valid, we are able to use the supply curve to suggest the cost situations existing at various output levels. We have shown above that a producer's supply curve is really the positively sloped portion of his MC curve. The supply curve in figure 5–1 thus indicates that the producer incurred variable costs equal to area 0SJC as he produced three (0C) loaves of bread. Since the producer will sell those three loaves only if the price is $.32 apiece, he will receive $.96 (area 0HJC) in revenues, leaving him with the net area HJS that has been called the "producer surplus." Since only variable costs are reflected in area 0SJC, the supplier is in addition responsible for fixed costs, and thus we cannot view the producer surplus strictly as his profit. However, we may interpret the producer surplus as the amount by which the supplier is better off (having produced and sold three loaves) compared to his situation at zero output. With this notion of producer surplus in mind we can see that suppliers would prefer to have higher prices for their products. As the price of bread rises from 0H to 0F, producer surplus in creases from HJS to FES.

This description of the underlying bases of demand and supply demonstrates the conflicting interests of the two sides in the matter of prices, with demanders preferring lower prices and suppliers higher ones. A free market attempts a type of reconciliation of this conflict in the sense of establishing an equilibrium pairing of price and quantity that market participants are unable to improve upon. If DD' in figure 5–1 now represents the combined demands of all bread consumers and SS' the combined supplies of all bread producers, the market solution will be 0G units of bread at a price of 0F per loaf, an equilibrium at the intersection of the two curves. Price 0F is the only one for which the market will generate no forces for price change. At any other price there will either be too much output for the expressed willingness to buy (with price reductions being prompted) or more demand than there is output (with disappointed customers tending to bid up prices).

Economists have long viewed this market solution as being more than a mere impersonal reconciliation of conflicting interests. They have imbued the free market outcome with an aura of optimality, a decision that is capable of best serving the interests of a combined society of consumers and producers. This optimality is achieved when the sum of producers' surpluses and consumers' surpluses is as large as possible (under the assumptions that both surpluses are equally desirable and that we can add individual surpluses together). We can see in figure 5–1 that as output moves from 0C to 0G, the sum of these two types of surpluses increases from DBJS to DES, a clear gain to society of BEJ. As output expands beyond 0G, this total surplus will decline as units of production cost more than consumers are willing to pay for them.[5] Thus, not only is the free market solution of an equilibrium at point E the natural result of unfettered, self-interested behavior of many participants, it is also the result that provides the maximum welfare for society. This is the outcome described by Adam Smith in his famous reference to the "invisible hand" of the market that leads a producer or a consumer "to promote an end which was no part of his intention."

We can get a fuller understanding of the meaning of this optimal (most efficient) point by realizing what is happening at point E in figure 5–1. At that point the preferences of society as consumers of goods and services (and as revealed in the demand curve) are matched with the preferences of society as providers of productive inputs (as revealed in the supply curve). Only at point E is the value of the last unit of output just equal to the cost of producing it. For lower quantities the value to consumers is greater than production costs, and therefore expansion of output is justified. For higher quantities the costs of production exceed the value to consumers, and a cutback is in order. Thus, a free market achieves an optimal solution for society by the simultaneous consideration of consumer evaluations of goods and the costs of production.[6]

Let us digress briefly to explain why the supply curve (or the cost side of a market) should also be viewed as satisfying preferences. Consider the supply and demand curves of figure 5–1 as applying to a labor market case. The quantity axis is the quantity of labor services (perhaps enumerated as person-hours of work) and the price of labor is the wage rate. The demand curve now represents the willingness of business to hire workers to produce goods and services and reflects the preferences of consumers for the respective products. On the other hand, the supply curve indicates the willingness of potential workers to exchange leisure for wages and thereby reflects the relative preferences of laborers for goods (to be bought with income) versus leisure. The resulting equilibrium labor price then enters as an element in the goods supply decision and is indicative of the desires of society to consume goods. In the same sense the amount of wage income that labor market demand and supply show as being paid to workers becomes a key element in the economic resource base from which consumers express an interest in goods and services. Similar discussions could be used to analyze markets for natural resources or financial capital. With this understanding of other market elements of the economic picture it should be clear that both the demand and supply sides of an economy reflect preferences, so that the operations of a free market are tied into the ethic of preference satisfaction in many dimensions and at many levels.

CONDITIONS FOR FREE MARKETS

Up to this point very little has been said about the conditions that must exist if this free market solution is to be legitimately viewed as an optimal reflection of preferences. The most familiar of these conditions specifies that both the buyers and the sellers must be so numerous in each market that no one of them can exert an appreciable influence on the resulting price. This requirement of competitiveness means that each market participant will be merely responding to a price situation, rather than being able individually to determine those prices. As a result, the price signals become accurate reflections of the participants' preferences. In order for a free market system to be capable of adjusting to changing conditions and preferences, participants must not only be restricted to having small shares of the market but also be able to enter or leave markets freely.

Another key condition concerns the sort of information that demanders and suppliers must have. If that information is inadequate by being either false or insufficient, the resulting decisions will not truly reflect the interests of participants. The scope of desired information is broad, including the prices and characteristics of prospective purchases as well as any price differentials that might exist among alternative demanders or suppliers. Although this may appear to be suggesting that complete information is required, we should keep in mind that information is rarely costless. Whether we are analyzing optimal free market structures or discussing the most appropriate data inputs relative to public policy matters, information should be sought only so long as its acquisition costs can be justified by an expected improvement in results. This is essentially the meaning that should be attached to the requirement of "perfect information" in an ideal free market.[7]

A third critical condition for free market optimality requires that the interests and preferences of all concerned parties be reflected in the market's decision. This stipulation means that there are no unaccounted-for "external effects," which operate outside the market to affect people's preference satisfaction. We shall turn our attention to these external effects in the next section when cases of market failure are discussed, but let us first emphasize that there are a great many effects of the workings of a free market that should be considered as internal rather than external to the market.

Suppose once again that figure 5–1 summarizes the demand and supply situation in the bread market. If new bread consumers enter the market, the demand curve will shift to the right, and a new equilibrium will be established with a higher price of bread and more bread production. A change in behavior by some consumers can be expected to have widespread impacts on other people associated with the bread market. Other bread consumers, faced with a higher price for a desired commodity, will be losers regardless of their purchase response to the price change. Bread manufacturers will gain increased profits as the price rises. Bread-industry workers, wheat farmers, and plastic-bag manufacturers may all experience some gain from the expanded bread market. Similarly, producers and consumers in the market from which these people diverted demand (e.g., the potato industry) can be expected to experience negative and positive impacts respectively as a result of this initial action.

All of these impacts, though external to those who set off the chain reaction, are internal to the markets in which they are participants. It is precisely such effects, working through the system of price signals, that are the essential *modus operandi* of a market system. Without them the market would be unable to reflect participant preferences accurately, to relate costs and benefits in a decentralized decision process. It is important to distinguish between the internal effects, which markets can reflect, and the external effects, which are usually not well reflected in the market and which will be discussed more thoroughly as we turn our attention to cases of market failure.[8]

A free market, operating under the ideal conditions we have described, has been shown by economists to produce a set of results that is a benchmark for comparison. As Francis M. Bator expresses it, "It is the central theorem of modern welfare economics that under certain strong assumptions about technology, tastes and producers' motivations, the equilibrium conditions which characterize a system of competitive markets will exactly correspond to the requirements of Paretian efficiency."[9]

This concept of efficiency involves two different applications of Pareto optimality as we have already outlined it. First of all, the goods that have been produced have been so distributed among the various consumers that no further mutually beneficial trades are possible. Secondly, the factors of production (inputs) have been so distributed among the various industries' products (outputs) that any reallocation would harm at least one consumer. These twin achievements are the results of a competitive market system that uses price signals to guide the behavior of consumers and producers and that uses the preferences revealed in response to those signals to make the ultimate price and output decisions.

If any of the assumptions underlying the free market model fails to hold, then a *prima facie* case can be made for remedying it through collective action.[10] Although the term "collective action" is most often interpreted as meaning legislative, judicial, or administrative decision by government, we should not forget that collective actions are also performed by such groups as "co-ops, unions, vigilante organizations, country clubs, carpools and trade associations."[11] Collective action is distinguished from the individual action characteristic of a free market. However, economic theory has traditionally treated the firms and households operating in the market as individuals. More recently, there has been considerable research into the roles and motivations of various members of a family or of people within the corporate hierarchy, research that should greatly increase our awareness of the complexity of the decision process within the private sectors of the economy.

The case for collective action of the governmental variety is most compelling in large-scale economies where private bargaining among a few participants (such as college roommates) cannot easily alleviate the principal market failures.[12] This case becomes more compelling to the extent that we can expect the governmental remedy itself to be carried out efficiently. Buchanan has pointed out, however, that majority decisions may fail to maximize welfare and has described the "burden of bureaucracy," which includes the negotiation and decision-making costs (or transactions costs) that are inherently required in any collective decision process, whether public or private.[13] The multistage process of policy consideration at the federal government level—starting for instance with proposals from the Department of Health, Education, and Welfare and moving to consideration by appropriations subcommittees and committees, to votes by House and Senate and possible conference compromise between two versions, and then to ultimate signing (or perhaps veto) by the president—may be more involved and costly than exists elsewhere. However, the essentials are likely to be duplicated by other units of government, by churches, or by tennis clubs. Even after collective decisions are made, it is usually up to the government bureaucracy to implement them. If the incentives that are in effect in a bureaucracy run counter to efficient operation, this implementation may be unduly burdensome to society. In addition to these possible drawbacks to the collective action alternative, we should realize that governmental activity may entail the "costs" of a loss of personal freedom. But the costs of collective action should be compared with the costs of market failure—that is, the losses due to reliance on individual action—if the scope of the market and its alternatives are to be appropriately outlined. We turn next to a discussion of the principal causes of market failure.

The major departures of actual markets from the assumptions of the free market model that have prompted calls for collective action are as follows:

1. Force and persuasion: activities by producers or consumers that influence the market other than the activities of production, sale, and purchase of goods and services.
2. False or insufficient information about goods and services or the conditions of exchange.
3. Lack of competition: monopoly and barriers to entry or exit from a market, which may be the result of either natural market conditions or intentional collusion.
4. Effects external to the market: influences of production or consumption on third parties, affecting their welfare without their having entered into the relation through voluntary exchange.
5. Collective goods: goods of such a nature that one individual's consumption does not subtract from any other individual's consumption.

In addition, two other considerations have led to advocacy of collective action to modify the working of markets:

6. Dynamic problems: influences on welfare in the transition between one equilibrium and another and the related consequences of market instability.
7. Other ethical criteria not reflected in Pareto optimality, such as equity, merit goods, and nonteleological criteria.

The first five of these departures can be classified as types of market failure as they can lead to equilibria that are not Pareto efficient. The last two involve situations other than equilibria. They concern the application of additional or alternative standards to the market's behavior.

FORCE AND PERSUASION

A major assumption of the free market model is that exchange will be free, without force or coercion. Buyers and sellers enter into exchange voluntarily and therefore presumably emerge from it in a preferred situation. There are, to be sure, inequalities after exchange, but ideal exchange does not make the poor person worse off. To this end, the legal enforcement of property rights is advocated.

Either seller or buyer, however, can sometimes violate this assumption by the use of force. The robber's threat, backed by a weapon, creates a new exchange situation in which goods are transferred on different terms. The threat on the part of a corporation to blacklist an employee, to withhold necessary raw materials from another producer, or to engage in price discrimination violates this assumption of the market model. Such departures from the model call for governmental intervention if the market model is to be approximated in reality. But at least one form of coercive economic activity, the strike, has been legalized in view of the previous inequality of bargaining power between labor and management.

Buyers and sellers, but especially producers, may also organize to make use of the powers available to the government to influence the market in their favor.[14] Insofar as this leads to a loss of welfare, it is a deficiency of the economic-political system and may be difficult to remedy by further governmental action. Case 5–B, concerning regulation in the oil industry is an example of collective action by producers.

A second assumption of the free market model is that the market is a device for satisfying given preferences on the part of the consumers. The market transmits information about the qualities of goods and the ways in which they may be expected to satisfy these preferences. Some of this information is transmitted simply by sale and consumption. Consumers' experiences with goods influence their later purchases, and information about products may be circulated among consumers as well. But the equilibrium may also be hastened and unpleasant trial and error eliminated if sellers communicate full and accurate information at the time of the sale so that buyers may establish their preferences for goods sooner. In the case of the labor market the same considerations apply to the buyers as well as the sellers of labor.

The communication from seller to buyer may, however, go beyond mere information to persuasion that alters the buyer's preferences. Much contemporary advertising is alleged to have this effect.[15] In other cases the mere increase in supply appears to have had an impact on demand. Even without advertising, the larger supply of physicians in some parts of the country seems to have led to increases in the demand for medical care. But the acknowledgement of such effects would contradict the assumption that the market satisfies given preferences that originate outside the market, and is thus resisted by many economists. It would be harder to argue that the market furthers consumers' welfare, if the market functioned to change their notion as to what goods satisfied them. This problem involves both philosophical questions concerning the nature of "welfare" and empirical ones concerning the actual effects of advertising and other communications on the market. Persuasion that changes preferences is not necessarily bad; but it requires ethical justification similar to that used in the case of "merit goods," which we shall discuss in this chapter.

FALSE OR INSUFFICIENT INFORMATION

A market system rests on legal foundations. The laws that permit exchange serve to control fraud as well as force. Exchange assumes an agreement between two parties, a contract involving obligations on the part of buyer and seller, such as we discussed earlier. Thus, if goods as delivered differ from those promised, there is ground for legal remedies. An insufficiency of information thus shades into a condition under which either sellers or buyers fail altogether to live up to their side of the bargain. One of the functions of legal systems is to sustain the conditions under which contracts will be kept.[16]

The provision of a legal framework controlling force and fraud constitutes the minimum condition for the existence of a free market. In the view of the strongest partisans of a free market, we should be cautious before undertaking further collective action. Some governmental actions can serve only to distort the operation of the market and, in economic terms, to reduce efficiency. But whether such actions are to be attributed to government, to economic interests, or to nonmarket values that we may support is a question for more detailed analysis in particular cases.

The information supplied by a market may be insufficient in several ways. Consumers may be unaware of the relevant characteristics of products or of the long-run consequences of consuming them. Consumers of health services and drugs have particular problems of this kind. Thus, the government may intervene in the market by requiring that users of birth control pills be informed of possible side effects, by regulating the claims of effectiveness of cold remedies, or by barring the sale of supposedly ineffective drugs, such as laetrile. Workers may similarly be insufficiently informed about the long-run consequences of working in a particular industry as regards their health, their chances for advancement, or their security. Producers may also lack information; but because of the great value of information to them (e.g., regarding the quality of raw materials), they are more likely to be able to devote resources to seeking it out. Each participant in the market seeks out information to the extent that he or she deems this search valuable. But especially in the case of the less educated consumer, it is likely that opportunities for search will be overlooked. For these reasons Anthony Downs considers that a function of government may be "protection of consumers from their own ignorance or incompetence." Among the products thus regulated have been "foods, drugs, water supplies, and cigarettes." [17]

LACK OF COMPETITION

Even if goods are sold under conditions of voluntary exchange and accurate information is provided about them, the free market model may still fail to hold because of lack of competition. This situation arises when there are an insufficient number of either buyers or sellers in a market, with the result that an individual participant's actions can have a significant impact on the market outcome. In the case of a producer this means that a decision to change his output will influence the price he is able to get for that output. His market power is indicated by the fact that he no longer merely responds to a market price but rather plays a role in determining that price. With this degree of "control" over his market the monopolist's price is not only higher than it would have been in a competitive context but also fails to reflect accurately the costs incurred in producing the goods. This failure to reflect costs thus undermines the key role of the price system in coordinating the preferences of producers and consumers.

The absence of sufficient competition on the buyer's side of the market rather than the seller's side is called "monopsony." This is illustrated in the one-company town where one firm is the only significant employer in the labor market. Prospective employees have few alternative job opportunities outside of that firm. Only through costly commuting or migration can workers avoid the market dominance of the single employer whose wage offers may understate the productive value of the employees to the firm. With this kind of "control" over the labor market the monopsonist injects a degree of inefficiency into the economy.

It is important to point out that monopolistic conditions may naturally arise in markets in which there are "economies of scale," that is, where there is a range of output over which average costs decline as output increases, as we discussed in connection with figure 5–2. In such a case there is a clear incentive for any producer to expand production and therefore the scale of his operations in order to take advantage of the lower costs. How many producers remain as suppliers to a market after all the economies of scale have been exhausted (and costs begin to rise again) will depend on the state of technology (determining the range of falling costs) and the amount of demand for the product.

In some situations a single firm may be the least-cost means for producing a given good or service. Such cases are often called "natural monopolies" and include such commodities as telephone service, water supply, and electricity. Consumers clearly have an interest in seeing that these natural monopolies fully exploit the cost-saving possibilities as long as the prices charged reflect those cost savings and not monopolistic control of the market. The customary solution is to grant franchises to public utilities whose size enables them to achieve cost savings but whose prices are subject to the regulation of utility commissions.[18] This obvious remedy may not successfully achieve preference satisfaction if, as many have charged, the regulated utilities are able to dominate the regulatory agencies politically.

The granting of franchises to public utilities nevertheless involves dilemmas, which can be discovered by referring back to figure 5–2. Suppose that demand for the service in question is small enough that the demand curve (as shown in figure 5–2) intersects the cost curves to the left of Q_0, the point of minimum average cost. We noted in our earlier discussion of figure 5–2 that such a market reached a natural equilibrium where the price of a good was equal to its marginal cost. Moreover, this result of marginal-cost pricing was clearly optimal in an efficiency sense since it increased production up to but not beyond the point at which an extra unit of the good cost just what it was worth to the consumer.

If the regulatory commission for a public utility enforced marginal-cost pricing in view of the demand and cost curves in figure 5–2, the public utility would be forced to charge P_4 for its services. A public utility that charged P_4 for each of the Q_4 units of, for example, electricity would find itself losing money since its average costs would be above price (and revenues) at that level of production. The regulatory commission is faced with the dilemma of trying to assure an efficient level of electricity output while assuring that the private electric company makes a sufficient profit to stay in the business. One possible solution is to maintain efficiency at P_4 and Q_4 but to ask the government to collect enough taxes so that a sufficient subsidy can be paid to the public utility to offset the losses that would otherwise result. This solution has not been frequently used for cases of privately owned utilities.

A second pricing alternative is to permit the utility to use a more complicated, multipart pricing scheme, rather than simply charging P_4 for each unit of electricity. Through a system that charges each customer a higher price for the first few units bought, the utility may be able to approximate efficient pricing while collecting sufficient extra revenues to avoid the necessity of tax-financed subsidies. This technique is widely used in energy industries (electricity and natural gas) and by transportation services, where annual passes may be sold that entitle the buyer to a zero fare per bus ride or a zero toll per bridge crossing. A third solution is to sacrifice allocative efficiency by permitting the utility to charge a uniform price equal to average cost (P_3 at suboptimal output level Q_3 in figure 5–2). This strategy is widely used in transportation situations.

One of the biggest problems with all three of these solutions is the selection (and enforcement) of a fair rate of profit for the privately owned public utility. The very mechanism of a price-regulating commission provides a clear inducement for the utility to seek sufficient political power to influence commission decisions and thereby achieve undue profits. Even beyond this, productive inefficiencies may arise since a firm that is essentially guaranteed a particular profit rate may have little incentive to produce in the least-cost manner.

A fourth method for dealing with the decreasing-cost, or natural monopoly, phenomenon is to have the government own and operate the facility. In this case price setting is usually done by the operating agency itself (e.g., recreation or transportation department), rather than an independent regulatory commission. Although the basic principles of efficient pricing are the same as in the first three cases, they are often more difficult to implement because of the primitive state of public accounting, particularly with respect to capital expenditures. In any event some of these public enterprises charge for their services (fares on buses) and others do not (free tennis courts). These last types of public activities are not monopolies since the town pool is probably not the only one in town and the city buses compete with family cars, taxis, and bicycles. However, we mention them here to emphasize the large fixed-cost element of so many of these publicly run enterprises.

Cases of decreasing average costs usually involve production processes with very large initial capital outlays and relatively small operating costs. A clear example would be a hydroelectric dam, which is very expensive to construct but quite cheap to operate. The same might be true for a tennis court or a highway, where maintenance expenses are small in comparison to construction costs. The high initial costs make it infeasible for single consumers to purchase such products on their own. But if there were some way of sharing facilities, many consumers could effectively be brought into the market. In fact, the "sharing" of highways by drivers is quite similar to the "sharing" of hydroelectric dams by electricity users and the "sharing" of auto assembly plants by car buyers. In the case of tennis courts private collective action in the form of tennis clubs has been used to achieve cost and facility sharing, and many localities have public tennis courts. We shall consider situations of this kind further in the section called "Collective Goods."

One major reason why such cost and facility sharing is carried out through governmental action is that it is very expensive to use the price mechanism of the market to divide production costs among users. In a market demanders must reveal their preferences through an observed willingness to pay a price. People are excluded from the benefits of those commodities whose price they are unwilling to pay. But the process of exclusion involves some amount of expense, as in the costs of checkout procedures in grocery stores. The costs of exclusion vary from product to product. It is relatively easy to exclude people from an opera performance but much more difficult to do so from a fireworks display. Thus, although most goods carry price tags related to the possibility of exclusion, others, such as local roads, most bridges, and some playground equipment, are made available at zero price and financed out of tax revenue.

Decreasing-cost situations have the further interesting characteristic of creating a desire among consumers for a bigger market brought on by higher demand. Remember that in our earlier discussion using figure 5–1 higher demand meant higher costs and a resulting loss for prior consumers. But suppose that the average cost of automobile seat belts falls as output rises, and especially if seat belts are placed in all new cars. A clear incentive is provided for those wanting seat belts to attempt to bring into the market others who have been unwilling to pay for seat belts at market prices. Thus, as a matter of self interest the seat belt demanders could advocate collective action in the form of a statutory requirement that all new cars be equipped with the belts. This possible explanation for the seat belt law differs significantly from the "merit good" case that we shall discuss.

The fluoridation of public water supplies may be similar to the seat-belt case. Individual home fluoridation equipment is available, and the price system is quite capable of excluding nonusers. Yet, by adding fluorides to a locality's water supply system, we can obtain the ultimate dental benefits at a greatly reduced cost per person. People cannot then be excluded from the benefits of the fluorides except by excluding them from water as well. In fact, with a fluoridated water supply individuals who disliked the chemical would be forced to bear additional expenses to avoid it, as through the purchase of bottled water or a chemical filtration device. Thus, a situation in which collective action is employed to exploit cost reductions for some may impose increased costs (above and beyond higher taxes) on others. Both equity and efficiency criteria are likely to be cited in the search for a solution in such a case.

Although many monopolies are created by the lure of cost reductions, others are less benign. There are cases in which the exploitation of economies of scale results in a small number of competing suppliers, who then may further combine or coordinate operations to increase the degree of monopoly control. A remedy for monopoly is government action to break up the large monopolistic firms, if production can be divided up among more numerous (and smaller) firms and if this breakup can be carried through in view of the monopolistic firms' political influence. Even in the absence of political influence, it is difficult to specify how far to push the breakup of monopolistic industries.

A degree of monopoly in terms of the free market model may also be attained through product differentiation and brand-name loyalty. If consumers are led to demand only a particular brand of product, even as an information-gathering economy to themselves, the result is to create a new product category within which the seller exercises some of the privileges of monopoly. He may, for example, raise his price relative to other sellers of what was previously considered the "same" product. This type of monopoly has not ordinarily met with regulation. But the subjective difficulty that a buyer may experience in shifting from one product to another is analogous to the costs of migration. If a buyer's attachment to a given product is based only on its qualities, the calculations of the free market model are being made. But if buyers come to believe that one product constitutes a market category by itself, then a case may be made that free entry into a particular part of the market is constrained.

Free entry of producers into the market is essential if supply is to increase in response to increasing demand. Thus, the regulation of entry to professions by their own members is a type of collective action, private or public, that is difficult to justify in terms of the free market model. Similarly, free exit from the market is a condition for the contraction of supply in response to reduced demand. Here the problem is not so much that of allowing businesses to leave the market, as that of preventing them from using political processes to remain in operation when their output is not demanded at a price corresponding to their costs of production.

EFFECTS EXTERNAL TO THE MARKET

Even when producers' and consumers' motivations conform exactly to the free market model, their activities may have consequences that are not reflected in prices and exchange. Such consequences are termed "externalities" because they involve people who did not participate in the market decision and thus are experiencing impacts external to the voluntary exchange mechanism. These externalities can be either positive or negative. If a producer or consumer creates undesirable sights, sounds, smells, or water conditions that reduce the welfare of another producer or consumer without appropriate compensation for these effects, a negative externality or "external cost" is said to have been imposed. Conversely, the production by one producer or consumer of effects that are deemed beneficial by another who has not paid for them is said to involve positive externalities or "external benefits." In either case the externalities entail impacts on nonparticipants that are not reflected in anyone's market decisions. The result is that market prices fail to reflect all relevant preferences and therefore send out inaccurate signals to guide the economy. Pareto optimality cannot then be achieved.

The various sorts of pollution provide the best-known examples of external costs. When the full costs of production are not borne by the manufacturer —indeed, the profit maximizer may have a clear incentive to "externalize" as many costs as possible—it may appear logical for the harmed party to be able to seek compensation or to use legal means for reducing the damage. When this stand is based on equity considerations (e.g., "It is not fair for your lawn mower to disturb my peaceful Sunday afternoon") the legal entanglements of property rights become involved. In setting up a legal system and set of such rights any society establishes a whole range of expectations about what individuals can and cannot do. Thus, a property owner may not be able to sue an airport authority for sound and smoke damage if he should have been well aware of the airport's existence when he built his home. Expectations may be more formally specified through zoning laws that could, for instance, prevent someone from raising pigs in the midst of a residential development.

From the economic point of view of efficiency the selection of remedies for external costs must be made on different grounds. As R. H. Coase points out, "What has to be decided is whether the gain from preventing the harm is greater than the loss which would be suffered elsewhere as a result of stopping the action which produces the harm."[19] By this standard the solution of prohibiting pollution is brought into question, for it may be more harmful to stop production at a polluting steel mill, thus reducing the well-being of users of steel products, than it would be to continue to pollute. Moreover, the most efficient outcome, reflecting all relevant preferences in the economy, may not entail the complete elimination of the external cost. Cleanup technology may be so expensive to utilize that it is more efficient for the polluter to compensate the damaged parties fully than to prevent the externality through total pollution control. However, we would expect that the polluter who now bears costs commensurate with the damages he has caused will adjust his supply relationship to reduce the output of the offending activity. It is this expectation that causes many economists to favor market-type solutions (referred to as "quasi-market policies" in chapter 7) that will work through the price mechanism instead of the alternative strategy of statutory controls that may poorly reflect true preferences. An example is an effluent charge related to the amount of pollutant a producer emits into a body of water. We may compare these two types of policies by analyzing the deposit-bottles case (case 5–A).

The problem with external costs is that the producer will not have adjusted his level of production and his choice of inputs to take these costs into account. He will not be an effective calculator of his own contribution to social costs and benefits. By matching up market demand only with his own internal costs rather than with full social costs, he is likely to produce more, both of his own product and of the unwanted by-product, than optimality would require. The market supply curve understates true costs, and inefficiency results.

The case of external benefits from consumption is fairly symmetric with that of external costs. Since there are benefits accruing to others as well as the direct purchaser of a particular good, the market demand curve understates the true preferences for that good and the equilibrium output that results is below the efficient level. This result stems from the inability of a direct consumer to reflect any benefits other than his own in his market behavior so that external benefits are not taken into account. The education of a child in North Carolina may be of value to residents of California, who would be willing to help pay for that Carolina education. However, unless some way is found to reflect these California preferences, too little education may be provided in North Carolina.

COLLECTIVE GOODS:
THE EXTERNALITY TYPE

We next consider a broad category of market imperfections that overlaps in part with the cases of decreasing costs and external benefits. The term "collective goods," which refers to this category, may be defined as goods that are consumed collectively, rather than separately, by two or more consumers whose consumption cannot easily be separated. We shall define collective goods more clearly in the following discussion. We shall view this section not as identifying a new case of market failure but as more clearly contrasting previous cases and outlining combinations of cases.

In a classic public-finance article Paul A. Samuelson has defined collective goods as those "which all enjoy in common in the sense that each individual's consumption of such a good leads to no subtraction from any other individual's consumption of that good." [20] This definition emphasizes the *rivalness-nonrivalness* distinction between private and collective goods. In stating that private goods are characterized by rivalness we mean that for one person to enjoy the benefits of a shirt, some productive resources or inputs must be used up that can then not be used to satisfy the shirt preferences of someone else.[21] The two shirt demanders thus are rivals for the productive resources, and two sets of inputs would be necessary to satisfy both demands. In the case of a collective good such as national defense the resources needed to provide one submarine's worth of protection for one person can simultaneously provide protection for other individuals. Consumers of national defense are nonrivals for national defense inputs, sharing rather than competing for resources.

National defense as a nonrival good is an extreme (or polar) case of positive (or benefit) externalities. If we were to array all goods and services along a continuum that indicated the importance of positive externalities,

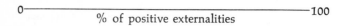

bread and shirts would be at the left end and national defense at the right end. (We shall return to intermediate cases later.) The individual bread consumer definitely cares about "whose bread it is" because only his own bread increases his well-being. However, the national defense consumer (enjoyer) does not need to distinguish between his own submarine and other people's submarines because the latter provide him with as much protection as if they were his own.

National defense is an example of one type of collective good, involving externalities, that is not only nonrival in consumption but also *nonexcludable.* When positive externalities exist, this lack of rivalness also exists and is inevitably accompanied by the characteristic of nonexcludability. A seller can exclude a buyer from consuming private goods by means of charging him a price. The exclusionary function of a price system, enforced by such things as toll booths and antishoplifting devices, seeks to prevent those who do not pay from enjoying the benefits of private goods. Prices may also be supplemented by such elements as the admissions requirements of universities in excluding potential beneficiaries. If goods provide external benefits, however, potential beneficiaries cannot be prevented from enjoying these benefits if others are already receiving them. The inapplicability of exclusionary devices is at the heart of market failure in the case of positive externalities. Although an individual could express his own interest in a market for such externality goods, his offer to buy would not reflect the benefits that would simultaneously be going to others, who would thus be able to free ride on his purchase. The automatic ability to free ride on nonexcludable goods clearly makes the market a poor means of reflecting all of the benefits forthcoming (particularly where large numbers of beneficiaries are involved) and therefore causes us to look for an alternative decision framework in an attempt to achieve efficiency in the amount of resources devoted to externality goods.

Other polar examples of externality goods are worthy of mention. Buchanan cites a case of such goods from David Hume, a case dealing with families living around a meadow that could be dredged and drained.[22] If all those families owned a portion of the soggy territory, all would simultaneously enjoy the benefits of additional agricultural property if dredging were done. It is entirely possible that although the aggregate benefits for all affected families would exceed the cost of dredging, no single family would individually receive sufficient benefits to hire the dredger on its own. Worthwhile dredging would be possible only through some collective purchase arrangement. Even if a dredging of the meadow did not improve the physical characteristics of the land, it might reduce or eliminate mosquito-breeding capabilities, thereby providing benefits to families with no property titles in the meadow itself. In such a case the dredging becomes an externality case with nonrival and nonexcludable benefits to a wider group.

Similarly, consider the case of rainmaking for a drought-stricken valley. If the technology of rainmaking is such that when it rains on one farm in the valley it rains on all, a market system based on purchases by individual farmers is unlikely to produce sufficient rainmaking services to satisfy true preferences. The same inefficient market result is apt to arise in the cases of externality goods such as law enforcement and cancer research.

The expression of "true preferences," as contrasted with falsified or strategically inaccurate preferences, is especially important in the externality good case. If farmers cannot be excluded from the benefits of rain merely because of nonpayment, they have built-in incentives to become "free riders." Attempts to obtain information about the value of rain to the farmer are likely to result in inaccurate answers, and especially answers of low monetary amounts if the response is expected to lead to a future financial obligation, such as a tax. The opportunity for free ridership with externality goods affects both the efficiency and the equity of policies made for goods of this type. Since the free rider's true preferences are not being taken into account sufficiently in the decision process, an inefficient underprovision of such a good is the likely outcome. Moreover, we may think it unfair for some people to receive benefits from activities to which they have made no contribution.

COLLECTIVE GOODS:
THE DECREASING-COST TYPE

Let us turn our attention next to examples of decreasing-cost situations, once again focusing initially on extreme or polar cases. Recalling that in decreasing-cost situations fixed costs of production dominated variable costs, we may move to a polar case in which there are no variable costs at all (marginal costs are zero). Consider the case of a bridge for which the relevant unit of output will be the number of crossings. If there is no wear and tear on the bridge from the crossings of vehicles or pedestrians, then we can say that the marginal cost of crossings is zero and that the average cost per crossing declines continuously as the output rises. Assume for simplicity that there are no congestion problems on the bridge.

In the bridge situation just described it seems clear that bridge crossings are nonrival with each other. Any single crossing imposes no resource cost on the bridge authorities and therefore does not impede or prevent further crossings. In this instance a bridge perfectly fits Samuelson's definition of collective goods. One person's crossing does not reduce at all the opportunities of others to cross the bridge. The nonrivalness of the bridge case, however, is quite different from that of the externality case. Here the nonrivalness stems from the particulars of the cost situation. For the externality case the nonrivalness is due to the interdependence of benefits.

To understand this distinction fully, let us see what would have to be true if the characteristics were reversed. A bridge could be said to have externality nonrivalness if one person's crossing automatically increased the well-being of other people, including those who never crossed the bridge. National defense would have decreasing-cost nonrivalness if the second submarine could be produced at lower average cost than the first. This type of nonrivalness would be complete if the second submarine could be produced at zero marginal cost. Without commenting on the accuracy of these revised "descriptions" of bridges and national defense, we should be able to see the importance of identifying the source of nonrivalness for all cases of collective goods.

The contrast between the decreasing-cost and externality situations is increased when we realize that bridges are *excludable* rather than *nonexcludable*. The bridge authorities are able to impose tolls and thereby exclude from the benefits all those unwilling to pay the toll. Thus, a market-style exclusionary device could be used to obtain information about the public's interest in bridge crossings (and thus bridges). The irony of the case is that the exclusionary toll, which generates market data for policy evaluation of the efficient number of bridges, itself undermines the efficient utilization of the existing bridges. In attempting to find out how many crossings would take place at $.10 each, the analyst prevents from enjoying the bridge all those who are willing to pay something less than $.10 for a crossing. In view of the presumed zero marginal cost such exclusions are inefficient.

A swimming pool may be very similar to a bridge. Once the pool is built, the water pumped in, the chemicals added, and the lifeguards hired, the marginal cost of extra swimmers may very well be zero (assuming again no congestion or maintenance costs that increase with the number of consumers). A pricing mechanism (including a high fence) could be used to exclude potential swimmers, but under these conditions it would be inefficient to do so.

There are other examples of decreasing costs that have different exclusionary possibilities. A lighthouse has relatively high fixed costs of construction and relatively small costs of operation. However, without some technological breakthrough, it would seem impossible to keep sea captains from seeing the light and thus enjoying its benefits. There are large costs of program production and transmission equipment in the television industry, but more viewers can be added without any increase in costs once the program has been broadcasted. The consumption of television programs does require the participation of viewers in the form of a television set purchase, just as highway users must buy either cars and gasoline or bus tickets. The viewer himself bears the opportunity cost of time in watching the program and of extra electricity, but the television station has no higher costs due to having more viewers of its program.[23] The nonrivalness of television does not mean that it is impossible to exclude viewers from programs. In addition to pay cable-television there is a technology to scramble broadcast television signals and to provide coin-operated descramblers, which can be attached to ordinary sets. Such systems have been used to place a price on special programs, but they have been found to be very expensive exclusionary devices for use on a continual program-by-program basis.

GOODS THAT COMBINE PRIVATE AND COLLECTIVE FEATURES

We have thus far considered only completely nonrival cases of different types of collective goods based on externalities and decreasing costs. And yet many real world situations are more realistically thought of as a mixture of private and collective characteristics. Let us begin our analysis of such in-between cases with a discussion of education. The immediate benefits of the joy of learning and the long-term value of improved earning potential are primarily available to the student. In using learning resources the student is usually a rival with others, since his being in the classroom likely prevents another from being in that same place or decreases another's chance for participation. (However, we should note that technology has somewhat blurred neat distinctions, for education by television lecture may greatly reduce the rivalness characteristic.) At the same time that these excludable benefits are being produced the rest of society (whether defined by neighborhood, city, state, national, or world limits) is probably valuing the improvement in society brought about by the production of education for individual students. Students who are better educated will presumably make that society work better, and in a democratic system their votes will influence the type of world others will live in. The production of these external benefits requires little or no extra resources beyond those needed to educate the student. Moreover, there is little way for the student or anyone else to exclude the rest of society from these external effects. Thus, some of education's benefits are rival and excludable, and others are nonrival and nonexcludable. Mixed private-collective goods have such a combination of characteristics.

The education case is one in which the nonrival external benefits are of a different sort from the rival ones. This need not always be true as is indicated in the case of garden flowers. If I plant roses in my front yard, I am able to enjoy both the visual and the olfactory beauty of the flowers together with the property right to pick them for inside use. My planting of the roses is rival to anyone else's planting of those same flowers in his own garden. However, my neighbors will likely enjoy the visual beauty of my garden, and unless I spitefully build a high fence or move the roses to an obscure corner of the backyard I will not be able to exclude my neighbors from those external benefits. In this sense roses become a partially private and partially collective good. The ability of a homeowner and passerby to enjoy garden flowers simultaneously instills a nonrival character into that product. However, the resident's right to pick those same flowers for the dining-room table adds a rivalness dimension.

In cases of a mixture of private good and external benefit characteristics we must realize that all benefits must be taken into account if we are to be faithful to the objective of satisfying preferences. This can be most accurately done through a mixed financing scheme, one that charges a price to consumers of the excludable benefits and adds a tax-financed subsidy from the public sector to reflect the nonexcludable attributes.

The case of a mixture of rivalness and nonrivalness in the decreasing-cost model was outlined earlier through the analysis of figure 5–2. This mixture corresponds to the fact that although average costs decline up to an output of Q_0, there are positive marginal costs of production. Tennis courts have high fixed costs of construction, and certain types of surfaces require periodic rolling and watering to maintain the playability of the surface. Because maintenance should be more frequent the more often the courts are used, it can be thought of as a marginal cost. The use of tennis courts by one person is then rival to some extent with other players' usage. Either the maintenance is carried out through the employment of labor, which would then be less available for other activities (e.g., tennis lessons), or maintenance is not done and later players confront deteriorating courts. Similar mixtures of rivalness and nonrivalness probably exist with highway wear and tear and maintenance. The determination of positive marginal cost permits us to prescribe the application of excludable pricing equal to that marginal cost so that efficiency norms can be adhered to, as long as the collection of the price is not itself too expensive.

The road and bridge cases have been discussed so far in terms of uncrowded conditions, which means that if marginal road maintenance costs are truly zero, usage of these facilities by travelers is nonrival. However, the situation becomes different as soon as congestion occurs. The occupation of the road by one car prevents other cars from using that same place in the line of traffic and slows down other travelers, also increasing the risk of accidents. Even though both toll collection and maintenance costs per car have not changed, congestion means that all drivers are imposing the increased costs of more expensive travel on each other. Congestion thus becomes a case of negative externalities that should be reflected in pricing if roads are to be used efficiently. Tolls that are inappropriate on uncrowded roads become more appropriate at congestion times.

This same principle can be applied in electricity rate cases where experiments in peak-load pricing are being conducted. If electric meters can be built with timing devices to provide an inexpensive exclusionary device, variations in the price of electricity among different times of the day may induce consumers to move their use of electricity to portions of the day when the company has excess generating capacity. This could reduce electricity congestion (and the possibility of blackouts or brownouts) and assure that only the users who value the product most (and are willing to pay the higher peak-load price) will receive electricity during peak periods.

There are probably a large number of examples of collective goods of the decreasing-cost type. Parks, museums, and bus transportation appear to belong to this group. Exclusion is possible for most of the benefits of these services but often not applied because it would be inefficient to do so. The possibility of exclusion is shown most clearly by the coexistence of private alternatives. Private taxicabs drive side by side with public buses. A town may provide free tennis courts even though a private tennis club already exists. A public swimming pool will be built if the political mechanism detects a sufficient willingness to share the cost through a combination of property taxes and admission fees. A private swimming club may be formed because some are willing to pay more for greater quantity or quality, less congestion, or congestion with the "right people." A family building a backyard pool is likely to have a lower "congestion threshold" or a desire to swim only with those of their own choice.

The nonrivalness of decreasing-cost services very often requires the direct participation of beneficiaries in choosing whether to consume these services. Benefits are largely provided only to the users of buses, parks, roads, and museums. This is in contrast with the nonrivalness of positive externalities, since the benefits of national defense, law enforcement, pollution reduction, or mosquito control may require no direct participation. However, there are likely to be instances that combine both decreasing costs and positive externalities. People who never visit a park may value the reduced juvenile delinquency that recreation can cause. Car drivers may enjoy the reduced traffic and pollution associated with bus systems. And the cultural heritage fostered by art museums is available even to those who do not visit the museums.

The term "collective good" thus encompasses a variety of different combinations of nonrivalness and nonexcludability. Each case deserves a full analysis to discover its attributes. Moreover, if governmental participation is involved, the type of governmental involvement should be appropriate to each service's characteristics.

DYNAMIC PROBLEMS

The theorem underlying our discussion of market failures so far concerns the comparison of various equilibrium situations in which markets may exist. It embodies the assumption of "comparative statics," according to which we ignore the processes of transition from one equilibrium to another. These transitions, however, give rise to increases or decreases in welfare and cannot be ignored in our comparison of policies.

An obvious aspect of these transitions is that they may delay the realization of welfare. Thus, as Peter O. Steiner points out, "If resources respond to market signals surely but slowly, the market process may prove an expensive way to achieve resource shifts. . . . It may well be that public policy can increase the supply of physicists [persons in a needed occupation] more quickly and more cheaply by fellowships, by research grants, etc. than the unaided market." [24] John Kenneth Galbraith points out that investment in technology necessarily slows a firm's response to the market and leads it to seek stability in other ways. [25]

The concern of economists with economic growth may be merely a matter of seeking a continual sequence of new and presumably better equilibria. [26] But if there are features of the growth rate itself that are judged to affect welfare, then this goal cannot be subsumed under the static comparison of states of the economy. Similarly, inflation not only involves transfers of real income away from those with fixed monetary incomes but also disappoints the expectations of real income to which persons may have felt they were entitled.

Economists have also been concerned with stabilization of the economy against fluctuations, especially depressions. The possible reasons for stabilizing the economy are several: Depression may be undesirable as an equilibrium state since it fails to meet the work and income preferences of many people; the total welfare resulting from boom and depression may be less than that of an average or intermediate state; and persons may be low on their preference scale because of a rapid decrease in their access to goods. They might even value stability to such an extent that they would be willing to place a monetary value on such decreases, as by purchasing insurance. The unemployment compensation program is an illustration of this.

We have noted the difficulty for workers concerning relocation and the costs thus associated with the job market. Such costs include those of "frictional" unemployment, which results from the movement of industries from one area to another or resources from one industry to another. The welfare costs of such transitional "friction" may be such that government should alleviate them, as through unemployment insurance, job training, or government payments to industry to switch product lines as imported goods take over former markets. But in anticipation of such costs those potentially affected may also act politically to prevent the transition from occurring. The promotion of the political feasibility of policies can thus involve compensation to persons potentially harmed by reallocation of resources or gradual changes from one equilibrium state to another.

OTHER ETHICAL CRITERIA

Beyond the criteria of preference satisfaction and Pareto optimality are others that are commonly used in policy choice—and indeed, that are essential if we are to make the frequent policy choice in which we are not indifferent to transfer of money or resources from one person to another. We have referred to several of these criteria in chapter 3.

"Horizontal equity," or the dictate that equals be treated equally, is a point of entry for the norms of the society that define categories within which persons are viewed as equal. Thus, if we wanted to increase productive efficiency, we might consider a selective taxation system that would motivate people who were most sensitive to the inducement of lower taxes. But such a system would be considered unjust if it penalized people who were already producing efficiently, without need of inducement. This judgment of injustice involves an aspect of horizontal equity.

"Vertical equity", the unequal treatment of unequals, includes possible justification of the transfer of income from rich to poor, which has become an increasing concern in industrial societies. To a limited extent this can be justified (or explained) as collective action to produce not only benefits to the poor but also collective goods to taxpayers in the form of social stability, a more competent labor force, and less unsightly cities. Buchanan explains the willingness of taxpayers to support such redistribution on the ground that they experience a "net utility gain." [27] But such explanation is not the same as justification. Such an observable willingness of taxpayers to give is likely to place particular emphasis on the welfare of others near to the giver, as contrasted with those far away. Thus, taxpayers or donors are usually more willing to foster the welfare of family members or citizens of their own community than of persons of another race on a distant continent. An assistance program based on such preferences would probably be geographically limited. The justification of broader transfers on ethical grounds may, however, have to be argued in noneconomic terms related to judgments that an additional dollar produced different amounts of welfare in rich and poor recipients, as we mentioned in chapter 3.

A variety of ethical criteria that run counter to the ethic of preference satisfaction may ge grouped under the economic concept of "merit goods" or its opposite, "demerit goods." These concepts refer to goods that are judged to be good or bad for consumers, *regardless* of the consumers' preferences. Health and education are examples of goods that may be involved in judgments of this sort. In either case consumers may not wish to expend the effort or resources to obtain goods or services that will benefit them only in the long run. Conversely, they may purchase products that are pleasant to use, even though the products will impair their health in the long run. Conceivably, these problems might be dealt with by supplying more information about long-run consequences. But when that is not possible, these problems involve judgment by one segment of society (or by the analyst) that run counter to the preferences of the persons affected. Thus, the Social Security program may in effect force some people to "save" more for future use in their retirement years than they would on their own, such saving being considered a merit good. The ban on laetrile was advocated by persons who felt that consumers of laetrile were harming themselves by their choice to use it, that is, laetrile was considered a demerit good.

Among the ethical criteria that run counter to preference satisfaction is the valuation of benefits to be received in the long run. For persons now living these benefits include long-run health, as in programs for compulsory health insurance or preventive medicine. The ethical criteria that relate to these long-run benefits include notions of the good life and the healthy personality, and those notions may entail efforts to persuade or educate persons to change their preferences concerning goods and styles of life. These nonpreference criteria also include some bases of justification for population policies in which not merely preferences but also persons having preferences are the subject matter of policy.

To classify a particular good as a merit or demerit good is an ethical judgment involving a conscious attempt to ignore some people's preferences. In this respect it has the same status as the economist's judgment that the satisfaction of an individual's preferences makes him better off; this, too, is an ethical judgment. These are judgments that a citizen policy analyst must make. You may decide to impose your own preferences on others, declaring in effect that "I would have bought those seat belts (or fluoridated water, or food, or education) if I had been in your shoes" or, in the case of demerit goods, "I would have abstained from smoking cigarettes." The judgments depend on the ethical systems or criteria that you have chosen for comparing policies. We can also ask whether particular collective or community decisions treat goods as merit or demerit goods. But this does not absolve us of our responsibility, especially as citizens, to decide whether such judgments are justified.

One other realm in which ethical considerations run counter to the preference ethic concerns "preferences" based on moral feelings, which we might judge to be *unrelated* to the chooser's welfare. Moral indignation may be aroused by others' actions, which elicit negative preferences and thus produce apparent "external costs." But even if we should espouse an ethic of preference satisfaction, we might choose to omit some such morally based preferences from our computation of costs. Such an omission is implied by the notion of "crimes without victims," such as prostitution, that are judged not necessarily to harm the persons involved even though they produce moral indignation on the part of others.

A final exception to the teleological ethic of preference satisfaction lies in considerations of nonteleological ethics. We may depart from judgment in terms of preferences not merely because we feel that persons should consume other ("merit") goods, but because we feel that they should act rightly in certain ways that are not directly related to consumption, regardless of the consequences of these acts. Thus, we may adopt a "work ethic," under which all able-bodied people should have a job, and reflect this ethic in a work requirement feature of a proposed policy such as President Nixon's Family Assistance Plan.

GOVERNMENT ACTION TO CORRECT MARKET IMPERFECTIONS

If we observe an instance of market failure and conclude that collective action may be justified, we must still ask what form that action should take and whether it is likely to lead to improvement in the situation. A major form of collective action is government action, but private collective action is also an alternative.[28]

A major consideration when we compare government action with private action to remedy deficiencies of the market is the relative effectiveness of the two. Private action is likely to be less efficient as more people are involved and transactions costs are greater. Government action, however, usually involves imposition of the wishes of one group on another. In this case the latter group is likely to bear costs that they have not accepted in a voluntary bargain—other than the "bargain" of their participation in the voting process that left them in the minority. If we evaluate such collective action in terms of costs and benefits, we should include the costs that it imposes. These costs do not, however, correspond exactly to votes against the policy. Individuals may sometimes vote against a policy and yet benefit from it. Elected representatives may sometimes vote against a policy even when most of their constituents would benefit from it. They may also sometimes support a policy that harms their own constituents on grounds of the welfare gains to others outside their constituencies. In addition, a policy chosen by one political system (state or nation) may produce benefits or costs for persons outside that system, a relation that is especially characteristic of foreign policy.

Government action involves not only substantive remedies for deficiencies in the market but also the necessary "maintenance of the government itself."[29] Such maintenance includes the levying of taxes, the maintenance of the legal framework, the payment of public officials, and the support of the decision process, such as elections and legislative sessions. Substantively, government action can take the form of regulation of the economy through taxation, subsidy, price-setting commissions, or legal sanctions. Taxation or subsidy can be used to adjust levels of production of industries or activities that provide external costs or benefits respectively. Prohibition (the imposition of punitive sanctions or extreme costs) can be used to remove demerit goods from the market. Goods that are judged to have only a modest amount of demerit (such as alcoholic beverages) may be taxed rather than prohibited. These regulatory functions can be regarded as placing different costs on various activities and thereby reordering citizens' and consumers' behavior. Taxation can also, of course, be a means of redistribution of income. This economic perspective, however, neglects the change of preferences that occurs through learning, a change that is also a possible effect of governmental action.

There are a variety of ways in which the government may become involved in the provision of pure collective goods or mixed private-collective goods. It may purchase a commodity for public use, as in contracting for military equipment. It may choose to be the producer and not merely the purchaser of a commodity, as has been done with police and fire protection, postal services, military personnel, and most water supplies. It may select the amount of services that will be made available to its citizens, as with national defense, space exploration, public schooling, or public recreation, though citizens may either substitute or supplement some publicly provided services through a private market. Government may also participate in whole or in part in the financing of designated services through subsidies to agriculture, tuition subsidies, or total tax-finance of flu shots. The appropriate combination of these involvements should follow from a careful study of the production-cost situation, the nature of the benefits provided, and the costs of collective involvement itself.

A third type of government intervention, which is being considered increasingly, is the creation of incentive systems or quasi-market policies.[30] These include the attachment of prices to externalities and the creation of structures that function analogously to the market. Thus, government can attach prices to the emission of effluents or noxious substances emitted by factories.[31] In the delivery of public services it can also replace single organizations by competing organizations. Programs that pay rent subsidies to poor people in private housing and thus provide alternatives to publicly owned low-rent housing can create a broadening of opportunities similar to that of the educational voucher system we described earlier. Competition among government bureaucracies to increase efficiency has also been proposed.[32]

Although economic and market considerations provide a useful basis for classifying policies, there are other types of governmental policies that do not operate exclusively through the economy but affect attitudes or preferences directly. Most important are those that change (or maintain) preferences rather than simply being concerned with the satisfaction of preferences. Education, whether in the home or in schools, can involve changes of preferences that affect both the economy and the state. The administration of justice involves not simply placing prices or costs on crimes but stigmatizing them and influencing the strength of social norms. And policies that influence the conduct of public discussion as well as the level of public taste, policies involving issues such as freedom of speech, libel, obscenity, or the costs of communication, may also involve alteration of preferences and thus go beyond the economic framework.

Democratic government itself is often thought of as a market-like mechanism for making decisions. In this view citizens register their preferences for various policy alternatives by voting and other forms of participation. But in the citizen role that we ask you to assume here you are doing more than recording your personal preferences—your prospective gains and losses—with respect to alternative policies. You are comparing policy alternatives in view of standards of the general welfare, or general moral standards. When citizens make this sort of comparison, democratic choice is no longer completely like market choice. Citizens are required to make more complex calculations, taking others' situations into account as well as their own. They are expected to try to persuade one another of the rightness of their policy choices, rather than merely adding up disparate and selfish choices. To the extent that citizens agreed on their valuative criteria and agreed on the factual means for furthering them, the criteria would approximate consensus.

It is unrealistic to expect a high degree of consensus, however, because people's values differ, even when they are considering the general good; because people sometimes consider personal or group welfare rather than the general welfare; and because the sort of analysis with which this book deals requires time and effort and cannot always be carried out by all citizens. Nevertheless, even a modest increase in analysis by citizens in view of the general welfare can allow us to criticize the market sector of the economy in reasoned terms.

Our task in this chapter has been to criticize the market, judging when it functions better and worse. We might try to judge the democratic process or particular democratic processes as well. But reform of governmental processes is often more difficult than regulation of the economy, and our knowledge of types of shortcomings of democratic processes is less precise than our knowledge of market failures. We might be concerned with fuller participation and better information for the citizen, but in a sense this entire book deals with that problem. The modification of democratic decision procedures is thus a more difficult and less precise problem for the analyst than the correction of the market.

SUMMARY

This chapter has focused on markets, both those that work well and those that do not. The basic criterion used to evaluate market performance was efficiency, as defined in relation to the satisfaction of citizen preferences.

The fundamental outlines and workings of a free market system were described so that the relationship between its activities and participants' preferences could be clearly understood. Those preferences are revealed as people participate in the roles of consumers and producers. The equilibrium tendencies of the market were outlined so that the impacts that market participants have on each other as the market attempts to perform its resource allocation function could be understood. These impacts include effects on the distribution of purchasing power among the participants.

The major portion of the chapter was devoted to conditions that prevent a market from achieving Pareto-optimal efficiency. These conditions were: force and persuasion, false or inadequate information, lack of competition, external effects, and collective goods, which include various combinations of monopoly and externality traits. We discussed the way in which each condition detracted from efficiency objectives, and we analyzed alternative corrective measures.

Finally, we considered aspects of the dynamic, or transitional, behavior of a market economy and other ethical criteria that are not reflected in Pareto optimality.

In the following chapter we shall assume that analysis has led us to recommend a best policy, and we shall examine the problems of putting such a policy into effect.

GLOSSARY

Average cost: the total costs of producing a given output divided by the number of units produced.

Collective action: joint behavior in pursuit of mutually compatible goals.

Consumer surplus: the net gain to the purchaser of goods or services; the difference between the value of the purchased items and the value of resources paid to purchase them.

Comparative statics: the study of the differences between two or more equilibrium situations in a market. This ignores the dynamic process by which a market moves from one equilibrium to another.

Crimes without victims: violations of the law that involve no harm, damage, or disutility to anyone other than the violator.

Demand: a willingness to give up resources (usually money) in exchange for desired goods or services.

Diminishing marginal utility: the characteristic of a good or service in which additional units of the good successively yield smaller increments in value.

Economies of scale (decreasing costs): the situation in which the average cost of producing goods or services declines as output increases.

Efficiency: the state of making the best use of resources. Productive efficiency is achieved when least-cost methods or combinations of inputs are used in production. Allocative efficiency is achieved when resources are divided among industries so as to reflect all relevant costs and benefits.

Effluent charge: a levy imposed on polluters that directly varies with the quantity of pollutants.

Excludability: the quality of a good that allows its benefits to be kept from potential beneficiaries through a pricing mechanism or some other rationing device.

Exclusion: the act or process of preventing people from receiving the benefits of goods or services.

External effects (externalities): the impacts (positive or negative) of production or consumption incurred by people who have not received them through voluntary exchange.

Externality good: a good that produces (positive) external effects.

Fixed costs: those costs of producing goods or services that do not vary with the level of production.

Free rider: a person who is able to receive the benefits of a good or service without having to pay for them.

Frictional unemployment: the largely inevitable characteristic of a voluntary labor market in which the people who are without jobs spend some amount of time in searching for and accepting new employment opportunities.

Internal effects: the impacts (positive or negative) incurred by market participants (other than the buyer or seller) as markets adjust to changing demand and supply situations.

Marginal cost: the increase in total costs incurred in producing one additional unit of output.

Marginal utility: the value of an additional unit of a good or service.

Market failure: the condition in which the characteristics of a market prevent it from achieving allocative efficiency.

Merit good: a good that is deemed so worthwhile that it ought to be provided to a greater extent than the true preferences of beneficiaries would warrant; similarly, a *demerit good* is one deemed so lacking in merit that the amount provided should be reduced below the level warranted by true preferences.

Monopoly: the domination of the supply side of a market by one producer (or, in an approximate sense, by a relatively few producers).

Monopsony: the domination of the demand side of a market by one or a few buyers.

Natural monopoly: the dominance of a market by a single producer who has taken full advantage of economies of scale to drive smaller (higher cost) rivals out of the market.

Nonexcludability: the quality of a good that makes it impossible to exclude people from receiving the benefits of that good (or sometimes that possible exclusion is inordinately expensive to implement).

Nonrival consumption: the utilization of a good by one person that does not keep other people from enjoying the benefits of that same good.

Nonrival good: a commodity the enjoyment of which by one person does not reduce benefits to others.

Paretian efficiency: the state of having taken advantage of all possible Pareto improvements (see also Glossary to chapter 3).

Producer surplus: the net gain to the seller of goods or services; the difference between the costs incurred in producing commodities and the value of resources received in selling them.

Pure collective good: a commodity whose consumption by one person involves no reduction in the consumption opportunities of others.

Pure private good: a commodity whose consumption (utilization) by one person prevents others from receiving the benefits of that same commodity.

Rival consumption: the utilization of a good by one person that prevents others from enjoying that same good.

Social cost: the cost of a good that reflects not only the amounts paid directly for production but also the net external cost of production.

Supply curve: a line indicating the willingness of one or more owners or producers of goods to sell various quantities of those goods at various possible per unit prices.

Transactions costs: the costs involved in negotiating and reaching agreement with respect to exchanges, rules, or laws.

Utility: a measure of worth or value.

Variable costs: those costs of producing goods or services that vary positively with the level of output.

1. Consider figure 5–1. If a new producer enters the market, in what direction will the supply curve move? What will happen to the consumer surplus after this entry? What will happen to the producer surplus of all of the established producers? Will the producer surplus for the whole market be greater or smaller than it was before the new producer arrived?

2. Explain what will happen to the prices of bread and potatoes and to consumer and producer surpluses if consumers in figure 5–1 switch from potato consumption to bread consumption.

3. Suppose that artificial rainmaking takes place, as contracted for by a single lettuce farmer in a drought-stricken valley. Indicate whether the following people will receive costs or benefits from this action and whether those impacts should be viewed as internal or external to the market:

    a. fellow lettuce farmers in the same valley, who receive rain simultaneously

    b. lettuce farmers from another state

    c. salad lovers

    d. steak-restaurant owners

    e. lettuce pickers in the same valley

    f. lettuce-crate makers

    g. corn farmers

    h. tennis-club owner in the same valley, who receives rain simultaneously

    i. tennis-club owner in the next town, who does not receive rain

4. In figure 5–1 assume that the demand and supply curves are continuous, applying to fractions of a loaf of bread.

    a. (Requires calculus) Verify that the value to the consumer of three loaves of bread is \$3.30, using the expression

    $$V = \int_0^Q P_D dQ$$

    b. Using the area of the relevant trapezoid, find the total value to the consumer of two loaves; of five loaves.

    c. If the price of bread is \$.40 per loaf, find the consumer surplus when five loaves are purchased.

    d. Find the producer surplus if three loaves are produced at \$.32 each.

    e. Find the producer surplus if five loaves are produced at \$.40 each.

5. (Requires calculus) For the supply and demand curves (linear functions) given in figure 5–1, calculate the amount of bread that would be produced by a monopolist in the situations that follow.

   a. Suppose the monopolist has control of the price (but cannot engage in price discrimination) and wishes to maximize his total *revenue*, given by QP_D. (Hint: Solve the demand equation for P_D, multiply by Q, and differentiate with respect to Q.) Assume that the demand function is continuous.

   b. Suppose the monopolist wishes to maximize his *profit*, which is equal to revenue minus cost. To do so he must set the derivative of profits (or marginal revenue minus marginal cost) equal to zero. If we assume P_S reflects marginal cost, we can set it equal to marginal revenue to find the maximum profit point. (Hint: To find marginal revenue, differentiate QP_D with respect to Q.)

6. The following types of departures from the free market model may serve as justifications for collective action in furnishing particular types of goods and services:

   fp: force and persuasion

   lc: lack of competition

   i: insufficient information

   ex: externalities

   c: collective goods

   c_1: externality type

   c_2: decreasing cost type

   eq: equity

   m: merit goods

   dm: demerit goods

   dy: dynamic problems

   a. What types of departures from the free market model, if any, may be involved in the production and sale of the following types of goods?

   (1) lighthouses

   (2) national defense

   (3) telephone networks

   (4) telephone receiving equipment

   (5) fire protection

   (11) production of energy from coal

   (12) soap

   (13) dental services

   (14) inoculation against communicable disease

(6) tennis courts

(7) parks

(8) roadways

(9) bridges

(10) clean air

(15) automobiles

(16) fluoridation of water supplies

(17) law enforcement

(18) cancer research

(19) health insurance

b. What justification, if any, might be offered, in terms of departures from the free market model, for performance of each of the following functions by government?

(1) police protection

(2) firehouse protection

(3) postal service

(4) payment of mayor and city council

(5) regulation of foods and drugs

(6) prohibition of sale of laetrile

(7) public housing

(8) public education (and job training)

(9) regulation of discardable containers

(10) day care for children

(11) stabilization of the economy against depression, inflation, unemployment

(12) construction and maintenance of roads

(13) refuse collection

(14) public provision of radio or television

(15) zoning for residential, commercial, or industrial land use

(16) regulation of labor-management relations

(17) income redistribution

(18) provision of veteran's hospitals and pensions

(19) provision of electricity, gas, water

(20) elimination of monopolies

(21) provision of consumer protection agencies

(22) enforcement of truth in advertising

(23) building and maintenance of libraries

(24) enforcement of energy conservation measures

1. James M. Buchanan, *The Demand and Supply of Public Goods* (Chicago: Rand McNally, 1968), pp. 102–08.

2. Ibid., p. 108.

3. This estimate of $3.30 is based on the continuous linear demand curve DD′, which presumes that the good in question is infinitely divisible (i.e., that fractions of a loaf of bread may be purchased). The area-type measure becomes more accurate for such calculations as we move to market-wide demand curves that more closely resemble the continuous form.

4. We sometimes define the efficiency of a productive process as the ratio of output to input. But when multiple inputs or outputs are involved we have to measure them in common terms. Monetary measurement leads us to a calculation similar to that of cost-benefit analysis, comparing the amount of preference satisfaction provided by outputs with the amount forgone in order to supply the inputs. The free-market model assumes that competition results in maximum productive efficiency. But it is also possible that general productive efficiency may be limited by the norms or the level of skills of a particular society.

5. The exact calculation of the two surpluses as output exceeds OG is somewhat ambiguous. Suppose the market price continues to fall (along the demand curve) as output rises, so there are no unsold goods to worry about. Consumers gain not only through the lowered price on the first OG units but also from the new consumer surplus on purchases beyond OG. However, the gain to consumers on the first OG units is exactly offset by a loss (of revenue and profits or surplus) of the same amount to producers. With the combined surplus to consumers and producers being the same for the first OG units, what happens to society as production increases beyond OG can be determined by looking only at the extra output. All units to the right of point E show the value to consumers (the vertical distance up to the demand curve) to be less than the value to producers (the vertical distance up to the supply curve). Thus, the decline in producer surplus is greater than the increase in consumer surplus, so that the increase in output is unwise. An alternative method of calculation, which permits the price to be set along the supply curve, results in unsold goods. Since the evaluation of unsold goods is uncertain, this method is much less precise.

6. To relate this description of an optimal solution back to the efficiency criteria described in chapter 3, we can say that point E represents a Pareto optimum in the sense that it would be impossible to find any other price and quantity combination that would not harm at least one market participant (relative to his status at E). Point E is similarly a Kaldor optimum, and any movements from E would be criticized on benefit-cost grounds since the resulting benefits would be less than the associated costs.

7. The decision-tree model of medical screening in chapter 4 illustrated a calculation concerning whether the information available from a screening test was worth the cost. When information benefits persons other than the searcher, however, we cannot expect an optimum degree of search to be conducted on grounds of self-interest.

8. These internal and external effects have frequently carried the labels of pecuniary externalities and technological externalities in the economics literature. In the hope of avoiding confusions for the reader we shall confine our use of the term "externalities" to the case of technological externalities (or external effects).

9. Francis M. Bator, "The Anatomy of Market Failure," *American Economic Review* 72(1958): 351.

10. James M. Buchanan, *The Bases for Collective Action* (Morristown, N.J.: General Learning Press, 1971).

11. Peter O. Steiner, "The Public Sector and the Public Interest," in Robert H. Haveman and Julius Margolis, eds., *Public Expenditures and Policy Analysis*, 2d ed. (Chicago: Rand McNally, 1977), p. 32. Note that collective action need not serve an enlarged public interest; some policy problems involve reducing the harmful effects of collective action.

12. For further treatment of bargaining, see William H. Riker and Peter C. Ordeshook, *An Introduction to Positive Political Theory* (Englewood Cliffs, N.J.: Prentice-Hall, 1973), pp. 252–54.

13. Buchanan, *The Bases for Collective Action*, p. 16.

14. Mancur Olson, Jr., *The Logic of Collective Action* (Cambridge, Mass.: Harvard University Press, 1965); Charles E. Lindblom, *Politics and Markets* (New York: Basic Books, 1977), ch. 13.

15. John Kenneth Galbraith, *The New Industrial State* (Boston: Houghton Mifflin, 1967).

16. Buchanan, *The Bases for Collective Action.*

17. Anthony Downs, *Inside Bureaucracy,* (Boston: Little, Brown, 1967), p. 34.

18. Two studies recommending that cities sometimes purchase services on a scale less than that of the entire city are E. S. Savas, "Policy Analysis for Local Government: Public vs. Private Refuse Collection," *Policy Analysis* 3(1977): 49–74 and Roger W. Schmenner, "Bus Subsidies: The Case for Route-by-Route Bidding in Connecticut," *Policy Analysis* 2(1976):409–30.

19. R. H. Coase, "The Problem of Social Cost," *Journal of Law and Economics* 3(1960): 27.

20. Paul A. Samuelson, "The Pure Theory of Public Expenditure," *Review of Economics and Statistics* 36(1954): 387. This type of goods is also referred to as "public goods," "social goods," "group consumption goods," or "collective consumption goods" in other discussions of this subject.

21. We assume that the shirt becomes the property of one person, rather than being shared or worn alternately by two or more persons. Even in the latter case, there would be an element of rival consumption if two persons wanted to wear the shirt at the same time or if one person's use added to the wear and tear.

22. Buchanan, *The Bases for Collective Action*, p. 5.

23. The size of the *potential* viewing audience will depend on the strength of trans-

mitted signals, which in turn will influence costs. But once transmission strength is established, extra viewers cost the television station nothing.

24. Steiner, "The Public Sector and the Public Interest," in Haveman and Margolis, eds., *Public Expenditures and Policy Analysis*, pp. 36–37.

25. Galbraith, *The New Industrial State.*

26. This aspect is stressed by Walter W. Heller in *Economic Growth and Environmental Quality: Collision or Co-existence?* (Morristown, N.J.: General Learning Press, 1973).

27. Buchanan, *The Bases for Collective Action*, p. 11.

28. Otto A. Davis and Morton I. Kamien, "Externalities, Information and Alternative Collective Action," in Haveman and Margolis, eds., *Public Expenditures and Policy Analysis.*

29. Downs, *Inside Bureaucracy*, p. 34.

30. Charles L. Schultze, *The Politics and Economics of Public Spending* (Washington, D.C.: Brookings, 1968), pp. 103–25.

31. A. Myrick Freeman, III, *The Economics of Pollution Control* (Morristown, N.J.: General Learning Press, 1971), compares effluent charges with other approaches to pollution.

32. See William A. Niskanen, Jr., *Bureaucracy and Representative Government* (Chicago: Aldine-Atherton, 1971); Buchanan, *The Bases for Collective Action*, p. 17; J. A. Stockfisch, *The Political Economy of Bureaucracy* (Morristown, N.J.: General Learning Press, 1972).

Deposit-Bottles

This case is chosen to illustrate the types of policies that may be considered when production or consumption gives rise to an external cost. Since this article was written, several additional states have passed laws requiring deposits on beverage containers or enacted other related policies, and federal legislation has been proposed.

CITY DEPOSIT–BOTTLE PLAN FACES LOBBY THAT KILLED SIMILAR BILLS ELSEWHERE [1]

In the New York City Council, a proposed law to require returnable beverage containers has been sponsored by 28 Councilmen, well over a majority of the 44-member body.

The bill, known as Intro No. 345, has the enthusiastic backing of many Councilmen who say they would like to stop the growing litter and garbage problems caused by cans and bottles tossed away after one use.

But Intro 345 is given no chance of becoming law.

"It's going no place," said a source close to the Council. "It's politically dangerous."

Costs Are Raised

Bills almost identical to Intro 345 have been introduced across the country in the last few years as the tide of nonreturnables increased sharply, but most of these bills have died because of one of the most intensive lobbying campaigns in recent history.

The pressure against the so-called "bottle bills" has been mounted by a coalition of industries and unions that see their economic gains threatened. Its members include the steel and aluminum industry and can and bottle makers.

Many of the arguments against the bottle bills lean heavily on costs.

"There is no question that the Oregon law [which has required returnables for almost two years] and additional expenditures for highway cleanup have improved the litter situation there," said William F. May, chairman of the American Can Company, "But it has come at quite an increase—about $10-million a year—in the cost of beer and soft drinks for the people of Oregon."

Mr. May said the change-over to returnables meant added labor costs in bringing back the bottles. But supporters of the bill argue that the returnable system is cheaper because the bottles are used over and over again.

Rising costs of beverages, supporters of the bottle bills say, have been caused by other factors, such as rising prices for raw materials and even the arbitrary raising of prices by bottlers who wanted to prove their own point that going back to a returnable system would cost more.

It would be much too costly to go back to a returnable system all over the country, Mr. May said, because the nation's distribution system is now designed for a one-way type of container. Rather than destroy the current distribution system, Mr. May said, it would be more efficient to improve the collection of waste and then remake or recycle it into useful things—like new bottles and cans.

Much at Stake

Mr. May, who is also a member of the board of directors of The New York Times, said beverage containers represented $450-million worth of American Can's total sales of $2.5-billion a year.

The battle against the ban on nonreturnable beverage containers is so intense because the stakes are so high. The glass-bottle-manufacturing industry, which has been booming on the wave of nonreturnables, would produce many fewer bottles if they were used over and over again.

Cans virtually would be driven out of the beverage market, because no one has yet devised a way to make them reusable.

For the canmakers, a recent study showed that beverage containers represented $1.8-billion of their annual sales. About half of all cans manufactured in this country are for beverages.

The introduction of nonreturnable bottles—or "convenience packaging" as it is called in the industry—[coincides with and may be a major factor in] a sharp increase in beverage consumption. Between 1959 and 1972, consumption of soft drinks and beer rose by 33 per cent per capita.

U.S. Gives Figures

The increase has not been without its cost to the environment.

In testimony in favor of a nationwide bottle bill, John R. Quarles Jr., the deputy administrator of the Federal Environmental Protection Agency, said that during the time that beverage consumption had risen 33 per cent, the number of bottles discarded had gone up by 262 per cent—from 15.4 billion in 1959 to 55.7 billion in 1972.

While containers make up only 8 per cent of the solid-waste load, Mr. Quarles said, they now account for between 54 and 70 per cent of the volume of highway litter. Containers, he said, are also the fastest-growing segment of the waste load—increasing 8 per cent a year.

In addition, Mr. Quarles said, the use of throwaway bottles is a waste of resources and energy. He said that the making of beverage containers now con-

sumed between 1 and 2 per cent of the energy used by all of the nation's industries. Reusing beverage containers would save 92,000 barrels of oil a day, he said.

Used 10 Times

Nonreturnable bottles, because they only have to last for one time,
are cheaper to make than the sturdier returnables. A recent study by Beverage
Industry magazine put the cost of a thousand nonreturnable 12-ounce soft-
drink bottles at $42.33, compared with $83.42 for the same size returnable.

But the extra cost of a returnable is recouped with increased use. In
Oregon, studies have shown that returnables make at least 10 trips.

Lobbying pressure was brought to bear here in 1971, when the first
legislation against nonreturnable containers was drafted by the city's Environmental Protection Administration, then headed by Jerome Kretchmer.

"The opposition was very, very tough," Mr. Kretchmer recalled recently. "The beverage people said 'this will ruin our business, drive us out of
town and leave unemployment.' "

"Schaefer [the F. & M. Schaefer Brewing Company, one of the city's
two remaining breweries] threatened to cancel their sponsorship of the park
concerts," Mr. Kretchmer said, "and they said, 'Get this guy Kretchmer off our
backs; we're an important industry to New York City'."

Other Matters Involved

Alvin E. Heutchy, vice president of F. & M. Schaefer, said the other day
that it was more than just the park concerts that were in danger when the bottle
bill had a possibility of becoming law.

"We told them we would have to reconsider a lot of other things we
were doing to help the city if this [the bottle bill] went through," Mr. Heutchy
said.

"If you ban the cans and if you have only returnable bottles, then our
business would be so seriously hurt we wouldn't have the money to sponsor
anything."

As a result of this pressure, no bottle bill has even approached becoming
law here.

The coalition against Intro 345 is called the New York Industry-Labor
Committee for Resource Recovery. It is headed now by Sidney P. Mudd, president of the New York Seven-Up Bottling Company.

Early this year, just after Mayor Beame's administration came into
office, Mr. Mudd sought—through Paul Buiar, a public-relations man influential
at City Hall—an audience with Robert A. Low, the new Environmental Protection Administrator.

'Well-Organized Group'

"If you can sit down with a man in a private room and let him know how you feel," Mr. Mudd said, "you can generally get your idea across."

Mr. Mudd sat down with Mr. Low, and Mr. Low recalled later that he was impressed "that it was a well-organized group opposed to the bottle bill." "He [Mr. Mudd] said he represented a lot of people—the soft-drink people, the beer people—and that they were important to the city's economy," he added.

Mr. Low is responsible for getting rid of the city's garbage—and its quantity seems to grow constantly. After some study, he said he was in favor of a bottle bill, but not for New York City alone. He said it should be enacted by the Federal Government because "if it were enacted on such a narrow geographical basis, industry could pick up and move to another area."

This year, the principal sponsor of Intro 345 is Councilman Monroe Cohen, Democrat of Brooklyn. Mr. Mudd said he also had talked with Mr. Cohen.

"I told Cohen that if the bill were enacted, industries would shut down, thousands would be out of work and the city would suffer economically," Mr. Mudd said.

2d Councilman Comments

Mr. Mudd said that Mr. Cohen replied: "Oh my God, Sid, I didn't know anything like that could happen. I'm glad you told me."

Mr. Cohen said he had been told by bottling companies that they would go out of business, but said he had not really checked their contentions.

A Brooklyn Councilman, Frederick W. Richmond, said that while he is in favor of reducing the city's solid-waste burden, he is concerned about what he had heard from the city's two breweries, both of which are in Brooklyn.

"Conversations by members of my staff with both Schaefer and Rheingold indicate that such a law might force Schaefer out of New York City and Rheingold out of business," Councilman Richmond said.

"It is clear to me," Mr. Richmond said, "that while citizens will support any effort to clean up the environment, even if it causes inconvenience, the public also expects that government should insure that no one should be summarily forced into unemployment or welfare because of environmental efforts."

Some of those who believe they would be affected adversely by the bottle bill are angered by any show of support for it.

"I was incensed at The New York Times," Mr. Heutchy of Schaefer said, recalling editorial support for the bottle bill. "Those who live in paper houses are going to get burned," he added, saying that most litter is paper.

The opponents are now confident that the bottle bill is dead here, but heavier ammunition is available if it is needed.

"I think we've made our point," Mr. Mudd said. "I don't think anything is going to happen here now, but I have to run scared."

The caliber of that ammunition may be illustrated by what happened in Erie County, which includes Buffalo, where last May a bottle bill came to a vote in the County Legislature.

One of the major proponents of the Erie legislation was a group called Housewives to End Pollution. They gathered more than 14,000 signatures within two and a half weeks to show what support the bill had among the citizens.

"Then the thing that happened with the unions really scared us," said a leader of the housewives' group, who asked that her name not be used because she was still afraid of what would happen to her or her family.

Four-Hour Meeting

"I am now completely disgusted with the democratic process," the woman said.

The group's leader said A.F.L.-C.I.O. and Teamsters Union representatives had met with them for more than four hours, emphasizing that the legislation would not be allowed to pass.

"It was a chilling experience," the woman said. "They told us, 'We've checked you all out. We know who your husbands are and where they work and how many children you have.' "

The woman said a man who said he was from the Teamsters told them that even if the bottle bill did pass, it would have to be vetoed by the County Executive—"He's in the liquor business and he knows we'll get him."

The Erie County Executive is Edward V. Regan, who retains an interest in his family's wholesale liquor business, the Bison Liquor Company. Mr. Regan said the company dealt with the Teamsters but had received no pressure on the bottle bill.

Mr. Regan said he took no stand on the bottle bill because it had been voted down in the County Legislature. If the bill had reached his office, he said, he would have held a public hearing. He said he had taken no stand because "there's not much point in a public hearing if everybody knows where I stand."

'In Retaliation'

During the Erie County battle, Buffalo television station WBEN-TV ran an editorial favoring the bottle bill. George Torge, the station's general manager, read the editorial over the air and immediately several breweries canceled their advertising.

Did they say why they withdrew the advertising?

"They sure as hell did," Mr. Torge said. "It was in retaliation to the editorial."

Morley Townsend, an Erie County Legislator who also is a lawyer doing legal work for Pepsi-Cola, told friends privately that he had been warned that there would be "economic repercussions" for him if he voted for the legislation.

Last week, Mr. Townsend, who did vote for the bottle bill, refused to talk about the matter, other than to say he was still a lawyer for Pepsi-Cola.

"It's a private matter, and I'd rather not discuss it," Mr. Townsend said.

A key document that the Erie County Legislature used in support of the bottle bill was a detailed economic analysis by Dr. Clark W. Strausser, an associate professor of economics at the Johnstown campus of the University of Pennsylvania.

Stand Reversed

His study, a 200-page presentation, was paid for by a $4,000 grant from New York State's Council of Economic Advisers.

Although his report, published last November, favored a bottle bill for Erie County, shortly before the vote was taken in May, Dr. Strausser reversed himself and said he no longer favored the measure.

Puzzled supporters of the bill said they had some difficulty in reaching Dr. Strausser immediately for an explanation.

Last week, however, Dr. Strausser said, "I went at it in a relatively naive way when I did the study originally."

Dr. Strausser said that he had not been pressured by opponents, but that he had gotten "some new figures from the beer industry that I believed."

The figures were for the amount of solid waste caused by beer containers. Previously Dr. Strausser said he had used figures compiled by the Federal Environmental Protection Agency.

Dr. Strausser said he believed the beer industry figures more because "they were worked out on a state basis, while the E.P.A.'s were national."

Deposits Vary

Vermont has followed Oregon's lead in requiring mandatory return deposits on beverage containers.

Oregon's law has a two-tier system. A five-cent deposit is required on bottles that are distinctive to one brand. A two-cent deposit is required on standard beer bottles that may be used interchangeably by all companies.

The idea behind the lower two-cent deposit was to encourage the use of standard bottles that could be returned anywhere, making the returning job easier.

Vermont's original bottle law did not have the reduced two-cent feature, and bottlers, in an attempt to get the Vermont legislation repealed, made a strong point of the difficulty of returning bottles to different places.

In an attempt to strengthen the Vermont law this year, Sam Lloyd, a Vermont legislator from Weston, introduced amendments to institute the two-cent standard bottle deposit and to outlaw flip-tops on metal cans.

The night before the amendments were to be voted on, Mr. Lloyd said, he received a telephone call from John Carbine, a Rutland lawyer representing the Glass Container Manufacturers Institute. He said that $100,000 worth of "corporate money" would be available to study the whole situation if the amendments could be dropped.

Versions Differ

Mr. Lloyd said that he did not drop his support of his amendments, but that they were defeated in the Legislature anyway.

Mr. Carbine said he did not recall offering any set sum of money. He said he just wanted to say that the facilities of the National Center for Resource Recovery were available for help.

That national center in Washington is supported by opponents of the bottle bill who say that the way to control waste is to collect it and separate it and try to sell it for raw materials.

Legislators have regularly been given free trips to pilot plants set up at places such as Franklin, Ohio, and Elizabeth, N.J. to demonstrate the feasibility of this idea. So far the projects have not gone beyond the pilot stage.

Legislators in Vermont were also offered free trips to hockey games by brewers opposing the bottle bill.

But most of the free trips for legislators around the country are listed as strictly educational.

"All we do is give them a sandwich and a ride (often by private plane) to the facility," said Blair Smith, vice president of environmental affairs for the American Can Company in Greenwich, Conn. "There is no alcohol. It's not a wining and dining situation. We have tried to make an educational effort."

Prices Go Up

Proponents of the bottle bill say they have no such funds for educational efforts nor can they manipulate the market to make their point.

In Vermont, the opponents charged that returnable bottles would be more expensive, so they raised prices when bottles were required to be returned. In other places where both returnable and nonreturnables are sold, the beverage in bottles that can be re-used is cheaper.

"It's funny that the prices of all the companies went up uniformly," said Vermont's Attorney General, Kimberly B. Cheney, who is still looking into that situation.

"They're doing everything they can to defeat it [the bottle bill]," Mr. Cheney said, "but there's no question that it's working in cleaning up litter— and it's the first step in trying to do something about the throwaway society."

In New York State, Attorney General Louis J. Lefkowitz has, since 1972, proposed statewide legislation to ban nonreturnables. It has failed every year.

Connecticut Bill Fails

"Usually environmental cleanup has to be balanced off because it costs something to do the cleanup," says Philip Weinberg, Mr. Lefkowitz's assistant for environmental affairs, "but here is something that would save money [on the cost of beverages and the cost of handling solid waste] and still the legislation doesn't get any place."

Connecticut's House of Representatives last May killed an attempt to ban the throwaway containers.

William L. Churchill, chairman of the subcommittee on nonreturnables, said he went at the state's expense to study the Oregon experience.

"I found the situation there somewhat questionable," Mr. Churchill said. "There was an awful lot of false information on both sides."

Mr. Churchill and other Connecticut legislators also went down to Atlanta, to the Coca-Cola headquarters. The trip was paid for by Coca-Cola.

"It wasn't a social occasion at all," Mr. Churchill said. "We spent the whole day at the plant. It was really a good backgrounder for us. They were very concerned that we understand their marketing problem."

Note

1. David Bird, *The New York Times*, 8 July 1974. © 1974 by The New York Times Company. Reprinted by permission.

Oil in East Texas: Markets and Regulation

Late in 1930 a new oil pool was discovered in East Texas. It proved to be the largest known pool in the world at that time, and its exploitation caused economic chaos in the United States oil industry. In a matter of six months the price of crude oil fell from $1.00 per barrel to $.10 per barrel. As a result, great pressures were brought to bear not only in Texas but elsewhere to regulate oil production. After oil regulation was enacted, the governors of Texas and Oklahoma had to declare martial law in an effort to enforce such oil regulation.

A study by Warner E. Mills, Jr., emphasizes the legal and political aspects of this situation.[1] In the discussion that follows we will use the case as an illustration of the workings of a market and the interests of producers and consumers within that market. Relevant data will be used to show how we can estimate relationships that are important in this case. The importance of the political jurisdiction facing the regulation decision within a nationwide market is outlined. And finally, the relevance of externalities and monopolistic elements in regulation decisions is discussed. The East Texas case thus illustrates many of the principles and ideas of chapter 5.

History

At the time of the East Texas oil strike, the United States had already begun its economic slide in the Great Depression. The decline in the mid-continent price of crude oil from a 1929 average of $1.36 per barrel and a 1930 average of $1.23 to the January 1931 price of $1 was due in part to the weakening demand of the depressed economy.[2] The national crude-oil production of 2,100,000 barrels per day in January 1931 was also lower than it had been as both state regulatory authorities and producers themselves responded to the decline in demand and prices. In terms of figure 5–1, the reduction in demand shows up as a leftward shift in DD' and a new equilibrium at both lower price and lower quantity.

In January 1931 only three wells were operating in East Texas, and they were producing a mere 10,000 barrels daily. By the end of March East Texas crude-oil production had risen to 90,000 barrels daily from almost 100 wells. During that month the price of crude oil fell to $.70 per barrel, causing great consternation throughout the industry. Governor "Alfalfa Bill" Murray of Oklahoma convened a meeting of representatives from oil-producing states, but no concrete results were forthcoming. Governor Ross Sterling of Texas, founder of the Humble Oil Company, was so discouraged about the ability of the state regulatory authorities (the Texas Railroad Commission) to control the situation that he proposed that a new state commission be created to perform the task. Even before the East Texas discovery, Texas was by far the largest oil-producing state, accounting for almost one-third of the nation's output in 1930. Thus, the price decline caused a substantial reduction in the Texans' "producer surplus," the type of surplus described in chapter 5. The reliance of the Texas state government on oil-tax revenues and of the University of Texas on oil royalties meant that Governor Sterling also had to be aware of the public-sector implications of the oil market.

Early in April 1931 the Railroad Commission issued orders restricting East Texas output to 90,000 barrels a day, but those orders were ignored as more and more wells were brought into production every day. By May East Texas wells were producing more than 250,000 barrels daily, and the glut on the crude-oil market sent prices plummeting to $.40 per barrel. The Texas legislature adjourned without passing new oil legislation, and a Texas Oil Emergency Committee was formed by producers from other parts of Texas, calling for a special session of the legislature. With the price down to $.20 per barrel and East Texas production at 350,000 barrels, attempts were made to have the East Texas producers voluntarily restrict output since the Railroad Commission orders had been challenged in the courts and had not proved enforceable.

On 8 July 1931 Governor Sterling called a special session of the Texas legislature to consider new ways of dealing with the crisis. As this session struggled with the questions of defining regulatory standards and selecting the agency to carry the standards out, the price of oil continued to fall as output climbed, reaching a peak of 738,000 barrels daily in East Texas in early August. Governor Murray closed more than 3000 Oklahoma wells under martial law, cutting production by 300,000 barrels and threatening to keep them closed until the price returned to $1.00.

The Texas legislature passed a new regulatory law on 12 August. However, Governor Sterling, aware that it would take some time for the Railroad Commission to establish quotas and fearing that a wasteful surge of production would occur prior to the effective implementation of those quotas, declared martial law on 16 August. Troops were sent to East Texas to prevent acts of violence between producers and to shut down the 1600 wells of the world's largest known oil pool. The effect of martial law in the two largest oil-producing states was to reduce production by an amount equal to one-half of what the nation's output had been at the beginning of that year.

The curtailment of crude-oil production had a rapid impact on prices as oil buyers posted a price of $.68 per barrel before the end of August. The Railroad Commission set a 400,000 barrel per day limit on East Texas production, and the field was permitted to reopen early in September. With the market stabilizing and output remaining under tight control, the price of oil by January 1932 was $.83 per barrel and production was less than ten percent above the level of a year earlier.

REPRESENTATION OF KEY DATA

Table 5B–1 and figure 5B–1 provide the key data from the historical outline given here of one of the wildest years in United States oil-industry history. The various price and output observations are plotted in figure 5B–1 under the assumption that they are different points on the same demand curve. There are two major reasons why this assumption may be incorrect. On the one hand, some of the production may have gone into involuntary storage and was not used to meet the immediate demands of oil consumers. Secondly, the demand curve may not have remained unchanged over the twelve-month period shown, especially since the national economy was contracting during this time, and we might expect the demand curve to have gradually moved leftward. Nonetheless, it appears reasonable to assume that the demand for oil was relatively stable over the short period covered. The demand curve is drawn to approximate the observed points shown in figure 5B–1.

In figure 5B–1 we are assuming that each of the six observed points represents one point on six separate supply curves. In other words, as more wells began producing oil in East Texas, we can say there is a new supply relationship, representing a new willingness on the part of producers to put this good on the market. However, this view may be inaccurate since it is apparent that state regulatory authorities influence, if not set, outputs in many parts of the industry. Where this is the case, the supply curve shown may not represent the profit-oriented decisions of the producers themselves.

A further complication of interpretation arises if the six points each belong to one of six different supply curves, for then we have no knowledge of the

Table 5B–1.

Oil Prices and Output Levels, 1931–1932

Date	Oil Price per Barrel	US Daily Oil Output	East Texas Oil Output	Other Texas Oil Output	All Texas Oil Output
January 1931	$1.00	2,100,000	10,000	670,000	680,000
March 1931	$ .70	2,260,000	90,000	650,000	740,000
May 1931	$ .40	2,430,000	256,000	665,000	921,000
July 1931	$ .20	2,540,000	380,000	720,000	1,100,000
October 1931	$. 68	2,360,000	400,000	600,000	1,000,000
January 1932	$. 83	2,200,000	290,000	515,000	805,000

Source:
Various 1931 and 1932 issues of the *Oil and Gas Journal*.

Figure 5B–1.
*Supply and Demand Curves for Oil, 1931–1932.**

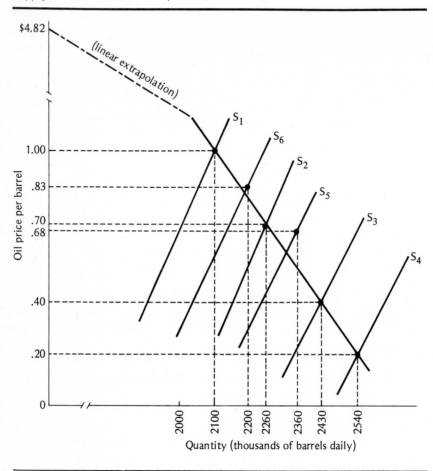

* Plotted from table 5B–1.

shape of the shifting supply curves. It seems clear from news reports for that period that many oil producers were inclined to produce less at lower prices, a relationship in line with the analysis of ordinary supply curves in a free market model. However, there were some producers whose decisions seemed little affected by the price situation, for reasons to be discussed later that are peculiar to the oil industry. We follow the standard market model in assuming positive-sloped supply curves in figure 5B–1.

The description given of the oil industry in 1931 does not mention the situation faced by petroleum consumers. The demand curve shown in figure 5B–1 provides a means of estimating the impact on consumers as the price of oil fell from $1 to $.20. Prior to the East Texas discovery, the consumer surplus can be shown to be the triangle under the demand curve and above the $1 price, or an amount of approximately $4 million per day. The fall in price to $.20 expanded the consumer surplus by the area of the trapezoid between $1 and $.20 and over to the demand curve. This additional consumer surplus can be estimated to be $1.86 million per day.

Because of the lack of data concerning costs and the true supply relationships, it is not possible to provide estimates of the impact of price declines on producer surplus. However, we can observe from table 5B–1 that production in other parts of Texas and in other states was very similar in July to the January totals of 670,000 and 1,420,000 barrels respectively. If we assume that production elsewhere was unaffected by the price, then in this case the price reduction of $.80 per barrel could be translated into a $536,000 daily loss for other Texas producers and a $1,136,000 daily loss for producers in other states. In the light of these figures it is small wonder that oil producers were up in arms all over the country.

Jurisdictional Considerations

But what was the reason for governmental involvement in the oil industry? To understand the issues more clearly, let us first ignore the existence of state boundaries and think only of a national market. And let us also change the product to coal, assuming that new coal deposits had been discovered. To show this situation, let the coal market be in initial equilibrium at point F in figure 5B–2. Prior to the new coal discovery there is a combined consumer and producer surplus (or net gain from having the coal industry) of triangle AFD. If the newly discovered coal can be mined more cheaply than previously known deposits, the supply curve will shift down to curve S_2 and a new equilibrium will be established at point G. At the lower price and higher output of coal, the combined consumer and producer surplus becomes BGD, a clear improvement for society as a whole. Any attempt by society to restrict production to some amount less than that indicated by point G can only reduce the overall gain. However, this does not mean that everyone gains from the new coal discovery. In particular, the established coal producers, who used to have a surplus of triangle AFE will find that surplus reduced to triangle AHC after the new mines begin to produce coal. There is thus strong motivation for established producers to attempt to prevent or minimize the extra output from cheaper mines, just as Texan oil producers in areas other than East Texas did. However, if the government is to take account of the economic interests of society as a whole at equilibrium, it should reject those producer pressures for output restrictions.[3] In this case it is not economically wasteful to permit new coal operators to supply the market up to their maximum willingness.

This conclusion about the welfare of society may need to be modified if

Figure 5B–2.
Supply and Demand Curves for Coal.

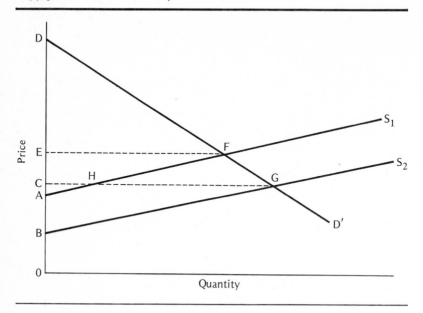

the society under consideration constitutes a political jurisdiction that is only a portion of an economic market. Returning to the Texas oil case, let us recall the estimated loss to producers in other parts of the state as oil prices fell off $536,000 per day. East Texas producers may have been gainers as they brought their newly found product to market. But that gain cannot have exceeded their oil revenues of $76,000 per day (380,000 barrels at $.20 per barrel), and this figure can be accurate only if such production was costless. There were of course gains available to oil consumers in Texas, but the latter were clearly only a small portion of the oil-consuming public. Census figures for 1930 show that Texans comprised five percent of the United States population. We could thus estimate consumer surplus gains by Texans to be five percent of the $1.86 million per day figure calculated above, or $93,000 per day. These three estimates together show that Texans as a group would seem to have lost at least $367,000 per day as a result of the oil price decline following the East Texas discovery. This suggests that a governor of Texas need not think of narrow interests of one group of constituents but could be considering the overall welfare of Texas in advocating controls on oil production. Where production is more heavily concentrated than consumption, it is not surprising that political subunits will have incentives to become involved in production and pricing controls. The recent examples of oil in the Middle East and coffee in Brazil illustrate this point very well.

The Nature of Oil
and the Presence of Monopoly

If we return to the broadest societal perspective, is there any reason for governmental involvement in the oil industry? Are there significant differences between oil and coal? The answer to the second question is yes because the liquid nature of petroleum and its resulting underground mobility create some rather unique problems in that industry. The physical nature of oil is largely responsible for its property-right link to the "rule of capture," which states in essence that the person who possesses the oil shall own it. Such a ruling was handed down by a Pennsylvania judge in the mid-nineteenth century when he asserted that oil was like a wild animal, it was no one's property until captured. This meant that a person was entitled to keep all oil coming from his well, regardless of whether it had physically been drawn from under his own land or the land of his neighbors.

This rule of capture has characterized and plagued the oil industry ever since. It clearly provides an incentive to "take from your neighbor before he takes from you." This legal precedent appears to inject an element of negative externalities into the process of oil production. If one person draws oil from his well, he is almost certainly drawing oil from under the property of his neighbors. In so doing he is imposing a cost in the form of reduced assets of oil reserves on his neighbors without their participation or consent. In addition, removal of oil by one producer reduces the underground pressures that assist all petroleum production and thereby increases the production costs of all other drillers into the same pool. Note that these negative externalities among producers are separate from and in addition to the internal effects of output on the prices received by other producers. Those internal effects could occur in oil, coal, potato chips, or toothpaste and are part of the natural equilibrating mechanism of a market. On the other hand, the external effects (in this case negative ones) caused by the underground mobility of oil, natural gas, and water are an example of market failure. This means that the supply behavior of individual oil producers fails to reflect the full costs of producing the good since some of it is essentially "stolen" from others. Therefore, the supply curves are too far to the right, and some means of restricting oil output may be in order if a proper balancing of consumer values and true producer costs is to be achieved.

The most obvious way of avoiding these negative externalities in oil production would be by single ownership of each oil pool. This clearly was not achieved in the East Texas case, to some extent because of the huge size of that pool and the reluctance of the major oil companies to become involved soon after the discovery. With so many owning property above the pool, many thousands more wells were drilled than were necessary for the oil ultimately recovered. Yet each producer viewed each well as essential to protect his own stake in the pool. The excessive drilling was made worse when the Texas Railroad Commission attempted to set production quotas (proration) on a per well basis. The initial

East Texas allotment in September 1931 was 225 barrels per well daily. This encouragement for further drilling into the same pool was so great that in order to keep output in line the quota had to be continually reduced. By the end of 1932 each well was allowed to produce only thirty-three barrels a day. This is indicative of the excessive drilling costs caused by the chosen method of prorationing production.

In the absence of single ownership of an oil pool the externalities resulting from the rule of capture can largely be eliminated by so-called unit production, which had worked successfully in West Texas and had been instituted early in 1931 in a large California pool. Under unit production all owners of property over a given pool share in the production of that reservoir of oil. Output decisions for the whole pool are made to take maximum advantage of underground pressure and thus maximize total recovery. This voluntary method of prorationing output provides assurance that one producer's stake in the pool cannot be "stolen" by his neighbors. The poor reception that suggestions of this sort received can probably be traced to the fact that many of the East Texas drillers were newcomers to the oil business and unfamiliar with the feasibility of such sharing arrangements. In addition, many of them had financed their drilling operations with short-term bank loans. There was therefore a fear that output restrictions might so reduce income that they would be unable to pay off those loans. The difficulty of achieving voluntary collective action in the form of unit production in East Texas illustrates the importance of a mutual sense of confidence in other participants and of some mechanism of enforcing agreements.

Although we have suggested that the rule of capture tended to place the supply curve for oil too far to the right and thus encourage production beyond the level that true costs would permit, there is a possibility of tendencies in the opposite direction. Many of the small East Texas producers viewed attempts at prorationing as a strategy by the large oil companies to monopolize the business. They thought the enforcement of output quotas would mean bank-loan defaults, with the major oil companies then being in a position to take over the wells at a very low price. Thus, the major oil companies could have had a dual objective in advocating production controls: first, an immediate rise in revenues and profits as oil prices rose and, secondly, the chance to buy up more East Texas wells quite cheaply and so extend their dominance in the industry. As we indicated earlier in the discussion of market failures, the existence of monopolistic elements is usually interpreted as restricting output in the attempt to maximize profit. This would mean having a supply curve that is too far to the left relative to the true cost environment.

We are thus left in this East Texas oil case with a great need for data to analyze divergent forces generated in an imperfectly operating market. Even if the decision unit was not the individual state but the nation as a whole (today, that might more properly be the world), the restrictive tendencies of monopolistic elements would have to be weighed against the excessive output tendencies brought on by the rather unique property rights of oil itself. The ultimate efficiency level of oil output selected from society's broadest perspective might be either above or below the output equilibrium established in a not-so-perfect market.

Notes

1. Warner E. Mills, Jr., "Martial Law in East Texas," Inter-University Case Program 53 (Indianapolis: Bobbs-Merrill, 1960).

2. Temporary National Economic Committee, *Petroleum Industry Hearings* (New York: American Petroleum Institute, 1942), p. 226.

3. This assumes, of course, that all dollar gains and losses are equally weighted in society's overall calculations.

6

Political Feasibility: Enactment and Implementation

As a policy analyst, you cannot be content to choose the alternative that would produce the best results *if* carried out. You must also examine the conditions under which a policy alternative is likely to *be* enacted and carried out, including the effects of your own activities.[1]

We refer to these conditions as the conditions for *political feasibility*— the degree of possibility that the policy will be carried out. Political feasibility, which depends on the actions and interactions of human beings, may be distinguished from technical feasibility, which involves our capacity to design and produce devices that will perform given tasks.

In this chapter the term "political" will be interpreted broadly to refer to the exercise of influence or power. It will not be restricted to the actions of governments, but will extend to influence within organizations and among persons. It thus includes all the types of influence that an individual or group may mobilize in support of a proposed policy. Your influence as a citizen is not restricted to voting. You also have the opportunity to communicate orally or in writing, to publicize your case through the mass media, to recruit support, and to persuade groups and officials to support your proposed policy.

The problems of putting a policy into effect are so important that some experienced observers see them as dominating the entire process of analysis. Graham T. Allison, for example, asks, "What percentage of the work of achieving a desired governmental action is done when the preferred analytic alternative has been identified?" He estimates "about 10 percent in the normal case," implying that problems of feasibility can require as much as ninety percent of the work. A half-century earlier Max Weber cautioned his students who were considering politics as a vocation that "politics is a strong and slow boring of hard boards." [2] If you take these admonitions seriously, you can understand why the advice given to the citizen, or to anyone who wishes to influence policy, is often *entirely* political or administrative—how to gain access, how to organize groups, how to protect oneself from the tactics of others, how to make sure that organizations put policies into effect. Even with this advice, we must recognize the great complexity of large political systems and their resistance to change.

The assessment of feasibility must actually begin from the moment that you consider working on a problem. You must make an initial estimate about whether the analysis is worth your time and effort. Part of this estimate may be a quick assessment taking into account the resources that must be devoted to the analysis.[3] But another important part is your judgment of the chance that people will act on your eventual recommendations. This latter judgment may lead you to consult others who are familiar with the political system in question, who control valuable resources, or who can make decisions.

Even while you are carrying out your analysis, you will be wise to be aware of possibly changing conditions of feasibility that will influence the response to your recommendations. If a key official is replaced while you are conducting your analysis, it may be worthwhile to take time out to acquaint the new arrival with the problem and your part in it. If you are working in a community or heterogeneous group, you may wish to report to them periodically in order to be sure that their view of the problem has not changed or the priority they give to it been reduced. Rules, regulations, deadlines, and action-channels also often change during your analysis, and you must check these conditions periodically.

FEASIBILITY AND THE SOCIAL ROLES
OF THE ANALYST

The interaction between the analyst and those who make and implement the policy is thus a process that goes back to the first stage of analysis. In definition of the problem, formulation of criteria, choice of alternatives and models, and collection and interpretation of data, the analyst may well improve the results if he consults with the clients or public whom he wishes to serve.[4] Among the persons he consults, he must also judge who can be most influential in aiding or blocking his proposals.

You may, of course, become part of an organization in which it is your responsibility to assess the desirability of alternative policies and someone else's to assess policy feasibility. But even in this situation, some attention to feasibility can be useful.

In the type of course for which this book is intended, you may be asked to analyze and report on particular cases. This type of assignment relieves you of the responsibility of deciding whether a given problem is worth your effort. But the artificial aspects of these classroom exercises should not lead you to forget that in real life the decision whether a problem is worth analysis, in view of your time and other resources, is often yours.

The social roles that you occupy are of central importance in your decision concerning what you can effectively do. The role of citizen, which we all occupy, might appear to be that of an isolated individual. But if we wish to influence a collective decision, we must ordinarily join with others to do so. We may try to take advantage of group memberships that we already possess, persuading our neighbors, fellow employees, or fellow members of a political group that a problem exists and that certain policies should be adopted. We may also form new group ties in seeking support. Our involvement in these groups exposes us to the views of others, who present their own definitions of problem situations. We may respond to these definitions by acting in agreement with them; by trying to change them; or by inaction, if we find insufficient support and judge other activities more important.

One particular role we may occupy, which is more constrained than that of the citizen, is that of the employee. We have centered this book about the citizen-analyst because only the citizen is truly free, in principle, to choose the system of values that he wishes to further through policy choices. Once we accept employment we enter into a contract to further the goals of the employing organization through our work. Especially in political organizations aimed at general values, we may engage in policy analysis as employees. When we do so, however, our problem situations are likely to be defined by our superiors, and our opportunity to redefine problems may be limited.[5] Yet if our values have entered into our choice of employment, our actions in our jobs may still serve the values that guide us as citizens.

When you try to increase the feasibility of a policy proposal, we assume that the principal means you use will be persuasion, communication, and organization. The range of actual means for furthering policies, however, is far wider. It includes the mobilization of public support by organized lobbying, publicity, or campaign management; the use of threats or rewards in bargaining; public demonstrations including civil disobedience; and the ultimate use of deception and force in espionage, guerrilla warfare, and outright warfare. Analysis can precede the use of any of these approaches to feasibility. But as we move toward the use of threats and force, we are using analysis itself less and less as a means of obtaining support. A tacit assumption of this book is that analysis is valuable in public communication. We thus stress those approaches to feasibility that are more likely to incorporate the use of analysis in persuasion.

The role of the advocate differs somewhat from that of the analyst. An advocate is committed to a particular type of policy or to the interests of a particular group. Conceivably, one may be an advocate of the public interest. But commitment to a particular public-interest group can involve adherence to a narrow and particular ethical criterion—stressing, for example, the interests of consumers and not producers or one social class and not others. This commitment may be justifiable in the terms of this book if it is based on an ethical system. But it can sometimes lead to an unwillingness to reconsider policy positions that a group has chosen or a lack of openness to new analysis from diverse sources.

To maximize the feasibility of policies that you wish to put into effect, you must acquire some understanding of organizations, politics, particular political systems, and yourself, as well as skills of communication and influence. Later in this chapter we shall discuss some general features of this understanding, but much of it has to be learned through your own experience. Detailed case studies, internships, and actual participation can supplement the general principles that we present.

You must learn to assess the potential support and opposition to a proposed policy and to consider how support may be developed. This assessment involves judging degrees of support and the sources of possible change on the part of persons or groups, as well as more detailed judgments based on knowledge of the personalities involved and the particular past relations among participants. It also involves knowledge of potential modifications of policy proposals that will increase support or decrease opposition, as well as knowledge of arguments and counterarguments. You must learn the actual and prospective arguments of others, not only to influence them or anticipate their actions but also to respond to them rationally. The arguments directed by others against your proposed policy, even if they are related to material or organizational interests of their proponents, may nevertheless have merit and serve to test the validity of your analysis.

If you are a member of an expert or professional group, you may be tempted to regard your own profession as providing objective advice and others as revealing material interests or biases in judgment. But it is well to try to take a broader view, to see and understand the positions of various organizations and professions.[6] Such a perspective is important for assessing the feasibility of implementation as well as enactment, since special occupational groups are often involved in implementation.

ENACTMENT AND IMPLEMENTATION

Whether a desirable policy is put into effect depends on its being officially enacted and then on its being carried out, or implemented. Each of these two aspects of feasibility presents characteristic problems, and neither can be ignored.

We may say that a policy has been *enacted* when it has been approved at the necessary authoritative choice points.[7] For a state law these points might include approval by legislative committees, passage by two houses of the legislature, and signature by the governor. For an administrative regulation within an organization, only the approval of the president or administrative head may be required. If policy choices involve changes in the law, these may take place through changing precedents in court decisions. Constitutional provisions may be changed through amendment and sometimes by revolution.

The complexity of problems that can arise in the enactment of a law is illustrated by the history of President Nixon's Family Assistance Plan from 1969 to 1971.[8] First, the proponents of a negative income tax had to gain the ear of the president. Then, after the drafting of the proposal, they had the difficult task of seeing that it was approved by the Ways and Means Committee of the House of Representatives and by the House itself. After House passage, Senate passage seemed to the proponents relatively easy. But the bill was in fact defeated in the Senate Finance Committee, as it faced a combination of politically skilled conservatives and outspoken advocates of greater welfare aid to the poor. At each of numerous stages calculations of feasibility and efforts at persuasion had to be made. Systematic substantive analysis played a modest part in the arguments used, but problems of feasibility of enactment were far more difficult.

For the enactment of some policies, numerous people with authority to make choices must decide. Allison gives the example of a set of possible policies considered in 1969 for the creation of a new medical school in Massachusetts.[9] An early stage of enactment was the Medical School Bill of 1962, which authorized site selection and the appointment of a dean. The dean, once appointed, began expanding the existing plans. In 1968 the Board of Trustees of the University of Massachusetts chose Worcester as the site. Federal grant applications were submitted, and some were approved. But when Francis W. Sargent became acting governor of Massachusetts in January 1969, the question of whether the state should support the new school still remained open. A number of authoritative decisions had been made, but they were not sufficient to provide the resources for the school. In that sense the policy of creating the school had not yet been enacted.

The complexity of this public choice (of which we have reported only a part) illustrates that enactment can involve a long sequence of decisions. In this respect it resembles implementation. Some of the stages in enactment carry only part of the authority necessary for implementation. The approval of a plan by a legislature or a city council does not necessarily provide resources, and there may be expectations that the plan will be modified over time. We should not, therefore, think of enactment as limited to a single decision.

Formal choices are also supplemented by informal ones. Individuals who can gain access to officials may have more influence than others. The ability to telephone officials or call them by their first names can make a difference. Interest groups and political parties, even though not recognized in a constitution, have important influences on legislation. And some policies may in fact be made without official enactment, through the development of informal agreement on a new way of treating or deciding cases of a given kind. The informal development of compliance or support for a policy is often as important as the formal expression of the policy on paper.

The mere enactment of a policy does not insure that it will be put into effect. Enactment corresponds to an initial general authorization on paper of a policy or program. The *implementation* of this policy comprises all the further steps for the provisions of the policy to be put into effect. Some of these steps may be additional written statements from superiors to their subordinates for the detailed carrying out of particular parts of the policy. Lowering the speed limit, for example, requires not only the posting of the new limit on road signs but a change in enforcement practices if most drivers are to reduce their speed. A new mode of teaching may be officially chosen by a school board, but will not necessarily be adopted by teachers unless they have learned how to teach in the new way and are motivated to do so.[10] Not only administrators (police, teachers) but also their clients (drivers, students) must learn to comply with the new policy.

Only when the activities specified in the policy have been carried out can we say that the policy has been implemented. But the examples of speed limits and teaching show that we need to make clear what these activities are. Do they end with police chiefs' telling their officers how to enforce the limit, or with the officers' actual enforcement activity, or with a change in behavior on the part of drivers? In case 4–A we assumed that implementation ended with enforcement activity and that driver compliance was involved in a model of *consequences* of the policy, not a part of the policy itself. Similarly, a policy that affects teaching can be taken to include the implementation of changes in teachers' activities, but not changes in student behavior. We need to make a clear distinction between the implementation of a policy and the consequences of the implemented policy, in order to understand just what our models of consequences include.

The implementation of a policy, like its enactment, can involve either one, a few, or many decisions or actions. When a community decides to fluoridate its water supply, implementation of this decision requires only the placement of the required amount of fluoride in the water periodically. Other policies, however, require the participation and cooperation of numerous organizations.

The decisions made in implementation differ from those in enactment in that they do not involve authorization by the entire community. Rather, the necessary actions may ramify out into smaller agencies and bureaus, each of which is expected to carry out part of the overall policy. These smaller parts of organizations, whether newly established or already existing, usually operate independently of one another. They do not have to come together to carry out their parts of the process, as representatives in a legislature come together to pass a law.

Once a policy is communicated to the organization that is to carry it out, persons at numerous levels in that organization must do what is required. The organizations that carry out policies are typically bureaucratic—that is, people in them are employed and paid to carry out their superiors' instructions —but this does not guarantee that they will do so promptly and faithfully.[11] If a new policy runs counter to the values or habits of those who are to carry it out, it may be delayed or modified.

We have considered a policy to be a written statement that is enacted and implementation to be a process leading from that statement to a later state of affairs that we can describe. We expect most policies to be put into effect only partially or with some delay. The later state of affairs will in turn have consequences that we value or disvalue. For example, a policy for desegregating schools may specify that certain racial proportions be obtained. Several years later the proportions may still not be exactly as specified. The consequences of obtaining these actual proportions may include changes in students' test scores, intergroup attitudes, and their earnings and civic participation in the longer run.

The models that we use to choose policies are usually aimed at predicting these later consequences in relation to our criteria. We can try to predict these consequences in two ways: from the enacted policy or the implemented policy. What we really want to know is the entire causal relation from the proposed or enacted statement to the ultimate valued consequences—for example, from the requirement of racial mixture to long-run patterns of earnings. If we predict the valued consequences from policies *as if* they were implemented, we are omitting the process of implementation as it transforms the enacted policy. We thus need to combine two kinds of models: a model of implementation and a model predicting the valued impacts of the policies implemented. We can study these two models separately or try to combine them in one larger model.

Regardless of whether we analyze the enacted policy or the implemented policy, however, the implementation of a policy is not to be taken for granted. It requires positive cooperation on the part of some persons and requires that others refrain from opposing it. The same sources of opposition that appeared in the enactment process may reappear during implementation.

COLLECTIVE DECISION SYSTEMS

When you as a citizen are seeking the enactment of a policy, you will be involved in the decision system of a political community. To assess the feasibility of enactment of a policy, you must form a picture of the system within which this process occurs. Some political communities are hierarchical. Examples are a company town or a city tightly controlled by a political machine. Others are looser in structure, involving numerous uncoordinated organizations and associations. It is with this latter type that we shall be largely concerned.

Political systems may also vary in their degree of consensus or conflict, ranging from a community agreed on the values relevant for a problem to a system of nations in conflict about their vital interests. In the case of extreme conflict any decisions that may be reached cannot be said to be collective or authoritative as much as the result of bargains accepted by each participant in terms of its own interests or as the result of force.

Among these systems of collective decision it is sometimes suggested that democratic political processes reflect and combine preferences in a fashion similar to the market. Yet democratic and representative politics, like the market, can sometimes fail to further the general good, even in terms of an ethic of preference. Individuals or groups may be threatened by a prospective policy and may have the power to block it even though it has aggregate advantages for others far greater than prospective costs to the threatened groups. Groups with special resources may also cause policies to be enacted that further their particular interests to the detriment of others. Thus, we cannot take the results of a given political process as automatically furthering the general welfare or the ethical system we support.

We assume that you are seeking enactment of a policy in a democratic system that is not extremely hierarchical or conflictual. The most general task you will then face will be to induce various supporters of your policy to act together. You may take actions aimed at influencing only one decision center or group, such as lobbying with a state legislative committee or trying to influence the position of one important group. But the distinguishing feature of citizens' activities for enactment of policies is their *collective* character—the drawing together of groups.

This collective feature is less characteristic of decisions taken within bureaucratic structures. In implementation of policies we more often seek out persons in bureaucracies who control particular parts of a policy, and we are less likely to have to draw these people together than when seeking enactment. Even when we seek enactment, a highly organized governmental structure such as that of the federal executive provides less opportunity for drawing groups together than do most local communities. Thus, in writing of bureaucratic governmental politics, Allison points to well-defined action-channels, to players in positions, and to relatively formal rules of the game.[12]

Organizations

The community in which you are seeking enactment will usually include organizations as well as individuals. These organizations, private or public, are involved as parts of the collective decision system. But for enactment we assume that you are not operating entirely within a bureaucratic organization. A central aspect of your assessment of feasibility of enactment is thus your judgment regarding how persons in organizations will act.

The political world of the late twentieth century is largely a world of organizations, both bureaucracies and voluntary associations.[13] There are and have been political worlds where the most important participants are individuals rather than organizations, as, for example, in small towns, college departments, fraternities, or medieval kings' courts. But here we are concerned mainly with policy choices in which individuals participate through their roles in organizations. These roles provide them with incentives that are internal to their own organizations, and these incentives in turn lead them to choose certain external strategies for their organizations.[14] The bureaucratic organizations that enter politics may be either private (firms) or public (parts of government). The voluntary associations in politics include interest groups, groups organized about notions of the public interest, and political parties.

Your own opportunities for action within an organization differ considerably depending on whether the organization is a bureaucracy or a voluntary association. In a bureaucracy if you are a member, you are an employee. You are not expected to organize your fellow employees to vote on changing the organization's policy. In a voluntary association in which you pay dues, you may try to organize fellow members to elect officers and vote on internal policy matters without risk of being fired.

To understand the actions of organizations, you may begin by considering their *typical* intentions—the goals, constraints, and tactics that are characteristic of, let's say, an elected official, a newspaper editor, the head of a chamber of commerce, an educational administrator, or the leader of a professional association.

Even though organizations have typical intentions, we must also remember that these intentions characterize them only in general and that specific exceptions exist. First, individuals in groups with special interests do sometimes act in the general interest. They are not simply economic or political men and women in a narrow sense. Second, individuals have unique personalities, goals, and resources, which cannot be ignored. This second corrective leads us to the case-study approach, to the viewpoint of the historian, to internship programs in policy training, and to consideration of "sensitivity training" for students of policy analysis. Thus, the intentions of groups may be studied and known by social science, but they also partake of voluntary choice and thus resemble strategies in games rather than determinate predictions.

A useful rule of thumb is to assess the expected positions of individuals and organizations, especially bureaucracies, in terms of careers, organizational interests, and constituencies. As Rufus Miles has expressed it, "Where you stand depends on where you sit." [15] This rule assumes that individuals and organizations will act to maintain or increase material rewards such as the budget share of an organization, the career prospects of an organizational employee, or the support of a group that will assure a politician's security or advancement in office.

These stands or positions do not result simply from a desire for material gain, however. They are supported by systems of ideas relative to what the organization's proper function is and how it relates to the larger society. For example, the central mission that the Air Force sees for itself may be "the flying of combat airplanes designed for the delivery of nuclear weapons against targets in the Soviet Union." [16] That which the Children's Bureau sees for itself may be to serve children, but to do so in a way viewed by outsiders as passive and quality-oriented. [17] In each case this central mission or "essence" comes to be supported and justified by persons in the organization; and, at least in the case of the Air Force, members come to believe that an increasing budget and more personnel for this purpose also serve the public interest. [18] This perspective also directs our attention to the standard operating procedures through which organizations are prepared to act. [19]

Organizations and persons in them also respond to the wishes of constituencies on which they depend. A legal constituency is the collection of citizens who are entitled to elect a representative. But in less formal terms a Republican congressional representative's constituency may consist primarily of the Republican voters in his district, of the organizational leaders in his party there, of interest groups whose support he expects, and of persons or organizations whom he expects to contribute to his next campaign. The notion of a constituency can also be extended to bureaucratic constituencies. The Joint Chiefs of Staff look to the Army, Navy, and Air Force as their constituencies. In the New York school system in the 1960s, one superintendent was regarded as a "high school man," enjoying particular support from the high school principals and encountering difficulties when his policies threatened them.[20]

Coalitions

We can then regard organizations, with their typical or actual goals, as analogous to building blocks or chessmen from which combinations may be formed in our quest for feasibility of enactment.[21] These combinations, or *coalitions*, involve mutual obligations assumed for the duration of the quest for enactment or longer. Coalitions may seek the majority needed for enactment or sometimes a larger consensus that will affect feasibility or their capacity to act together later.

Within this perspective various organizations and their members may be seen as seeking somewhat different goals within a larger political system. Each organization may be seen as playing in a "game" of its own. Thus, in a community there may be "a political game, a banking game, a contracting game, a newspaper game, a civic organization game, an ecclesiastical game, and many others."[22] In various political systems these games may be separate or coordinated, cooperative or competitive.

The case studies in this book provide examples of coalitions that might be formed between organizations. In the city-growth case (case 3–B) both minorities and realtors are interested in permitting growth. Their organizations, though not usually allied, might cooperate in opposing growth-control policies. In the Texas case (case 5–B) regulation of oil production would raise the price of oil, thereby benefiting both the established oil producers outside East Texas and the University of Texas, which derived revenue from previously existing oil pools. A natural affinity therefore existed between administrators at the University of Texas and established oil producers, whether they were actually allied or not. In the deposit-bottles case (case 5–A) managers and workers in the bottling and beverage industries were allied in opposing regulation of disposable beverage containers, even though management and labor are often in opposition on other issues.

These examples illustrate that organizations or groups of individuals may join with one another because of specific common interests they have in favoring or opposing a particular policy. These common interests may vary from material gain or resistance to threats to income, to commitment to ideas such as those of rights or the "essence" of an organization.

Your opportunities to form such combinations will vary from one situation to another. The relations among organizations and their resources and goals may allow greater or less latitude for the furtherance of a particular policy. In a monolithic or hierarchical power structure the goals of a dominant organization or person may be determining. In a highly polarized conflict situation, especially where two rival organizations have obtained commitment from nearly all participants on one side or the other, the opportunity for analysis or for proposal of new policies may also be small.[23] The possibilities for new policy initiatives may depend not only on available operating procedures but also on the categories in which policies are typically viewed.[24]

Though assessment of feasibility often takes existing political structures as given, it is also possible to try to change them. The founding of new organizations is an important political alternative. So is the reorganization or reform of existing structures. Examples are the reform in Congress of the Rules Committee and the later formation of the Budget Committees.[25] Among organizations with fixed structures and goals we may consider allocating a new function to the one with the most appropriate "essence," as we choose among action-channels within a larger structure. In addition, political action may be directed to cause internal conflict within an opposing organization or coalition, to cause it to lose membership, or to cause those on one's own side to become more united. Such options, though politically important, are extremely difficult to assess in terms of their ultimate costs and benefits to the public.

PROBLEMS OF IMPLEMENTATION

Although enactment and implementation take place within similar organizational environments, that of implementation involves public bureaucracies and deserves special attention in this respect.[26] The characteristic features of implementation are indicated by the following example involving solid-waste collection in New York City:

> The head of the Sanitation Department conceived the idea of adopting a new truck with a larger, mechanical container which would reduce the manual chores required in picking up materials and persuaded the Mayor to agree. This was followed by a press conference at a parking lot in Brooklyn in which the Mayor and Sanitation officials, including the head of the union, watched as the borrowed truck did its work for the television cameras. The Mayor made a speech and shook as many hands as possible. After that the trouble began. Union representatives and the department's chief medical officer challenged the safety characteristics of the new truck. The Bureau of Motor Vehicles challenged the size of the truck. But once this was settled the Purchasing Department held up the order of trucks because of an opinion of their own about the proper size. By that time the Mayor's office had lost interest in the whole thing and was deeply into the political campaign. The final implementation of the plan, promised for 1969, came in 1972.[27]

This example illustrates that numerous organizations have to do their part for a policy to be put into effect. Sometimes these organizations overlap one another, as the labor unions in our example overlap with the sanitation department. What is important is that each organization must concur before the policy can be carried out. Each has an effective veto, much as each of a number of officials must often "sign off," or give his or her approval, in order for a national policy to be approved by the executive.[28]

It also shows that the mayor's decision to "enact" the policy could be merely symbolic; he seemed to want the publicity more than the policy itself. Here, as in many other instances, enactment *and* implementation require *continued* commitment by leaders if they are to take place. The mayor's involvement in the political campaign changed his priorities and commitments. Thus, mere distraction can defeat the implementation of a policy. The same problem can arise for enactment. President Nixon's Family Assistance Plan was initially defeated by the Senate Finance Committee. The invasion of Cambodia, announced during the Finance Committee hearings, produced a wave of opposition to Nixon and the plan. International policy was higher in President Nixon's priorities than domestic policy. Later, the 1972 presidential election campaign also changed his priorities. It then became more important to him to oppose Senator George McGovern on the welfare issue than to push further for his Family Assistance Plan.

The fact that the policy for the new trucks *was* implemented in 1972 shows that sometimes the passage of time will allow a policy to be put into effect. As long as someone in authority continues to work for the policy, it may eventually return to high enough priority on others' agendas. Having once been considered, a policy may become familiar to participants, though because of its familiarity it may also find opponents with ready arguments and tactics as well. Its "seniority" may sometimes gain it priority relative to more recent proposals. Older "pending" policies may in fact be brought forth and discussed as a means to delay current ones. The passage of time is not always helpful to a proposal, however. It may allow opposition to grow or support to fade.

To cope with difficulties such as these, the first remedy is to try to anticipate them. The person who "has the action" for enactment, like the floor manager of a bill in Congress, must look ahead to avoid guiding the implementation of a policy into a lethargic, preoccupied, or resistant organization. Sometimes there will be little choice. The sanitation department, for example, collects solid waste, but for some related policies an analyst might consider private contractors instead. At other times, especially for a new program, he will be able to choose between two or more existing organizations as well as setting up a new one. If a new organization is set up, he will also have to see that it is viable.

An example of this type of anticipation was the struggle during the Nixon administration concerning whether policies affecting children should be placed in the hands of the Children's Bureau or elsewhere in the Department of

Health, Education and Welfare (HEW).[29] The Children's Bureau, established in 1912, was not a typically aggressive agency; it had made only modest claims on the federal purse when new opportunities arose. When the Nixon administration considered transferring the Head Start program from the Office of Economic Opportunity to some agency in HEW, a controversy arose about which agency should have the program.

> The traditionalism and maternalistic style of the Children's Bureau discouraged the child-development activists of the sixties from using the bureau as the focal point for an expanded program of federal intervention in early childhood. Neither aggressive in style not innovative in program, the bureau seemed out of touch with the issues of children in poverty, the special problems of black children, child-care programs for working mothers, early education for cognitive development.

The bureau did have "an outside constituency of middle-class matrons," which had some appeal to Republican administrators. Nevertheless, a new Office of Child Development was formed and given the responsibility for Head Start, and the Children's Bureau was bypassed.[30]

In addition, it is important to try to anticipate problems of implementation during the enactment process when you are seeking support. For formal enactment of a policy by a legislature, a bare majority may be all that is needed. But often if there are groups and organizations whose support is needed in implementation, their additional support may be important to obtain in advance. In the decision process during the Cuban missile crisis President Kennedy wanted to be sure that the armed services were adequately consulted, not merely because of their possible reactions afterward but in order to be certain that the plan adopted was properly carried out.

Implementation, though of vital importance, does not come as readily to citizens' attention as does enactment. Citizens who ignore implementation, however, may find themselves deceived by "policies" that are merely symbolic. In order to see farther than the early stages of policy enactment, citizens must take advantage of the intimate knowledge of federal, state, or municipal bureaucracy that insiders possess or, in the longer run, acquire this knowledge themselves. To some extent this information can be obtained from public documents, but a more reliable source is the advice of persons with long experience in government. In cities and towns this information is available locally. In a state or national capital it is available through lobbyists associated with citizen groups, through present or past officials, and through lawyers who work with government. If you are preparing a bill for the legislature, you may need to use this type of information to channel the policy to a receptive agency. If you are watching to see that a policy is put into effect, you will also want to know which persons or groups in the implementing agencies are likely to favor or oppose the policy.

A final condition for implementation (and for a continued campaign for enactment as well) is the monitoring of outcomes.[31] You must find ways of checking regularly on the progress of the program and make sure that this information is not biased by any "dressing up" of the program for the benefit of outsiders like yourself. Organized interest groups, with active supporters in the legislature exercising "oversight of administration," have advantages in carrying out this sort of monitoring. Systematic research on the impact of a program, taking the form of evaluation studies, is a way of checking both on implementation and on the adequacy of the model underlying the program. We shall consider this type of research in more detail in chapter 7.

We have now discussed the processes of enactment and implementation separately, including particular ways in which you may approach each process. Bureaucracies, though they play a part in both processes, enter into them differently. In enactment these organizations operate as parts of a larger decision system in which coalitions may be formed. In implementation each bureaucracy is more likely to function separately.

We next consider three problems that arise in similar ways in both enactment and implementation of policies: agenda setting, indirect influence, and personal feasibility.

AGENDA SETTING

Regardless of whether you are seeking enactment or implementation of a policy, you are likely to face the task of getting your policy on the agendas of people who are to act on it. This means more than simply influencing a general public definition of the problem situation; it concerns the specific priorities of legislators, executive officials, and administrators. (Courts also have dockets and priorities. Their decisions may further policies, stop their implementation, or compensate people who have been harmed by them.)

Such a set of specific priorities has been referred to by Roger W. Cobb and Charles D. Elder as the *institutional agenda*—"that set of items explicitly up for active and serious consideration of authoritative decision makers."[32] Examples are the agendas of "a township meeting next Wednesday evening, [and] the President's State of the Union message."[33] You will be primarily concerned as an analyst with items that are to be considered for action, not merely for bargaining, symbolism, or study.

You must be aware of your opportunities for influencing a decision system in order to choose among the possibilities. You may try to influence the public definition of the problem situation. However, a proposal may be widely supported yet not be officially before any decision makers for action. Conversely, it may come before a decision maker even though it is not widely known by the public. Thus, you must be concerned with the channels through which action can occur.[34] It is possible that several alternative action-channels exist, in which case you must choose which one or ones are most appropriate.

If we are acting as citizens in a democratic system, placing a proposal on the agenda of an elected official is usually closely related to developing or sensing popular support for it, especially support within that official's effective constituencies. To develop support, we may consider various methods of redefining problems such as we discussed in chapter 2. In a campaign for fluoridation of the water supply (case 6–A), for example, proponents conducted studies of the extent of tooth decay and arranged to have the results presented in the press. Proponents may also publicize the extent of concern with an issue to increase this concern, present individual cases of personal hardship related to the problem, or relate new problems to old ones with which people are already concerned. In all these sorts of communication, however, we face a dilemma between using more and less rational means of persuasion.

Whether or not the decision system is democratic, we may wish to gain the cooperation of persons or organizations with various goals and perceptions of the problem. In a system with such diverse centers of influence, it does not suffice to place an item on the agenda of a single decision maker. The diverse participants must make their own decisions. Our task may then be to place the item on the agendas of various people or groups, taking into account the distinct emphases that each places on particular aspects of the problem. Even if the decision system centers about one or a few persons, the press may still sometimes be used to gain their attention.[35]

When you wish to see that a program is implemented in its various aspects, you may have to follow it up to see that it remains on the agendas of various organizations and groups. School busing and desegregation, for example, require action by planners, school administrators, teachers, and bus drivers as well as cooperation by parents and children. The blockade initiated during the Cuban missile crisis required coordination of numerous naval vessels and their crews.

Ordinarily, we expect that decisions and orders from the person in charge of a bureaucratic organization will assure that the agendas of all participants give priority to the policy as initially defined. If, however, you suspect as a citizen that an organization is redefining a policy or giving it lower priority, you need to find out what various parts of that organization are doing. President Kennedy faced such a problem in making sure that the 1962 blockade of Cuba was not unduly provocative to the Russian ships approaching Cuba. He therefore monitored the actions of individual ships and their commanders.[36] He had to make sure that the agenda of the ships' commanders included not simply a "blockade," as interpreted in the *Manual of Naval Regulations*, but also the communication to the Russians of a precise degree of concern by the United States government.

Your task as a citizen, in bringing your policy to the agenda of an organization, is not the same as that of an employee or official *in* the organization. If you were a governmental official who wanted to involve the president in furthering a policy, you might seek his attention by going through channels, starting with your superiors or an official decision-making group. You might also be able to go to him alone and persuade him, or you might go through his staff or others who have access to him.[37] Similar approaches are needed for lower ranking officials.

As a citizen, however, you approach officials from outside their organizations. In a democracy your opportunity for influence derives more from your potential for influencing electoral support. You can expect greater access to a legislator if you are one of his or her constituents. Even an expert will often find it easier to gain the ear of a congressional representative if the expert comes from the representative's district. National organizations trying to influence Congress often develop campaigns of persuasion through their members who are leaders or campaign contributors in individual representatives' districts.

If you approach the executive branch, your approach is more likely to be through agencies that are divided in terms of function—health, education, welfare, commerce, labor, energy, agriculture, science—than through geographical constituencies. Interest groups develop ties with executive agencies that serve them, agencies that they can also support at budget time through legislators allied with them. You may be able to make use of channels of this sort to see that a policy is being implemented, if you have the support of the relevant interest group. This sort of commitment may not always be consistent with the general interest, however. A group with ties of this kind may be unwilling to criticize policies by which it itself gains at the expense of the taxpayer.

The priority that a policy occupies on an official's agenda may also vary with the general sense of importance that people attach to that policy. Early in a new administration its leaders' sense of the importance of certain policies is communicated to government officials, especially when the executive has many jobs to offer as rewards. As enactment proceeds, participants also sometimes gain a sense of "momentum" for a proposal and are more inclined to see their own participation as effective. A proposal that loses this sense of momentum usually loses supporters and moves down in the priority of its remaining supporters, receiving less of their energy and attention. The symbols that define a problem situation also affect people's enthusiasm, as we noted in chapter 2. Presidential speeches have this effect, and public evidence that a group has popular support may produce similar results.[38]

The choice of agenda items for enactment or implementation thus involves organizations, constituencies, persuasion, and symbolism. Your own skills in oral and written communication of the results of your analysis can play a part in this choice. You will need to speak and write clearly, to write brief memoranda for busy officials, to present data in readable tables and graphs, to adapt your message to your audience and to sense an audience's reaction, to meet counterarguments, and to communicate to the public as well as to leaders.

INDIRECT INFLUENCE

We have noted that if you want to influence a decision you may be better able to do this by working through an intermediary than by attempting to influence a decision maker directly. You may be able to influence the intermediary, who can in turn influence the decision maker. Such indirect influence is common in politics. You should be aware of it, and be able to judge when it should properly be used.

An example of an effort at indirect influence is the following account of attempted influence by General Motors and Procter & Gamble, through Blue Cross as an intermediary, on the enactment of a proposed Consumer Protection Agency.

> Two corporate giants, General Motors and Procter & Gamble, have used their economic clout to block the establishment of the proposed Consumer Protection Agency.
>
> White House sources tell us that both companies threatened to withdraw business from Blue Cross unless the medical insurer softened its support of the consumer agency. Blue Cross insures approximately 750,000 General Motors workers and about 50,000 Procter & Gamble employees.
>
> President Carter has endorsed the Consumer Protection Agency, which would become the consumers' official advocate in Washington. But many corporations fear it would develop into a bureaucratic Ralph Nader that would constantly hound them. Business lobbyists have been swarming over Capitol Hill, therefore, to oppose the creation of the new agency.
>
> But the Blue Cross Association, in behalf of its 84 million members wrote a strong letter to President Carter on June 1 supporting the proposed agency. "We do not look upon the Agency for Consumer Advocacy as a potential opponent," declared the letter, "but as a partner in identifying consumer issues and meeting consumer needs."
>
> We have checked out the next development carefully with trustworthy sources. They say that Blue Cross executives heard from both General Motors and Procter & Gamble.[39]

We use this example to illustrate indirect influence, regardless of whether it is an exact report. The corporations in question had potential influence over

Blue Cross because they could threaten to withdraw business from Blue Cross by taking their employees' insurance elsewhere. This influence had nothing to do directly with the proposed Consumer Protection Agency. But since Blue Cross was a potential supporter of that agency, the corporations could try to use influence to reduce Blue Cross's support for it.

The cases included in this book provide other examples of indirect influence. In the deposit-bottles case (case 5–A) a group known as Housewives to End Pollution was organized in Erie County, New York, to favor legislation for deposit bottles. But union representatives from the affected industries met with the housewives' group. One housewife who was afraid of what would happen to her family reported that union representatives had told them, "We've checked you all out. We know who your husbands are and where they work and how many children you have." The threat was not explicitly reported, but the unions were apparently threatening personal or economic harm to the women's families.

In the fluoridation case (case 6–A) the proponents of fluoridation obtained the aid of a newspaper writer who lived in their Massachusetts community. As a result, "a series of articles on fluoridation was published in one of the major Boston daily newspapers." But earlier in the campaign for fluoridation, "it was discovered that every week anti-fluoridation material was included as part of a regular radio broadcast on a major Boston station. Through contacts with the radio station and certain advertisers, it was possible to secure the removal of this highly biased material from the series of programs." The proponents used both direct and indirect influence here. But influence through the advertisers was more indirect, since the advertisers' influence on the radio station's revenues was not connected with the fluoridation issue.

Indirect influence, as shown in these examples, sometimes seems improper. Examples of this sort are often cited to show that large and powerful organizations use their resources unfairly or unethically. But our purpose in discussing indirect influence is to lead you to consider using it yourself. Although you may not have the resources of a corporation, a labor union, or an advertiser, you may still command friendship and obligation that can be used to support a policy you favor. You should be aware of the possible use of resources of this sort either for or against your policy and consider whether you should use them yourself.

You may in fact develop resources for indirect influence by political or organizational efforts over a period of time. A skilled politician once defined politics as "the art of putting people under obligation to you." From the earlier leaders of Tammany Hall to contemporary leadership in the House of Representatives, such obligations have been used to promote policies.[40] The obligation may be generated by one sort of favor, such as attending a funeral or providing a political appointment, and used for quite another sort of policy.

Obligations of this sort are not only created by skilled politicians but they are also honored, and a politician who fails to honor obligations loses much of his reputation and thereby some of his influence. One is obligated to repay key supporters, especially those who have been of aid at crucial times. One is obligated to show loyalty to one's own followers, whether in a bureaucracy or in the coordination of a campaign for the enactment of a policy.[41]

In the last analysis, however, as you consider using indirect influence, you must consider not only whether you can do so but whether you should. The issues involved are those of "personal feasibility."

PERSONAL FEASIBILITY

These pictures of influence may differ from those of nonpolitical life in seeming Machiavellian. They may seem to involve an amoral or manipulative view on your part. We have tried to compensate for this by explicit attention to ethics at the start. These ethical considerations must include the creation or maintenance of norms, or of "rules of the game." Though we cannot say that a particular set of rules is necessary, certainly *some* rules are necessary. But systems differ in their rules. Members of some systems may indeed be devoted to a common cause or to the general welfare. In these systems it might be inappropriate for us to assume a suspicious stance as professional politicians often learn to take. The decisions within a family or a group of friends may be of this sort, while international politics lies at the other extreme.

A central aspect in which personal ethics concerns you as a policy analyst is your choice of persons with whom to work—community, group, or employer. If your work is to be effective, and if you are to earn a living as an analyst (rather than simply evaluating policies as a citizen), you must normally gain the assent of other persons and organizations in order to conduct your analysis. Your agreement with them typically specifies the purpose of your investigation and advice and provides access to necessary data. Some policy analysis can be done without commitments of this kind, but much analysis requires them. Both analysis and political feasibility can benefit from the resources you gain by group membership and leadership roles.

The skilled policy analyst or evaluator will recognize that organizations do not always want thoroughgoing investigation or analysis.[42] Persons at various levels in an organization will have understandable fears that evaluation can threaten their own positions, sometimes unjustly. Thus, the analyst must learn to see whether his or her advice will be consistent with the client's goals. If the client is an organization, the analyst must learn to see at what level in the hierarchy advice will be most welcome. This initial assessment will guide the analyst in deciding whether or not to agree to undertake analysis for a particular client. The agreement to work with a given client, like the founding of an organization, creates contractual or nonteleological commitments that constrain one's subsequent goals and choices. Thus, personal ethical reflection, political sensitivity, and clear definition of the problem (at least for the analyst personally) are essential at the very start of the process of analysis.

We have repeatedly contrasted a relatively selfish model of organizational participants in the policy process with our insistence that you as policy analyst be guided by considerations of the general welfare or other ethical standards. Yet we would be blind if we denied the same motivations and impulses in ourselves as we observe in others. We all have inclinations to further the welfare of nearer groups—families, employing organizations, professions, political communities—as well as our personal welfare, when we might instead sacrifice these values to the welfare of more distant groups. We learn to justify these choices in terms of the values that our groups support, our obligations to nearer groups, or the apparent unreasonableness of the demands that an ethic requiring self-sacrifice might make. For these reasons another aspect of ethics often enters policy choice: the conflict between notions of the general welfare and our own personal or group rights or welfare. The most conspicuous case of judgment in favor of the organization is *raison d'état*, the justification of governmental acts simply in terms of the national interest.

Over the long run we often acquire organizational commitments in the hope of doing good. These commitments are less visible in the artificial classroom exercise in which you are asked to imagine that you are a mayor, the president, or a group leader. But in life outside the classroom we must pay personal costs and incur obligations in seeking leadership roles. To occupy such positions or to gain access and influence to persons in them usually requires the expenditure of options or resources. We may have to commit ourselves to organizational goals that are not wholly consistent with our ethical systems. These may be the goals of others who control our advancement from one role to another or the advancement of our supporters.

We cannot, therefore, ignore conditions of *personal* feasibility. The sacrifice and effort that the pursuance of some policies requires cannot be expected from everyone. An older politician cannot be expected to muster the personal physical resources for a struggle that a younger one might.[43] A person or group willing to sacrifice and expend effort for an ideal may come nearer to accomplishing it than another person or group of apparently similar resources.

Because personal feasibility is so important a feature of any choice and because our interventions in policy choice always involve this personal element, some writers have in effect combined desirability with personal feasibility in a single calculation.[44] But desirability, as we have described it, derives from general ethical positions that are argued and supported through collective discourse about the general welfare or about what is right. These ethical positions are not merely personal preferences and are expected to transcend personal and organizational interests. Thus, we may discuss collectively what policies are preferable or desirable in a particular situation, even though there are also particular elements of feasibility that differ among individuals.[45]

SOCIAL SCIENCE AND MODELS
OF FEASIBILITY

In this chapter we have discussed feasibility from your standpoint as citizen and analyst. But because we are also relating policy analysis to the contributions of the social sciences, we must raise the special question whether scientific models of feasibility are possible and, if so, to what degree. We noted in chapter 3 that feasibility cannot be expressed as an objective probability as long as it depends on our own actions and the actions of those whom we are persuading. This is why we cannot attain the same degree of objectivity in assessing feasibility as in other models of cause and effect.

Because analysts seeking to put a policy into effect are typically interacting with those who decide and who are affected, their analyses of the conditions of feasibility cannot have the detachment of pure natural science.[46] They must expect to consult, persuade, receive counterproposals, be criticized as regards both the facts and values they advance, and be the object of political action. Whatever difficulties we saw in the establishment of models regarding the consequences of policies, the difficulties of formulating the conditions of feasibility are far greater. Indeed, we may find it self-defeating to seek to express them in scientific laws and formulas because of our own involvement and the need to treat our fellow participants like ourselves.

The objective calculation of feasibility is also difficult because of its dependence on our roles as participants or analysts. What is feasible for one person is not for another. For the person who is authorized to decide, feasibility of enactment is no problem. What is infeasible at one time may become feasible at another, not merely because of changes in the situation, but because of a decision by key participants to mobilize necessary resources or to give priority to a particular problem. The mixed-scanning perspective suggests that when we (or important participants) move from the smaller to the larger perspective, some possibilities suddenly appear more feasible. If we wish to ask whether a policy is feasible, therefore, we must give meaning to the question by specifying the participant who is to act, the time, and the precise form of the policy proposal.[47]

We must consider not only the reactions of those affected but also the anticipatory reactions of those who *might* be affected or who fear that a particular policy alternative may be tried. Thus, whether in a game such as chess or in international politics, one player is typically concerned with the other's capabilities and intentions. Other players in a political game react to something more than policy proposals.

Our assessment of political feasibility is thus different from a scientific view of the social world—not only in its specificity but also in its short time perspective and its often lesser standards of rigor. The analyst's judgments must be furnished in time to be useful for decision, whereas a scientist must suspend judgment if he or she deems the data insufficient.

The pictures of individuals and groups that we form when assessing feasibility also differ from those furnished by social science in that they are not always potentially public, at least in the short run. One cannot say to a prospective ally or opponent that one has plotted his position on a diagram. Rather, one must treat him as a free and reasonable human being, entitled to the same consideration as oneself. If one contemplates manipulation or half-truths, one must expect to be dealt with in the same way. Thus, to characterize one's own organization, in a meeting of that organization, as having a "power structure," is somehow inappropriate even among social scientists.

The analysis of power structures by sociologists and political scientists is relevant to feasibility, however. We must know who is likely to be able to further a proposal or to block it. This requires knowledge of both formal positions (What legislative committee will hold hearings?) and informal influence (Who could persuade the head of the committee to take the bill up sooner? Who could induce the mayor to make a public statement?). It also requires analysis of the real structures of influence in organizations as well as in communities. We must learn who can supply us with information, who can take an issue to the top of an organization through informal channels, and which branches of an organization are lacking in skills or motivation.[48] Not all of these questions have been addressed in academic studies of power structure, but they need to be considered together in our tasks of influencing enactment and implementation.

SUMMARY

An essential part of policy analysis is your assessment of and influence on political feasibility—the possibility that the policy you choose will be carried out. Your chance of influencing this possibility depends on the social roles that you occupy. Feasibility depends on a policy's enactment, or its being authoritatively chosen, and its implementation, its being put into effect. Each of these aspects of feasibility can itself involve numerous stages or choices.

In order to assess the feasibility of enactment of a policy, you must understand the decision system in which you wish to enact it. As a citizen you are normally involved in a political community that makes collective decisions involving combinations of groups. Such communities include organizations as major elements. These organizations are of two kinds: bureaucracies and voluntary associations. You may begin your assessment of feasibility by judging the typical intentions of organizations and of persons in them. These typical intentions are related to organizational missions and resources, careers, and constituencies. In seeking to increase the feasibility of enactment of a policy, you may try to encourage coalitions between organizations.

Implementation of policies that have been enacted requires anticipation of implementation problems while you are seeking enactment. The policy has to be referred to the right organization, or the right kind of new organization has to be created. As the organization carries out the policy, the results should be monitored.

To increase the feasibility of enactment or implementation, you will have to act so as to place that policy on the agendas of one or more decision makers. This means encouraging decision makers to give it serious consideration and high priority and to interpret the policy as you intend. As a citizen, you will ordinarily approach decision makers from outside their organizations, often in connection with their electoral constituencies or the constituencies of elected officials who influence them.

The influence you exert can sometimes be indirect, that is, exercised on others as intermediaries and based on rewards or threats that are not directly related to the policy. You may be able to induce these others to influence policy makers' decisions about the policy. Examples of indirect influence often concern the actions of large organizations with control over the jobs and markets of other organizations, but you may consider using this sort of influence as well.

In seeking influence you may have to create and comply with obligations. These obligations may create ethical problems that you will have to evaluate. Such ethical problems are part of the larger problem of personal feasibility, involving your willingness to sacrifice your personal welfare for the general welfare.

Feasibility is not easily assessed by rigorous scientific models because we are involved closely with the other citizens whose acts affect it. This involvement makes it difficult to take the detached role of the scientific observer.

If we are successful in implementing a program, later analysis of the value of the program will assume a different form. These later cycles of analysis are the subject of chapter 7.

GLOSSARY

Action-channel: a legitimate channel of communication through which proposals can be placed on the agenda of a decision maker.

Agenda: a set of items up for consideration by a decision maker.

Bureaucracy: a private or public organization with hierarchical authority, in which participants are paid to perform fulltime duties.

Choice point: a place (social role or institution) at which a decision is made— for example, a legislature, legislative committee, executive, or administrator.

Coalition: a lasting agreement between individuals or organizations to act together for political purposes such as enactment of a policy. Its duration must be at least the interval required for enactment of the policy (though we can also say that a coalition is broken).

Collective decision system: a collection of persons, who may also be grouped together in organizations, who join together to make decisions binding on themselves. (See also political community in Glossary to chapter 1.)

Constituency: a set of persons on whom a public official or participant depends. This term includes the formal constituency defined by legal voting requirements, for an elective official, and informal constituencies defined by resources, informal social ties, or similarity of political interests.

Enactment: approval of a policy at the necessary authoritative choice points. The result of enactment is a policy in the form of a document, but without the additional activities needed to convert that document into operational form.

Essence of an organization: the set of goals, ideals, and self-concepts held by members of an organization that determines what organizational activities they consider most important.

Feasibility: the degree of possibility that a policy can be put into effect (enacted and implemented), through your efforts or the efforts of its proponents.

Implementation: the steps necessary for the provisions of a policy to be put into effect.

Indirect influence: the influence exercised by an actor A on actor C through the action of an intermediate actor B. In the typical case, the substance of the A–B relation is different from that of the B–C relation.

Organization: a social system set up intentionally to serve some goal; includes bureaucracies and voluntary associations.

Personal feasibility: the degree of possibility that you will act to further a policy, taking into account your personal priorities, allocation of resources and effort, and ethical judgments as to proper modes of personal action.

Political: having to do with the exercise of influence or power.

Political system: a collection of persons who interact, exercising power or influence on one another, to produce resulting events; includes collective decision systems but also systems in which the resulting events are not normatively binding, as in the international system.

Standard operating procedure: a coordinated set of activities that an organization is routinely prepared to undertake.

Voluntary association: an organization that members usually join by paying dues and in which members have the right to elect the officers.

1. You are considering possible state legislation that will affect the availability of medical records to patients. In order to be enacted, such legislation must be reported from committees in both houses of the legislature and signed by the governor. Name six choice points that affect feasibility of enactment, one of which is not a point of formal governmental choice.

2. What is the smallest number of choice points at which approval is necessary for an amendment to the United States Constitution? Consider a decision by a legislative chamber as a single choice point.

3. You are considering the possibility of establishing a new, lower speed limit for your state. In your analysis of the consequences of this policy, what difference does it make for your model whether you consider the policy to be defined by enactment of the new speed limit or by enactment together with implementation?

4. You are considering working for enactment and implementation of a given policy in two communities of comparable size. One of them is loosely organized and includes a variety of relatively independent groups. The other has been dominated by an organized local political party with control of patronage for over two decades. How would your approaches to feasibility of enactment and implementation differ in the two communities?

5. You are interested in finding out how fully a recently enacted federal policy is being carried out. What means are available to you to seek out this information?

6. How do we estimate the typical intentions of an organization?

7. How does your role in a bureaucracy or an association affect your possible personal alternatives for furthering policies?

8. Classify the following organizations as bureaucracies, voluntary associations, a combination of the two, or neither:

    a. the AFL–CIO

    b. the Democratic party

    c. General Motors

    d. the Social Security Administration

    e. a local chamber of commerce

    f. the American Political Science Association

    g. Congress

    h. a multicampus state university system.

ADVANCED EXERCISE

9. In case 3–A concerning the laetrile controversy James J. Kilpatrick writes: "Over the years I doubt that any columnist has been more friendly to the medical profession than I have been. In season and out, I have fought the doctors' battle against overweening government." This statement reflects a larger political coalition between advocates of the free market, as against government intervention, and the medical profession. If this coalition has been altered in the laetrile case, why has this change occurred?

NOTES

1. Arnold Meltsner, "Political Feasibility and Policy Analysis," *Public Administration Review* 32(1972): 859–867.

2. Graham T. Allison, *Essence of Decision* (Boston: Little, Brown, 1971), p. 267; Hans H. Gerth and C. Wright Mills, eds., *From Max Weber: Essays in Sociology* (New York: Oxford University Press, 1946), p. 128.

3. James W. Vaupel, "Muddling Through Analytically," in Willis D. Hawley and David Rogers, eds., *Improving the Quality of Urban Management* (Beverly Hills, Calif.: Sage Publications, 1974).

4. This process of consultation and reciprocal influence has been incorporated in Kurt Lewin's procedures of "action research," as described by Alfred J. Marrow in *The Practical Theorist: The Life and Work of Kurt Lewin* (New York: Basic Books, 1969), ch. 14, ch. 21; in Jürgen Habermas's notion of "discursive formation of the will," in *Theory and Practice*, trans. by John Viertel (Boston: Beacon, 1973), p. 26; and in Robert W. Friedrichs's notion of "dialectical sociology," in "Dialectical Sociology: Toward a Resolution of the Current 'Crisis' in Sociology," *British Journal of Sociology* 23(1972): 263–274. It is also part of the process of "participatory planning," used in decisions such as the location of highways.

5. A hypothetical example of this sort of analysis by a member of a state official's staff is Graham T. Allison, "Implementation Analysis: 'The Missing Chapter' in Conventional Analysis. A Teaching Exercise," in Richard Zeckhauser et al., eds., *Benefit-Cost and Policy Analysis 1974* (Chicago: Aldine, 1975).

6. See Robert S. Friedman, *Professionalism: Expertise and Policy Making* (Morristown, N.J.: General Learning Press, 1971).

7. Enactment corresponds to the process of legitimation of proposals described in Charles O. Jones, *An Introduction to the Study of Public Policy*, 2d ed. (North Scituate, Mass.: Duxbury Press, 1977), pp. 92ff.

8. See Daniel P. Moynihan, "Income by Right," *New Yorker* 48(1973): I, 13 Jan.,

34–57; II, 20 Jan., 60–79; III, 27 Jan., 57–81; and Moynihan, *The Politics of a Guaranteed Income* (New York: Random House, 1973).

9. The following account is drawn from Allison, "Implementation Analysis," in Zeckhauser et al., eds., *Benefit-Cost and Policy Analysis 1974*, p. 374.

10. Willis D. Hawley, "Horses Before Carts: Developing Adaptive Schools and the Limits of Innovation" (Durham, N.C.: Duke University, Institute of Policy Sciences and Public Affairs, 1976).

11. A bureaucratic organization is one in which members are full-time employees and each has a single superior to whom he is responsible. A single superior may thus have several subordinates, and these may have other subordinates in turn, constituting a "bureau" or "agency" within the larger organization. Sociologists define bureaucracy in further detail, but these are the essential features for our purposes.

12. Allison, *Essence of Decision*, pp. 164–171.

13. An association is a voluntary organization into which members enter freely without monetary recompense and in which members at least nominally have some control over the organization's policies. Members of associations typically pay dues. Examples are sports clubs and political interest groups. Conceivably, new organizational forms with different characteristics could be created. But in the short run we consider existing forms.

14. See Norton R. Long, "The Local Community as an Ecology of Games," *American Journal of Sociology* 44(1958): 251–261. James S. Coleman has also suggested the importance for individuals of learning about their relations to organizations; see his *Power and the Structure of Society* (New York: Norton, 1974), pp. 99–100.

15. Allison, *Essence of Decision*, p. 176.

16. Morton H. Halperin, *Bureaucratic Politics and Foreign Policy* (Washington, D.C.: Brookings, 1974), p. 78.

17. Gilbert Y. Steiner, *The Children's Cause* (Washington, D.C.: Brookings, 1976), p. 9. We discuss the Children's Bureau further later.

18. For central mission or "essence" see Halperin, *Bureaucratic Politics and Foreign Policy*, p. 28.

19. Allison, *Essence of Decision*, ch. 3.

20. David Rogers, *110 Livingston Street* (New York: Random House, 1968), p. 254.

21. See William D. Coplin and Michael K. O'Leary, *Everyman's Prince: A Guide to Understanding Political Problems*, 2d ed. (North Scituate, Mass.: Duxbury Press, 1976).

22. Long, "The Local Community as an Ecology of Games," p. 253. Further detail on implementation games is given in Eugene Bardach, *The Implementation Game* (Cambridge, Mass.: M.I.T. Press, 1977), chs. 3–6.

23. James S. Coleman, *Community Conflict* (New York: Free Press, 1956); Theodore R. Marmor, *The Politics of Medicare*, rev. ed. (Chicago: Aldine, 1973), p. 109.

24. Ralph K. Huitt, "Political Feasibility," in Austin Ranney, ed., *Political Science and Public Policy* (Chicago: Markham, 1968).

25. On committee reform, see Marmor, *The Politics of Medicare*, pp. 59–60, 106.

26. See Jones, *An Introduction to the Study of Public Policy*, ch. 7.

27. This case was originally presented by Jerry E. Mechling in "The Roles of Policy Analysts in Large Public Organizations," Ph.D. dissertation, Princeton University, 1974. It is summarized in Erwin C. Hargrove, *The Missing Link: The Study of the Implementation of Social Policy* (Washington, D.C.: Urban Institute, 1975), p. 28. Reprinted by permission of the Urban Institute, © 1975.

28. Halperin, *Bureaucratic Politics and Foreign Policy*, p. 107.

29. The following example is based on Steiner, *The Childrn's Cause*, pp. 5–9 and passim.

30. Ibid., pp. 36–37, 41–42.

31. These problems are discussed from an administrator's viewpoint in Herbert Kaufman, *Administrative Feedback: Monitoring Subordinates' Behavior* (Washington, D.C.: Brookings, 1973).

32. They contrast the institutional agenda with the *systemic agenda*—similar to our "problem situation"—which is "all issues that are commonly perceived by members of the political community as meriting public attention and as involving matters within the legitimate jurisdiction of existing governmental authority." See Roger W. Cobb and Charles D. Elder, *Participation in American Politics: The Dynamics of Agenda-Building* (Boston: Allyn and Bacon, 1972), pp. 85–86; and Jones, *An Introduction to the Study of Public Policy*, p. 40.

33. Jones, *An Introduction to the Study of Public Policy*, p. 40.

34. Allison, *Essence of Decision*, pp. 169–170.

35. Halperin, *Bureaucratic Politics and Foreign Policy*, p. 177.

36. Allison, *Essence of Decision*, pp. 127–132.

37. Halperin, *Bureaucratic Politics and Foreign Policy*, pp. 196–207.

38. On presidential speeches see ibid., pp. 189–192.

39. Jack Anderson and Les Whitten, " 'Human Error' Labels Guns as Books," Raleigh, N.C., *News and Observer*, 22 July 1977. ©1977 United Feature Syndicate, Inc. Reprinted by permission.

40. The politician quoted was Jake Arvey, a one-time Chicago Democratic leader. The quotation and a reference to Speaker O'Neill in similar terms appear in Martin Tolchin, "O'Neill's Role as Speaker Draws Praise," *New York Times*, 2 Jan. 1978. See also William L. Riordan, *Plunkitt of Tammany Hall*, 1905 (New York: E. P. Dutton, 1963).

41. Allison, *Essence of Decision*, p. 166.

42. Regarding the evaluator, see Carol H. Weiss, *Evaluation Research* (Englewood Cliffs, N.J.: Prentice-Hall, 1972).

43. Edward C. Banfield, *Political Influence* (New York: Free Press, 1961), p. 18.

44. Vaupel, "Muddling Through Analytically," in Hawley and Rogers, eds., *Improving the Quality of Urban Management.*

45. This distinction is analogous to that between objective evidence and personal *a priori* judgments of probability, as they enter into Bayesian statistics.

46. See Morris Janowitz, "Sociological Models and Social Policy," in Morris Janowitz, *Political Conflict* (Chicago: Quadrangle Books, 1970).

47. For President Nixon's Family Assistance Plan, a prediction of feasibility by Bill Cavala and Aaron Wildavsky was in error partly because Nixon altered the symbolism of welfare reform. See Moynihan, *The Politics of a Guaranteed Income*, pp. 7–12.

48. See Downs, *Inside Bureaucracy*, ch. 13.

Fluoridation in a New England Town[1]

This case is presented to illustrate problems of feasibility of enactment in a community situation. It was prepared by Thomas F. A. Plaut, not long after the 1961 referendum described, for use at the University of Michigan School of Public Health.

Proponents of fluoridation organized support over a two-year period culminating in a referendum. Because the major decision involved a vote by the public, much of the activity of the proponents centered about informing and persuading the public. This case therefore differs from many other community issues in which decisions are made by government organizations and representatives rather than directly by the public. It also involves less bargaining among groups than many other issues because the policy of fluoridating the water supply did not involve detailed negotiable changes.

In addition to mounting a broad information campaign, the proponents also aimed at leaders and organizations in the community. They were largely successful in gaining the support of community organizations, but occasionally a group such as the League of Women Voters, through its internal decision processes, failed to support them. They were successful as well in reducing the opposition to fluoridation that might have come from health professionals and other leaders in the community.

To carry out these activities, they had to form their own group, the Newton Citizens' Committee for Dental Health; gain resources for it, including money, time and effort, and an office; and organize it internally into committees for effective functioning.

To a very limited degree they also engaged in tactical planning and the gathering of intelligence. They anticipated that there would be controversy about fluoridation and sought political advice from persons with experience. They avoided associating advocacy of fluoridation with particular groups in the community (for other types of policies, however, such group alliances can be helpful). They anticipated possible counterarguments that might be directed either to experts or to citizen supporters. During their petition campaign they obtained information about where support and opposition were localized. Also important was their ability to respond to new problems of feasibility as they arose, such as the need for a petition, or suddenly publicized claims by the opposition.

The above steps are common to many efforts to cope with the problems of feasibility. But although the proponents worked hard to win the referendum, enactment in this case was far simpler than in many others. The fact that this movement could be led by political amateurs suggests its relative simplicity. Many operations in Washington or in large cities are impossible without substantial experience and resources. The task of citizens in such cases may be to try to obtain the active support of experienced politicians. A somewhat more complex example of feasibility was given in the deposit-bottles case.

Background Information—Newton, Massachusetts

The city of Newton, with a population of 92,384 (1960 Census), is part of the metropolitan area that surrounds the city of Boston. Newton is the eighth largest city in the state and the only city of its size that is primarily residential, rather than industrial or commercial. Newton, often referred to as the "Garden City," is one of the wealthier communities in the state with a high assessed property valuation per person. It particularly prides itself on its public school system which has the fourth largest enrollment in the state.

Newton is governed by a Mayor and a Board of Aldermen. City elections, on a non-partisan basis, are held every two years. As recently as six years ago, registered Republicans outnumbered registered Democrats by better than three to one. In 1961 this margin has been narrowed to less than three to two. The City remains primarily Protestant in its composition, although the proportion of both Jewish and Catholic families has increased in recent years.

Many physicians and dentists reside in Newton and the city has a public health department with 25 full-time employees, including a medical health officer. There are an unusually large number of civic, educational, social, and recreational organizations in the city. On any day, Newton residents have at least fifteen different meetings to choose from. Through the local Community Council, a clearing house service has been set up to reduce conflicts on meeting dates.

The Fluoridation Campaign

Initial Interest and Early Organization: January to March 1960 (3 months) Late in December of 1959 a young Newton mother, wife of a psychiatrist, heard at a social gathering about the results of the November 1959 Cambridge [Massachusetts] fluoridation. In December a recount in Cambridge had confirmed that fluoridation was approved by an extremely narrow margin. Within a few weeks this Newton mother had contacted several public health authorities to obtain information on the technical as well as political-legal aspects of water fluoridation. She also contacted a social scientist who had been active in the Cambridge campaign and several other persons—including the wife of an expert in dental research. Very quickly this group discovered that the earliest possible date for a fluoridation referendum in Newton was almost two years away, i.e., November of 1961. However, there was agreement that initial organizational and educational efforts should begin immediately without public fanfare.

Before the end of January (1960) an informal half-hour presentation on fluoridation was made to the Governing Board of the Newton Community Council. (Most of the numerous organizations in the city of Newton are affiliated with the Community Council. For a number of years the Council has had full-time professional staff and had been active in various aspects of health, welfare and recreation in the city.) This initial step was undertaken because it was realized that the backing and support of many organizations in the city would be needed in order to develop a successful fluoridation campaign. Because of the relation of most organizations to the Community Council, it seemed logical to begin an educational campaign with this group.

During January various approaches were also made to key persons in the city-wide Council of Parent-Teacher Associations. Material on fluoridation was sent to the chairman of the Health and Safety Committee of this PTA Council for distribution to the many school PTA's in the city. The Director of Public Health for the city of Newton was informed of the citizens' interest in fluoridation and he indicated his eagerness to be of assistance. He did point out that experiences of other communities indicated that the leadership in a fluoridation campaign should not come from the professional public health persons, but should be in the hands of a group of interested citizens. The Director of Public Health also had available from the Newton Water Commissioner information on the cost of installing the necessary fluoridation equipment.

The first meeting of persons interested in developing a Newton fluoridation committee was held early in February (1960). This meeting was attended by about a dozen persons, including a dental researcher well qualified to answer scientific questions and a person familiar with the political and social-psychological aspects of the controversy. At this meeting it had been planned to begin the actual organization of a fluoridation committee for Newton. However, virtually the whole evening was spent in a general discussion of various aspects of fluoridation and little organizational progress was achieved. In every subsequent meeting which was attended by persons who had not previously been involved in the work of the group, it was found necessary to spend a considerable period of time answering the many questions that were raised about various aspects of fluoridation. Until persons had at least an initial understanding of the scientific and political aspects of this issue, they were not ready to become involved with the committee and participate in its plans for the campaign.

At this first meeting it was also pointed out that in most communities the fluoridation question usually engendered much feeling and excitement. The group agreed that there was little reason to believe that Newton could approve fluoridation without some controversy developing. The very rough outline of an initial, quiet, educational campaign, with later increasing involvement of community leaders and community organizations, was sketched at this meeting. Various persons agreed to undertake tasks in relation to these objectives. One lady explored ways in which the Newton League of Women Voters and the PTA's could be useful as channels for community education on fluoridation. In the period of the next few months, she contacted many persons in these two groups and explained to them the value of water fluoridation and the steps that

Newton would have to go through to obtain it. This work proved to be invaluable in the later development of many PTA meetings on fluoridation. Much interest was also developed among some groups in the League of Women Voters and it was only by a small margin that the League decided not to study fluoridation as one of its two or three issues for the coming year. The Spring 1960 Bulletin of the Newton League of Women Voters indicated that much interest had been expressed in fluoridation but that the decision had been made not to study this issue. The Bulletin explained that if the matter did come before the voters, the League would then present the facts on it to the people of Newton. It is interesting to note that in the fall of 1961, i.e., just prior to the referendum vote, the Newton League of Women Voters did *not* present any facts on fluoridation because the issue had become too controversial!

A basic principle of the operation of the Newton committee was developed at this stage. It was decided that members of the group should each try to interest and involve friends and neighbors in the work of the committee. This was usually done by asking persons to attend one of the monthly meetings of the group, or by holding a small meeting in a home as a sort of "coffee-hour." In this fashion a core group of interested and well-informed persons was gradually developed. During the first few months it was also possible to secure the support and participation of several experienced persons from the health and welfare field who were residents of the city of Newton. Particularly invaluable were persons who had understanding of principles of community organization and public education. Preliminary informal contacts were also made with several key political leaders in the city. It was hoped that these persons might be sufficiently concerned about fluoridation to give their support to the group. Some of them gave invaluable suggestions to the group regarding how it should plan its organization and campaign activities. With these objectives in mind, various conversations were held with selected leaders of the Republican and Democratic Parties in the city.

Since fluoridation is a dental-medical issue, the support of physicians and dentists in the city had to be secured. The leadership of the county medical society was immediately informed of the plans of the citizens' group, and the group was asked to give its support. Very shortly such support was given and a financial contribution was made. In early March a meeting of the local dental society was entirely devoted to fluoridation. At this meeting the scientific and sociological aspects of fluoridation were each discussed by a person familiar with that element of the problem. Although only a small proportion of all the dentists in Newton attended this meeting, many of those present worked actively in the subsequent campaign and also recruited other dentists to help.

In these early months the group adopted a name—Newton Citizens' Committee for Dental Health—met with the Director of Public Health, and began to accumulate pamphlets and books that could be used in the orientation and education of interested groups and persons. One member of the Committee, the lady who had initiated the whole project, agreed to serve as temporary chairman and as a communications link between all persons in the group. Although eventually the Committee became so large and complicated—especially in the hectic last six weeks of the campaign—that communication and coordination did at times break down, it was understood right from the start that the whole operation would have to be held together in some fashion. For most of the 23 months of the campaign, excellent communications were maintained among members of the core group who were called upon to make major decisions. While countless hours were spent on the telephone—without this electronic device the campaign could never have been carried out—such conversations frequently obviated the necessity of far more time-consuming meetings. On many occasions the chairman informally polled the steering committee by phone in order to decide on a particular course of action.

Second Phase—Expansion of Committee and Its Work: April to September 1960 (6 months) Very early during this period, all persons who had expressed interest in the fluoridation Committee were invited to a meeting which was addressed by a professor from a nearby dental school. At this meeting, attended by about thirty persons, a detailed presentation was made on the scientific facts of fluoridation. Particular emphasis was placed on some of the arguments that had been raised by opponents of fluoridation. The purpose of the meeting was to increase the competence of committee members to answer a broad range of questions of fluoridation.

In the spring of 1960, a beginning was made by the Committee in the development of informational sheets that presented material specifically focussed on the Newton situation. Through contacts with persons in local and state water departments, basic engineering and cost information on water fluoridation for the city was obtained.

Close contact was maintained with the Health Department, which undertook a study of dental decay among Newton school children. This survey was done in 4 schools—two in wealthy areas of the city and two in poorer sections. The findings of this study, pointing to the major problems of dental decay among *all* Newton children, were reported in front page stories by the three local newspapers. In these newspaper reports no reference was made to the value of fluoridation in preventing dental decay. Throughout the campaign the city Health Department remained in the background and left the leadership and organization in the hands of the Citizens' committee. In this manner the findings and reports from the Health Department could function as "expert" evidence and testimony rather than being subject to any criticism of bias or partisanship. Later in the campaign, of course, the results of this dental survey were very effectively used by many speakers as pointing to the great need for fluoridation in the city.

While gradual recruitment of new members was achieved through personal contact and additional "coffee hours," the major activity of the Committee during the spring of 1960 was devoted to a carefully planned meeting to which representatives from several hundred Newton organizations were invited. It was felt that if the interest and support of even a fraction of these groups could be obtained, subsequent educational and organizational work in the city would be greatly facilitated. Invitations were sent to the leaders of each of these groups— as well as to all elected city officials. Most of these invitations were then followed up by personal telephone calls. A conservative estimate would be that close to 500 phone calls were made to persons inviting them to the meeting. No general publicity was given to this meeting since it was intended primarily for the education of the invited community leaders.

A prominent research scientist was the speaker at this meeting and his presentation covered the basic historical and scientific facts on fluoridation and also stressed many of the arguments and objections of opponents of fluoridation. Following his presentation there was a question period. While no public announcement had been made of this meeting, it was expected that some local opponents of fluoridation would appear. Members of the steering committee discussed at length how to handle this eventuality. Suggestions ranged from placing no limitations on attendance or participation in the discussion to hiring a policeman to exclude persons who had not been invited! Exclusion was decided against as it might well give the opponents an issue that they could use to advantage. However, all persons entering were asked to sign a register and it was agreed that questions from the floor would be restricted to Newton residents. Approximately 100 persons attended the meeting—including about half-a-dozen persons opposed to fluoridation. These persons were particularly active during the discussion period and it was necessary to restrict the number of questions that they could ask.

Subsequent to this meeting, efforts began to develop a list of endorsers for the work of the Committee. The plan was to secure endorsements of fluoridation from a broadly representative group of community leaders. At all times care was taken to ensure that the Committee did not become identified with any particular political, religious or ethnic group within the city. During the period of spring and summer of 1960, persons were also asked to indicate their willingness to work for fluoridation. By the early fall of 1960, over 50 persons had agreed to assist in the campaign. First efforts at collecting funds were also undertaken during the early summer, with all members of the "core" group sending out fund-appeal letters to a number of their personal friends. In this manner, several hundred dollars were obtained.

In preparation for public meetings that it was anticipated would be held starting in the fall of 1960, a Speakers' Bureau was developed and many Newton physicians, dentists and other scientists were asked whether they would be willing to address groups on various aspects of fluoridation. Eventually a list of over 40 speakers was compiled and close to twenty of these persons were actually used at one time or another during the campaign.

In the middle of June, the opposition presented itself in organized fashion for the first time. They announced that a public meeting, with "expert" speakers, would be held. This meeting was attended by about 40 persons—almost half of them proponents of fluoridation! Less than 10 Newton persons opposed to fluoridation were present and all four of the speakers came from outside the community. Members of the Newton fluoridation Committee who attended this meeting obtained an understanding of the kind of opposition they were dealing with. The meeting also functioned to increase the motivation and interest of these persons to work more actively in obtaining fluoridation for Newton.

In conjunction with these two meetings, the fluoridation Committee began a steady series of contacts with reporters and editors of the local papers. It was soon determined which newpapers were interested in material on fluoridation, and much good publicity was obtained in this manner. Attention was also paid to the occasional letters expressing opposition to fluoridation that appeared in the Boston papers and sometimes these letters were "answered." It was discovered that every week anti-fluoridation material was included as part of a regular radio broadcast on a major Boston station. Through contacts with the radio station and certain advertisers, it was possible to secure the removal of this highly biased material from the series of programs.

In the regular monthly meeting of the Steering Committee of the Newton Citizens' Committee for Dental Health, it became apparent that there was need for some form of committee structure. Mainly through the efforts of one member of the Steering Committee, a person with much experience in community organization, a detailed organizational structure was developed. Separate areas of activity, such as public relations, membership, fund raising, political organization, educational materials, etc. were outlined in this report. While there was no disagreement on the necessity for these specialized sub-groups, it was not possible to put most of them into actual operation at this time. There continued to be a relatively small group of persons who undertook a variety of responsibilities; however, gradually over the next 16 months, an approximation of this structure was achieved.

Third Phase—Active Public Education and Political Organization: October 1960 to August 1961 (11 months)   It was during this period of almost a year preceding the last hectic final 10 weeks of the campaign that the bulk of real educational work for fluoridation was done. Starting with five PTA meetings in October, a large number of meetings were arranged by the Speakers' Bureau. While a variety of different organizations were reached in this fashion, the largest number of presentations were made before PTA meetings. Because it was soon realized that few physicians or dentists are prepared to address lay groups on fluoridation, a kind of training program was instituted for potential speakers. A special evening meeting was held to train speakers and this was attended by over 30 physicians and dentists. At this meeting the historical and technical aspects of fluoridation were covered, as well as the arguments and points frequently raised by opponents. In addition many pages of carefully documented material were distributed to assist speakers in their preparation for meetings. At each meeting where a speaker was supplied by the fluoridation Committee, the arrangements for the meeting were carefully worked out with the sponsoring group. It was known in advance what kind of an audience was expected and speakers were chosen accordingly. A definite agreement was reached with the group as to the format of the meeting, i.e., how long the presentation was to be, the nature of the question period, etc. At a minority of these meetings, presentations were also made by persons in opposition to fluoridation. The Committee agreed to participate in such meetings, but only under the condition that the "anti" speakers be drawn from Newton residents. This policy was adopted to ensure that a platform would not be provided for one of the two or three nationally known physicians or dentists opposing fluoridation who have been used throughout the state by the "anti's" for many years. Since no Newton physician or dentist took an active role in opposing fluoridation, the "anti" speakers were lay persons. For only one meeting, very late in the campaign, were the opponents able to secure a physician to present material against fluoridation. Every speaker was thus well briefed on the kind of presentation expected of him, the audience he would be addressing, and who, if any, his opponents would be.

In addition a representative of the Committee was sent to every public meeting where there was any expectation that the fluoridation issue might be discussed. The purpose of this was (1) to obtain information on sentiment in the group on fluoridation, (2) to present information of fluoridation, (3) to seek the support of the group for the work of the Citizens' Committee for Dental Health, and (4) to try to prevent the group from taking a stand in opposition to fluoridation.

During this period regular meetings of the Steering Committee were held at least monthly and the telephone used for contact in the time between meetings. The agenda at these meetings usually included problems of organization, of fund-raising, of preparing educational material, or strategy in relation to key persons or groups within the community. A carefully prepared "fact-sheet" on fluoridation was finally completed in the early fall of 1960. It summarized the facts on fluoridation, indicated the broad scientific and organizational backing for fluoridation and particularly stressed information on Newton (the need, the costs, the method of fluoridation, and the forthcoming referendum). At one of the meetings of the Steering Committee, it was suggested that copies of this information sheet be distributed to the voters as they *left* the polling places after casting their votes in the 1960 presidential election. Since the turnout would be heavy, it was felt that this was an unusual opportunity to reach a large proportion of the persons who would be voting in the municipal election (and on fluoridation) the following year. Opposition was expressed to this proposal on the grounds: (1) that it was in bad taste, (2) that it would link fluoridation to political issues, and (3) that it would not organizationally be feasible to obtain the persons required for this kind of mass distribution. After much discussion, it was decided to try to cover only certain of the eight wards in the city.

Lists of persons who had agreed to work for the fluoridation Committee were used to obtain workers for the distribution of the "fact-sheet" at the polls. Four members of the Steering Committee each agreed to take responsibility for one ward. An organization plan was developed with ward captains, precinct captains and poll workers. Instructions were mimeographed for each of these sets of persons. These instructions dealt with recruitment of workers, keeping of records, and manner of distribution at the polls. On Election Day (1960) about 3,500 copies of the Newton "fact-sheet" were distributed in various parts of the city. Most of this distribution was done during the early morning hours and particularly in the evening when the voting was heaviest. It was not possible to obtain coverage of all the precincts in the four wards, even at these hours. Nevertheless a large number of persons were reached with educational material at this time. Since the sheet was given to persons as they left, there were no other "competing" handouts and virtually all voters took the material with them. Publicity was also given to this poll distribution in the local press on the following day.

Continuing efforts were made to expand the list of groups actively supporting fluoridation and to obtain the endorsement of more community leaders. By the fall of 1961, a list of 50 community leaders had been obtained—this included six of the 24 aldermen, several school committee members, prominent clergymen from all three major denominations, business leaders, and key persons from both political parties. Particular emphasis was placed on trying to prevent the recruitment of community leaders by the "anti" group. When the Committee heard that a key person in the community had doubts about fluoridation, he was immediately contacted by an appropriate proponent of fluoridation. The objective of these contacts was to bring information to the person, to indicate the support that the Committee already had in Newton, and to ensure that this individual would not take the lead in organizing opposition to fluoridation. Through these efforts it was possible to "neutralize" persons who otherwise might, on the basis of limited information, have taken a public stand against fluoridation. It was not, however, possible to convince all such persons that they should support water fluoridation for Newton. But with one exception, none of them took an active role in working with the Newton anti-fluoridation group. Organizational endorsement was finally obtained from a number of local groups including the following: Visiting Nurse Association, medical and dental societies, Community Council, Tuberculosis and Health League, pharmacists' association, Lions, Junior Chamber of Commerce, Board of Health, and Kiwanis.

In May of 1961, the anti-fluoridation group publicly announced its formation and the names of its leaders. *None* of these persons had ever previously taken an active role in community affairs. Later in the campaign one individual, who had been a member of the City Committee of one of the two major parties, did work strenuously against fluoridation. This person, while cooperating with the anti-group, did function somewhat in isolation from it. Until the last two months of the campaign, the opponents restricted their activity to an occasional newspaper advertisement and limited mailings of "anti" literature in a few parts of the city.

Late in the fall of 1960, the fluoridation Committee's efforts to raise funds were lagging badly and it was decided to run a house party to obtain money. A large home was made available for this purpose and printed invitations were sent out to a selected group of persons. These invitations were followed by personal phone calls, and a large proportion of those invited either attended or made voluntary contributions. While the catered meal and refreshments had to be covered out of the proceeds, a total of $650 remained to be added to the treasury of the Committee. This house party had the additional benefit of interesting and involving a number of persons in the work of the Committee.

In the early spring of 1961, an approach was made to the Mayor of Newton requesting that water fluoridation be placed on the ballot in the fall of 1961. He indicated that if there was genuine interest in fluoridation, the matter would be placed on the ballot. The Mayor suggested to the Committee members that they obtain the signatures of 5% of the registered voters in the community to a petition asking for a fluoridation referendum. Since the total number of registered voters in Newton was almost exactly 50,000 this meant that 2,500 signatures would be required. Initially the Steering Committee was distressed to find that this additional effort would be required. However, it soon became clear that this was a remarkable opportunity to develop a city-wide organization that could be used later in the campaign, and also that education on fluoridation and recruitment of workers could be undertaken in conjunction with the gathering of the needed petition signatures.

It was this petition campaign then that occupied the major efforts of the Committee during the first four months of 1961. An active member of the Newton Democratic Party and one from the Newton Republican Party became actively involved. These two men, because of their knowledge of many persons throughout the city, were able to assist greatly in the recruitment of ward captains, precinct captains and street workers for the petition campaign. A great deal of effort went into organizing this petition drive and it proved possible, after much effort, to obtain captains for almost all of the 36 precincts in the city. The recruitment of street workers was left, wherever possible, in the hands of the precinct captains. It was from the previously accumulated lists of volunteers and from the many contacts of the two political leaders that these persons were recruited. Five-hundred petitions were printed up (with room on each for 50 signatures). For record-keeping purposes, these petitions were numbered and then distributed among all the 36 precincts of the city in relation to the population of each precinct. Hundreds of record and instruction sheets for ward captains, precinct captains, and street workers were prepared. Many pieces of educational material on fluoridation that were also placed into the kits were prepared for each of the 36 precinct captains and for the street workers.

Ward and precinct captains were invited to a "kickoff" meeting for the petition campaign. A prominent university scientist spoke about fluoridation at this meeting and detailed instructions were given on the organization and operation of the petition drive. This meeting was well-publicized in the newspapers. The actual petition campaign lasted far longer than was expected and at times the organizational structure did not function too well. However, in the end a total of over 6,000 signatures was obtained—more than twice as many as the Mayor had requested. A total of over 75 workers participated in the petition campaign, hundreds of persons heard about fluoridation for the first time, and many additional workers were recruited. Just as the drive for signatures was getting under way, a front-page newspaper story reported that a poll of persons attending a dinner of the Newton Republican Club showed a vote of 190 to 56 in favor of fluoridation. However, the favorable effect of this publicity was more than counteracted when two adjoining communities (Brookline and Wellesley) voted against fluoridation in early March of 1961. Both of these towns are also rather wealthy suburbs of Boston. In Brookline the margin of defeat was 500 votes out of about 12,000 and in Wellesley fluoridation was beaten by a 2 to 1 margin. The results of the referenda in these two nearby towns forcibly brought home to the Newton Citizens' Committee for Dental Health the formidable organizational and educational task that it faced. For weeks after these votes, petition workers were asked why fluoridation had lost in these two communities.[2] One of the lessons that the Newton group learned from these two fluoridation defeats was the necessity of building into people "resistance" against the emotional arguments that were sure to be used by the opponents in their last minute appeals. It became clear that it would be advantageous for the proponents to raise some of these arguments themselves and then proceed to show that they were fallacious. In this manner persons could be prepared for the last minute appeals that they would be flooded with.

While the Committee members undoubtedly were pleased with the success of the petition campaign and while the number of signatures must have impressed the Mayor and other community leaders, an extremely important side-effect was the experience that the committee thus had in developing, nurturing and running a city-wide organization. Without this prior experience, it would not have been possible to undertake the intensive efforts that characterized the last two months of the campaign. From the petition drive, information was secured on which areas of the city were most favorably disposed to fluoridation and which were opposed. Ward and precinct leaders obtained valuable experience in this type of activity; for most of these persons it was entirely new. Weak points in the organization were detected and efforts made to overcome them in the final efforts of the fall of 1961.

Concurrent with the activity of the Newton fluoridation Committee was the development of a Massachusetts Citizens' Committee for Dental Health. By the early summer of 1961 this group had obtained the support of hundreds of persons from various parts of the state, including a former state governor, a former mayor of Boston, presidents of major universities, labor, religious, and industry leaders, and countless physicians and dentists. This Massachusetts Committee also began to make educational material available to the Newton group. In the early summer the Newton Committee sent out a fund-raising letter using the stationery of the state Dental Health Committee. This stationery contained the names of hundreds of Massachusetts citizens supporting fluoridation.

The fund-raising letter was sent to several hundred persons who it was felt might be interested in making contributions. A city-wide mailing of educational material had also been planned for this time but was not undertaken, mainly because of the lack of funds. During the summer of 1961, Committee activity was reduced, although a large number of stories on fluoridation were sent to the three local newspapers. Two of these papers were very cooperative in printing these news releases.

Fourth Phase—Final Intensive City-Wide Campaign: September 1961 to November 1961 (3 months)   During the last months of the campaign more, many more manhours were spent in working for fluoridation than in the whole previous twenty months! A large number of Newton citizens who previously had not worked for the fluoridation Committee contributed time, effort, and money. About 40% of the $5000 that was spent by the Committee was raised in these three months. Total campaign costs actually were far greater. It is impossible to determine exactly the "cost" of the secretarial services, postage, and printing that was absorbed by (1) members of the Committee (either at home or their offices), (2) other Newton residents interested in fluoridation, and (3) other persons also interested in the Newton fluoridation fight. A conservative estimate of the cost of these "free" services probably would be $2,500 to $3,000. Thus the total money cost of the campaign was close to $8,000.

Shortly after Labor Day 1961, a city-wide organization was developed for the "final" push. This again was based on the ward and precinct breakdowns that had been used for the November 1960 poll distribution and the spring 1961 petition campaign. Ward captains, precinct captains, and street workers were recruited, trained and supplied with materials. Kits which included a variety of instruction sheets were prepared for these workers. Each precinct captain was also supplied with a list of registered voters in the precinct. These lists had previously been checked to indicate the 6,000 persons who signed the petition. Workers were instructed to direct their initial educational efforts to the persons who had signed the petition. Since a turnout no larger than 20,000 voters was anticipated, it was felt that if each of the petition signers would vote for fluoridation and would make sure that one additional person also voted for fluoridation, a minimum of 12,000 votes would be cast in favor. This would then be more than enough votes to secure a favorable result.

Street workers were asked to call on as many of their neighbors as possible. If they could not do this, they were asked to phone their neighbors and also to distribute material on a door-to-door basis. It is impossible to know how many calls were made but close to two-thirds of the 25,000 households in the city [received] either a personal visit from a fluoridation worker [or] a call from a worker, or had material placed under their door. Over 60,000 pieces of educational material were placed into the hands of voters in this fashion. In the very last week of the campaign a city-wide mailing was sent by the Citizens' Committee for Dental Health to each household in Newton. This piece of literature included a long list of Newton physicians and dentists who supported fluoridation. In addition, a special mailing list of about 5,000 persons received a newspaper reprint that described and analyzed some of the organized opponents to fluoridation. This article pointed out that some of these opponents represent extreme, conservative groups, including the John Birch Society.

Wide publicity was given to the Advisory Board of the Newton Committee [a number of prominent citizens who lent their names to the Committee's efforts] and many statements were released by the Honorary Chairman of the Committee. This person, long active in city affairs, was a former representative in the Massachusetts legislature and greatly respected in many parts of the city. Through the assistance of a nearby dental school, it was possible to have dental hygienists visit almost every physician and dentist who had an office in the city. These visits were for the purpose of informing doctors and dentists about fluoridation and also to encourage them to speak to their patients about fluoridation. In addition, material was left for the waiting rooms of these men. Well over a hundred Newton physicians and dentists were visited.

Press coverage was expanded at this time and stories in support of fluoridation were obtained from sources such as the State Health Department and the Medical Society. When some questions were raised about the possible effect of fluoride on pipes, a report on this question was obtained from the State Health Department and printed in the newspapers. Through the efforts of a newspaper writer who lived in Newton and was interested in fluoridation, a series of articles on fluoridation was published in one of the major Boston daily newspapers.

In October the city solicitor ruled that a favorable vote on fluoridation would not be binding on the Newton Board of Aldermen, i.e., that this group could still refuse to appropriate the necessary funds. This decision was headlined on page one of the only Newton daily newspaper. Because of the many community leaders working with the fluoridation Committee, it was possible to obtain a statement from the Mayor that he would consider a favorable vote on the referendum to be binding on him. This statement by the Mayor appeared on page one of the paper on the very next day. In this manner the possible harmful effects of the original newspaper story were greatly reduced. Right at the end of the campaign a similar "quick answer" had to be prepared. The second city-wide mailing by the opponents of fluoridation stated that "State Health Director Regrets Approving Fluoridation." The implication here was that the man in question was the current Massachusetts Commissioner of Public Health. Actually the reference was to a former state health commissioner from another state. Again the extensive organization of the Newton Committee enabled it to obtain an immediate strong refutation by the Massachusetts Commissioner of Public Health. This answer was not only printed in the newspapers, but was also broadcast over several radio stations.

It was not until the last two months of the campaign that the Committee obtained an office of its own. From this location, in the basement of a Committee member's home, a great deal of organizational work was done. The telephone there was in constant use and thousands of pieces of literature were distributed from this location. Extremely important also during this period was obtaining the part-time paid services of a man who had had extensive experience in community education and community organization in the field of public health. His efforts were an invaluable supplement to the efforts of the many Newton volunteers. In the spring of 1961, it had been decided to appoint co-chairmen of the Committee and these two women and this man sought to coordinate the many activities and persons involved in the later stages of the campaign.

Large advertisements in several newspapers were purchased for the last issue prior to Election Day. Both lack of funds and uncertainty regarding the value of this technique were the basis for the limited use of advertisements. The opponents also did not do extensive newspaper advertising in these last phases, although they had bought small amounts of space periodically during much of the campaign. The work of the opponents was restricted mostly to the intensive word-of-mouth efforts of a handful of persons and two city-wide mailings to every household in Newton. The material that was sent out in these mailings was developed with great care and avoided the hysterical emotional appeals of most anti-fluoridation literature used in other campaigns. It consisted mainly of references to one or another "scientific" article or report. A naive observer undoubtedly would have been very impressed by the many apparently convincing arguments against fluoridation. Unquestionably, these two mailings by the opponents were effective in raising doubts in the minds of countless Newton voters.

As part of the city-wide organization, poll captains were obtained for each precinct. These persons had the task of securing workers to distribute material on fluoridation to voters as they came to the polls. Instructions were prepared for poll captains as well as poll workers. Despite the fact that the weather on Election Day was poor, almost all polling places were covered during the hours of heavy voting and at many precincts, at least one fluoridation worker was present from the time the polls opened in the morning until they closed in the evening. Several thousands of pieces of material were distributed in this manner on Election Day. Poll workers wore large placards urging a "Yes" vote and many also had stickers or signs on their cars. Posters had also been placed in store windows throughout the city. Including material distributed at the polls the previous year, during the petition drive and sent out in the various mailings, over 120,000 separate pieces of educational material were placed in the hands of citizens of Newton during the 23 months of the campaign. Over two dozen different pieces of material were used. These included fact sheets, reprints of newspaper stories, magazine articles, pamphlets, etc. Half of the pieces were developed by the Newton Committee itself. Others included material from the U.S. Public Health Service, the American Dental Association, Public Affairs Committee, articles reprinted from *Good Housekeeping Magazine*, *Changing Times* (the Kiplinger Newsletter) and *Time* magazine. Some of this material was obtained free of charge, some was bought, and some reproduced by the Committee itself. Several flyers were used that had first been developed by fluoridation committees in other communities.

When the counting of votes was completed early in the morning on the day after the election, fluoridation had won by a margin of 1,240 votes. A number of persons long familiar with Newton politics commented that the Citizens' Committee for Dental Health had run the best city-wide campaign ever seen in the city. Several politicians wistfully remarked that they wished they could have this organization working for them! Particular reference was made to the exemplary behavior of workers at the polls who refused to be drawn into violent emotional arguments. This was in contrast to some of the opponents who behaved in near-hysterical fashion at the polls. At least 300 persons and probably closer to 400 persons worked with the fluoridation Committee in the last three months of the campaign.

Notes

1. Reprinted by permission of Thomas F. A. Plaut.

2. In one of these towns the fluoridation issue at the last moment became entangled with other controversies, and this was a major factor in the defeat. In the other town, which is basically more conservative, an extremely active and well-financed campaign was carried on by the opponents.

7

The Cycle of
Policy Analysis

We have described policy analysis so far as if each analysis were conducted largely in isolation from others. Actually, analyses are linked with one another in numerous ways. Parallel analyses may result from the same problem situation arising in different places. An increase in crime or a population congestion problem, for example, can lead to similar analyses in various states and localities. Problems of environmental quality and resource scarcity face many nations in similar ways. Various analyses may also be linked because they draw on common sources of information for their models of causation. Both the discoveries of basic science and the results of practical analysis may ultimately be shared by various analysts.

Analyses may in addition be linked together over time so that an earlier analysis affects the course of later ones. If the findings of one analysis are sufficiently general and lasting, they can be used later by others. One analysis, even if it does not result in a new policy, may also lead to knowledge of conditions of feasibility that can be used by others.[1] Moreover, people who work on one analytic team may develop skills there that are useful for later analyses. For example, a team developed at the Ford Motor Company moved into the Department of Defense under Secretary Robert McNamara in 1961, and other groups with transferable analytic skills developed in the Department of Health, Education, and Welfare and in the Office of Economic Opportunity in the 1960s.

An especially important relation between earlier and later analyses relates to the organizations that are created to implement policies. A successful analysis can lead to the creation of an organization. We often say that implementation of a policy has been successful when the organization created has become self-sufficient and is a going concern. Organizations can also be created without a great deal of systematic analysis; but regardless of how they come into existence, they give rise to special conditions affecting later analyses. They develop specific goals, activities, and interests that affect later definitions of the problem situation and conditions for feasibility.

Our goal in this chapter is to consider the second cycle of policy analysis, the analysis that occurs after an initial policy has been put into effect. We shall therefore be largely concerned with the constraints placed on our analysis by the existence of organizations that are carrying out programs related to the analysis. Analysts often wish to make use of the experience of existing programs to guide further choices. When these choices affect the existing programs themselves, analysis takes the form of "evaluation" of a specific program or group of programs. The organizations that are carrying out those programs are likely to be threatened by analysis of this kind. Their reactions will then affect the entire process of analysis in major ways. Such reactions might include resisting threats to their future existence, selecting the information that is made available, and defining the goals of the analysis in terms of organizational interests.

The commitment of organizations to their goals and activities seems a necessary condition for the implementation of policies. These goals do not always promote the gathering of information for future analysis. Future analyses and choices can benefit, however, from information that these organizations may generate. We may therefore wish to choose policies that produce not only substantive benefits but also information.

POLICIES THAT GENERATE
INFORMATION

In a sense every policy generates information that affects our choice of future policies. Policies chosen by private industry generate market information that affects consumers' choices and investors' decisions. A competitive market makes use of this information to provide one type of accountability. Public policies affecting citizens generate information that enters the political process. A successful or unsuccessful program affects voters and comes to the attention of legislators who, to satisfy their constituents, support it or criticize it. In this sense public policies face political accountability.

There is, however, a third type of accountability based on scientific or technical assessment of policies. Systematic information about the effects of consuming a product or about the working of a program, based on representative samples of persons affected and on reliable scientific inferences, can be a part of policy analysis and can also improve the decisions that consumers or citizens make about that product or program. This systematic judgment of public programs can be especially useful if the programs generate the kind of information that analysts need.

If policies and programs are designed to generate this sort of information, then subsequent analyses can be better informed. Some of our possible policies, such as that of conducting research, are aimed primarily at gaining information. We might decide after considering several policy alternatives that we needed information more than a large immediate public investment in a program. We would then choose to devote resources to testing and improving our models, hoping that not long afterward we could choose a better program. One of the costs of conducting this research would then be the forgone opportunity to aid people through the program that we did not immediately establish.

We can also establish a program and combine it with data generation and research in several ways. One way is to undertake an intervention, let's say, the development of one or more school programs, in which the effects of one policy are systematically compared with those of another. Such interventions vary in their degree of rigor, from true experiments with randomized controls to simple policy interventions whose results are compared with previous events or nonrandomized controls (quasi-experiments). We shall discuss some such studies later in this chapter.

In a well-designed experiment, the goal of the manager of the experimental program is to generate information. He does so by making sure that the program, including experimental and control treatments, is implemented in such a way as to correspond to specified policies. He also cooperates with the research part of the experimental team, allowing them to gather the information they need. He wants to make his program work, but he wants even more to make the research tell the truth about the sorts of treatment used.

An example of this procedure was the negative-income-tax experiment conducted in New Jersey from 1968 to 1971 and in other areas of the United States.[2] The policy being tested involved giving money to poor families, the amount being related to their earned income in such a way that the recipients would be motivated to earn money themselves. If this had been an established program, the program manager might have also tried in other ways to encourage recipients to work. Since it was an experiment, the manager had to make sure that no incentives to work were provided other than the payments themselves. He was expected to generate useful information, not merely to try to make the program a "success."

Managers of ordinary service delivery programs have different motives. They need not be opposed to research, but they know that their rewards lie in successful delivery of services, that is, on schedule, of quality that is viewed as satisfactory, and to all the clientele they are supposed to reach. In this perspective the need to gather and record accurate information is of lower priority. As a result, when citizens try to use the records of such programs for research, even if the managers make them available, the records may not be of high enough quality to aid analysis. Information on some students or patients may not be adequately recorded. Personnel needed for urgent tasks may be diverted from data recording. Recording systems may be changed without adequate comparability being insured between the old and new methods of recording.

The problem is in effect one of information as an external benefit. The effort needed to provide information to other programs, or to citizen-researchers, may seem within the program as an imposition or a waste of valuable time and personnel. The responsibility of the manager is not to benefit other programs, but to benefit his or her own program. We thus need to devise incentive systems not only to make programs work better but to make them record better information about what they have done. The professionalization of managers with an eye to evaluation and the training of citizen-analysts who will reward public managers for keeping good data (even if the data are embarrassing) are among the types of incentives required.

An important source of information for analysis is therefore the keeping of high-quality administrative records in ongoing programs. The preservation of good organizational data can permit valuable evaluative studies. One such study dealt with the effects of an anesthetic, halothane, which could be compared to other anesthetics by use of data from "a particular group of 34 hospitals that kept good records and whose staffs keenly wanted to answer the very questions . . . asked" about the comparative effects of anesthetics.[3] These hospitals might have seemed to be diverting resources from the cure of patients in order to keep high-quality records. But the professionals in the hospitals realized that their capacity to treat patients in the long run rested on reliable scientific knowledge.

The data revealed on analysis not only that the anesthetics differed but also that the hospitals themselves differed in quality. These findings might have been embarrassing to some hospitals if they had been identified by name. However, if organizations are to keep good records, they must receive some reward for doing so and not merely be punished for embarrassing facts that are revealed. One of the worst reactions that citizens could give would be to condemn organizations that had allowed themselves to be scrutinized in terms of their own records, while letting other organizations with poor records go scot-free.

In another study well-kept records concerning land ownership, which were preserved by legal requirements, permitted an evaluation several decades later of one of the New Deal's programs of the 1930s. A program intended to allow blacks to own land in the South was regarded initially as a failure. But a reanalysis in the 1970s by Lester S. Salamon showed that in the areas where this program had been instituted, black land ownership had persisted and that owners in these areas may also have been more independent politically of whites.[4] Thus, the evaluation of programs in the longer run requires data series that are recorded and preserved over the long run.

ORGANIZATIONAL STAKES IN AN EXISTING PROGRAM

When we are engaged in a second or later cycle of analysis, we are usually evaluating a program set up to produce results rather than information.[5] In this case we must expect that the program under evaluation will have interests that affect not only policy choices but also every part of the process of analysis. Decisions about how to modify existing governmental programs are affected not only by interest groups outside of government but also by the organizations that carry out the programs themselves.

A program manager is usually chosen because he believes in the efficacy of the program and is expected to make it succeed. His career as an administrator will depend on the success of the program, which is normally judged by its reputation, its size, and its effectiveness. The size of a program is usually measured in terms of its budgetary allocation, the number of persons it employs, and its output (e.g., number of persons served). Its effectiveness may be judged in various ways, and it is in the interest of the manager to see that these judgments are made in ways that he considers just and favorable.

The program manager must not only believe in the program himself but must actively organize support for it inside and outside the organization. He must assure himself of the loyalty and efficiency of his subordinates in order to carry out the program's tasks. He may do this to some degree by his influence on employment and transfer of personnel. He may also foster employee morale by promotion and salary policies that his subordinates view as just. He may give public recognition to employees who render service that is especially valuable to fulfilling the goals of the program. At times he may have to defend the program or its personnel against criticism from outside.

An example of this responsibility on the part of the secretary of state is given by Allison.

> *When he defers to the Secretary of Defense rather than fighting for his department's position—as he often must—he strains the loyalty of his officialdom. In the words of one of his Indians: 'Loyalty is hilly, and it has to go down if it is going to go up.'* [6]

The secretary of state must defend his department against other departments, if only to insure the loyalty of his subordinates. In any public organization one condition for subordinates' loyalty is maintaining the budget that pays their salaries.

The manager of a program must also look outward to the constituencies that the program serves. He must encourage them to support the program politically if help is needed—for example, if the program comes under attack or needs active support in the legislature at budget time. The Head Start program exemplified this sort of support, whether organized by managers or others. "The Director of the Office of Child Development told a conference on early childhood that 'in communities where there is a Head Start Center, the entire community is being mobilized around the needs of children.'" In spite of the ambiguous results of a professional evaluation of the program, Head Start's demonstration "that public programs for children as young as three could be established . . . led to a willingness to accept public intervention in development of preschool children." [7]

A successful manager will therefore be wary of possible publicity that may harm his program. He may well ask why his program has been singled out for evaluation when others have not. He may try to see that evaluation is not conducted too soon, before the program has had what he considers a fair chance to produce its effects. He may channel evaluation into "formative" directions that help him to redirect the program as it develops, rather than "summative" evaluations that are given only at the end of a specified period and lead to recommendations to continue the program, expand it, cut it back, or eliminate it. The manager, like other persons working in the program and committed to it, will thus be a significant influence on not only the feasibility of changing the program but also the feasibility of gathering information about it.

We cannot say in general whether such attitudes on the part of the manager or his staff are justified or not. At times an evaluation study may be proposed in a fashion that is premature, technically inadequate, and designed to embarrass the program. At other times the program itself may be inadequate and its proponents obstinately blind to this inadequacy. Whether an evaluation is needed may have to be decided by an authority higher than that of the program itself. The public is such an authority, if it can be the source of reasoned and judicious evaluations.

CITIZEN ACCESS
TO EVALUATION DATA

Because of the stakes that an organization has in its evaluation, it will release data for that evaluation only with great care. The manager may wish under certain conditions not to generate such data at all, or to have them used only by "internal" evaluators who are employees of the organization, or to restrict their analysis to professionals with obligations to follow appropriate procedures and to interpret the results responsibly.

A difference therefore exists between prior analysis, which occurs in terms of general principles, and evaluation of specific programs, as regards the role of the citizen. Citizens are more often involved in the choice among new policies than in the systematic evaluation of existing ones. This is because evaluation studies are usually sponsored by government agencies or foundations who engage experts to perform the studies. The information needed to evaluate a program is thus initially the property of an expert group that has been called in to gather it. Only later, if at all, is it released in detail to the public.

The citizen's relation to program evaluation is thus more likely to involve reviewing someone else's evaluation study than gathering information for himself. An example is the series of studies made to evaluate the Head Start program for improving the educational opportunities of minority children of preschool age. An evaluation was carried out by Westinghouse Learning Corporation and Ohio University and then became the object of controversy.[8] A citizen trained in the methods of evaluation might be better able than other citizens to judge the merits of such studies after they have reached the press. A legislator might also be better able to understand the testimony and reports if trained in policy analysis. But neither would have conducted the study itself.

PROGRAM EVALUATION:
THE NARROWED FOCUS

The analysis that leads to initiation of a program can be connected with later analysis through evaluation of that program. This specific connection places the evaluator in a different situation, however, from that which we have described for policy analysis generally. The definition of the problem, the choice of criteria, the alternatives considered, and the models used will all be narrower than our previous chapters would suggest. The analyst who becomes an evaluator of a specific program must be aware of these differences.

Program evaluation is the systematic effort to judge the success of a program in order to see whether it has attained its goals. But concealed in this definition are important issues relative to how the *problem* is, and should be, defined.

Most important is the question concerning what programs come under scrutiny in the first place. In general, it is new programs or programs that have come under political attack that are evaluated. Crises or visible failures may also stimulate such reexamination. "Zero-base" budgeting principles, which ideally look at every program periodically to see whether it is functioning properly, are in fact more often directed at programs that have already been questioned on other grounds. The relation between such questioning and the decision to evaluate is an example of the frequently followed procedure of developing a detailed model of causation along the lines of an initial intuitive model of causation. If the relation between program and goals comes under question and a decision to evaluate is therefore encouraged, an intuitive model of low or absent causation is being substituted by some observers for the initial causal model on which the program was based. But political as well as causal considerations can lead to this negative preliminary judgment. A school program may be questioned, for example, either because parents feel their children are not learning as they should or because teachers consider that it threatens their autonomy and career prospects.

Many programs that cannot prove their efficacy statistically are nevertheless continued without question. The Head Start program had an enthusiastic constituency regardless of the results of the Westinghouse study. Established educational programs in public schools and colleges resist evaluation on the grounds of alleged teacher autonomy or presumed inappropriateness of rigid models of service delivery, even when their effectiveness has not been demonstrated by quantitative social or educational research. The delivery of health services also enjoys support even when its relation to improvements in health has not been demonstrated systematically.

The most thoroughly entrenched programs are those that have developed internal and external constituencies over a generation or more. To persons who saw them originate and have grown up with them, they are very unlikely to seem new or controversial. Such was the case with a variety of programs developed in the United States in the 1930s, such as Social Security and Aid to Dependent Children. These programs have nevertheless come under criticism in the 1960s and 1970s, in part because of demographic changes that were not fully anticipated at their origin.

When a generation or more has elapsed since the origin of a program, the organizational stakes of its proponents will be high, but the analysis that led to the development of the program may be ignored because of changes in public perspectives. Proponents of Social Security may even fear new analysis because such analysis might show the program to be not a "bank-deposit" arrangement, but a form of taxation that transfers resources from one generation to another. The "welfare" programs of the 1930s have also been challenged as reflecting mere organizational interests of social-work professionals, without consideration of the analysis that led to the development of those professional services in the first place. The study of contemporary history can thus reveal important features of the cycle of policy analysis.

An equally important aspect of problem definition in evaluation concerns the valuative *criteria* that are to be used. The criteria used in evaluation of existing programs tend to be specific rather than general. They are typically concerned with whether the programs met their stated goals. Was a training program effective in raising achievement scores or helping the unemployed get jobs? Did a program in intergroup relations improve the attitudes of members of one group toward another? Did a program in preventive medicine reduce the incidence of specified diseases? Did a program that was intended to control the costs of health services in fact reduce costs?

In many instances these criteria relate to programs for the delivery of human services and thus involve measuring relatively intangible benefits provided through human contacts.[9] We can more easily measure the effectiveness of weapons systems or transportation systems. But this latter sort of judgment, involving natural science and engineering as well as human reactions, may be called "technology assessment" rather than "evaluation."

The specificity of these criteria implies that in evaluation we are often measuring effectiveness rather than economic efficiency. A concern for efficiency leads us, as we have seen, to various forms of the ethic of preference satisfaction and to criteria that provide indications of tradeoffs between programs. If a program has been totally ineffective we may wish to terminate it and return its budgetary allocation to the private sector. But even if it has produced clear-cut effects, we still have to consider terminating it unless its benefit-cost ratio is greater than unity. Similar tradeoff questions can be raised for other teleological criteria.

Although the usual definition of evaluation implies that a program is to be judged in terms of its stated goals, if the public, clients, manager, or others affected by a program judge that the program has side effects other than the stated ones, the range of goals to be examined may be enlarged. A struggle may then ensue between proponents and opponents of the program. Proponents, especially program managers, may seek to avoid evaluation altogether or to choose criteria that will be favorable to the program. Critics, on the other hand, may try to see that data gathered bear strictly on the prescribed goals of the program, rather than new areas in which the program may be providing side benefits. Alternatively, critics may seek out negative unintended consequences of program operation.[10] This approach is characteristic of outside rather than in-house evaluation and may sometimes be the stance of the citizen as distinguished from the hired consultant.

The *alternatives* considered in program evaluation are usually focused on the program itself: to expand it, continue it, curtail it, or terminate it. These differ subtly from the alternatives we considered earlier. Previously, we stressed that the alternative of doing nothing must always be considered and is often a baseline for calculation, as in cost-benefit analysis. Now, an implicit baseline is the nonexistence of the program, the state of affairs that would have existed if the program had not been put into effect.

The alternatives are also narrowed in their focus on the particular program being evaluated. Evaluation asks whether a particular program should be expanded or reduced and tells us little about alternatives different from this program. Details of implementation must be specified if we hope to generalize the results and apply them to different programs. If the program under study has succeeded because it had an extremely skilled manager, we may be more justified in supporting him or her than in creating new programs based on the same organizational principles.

The *models* used in evaluation, like the criteria, tend also to be specific to the programs under study. Evaluation tends to ask whether a particular program worked, rather than whether a particular *type* of program (or policy) should be chosen in preference to others. If a program has been systematically instituted to provide information on the effects of various policy and nonpolicy variables, then its evaluation can more nearly be the test of a model. One of the best ways to achieve this generality is to institute a set of programs and controls in which variables are allowed to vary independently.

Because evaluation studies deal with existing programs, they encounter in sharpened form some problems of *feasibility* that characterize policy analysis generally. Effective managers and program constituencies will be alert to possible harm to their programs. They will thus exercise care not only in permitting evaluation but also in releasing data for such a study. They may release data only under the condition that the results be kept confidential subject to the manager's approval. Such requirements obviously limit the analyst's options in recommending and furthering new policies.

The feasibility of alternative policies is thus affected by the preparation and dissemination of the evaluation report. The summary of the Coleman Report, for example, was drafted and redrafted because of its potential threats to the positions of Washington agencies, civil rights activists, and others.[11] Any policy-related report needs to be edited carefully to remove errors or sources of possible misinterpretation. But an evaluation report will receive especially close scrutiny from supporters of the program. Closely associated with this scrutiny is the question whether the report will be made available to the public. Although many publicly disseminated reports are ignored, there is always the possibility that a particular report will be seized on by critics or the media and negative judgments publicized. This risk can be reduced if proponents of the program insure that the report is used only for internal purposes. Whether this can be done depends on the source of sponsorship of the evaluation and on the terms negotiated by an evaluator when he initially contracts for the job.

Perhaps the most difficult problem of feasibility that follows an evaluation is that of terminating a program that has been judged inadequate or unnecessary. Even though a new program may sometimes be endangered by evaluation, a program of long standing may have generated regular sources of budget and support, and its employees may expect continued work there, to such a degree that the program is nearly impossible to terminate. Successful termination of a long-standing program seems to require drastic, uncompromising action by a politically skilled outsider.[12]

METHODS FOR EVALUATION

A distinctive feature of the evaluation of programs is that it involves time series of data.[13] Variables indicating the expected outcomes of programs are often measured at regular intervals: Examples are students' test scores, citizens' satisfaction with municipal services, delivery of health services, and motorists' conformity with traffic laws. These series of measurements are then used to infer whether the program in question made a difference, how much of a difference it made, whether the effect lasted, and perhaps whether the difference was worth the expense.

Most of the models we discussed in chapters 4 and 5, however, assumed that the effect of policies on dependent variables was instantaneous. The statistical models we considered assumed that all variables were measured at the same time. The models of market equilibrium also seemed to assume that supply and demand attained their equilibrium immediately, though the example of change in supply in East Texas (case 5–B) suggested that processes of adjustment might take place even if the rate of supply became constant. Only in the speed-limit case (case 4–A) did we compare data over time as part of the evaluation of a past policy.

We thus find that many of the models social science provides us for policy choice involve cross-sectional data and notions of instantaneous causation. On the other hand, time-series data and the corresponding "dynamic" models are far less frequent in theoretical social science, even though changes in effects over time are often observed when we intervene in a social system by changing a policy.

A time-series evaluation of a policy is likely to yield useful results if we gather data on the relevant population both before and after the policy is introduced, if we know what the policy was that was introduced, if we introduce it at the right time, and if we make parallel measurements on a suitable control group. In studying the effects of the 55-mph speed limit, we did not have a control group. Changes in amounts of automobile travel occurred in part because of the shortage of gasoline and its increase in price. These conditions have to be taken into account when we assess the effect of the speed limit on possible changes in costs of accidents. Inflation also affected accident costs and the value of time and had to be taken into account. A problem in the use of time series is therefore that numerous events and changes occur over the same time period. In the absence of genuine control groups, we need to separate the effects of policy variables from other effects.

Government officials are likely to introduce new policies when the problem situation has become especially acute. The 55-mph speed limit was introduced in this way. But if the event that gave rise to a problem situation was a random one, then the trend that produced it is more likely than not to be reversed thereafter. For example, the state of Connecticut cracked down on speeding in December 1955 after traffic fatalities had reached a new high. In 1956 fatalities decreased, but such a decrease might have occurred anyhow. Therefore, a time series of fatalities for Connecticut alone for this period, without controls, is hard to interpret.[14]

Our task is to learn what difference, over an extended time period, a specifiable policy made. It is necessary that the policy be described in detail if the evaluation is to be useful to a wider audience than that interested in one specific program. Thus, we would like to know more than the effect of a crackdown on speed in Connecticut or the introduction of a "breathalyzer" test for drunken drivers in Britain.[15] We would like to be able to say more generally what features of these policies were responsible for the results so that we could predict the consequences of new policies introduced elsewhere.

We need to make measurements on the group that the policy is aimed to affect (the target group), as we noted in chapter 4, because often the effect of a policy on the entire population is so small as to be invisible. Careful consideration must be given to possible side effects, and the sample of persons affected must be chosen to reveal these as well as the main or intended effects. An extended time period is desirable in order to see whether the effects of the program persist; whether they decline, as when people became accustomed to a new law-enforcement procedure; or whether they develop slowly over a long period.

The most convincing evidence of the effects of a program or policy is provided by a well-designed experiment. In such an experiment variables are allowed to vary independently of one another. To learn the effects of putting school resources into improved textbooks rather than salaries for better-trained teachers, we would plan to introduce these two factors in different schools while also carefully observing student learning in "control" schools where neither was introduced. If we wish to discover whether textbooks and teachers together produce an effect more than the sum of the independent effects, we introduce both together in some schools.

In human programs there are especially likely to be nonpolicy variables that need to be controlled. In studying the effects of an educational innovation we might try to control for the socioeconomic composition of the student body by choosing schools that were alike in this respect. We might control for the students' prior knowledge by giving them a test before they entered the program. We might also try to measure their attitudes and motivation in advance.

There are usually additional variables, however, that we do not know and for which we cannot control. No matter how many known variables we have tried to control in our design, we always wonder whether we have controlled them all. The procedures we ourselves used in choosing schools for experimental and control treatments might introduce some bias, and even if they did not, critics of our results might claim that they did. For these reasons the ideal procedure for selecting experimental and control groups is randomization, the use of a table of random numbers or the equivalent. This procedure insures that the experimenter's bias or the self-selection of those studied does not bias the results and that the results have known statistical properties.[16]

ASSESSMENT OF QUASI-MARKET POLICIES

The cycle of policy analysis is ideally a process of self-correction. But some policies that set up procedures for decision making are themselves intended to have self-correcting features. The competitive market and representative government illustrate this type of self-correction. The consumers' or voters' dissatisfaction with the goods or policies they receive is expected to result in a change of the goods or policies offered. Because these sorts of procedures are intended to be self-corrective, we are less likely to try to evaluate them by examining whether they yield a higher level of preference satisfaction or other desired outcomes than alternative arrangements.

Policies analogous to the market, which we may call quasi-market policies, have been suggested to allow public policy outputs to respond more to consumer demand. In education, as we mentioned in chapter 4, two such approaches have been tried: performance contracting, or paying educational organizations according to how much the students learn, and voucher systems, in which parents have a chance to use vouchers equivalent to certain amounts of money to pay for their children's education at any of several competing local schools. In advance, it seemed almost certain to proponents that these systems would provide greater incentives for effective education than would noncompetitive local schools whose staffs were not paid in relation to productivity. Yet studies of the results of these two types of programs showed that they did not live up to expectations. Whether this apparent inadequacy should be charged to the model or to its implementation is perhaps not as important as our knowledge that even programs of this sort need to be evaluated.

During the 1960s an increasing skepticism developed concerning whether professionals, without the stimulus of the profit motive, could deliver services effectively. This skepticism was directed at social workers, as regards national welfare programs, and at school teachers, especially in view of the negative findings of several well-publicized research studies such as the Coleman Report (described in chapter 4). It was then suggested that public educational systems should be held accountable for their performance and that one way to accomplish this would be to pay them according to students' perform-ance.[17]

In 1970 the Office of Economic Opportunity notified potential contrac-tors of a one-year program of performance contracting in which private firms were invited to make proposals. Six firms that appeared best equipped were selected, and school districts were chosen from among those responding to an invitation to academically deficient school districts. The contracts drawn up provided that payment would be related to individual students' gain in achieve-ment. For students who failed to gain the equivalent of grade unit in the year, no payment was to be made, and for those who gained that much or more, pro-portional payments would be made. Control schools were also chosen, though on a basis of similarity rather than randomization. Twelve thousand experi-mental students and a similar number of controls in eighteen school districts were studied.

The one-year time span was seen, at least in retrospect, to be insufficient for an incentive system to draw new firms into the market. Nor did it allow the chosen firms to make major adjustments in their programs in response to experience. It was actually, therefore, "a test of learning technology and man-agement abilities." [18]

The programs started up rapidly, sometimes with difficulty in finding enough qualified local personnel. Parents' consent to the experiment was also obtained. At the end of one year the experimental pupils scored one-tenth of a grade unit better, on the average, than pupils in other local schools, a much smaller effect than expected. Some of the contracting companies did better than others. Part of the feeling of disappointment that resulted may have been due to the high initial expectations. Perhaps we should set our sights lower and expect only gradual improvement.[19]

An alternative approach—based on preference satisfaction rather than on achievement scores—was that of educational vouchers. The Office of Eco-nomic Opportunity was the sponsor of an initial demonstration of this concept in Alum Rock, California, beginning in 1972. Because there was no randomized control group, this policy was not studied in a fashion that could be called "ex-perimental." Other local schools were used for comparison of test scores, how-ever. The program was evaluated by a research team from the Rand Corpora-tion.[20]

The Alum Rock school district in San Jose, California, agreed to par-ticipate in a voucher demonstration that would include its public schools, pro-vide job tenure and seniority rights for its teachers, and allow pupils who had attended a given school to continue doing so if they wished. The unit or pro-gram that was to be offered for choice was the "mini-school," an educational program within a given school. In the first year of the demonstration, "at the six voucher schools, 22 mini-schools emerged." [21] Teachers, administrators, and students began getting accustomed to the new system in the course of the first year. But as often happens with new programs, this adjustment took time. Like the performance contracting experiment, the voucher demonstration aroused hopes of rapid and immediate change. It may, therefore, have been judged against unduly high expectations. Sometimes, however, high expectations have to be aroused in order to persuade sponsors to support such a program and subjects to participate in it.

One difficulty encountered in Alum Rock, which is generally characteristic of organizations, was that the schools (administrators and teachers) were not always anxious to compete with one another and to face the insecurity that competition would bring. A cohesive group of six principals determined some of the conditions of the demonstration. They insisted that test data not be released to the public till the spring of 1974. Many teachers felt that it was unprofessional for one school to compete with others by newspaper publicity or to engage in overt criticism of another school. Teachers were also concerned with possible status changes that might result if their own mini-schools were unpopular and teachers had to be transferred to other schools. In addition, the inflow of new discretionary funds was not always welcomed. This departure from the line-item budgeting procedure led to a failure to spend about thirty-five percent of the compensatory voucher funds at the end of the first year. Even if schools had wanted to grow in funds and enrollment, they would often have had to hire new staff, strangers to the group, and to put new classes in trailers. Trailers would add classroom space, but cafeterias, libraries, playgrounds, and bathrooms would become crowded.[22]

In its second year the demonstration expanded, and its potential for introducing competition remained. Data on student achievement were "somewhat contradictory" in comparison with data on other local schools.[23] But since parents chose schools without knowledge of test scores and because their preferences may have been based on other criteria, this is not necessarily a failure of the program.

In the second year one of the potential avenues for competition among schools was blocked. It was initially expected that programs whose enrollment increased would be able to expand into the buildings of programs whose enrollment was decreasing. Objections of the receiving schools made this impossible, however, and in the third year this feature was abandoned. At the end of the five-year period of aid from the Office of Economic Opportunity, the principle of competition had been implemented only to a limited degree. Robert R. Mayer attributes this to the fact that the intended competition was to be introduced only within a larger bureaucratic system and that "the interests of the larger system prevailed when they conflicted with those of the voucher experiment."[24]

Both performance contracting and vouchers have potential for improving public education, even though neither lived up to expectations. Each showed, in retrospect, that time was required for the model to become effective. If the performance-contracting experiment had continued longer, it might have encountered organizational problems similar to those of the voucher program, but it was not located entirely within a single bureaucratic system. Perhaps the expectations of instantaneous success were encouraged not only by a general hope that we have for a panacea and the enthusiasm of proponents, but also by the lack of consideration of time lags in the initial models that were used. If this is so, then these examples show that practical trials of implementation can contribute to the realism of our models in a way that can usefully supplement the study of nonexperimental data and enlarge social-science theory.

SUMMARY

These examples suggest that policy analysis assumes a different form once a policy has been embodied in a program. Its focus is narrower, though sometimes criticism of existing programs can lead us back to broader and more imaginative ways of devising new ones. In the interval after a new program has been created, analysis and evaluation pose special hazards for that program. The result is to introduce a new element—managers', employees', and clients' stakes in organizational survival—into the politics of feasibility. Evaluation research thus necessarily involves an element of "methodology under pressure" that, although shared by analysis generally, is especially focused on the interests of participants in the survival of their programs.

Social experimentation has increasingly provided one way to check the results of our prior analysis and improve it. This experimentation can be extended to quasi-market policies as well as others. It provides us with a keener sense of the time lags involved in implementing policies and thus should lead to the improvement of our models by inclusion of these time elements.

Our sense of processes operating through time goes hand in hand with our use of time series in evaluation. Some programs will prove to have a substantial effect only in the longer run, perhaps after the spotlight of attention has turned from them. Others may produce large initial effects that later decrease. But we shall never know how these changes occur without devoting time and effort to careful review of older programs. Analysts as a group cannot afford to work entirely on problems that are responses to mere enthusiasm of the moment. The problem situation defined by a public anxious for a panacea may have to be redefined for some analysts so as to permit the study of longer-term effects. For this purpose we also need data that are gathered repetitively, preserved, and made available for long-run evaluation.

Control group: a set of persons or units who receive no "treatment," chosen for study in parallel with an experimental program.

Control variable: a nonpolicy variable whose effect is set aside in an experiment or evaluation either by designing the study so that comparisons can be made without its effect entering or by taking its effect into account statistically.

Evaluation: a study of the extent to which an existing program has fulfilled its goals.

Experiment: the introduction of a policy on a small scale, ideally with a randomized control group, to examine its effectiveness and value.

Formative evaluation: evaluation whose results are fed back before the completion of the program so that the program may be improved.

Quasi-experiment: a study of the effect of a policy intervention, which falls short of the requirement of a randomized control group.

Quasi-market policy: a policy that sets up monetary or competitive incentives for performance analogous to those of the market.

Summative evaluation: evaluation of a program carried on unchanged for a specified period, reporting the degree of its success (often to outsiders).

Zero-base budgeting: examination of a program as a whole to see what aspects of its entire budget require change; in contrast to incremental budgeting, which examines only a limited number of small proposed changes.

1. What typical tactics are open to a program director when faced with a threat to his program from outside evaluation?

2. How are the definition of the problem situation, the criteria, the alternatives, the model, and the calculations of feasibility different in program evaluation from the corresponding elements in analysis conducted prior to the existence of a program?

3. In evaluation studies, what special problems are encountered concerning freedom of access to data and dissemination of results? Do these problems exist for analysis conducted prior to the existence of a program?

4. (See case 4–A.) If you are considering choice of an optimum speed limit, what relevant information is available from evaluation of the existing 55-mph speed limit that would not have been available in 1973, before this limit was imposed?

NOTES

1. Such a process of successive approximations is included in the strategy of "disjointed incrementalism" described by David Braybrooke and Charles E. Lindblom in *A Strategy of Decision* (New York: Free Press, 1963), ch. 5. Here we stress reasoned analysis more and leave open the possibility of applying it to large as well as small changes.

2. See Henry W. Riecken and Robert F. Boruch, *Social Experimentation* (New York: Academic Press, 1974), passim.

3. Quotation from Lincoln E. Moses and Frederick Mosteller, "Safety of Anesthetics," in Judith M. Tanur et al., eds., *Statistics: A Guide to the Unknown* (San Francisco: Holden-Day, 1972), p. 15.

4. Lester S. Salamon, "The Time Dimension in Policy Analysis: The Case of the New Deal Land Reform Experiments," Working Paper 8741 (Durham, N.C.: Duke University, Institute of Policy Sciences and Public Affairs, 1974).

5. For detailed treatment of political conditions surrounding evaluation, see Carol H. Weiss, *Evaluation Research* (Englewood Cliffs, N.J.: Prentice-Hall, 1972), and Charles O. Jones, *An Introduction to the Study of Public Policy*, 2d ed. (North Scituate, Mass.: Duxbury Press, 1977), ch. 8.

6. Graham T. Allison, *Essence of Decision* (Boston: Little, Brown, 1971), p. 166, citing Roger Hilsman, *To Move a Nation* (Garden City, N.Y.: Doubleday, 1967).

7. Gilbert Y. Steiner, *The Children's Cause* (Washington, D.C.: Brookings, 1976), p. 35.

8. See Peter H. Rossi and Walter Williams, eds., *Evaluating Social Programs* (New York: Seminar Press, 1972), chs. 8 and 11.

9. See Harvey A. Garn, Michael J. Flax, Michael Springer, and Jeremy B. Taylor, *Models for Indicator Development: A Framework for Policy Analysis* (Washington, D.C.: Urban Institute, 1976), pp. 13–17. This monograph also distinguishes between measures of "social performance" and measures of the narrower concept of "institutional performance."

10. Taking criteria outside the official goals of the program has been referred to as

"goal-free" evaluation by Michael Scriven. See Susan Salasin, "Exploring Goal-Free Evaluation: An Interview with Michael Scriven," *Evaluation* 2(1974): 9–16.

11. See Gerald Grant, "Shaping Social Policy: The Politics of the Coleman Report," *Teachers College Record* 75(1973): 22–29.

12. See Robert D. Behn, "Termination: How the Massachusetts Department of Youth Services Closed the Public Training Schools"; Behn and Martha A. Clark, "Termination II: How the National Park Service Annulled Its 'Commitment' to a Beach Erosion Control Policy at the Cape Hatteras National Seashore"; Behn, "Termination III: Some Hints for the Would-be Policy Terminator" (Durham, N.C.: Duke University, Institute of Policy Sciences and Public Affairs, 1975–77).

13. An experiment with a randomized control group may be possible with only one observation after treatment, but time series add information.

14. See Donald T. Campbell, "Measuring the Effects of Social Innovations by Means of Time Series," in Judith M. Tanur et al., eds., *Statistics: A Guide to the Unknown* (San Francisco: Holden-Day, 1972).

15. Ibid.

16. See Riecken and Boruch, *Social Experimentation.*

17. See Edward M. Gramlich and Patricia P. Koshel, *Educational Performance Contracting: An Evaluation of an Experiment* (Washington, D.C.: Brookings, 1975), pp. 5–8. The following account is based on this monograph.

18. Ibid., p. 10.

19. See John P. Gilbert, Richard J. Light, and Frederick Mosteller, "Assessing Social Innovations: An Empirical Base for Policy," in Richard Zeckhauser et al., eds., *Benefit-Cost and Policy Analysis 1974* (Chicago: Aldine, 1975), pp. 55–56.

20. See Daniel Weiler et al., "A Public School Voucher Demonstration," in Gene V. Glass, ed., *Evaluation Studies Review Annual,* vol. 1 (Beverly Hills, Calif.: Sage Publications, 1976). The following account is based on this source, which reports results from the first year of the program, and on Robert R. Mayer, *Social Science and Institutional Change* (Washington, D.C.: U.S. Department of Health, Education, and Welfare, 1978), ch. 7.

21. Weiler et al., "A Public School Voucher Demonstration," p. 289.

22. Ibid., p. 292.

23. Ibid., p. 300.

24. Mayer, *Social Science and Institutional Change,* p. 220.

8
Epilogue: The Field of Policy Analysis

Public policy analysis is a set of principles for dealing with public problems, large or small. Large problems are worth large analyses, but small problems can still benefit from smaller systematic studies.

These principles are especially worthwhile for citizens, although we hear more often of their use by staff aides to public officials or to group leaders who wish to influence public policy. We expect policy analysis by the citizen to be characterized by its guidance by systematic ethics, a notion of the public interest or the general welfare that the citizen chooses. Other aspects of policy analysis may be used by employees who are assigned their goals by others or by proponents of particular interests that are less inclusive than the general interest—a firm or an industry seeking profit; a group seeking income, security, or power; or a social class seeking gain at the expense of other classes.

Once you as a citizen have chosen your goals, you can then assess the problem situation, redefine the analyst's problem, use models of causation to estimate the effects of various policies on your goals, and plot a course of action that increases the feasibility of enactment and implementation of your proposed policy.

Each of these steps may seem complex to the beginner, though we hope that at this point you find them more familiar. We have introduced you to numerous technical terms, as you can see by looking back at the Glossaries, as well as to several systematic techniques for analysis. Many of the terms we have introduced are derived from existing academic disciplines and professions whose approaches we draw together and reorganize in policy analysis. You may have wondered at times why these terms and their reorganization were necessary. Our answer is that the reorganization provides a broader framework within which many choices facing the public can be seen to share common features. It is this larger framework that is relatively new. Analyses of particular problems or of aspects of them have often been done well in the past. But these analyses need to be viewed more broadly in relation to one another and the aspects of an analysis need to be combined.

This text is an introduction to policy analysis. Each chapter could be the subject of an advanced course or of advanced study. The redefinition of problems requires skills that anticipate the entire process of analysis. Your formulation of your system of values draws you into perennial questions of ethics and back again to political philosophy as it deals with basic agreements and disagreements in a political community. The free market model is not only an elegant model of a major sector of society; it also embodies a philosophy of the good life and a style of reasoning that are particularly significant in twentieth-century America.

The choice and development of models leads us into all the natural and social sciences and their applications. Engineering and the health professions, when they face major policy choices, engage in reasoning that largely overlaps with policy analysis. Statistics and decision theory can be studied in far greater detail than we have presented. Finally, the difficult problems of assessing and promoting feasibility lead us to seek common elements in major political struggles as well as in the shorter-run controversies and decisions of smaller groups. The study of feasibility also requires that you learn how others may act toward you, whether it be in cooperation or in hostility.

We have encouraged you to learn a rational and public-spirited view of public decisions. Yet this encouragement is in some ways utopian. Perhaps in an idealized ancient Greek city-state citizens used their reasoning and their rhetoric in quest of the common good. But in late twentieth-century America we continually hear accusations of corruption in high places, manipulation through the mass media, and selfish use of power by elites. Is there then a place for altruism and reason in a political world that sometimes seems to provide little room for them? We hope there is.

We cannot make a final judgment here regarding the fate of enlightened and public-spirited citizenship. We have tried, however, to prepare you for the political risks inherent in policy analysis. We have placed our account of them near the end of the book, in chapters 6 and 7, and we have illustrated them with relatively simple examples. They are near the end because we believe that teaching political skill or means to power, without the prior choice of right policies, will accomplish little. They are simple because our discussion of feasibility, like every other aspect of the book, is introductory. We encourage you to explore every aspect of policy analysis further if you wish.

A major problem affecting the viability of a political community of citizen-analysts concerns the coexistence of various value systems. We have encouraged you to formulate your *own* value system in a precise fashion in order to use it in analysis. Only rarely, however, will you find that all your fellow citizens in a political community share that value system, even if it aims at the public interest. You may sometimes judge that your opponents are narrow-minded and misguided, and you may try to prevail over them by sheer strength of resources. They may at times do the same to you. At still other times you may compromise on basic differences in order to prevail or to preserve your political community. We have not told you how to do this because these compromises may well run counter to rational policy analysis. In the relations among analysts with profoundly different values, therefore, there are major problems that we have not tried to solve here.

This disparity among value systems may be less among the young than among the old. Among students there is a considerable diversity of value systems. But many students, with the major choices of life ahead of them, are open to the comparison of various philosophies of life. Even though later life is said to bring equanimity and detachment, it also brings a multitude of commitments —to family, community, job, organizations, and systems of ideas. We hope, therefore, that the students who read this book will show greater mutual understanding than their elders do or perhaps than they themselves will in later life. Having had less experience of the seriousness of political conflicts may allow some of our readers to be more ethical, if less skilled at furthering political feasibility.

We hope that most of you will find that you can use the principles in this book in analyzing and influencing small-scale policy decisions in your city, neighborhood, or associations. These principles will also help you to take positions on larger issues, even when your influence is limited to voting or discussion. We also hope that a few readers will acquire the skill and resources to use these principles in larger decisions, having become leaders or statesmen who seek the common good, while recognizing that political struggles and maneuvers are often the condition for doing so. In periods before the lines of controversy have hardened you may even find that analysis can be persuasive. The field of public policy analysis actually has few distinguished leaders whose reasoning has led to new policies that are recognized as worthwhile in the long run. Perhaps some of our readers can accomplish this.

The prospects for effective policy analysis are not, however, a matter of individual action alone. They depend on the coordination of human energies in groups and organizations toward reasoned, public-spirited participation. Some of the energies of students and faculty in higher education are being coordinated in this way through the development of instructional programs in policy analysis and related fields. This development requires, however, that we channel those energies into thoughtful and disciplined participation. Mere ideological advocacy of causes in educational institutions fails to make use of their resources for analysis and can be harmful to them. This requires that we refrain from advocating a policy, in the *name* of analysis, simply because our group favors it, because our human sympathies seem to call for it, or because the symbols associated with it have a wide appeal. The same sort of reasoned discipline that prevents scientists and scholars from embracing conclusions hastily must often restrain us from embracing policies hastily in the name of analysis. We are thus left in a state of tension: seeking a sound basis for policy choice; knowing our analyses can never be perfect or complete; yet wishing to encourage a type of public debate in which some of our choices as citizens are conducted according to rational rules.

Types of Ethical Criteria and Answers to Exercises

APPENDIX

Types of Ethical Criteria

We distinguish in the text between criteria that depend on assessment of the consequences of acts (teleological) and those that do not (nonteleological). Although this distinction is well known to philosophers, it has not always been indicated by a consistent terminology. Apparently closest is the distinction between teleological and deontological ethical theories.[1] But the latter term has more often been used to refer to ethical systems that embrace principles that may or may not relate to the consequences of acts.[2]

Braybrooke and Lindblom make use of a distinction between meliorative and peremptory values but point out explicitly that this classification does not correspond precisely to one centering about consequences alone.[3] Peremptory rules prescribe or proscribe certain acts without comparing them with alternatives; meliorative rules require that any act be compared with available alternatives before it is judged right or wrong. This distinction overlaps to a considerable extent with the distinction between nonteleological and teleological criteria, since teleological principles generally require examination of alternatives, and conversely. Exceptions to this correspondence can be imagined, however.

Braybrooke and Lindblom distinguish elsewhere between ethics of utility and of duty.[4] But this distinction is not precisely the one we wish, since it may conceivably be our duty to promote certain types of consequences through our acts. Terms such as "welfare," "benefits," and "costs" typically refer to criteria related to the consequences of acts, but contrasting categories are not so easily identified. In economics a distinction is made between efficiency and equity. However, equity may well be a consequence of our acts and may not simply correspond to a moral rule about types of acts.

A further distinction that is partly relevant is that between ethical judgments based on our intuitions or convictions, on the one hand, and judgments based on systems of values that modify those initially given bases of judgment. But some of our intuitions about rightness may well relate to the consequences of acts, even though many are of the unconditional type that hold an act to be wrong, "no matter what."

In distinguishing teleological from nonteleological criteria we have implied that we can clearly separate an act from its consequences. But between pulling the trigger of a gun, causing it to fire, and injuring another person we might distinguish between act and consequences in various ways. It is for this reason that we also considered "intermediate goals" in the text.

1. David Braybrooke and Charles E. Lindblom, *A Strategy of Decision*, (New York: Free Press, 1963), pp. 256–257.

2. See for example John Rawls, *A Theory of Justice* (Cambridge, Mass.: Harvard University Press, 1971), p. 30; he defines deontological theories as embracing both sorts of principles but refers to these theories as "nonteleological."

3. Braybrooke and Lindblom, *A Strategy of Decision*, p. 257.

4. Ibid., p. 11.

Answers to Exercises

Many of these answers are subject to argument. We provide them, not simply for students to check their own responses as right or wrong, but to illustrate possible lines of reasoning and to stimulate discussion. The instructor should review the answers and decide whether he or she agrees with them before assigning the exercises to students or evaluating students' answers.

CHAPTER 1

1.   Policies include national policies, such as the Social Security Program, and local policies, such as an increase or decrease in the property tax rate. They include long-standing commitments, such as the Monroe Doctrine, and important individual decisions, such as President Kennedy's decision to blockade the Soviet ships carrying missiles to Cuba in 1962. Policies also include the decision to do nothing when an important change might be made, as in the defeat of President Nixon's Family Assistance Plan in 1970. In addition, they include some private as well as public actions.

   Nonpolicy choices include the decision concerning whether an applicant for a government position passed the Civil Service examination or the decision about what to have for breakfast.

   There is a gray area, however, including decisions of intermediate importance that cannot easily be classified as policy or nonpolicy decisions.

2.   One notion of democracy is based on citizens' voting and participating in view of self-interest or group interest. A second notion is based on citizens' participation in view of their notions of the public interest or general welfare.

3.   We stress the citizen's role because we emphasize systematic ethics as the basis of policy analysis—a starting point that can best be taken by informed citizens. We also wish to improve the quality of public discussion of policies and to provide a better basis for the public to review and control the choices made by experts in government.

4.   In the city-growth case terms such as "the general welfare" or "the public interest" may be interpreted in two ways. A narrower interpretation limits their meaning to the welfare or interest of present residents of the community. This is the interpretation given in the last sentence of case 3–B. A broader interpretation includes outsiders as well.

5.   The solid arrows refer to causal relations, knowledge of which allows us to estimate the consequences of alternatives. The dashed arrow refers to a direct judgment of alternatives themselves.

CHAPTER 2

1. Water shortages are listed in the left-hand column as a specific problem. A more general problem of which they are a part (to the left of the center column) is that of resource shortages. This more general problem can lead us (in the right part of the center column) to consider either the need for new resources, inefficiency in the use of resources, or population problems that create a demand for resources. These in turn lead to a larger set of interrelated problems concerning the earth's resources and the numbers and distribution of population.

Crime is listed in the left-hand column as regards the functioning of the justice system and the prevalence of crime itself. In the center column these problems are considered with respect to general problems of crime and justice and the question whether family disorganization is a cause of crime. In the right-hand column these problems are related to a more general one of disorganization in modern society.

2. One sociological definition of a social problem is that it is a significant and unwanted discrepancy between the standards of a collectivity and actual conditions. The analyst's problem can differ from a social problem in being more precisely stated; in focusing on more concrete alternative policies that are to be analyzed (though it need not specify alternatives at the start); and in being concerned with matters that are not subjects of public concern. The analyst's problem may also be more specific or more general than the socially defined problem.

3. Social change may not be directly relevant to our policy choices since often we cannot alter or reverse this change. Knowledge of the effects of social change can, however, alert us to the existence of particular groups who have been affected by such change and who define their aspects of the problem situation accordingly. These groups may play an important part in our estimation of the political feasibility of policies.

4. Among the arguments used to avoid action are the contention that a problem or difficulty is "natural," that the behavior generating it is normal or typical, or that a difficulty may be cured by the passage of time.

People who wish to increase concern with a problem may publicize examples of its undesirable human effects, stress prevalent values or expectations that are not satisfied by the existing situation, or introduce new phraseology that connects this problem with negative symbols. They may also try to convince others that action in a specific direction will be effective in coping with the problem. Blaming a specific person or source may channel attention to the problem by persuading an audience that it can be solved.

To increase understanding as well as concern, it is necessary to include some of the elements of policy analysis in the arguments used. These include systematic evidence of the extent of the problem, of its causes, and of the expected effectiveness of policies that are advocated.

5. Economic and social indicators provide baselines in terms of which people's expectations are formed. Statistics for an earlier period of time then lead to special concern when conditions, as measured by later statistics, have become worse.

6. a. The migration of poor people to cities, where a lack of family resources made them more dependent on government aid, accentuated the problem.

b. Five perspectives on the problem (aspects of the problem situation) include a concern for aid to the poor, a concern for incentives toward work by recipients of aid, a concern for alleviating dependency as well as poverty, a criticism of professionals who had administered previous programs, and a desire to reform the welfare system in order to remove inequities and abuses.

c. In 1963 Moynihan chose welfare dependency as a problem because it lay within the jurisdiction of the Department of Labor and did not overlap with the concerns of parallel organizations such as the Department of Health, Education, and Welfare.

d. Nixon's election called for new proposals and allowed more criticism of previous programs than would have been possible under a Democratic administration.

7. a. In deciding whether these means were justified, you must set forth your own criteria and evaluate these means according to whether they should be permitted in public discussions. Generally, the means used here include arranging for the publication of newspaper articles, restricting questions at a meeting, and using indirect influence to remove antifluoridation material in a radio broadcast.

   In our judgment no universal rule can be made as to whether it is proper to introduce data into the newspapers. If such data are introduced, they should be accurate. The participation of professions is often a guarantee that data have been subjected to tests of accuracy. Data should be subject to rebuttal. Letters to the editor and openness to information from other responsible groups are conditions that may permit cross-checking of such information. The weakest point of the proponents' use of this information was to conceal the purpose for which the information was introduced. The use of information to predispose readers to an undisclosed later policy can border on manipulation.

   Restriction of questions seems justified at a private meeting. Even at a public meeting open to all citizens, it could be claimed that only citizens of Newton were involved. Using indirect influence to control radio broadcasts through advertisers' influence seems to set an undesirable precedent.

b. Those who wish to alert others to a new opportunity have to publicize it. If the new opportunity is available as a product sold through the market, sales and use of the product provide a type of information by word of mouth that supplements advertisements. If the new opportunity requires public action, then the opportunity may have to be publicized by showing that it either responds to an unrecognized problem or provides potential gains that are worth its costs.

Advanced Exercises

8. a. The problem situation associated with the proposal for deposit bottles resulted from the increasing amount of roadside litter from disposable containers.

b. An "environmentalist" perspective on nonreturnable containers is that they represent an unjustified source of environmental pollution. The perspective of some producers and consumers is that "convenience packaging" represents an advantage to consumers, an improvement in the capacity of the economy to satisfy consumer preferences, and a source of jobs and prosperity.

c. The analyst's redefinition is an effort to include aspects of both the previous definitions and to weigh them against one another. In choosing overall efficiency as a criterion you are acknowledging that the satisfaction of consumer preferences is valuable, but that the dissatisfaction of the preferences of those who look at littered roadsides is undesirable. This latter effect represents a social cost that is not taken into account by the market and that therefore requires government intervention to produce greatest efficiency. When you choose this criterion, you are likely to compare the initial equilibrium of the economy with a later equilibrium, after some regulatory policy has been put into effect. This approach may neglect the costs of transition (referred to in chapter 5 as "dynamic problems"). The reallocation of resources and of persons to new types of production creates a short-run cost that is also related to political feasibility. The criterion of efficiency may also neglect problems of equity, but these problems are not brought out clearly in case 5–A.

9. a. The initial aspect of the problem situation was the concern of the oil industry, especially those parts of it outside East Texas, with a decline in revenues. A related problem was experienced by persons and groups deriving revenues from oil production outside East Texas, such as the state government and the University of Texas. A third perspective was that of the East Texas producers, who would lose revenue if the wells were shut down and many of whom thus opposed regulation. The consumers' view was not apparently part of the problem situation, as the gain to consumers was not strongly advocated within Texas as a reason against regulation.

b. The analyst's definition of the problem differs in that it considers consumers outside Texas. The analyst uses a notion of the public interest, or of overall efficiency, that includes outsiders as well as Texans. But just as in the preceding exercise, the analyst may be comparing one equilibrium situation with another and neglecting the costs of transition. These costs are particularly important in the oil industry because the "feast or famine" alternation was repeated with the discovery of each new oil field. In retrospect, of course, the need for conservation of resources such as oil looms much larger now than it did in the 1930s.

CHAPTER 3

1. "Greatest benefit" and "least cost" are two logically distinct criteria that may conflict for some choices. For example, if the analyst must choose between policy A, with benefits of $1000 and costs of $900, and policy B, with benefits of $5 and costs of $1, the former has the greater benefit and the latter has the lesser cost.

2. In any choice between two policies A and B, such that in going from A to B some people gain and others lose in their scales of preference, it cannot be a Pareto

improvement to go from A to B nor can it be an improvement to go from B to A. We may then say either that the Pareto criterion does not apply to the choice between A and B, or that it is indifferent to this choice.

If we apply the relation of indifference mentioned to the alternatives in table 3–1, we find five pairs of alternatives judged indifferent by the Pareto criterion. But day care is Pareto-superior to paving the street.

3. a. Present residents' welfare may be used as a criterion and, if expressed in sufficiently precise terms (e.g., benefits and costs), may justify restriction of in-migration. The welfare of outsiders may be included in a broader criterion of "general welfare" that includes outsiders and residents together. This latter criterion (again, if made more precise) may allow some balance or compromise between the interests of residents and outsiders, though in many cases it is likely to give much more weight to the interests of outsiders if considerations of vertical equity are included.

    b. Court decisions regarding constitutional limits on freedom to migrate have played an important part in limiting types of local policies that may be adopted.

    c. Present residents may have made earlier plans and decisions premised on expectations concerning the quality of life or property value in their communities and may claim that fairness requires the fulfillment of these expectations. These expectations, though used to justify public arguments, do not always have validity in legal proceedings.

    d. Vertical equity concerns the reduction of disparities between rich and poor. Some communities that have wished to exclude or limit in-migration have been wealthy suburbs that wished not only to avoid overcrowding but also to limit the in-migration of poorer people. Concern for vertical equity would lead us to give more weight to the claim for poorer in-migrants. The same sort of argument would seem to apply to the migration of persons from poorer countries to richer countries. However, residents of richer countries find it very difficult to apply the same principles of free migration to international as to domestic migration.

4. When one governmental unit is making decisions that fail to take into account the interests of outsiders, a possible remedy is to refer the decision to a more inclusive level of government (e.g., the federal government), which will presumably consider all the interests involved. Another remedy is for decision makers in the smaller unit to take the interests of outsiders into account.

5. The security of the United States, as a criterion for policy choice, does not relate directly to the security of outsiders. Nonresident citizens do receive protection from the United States government, and resident aliens may also receive security insofar as this is automatically available to all residents. But citizens of other nations who live in those nations benefit from American security only insofar as international alliances or geographical relations provide indirect benefit to them. If international policy were guided by considerations of the welfare or security of persons in many nations—whether a subset of nations or all nations—then the policies chosen would incorporate the welfare of nonresident noncitizens directly.

6. These losses of business and jobs would not be counted as costs if the analyst had reason to believe that compensating benefits would appear elsewhere in the economy. Diversion of resources from one sort of production to another would not necessarily be considered a net social cost when two equilibrium situations, before and after a change, were compared. If your ethical criteria included consideration of transitional costs or dynamic problems (chapter 5), you might include them.

7. a. Nonteleological.

b. Nonteleological.

c. Teleological.

d. Teleological.

e. Teleological, even though it does not compare alternatives.

8. Yes, its sale would be favored; preference satisfaction has no necessary connection with scientifically ascertainable effects. Opponents of its sale might argue that longer-run preferences would fail to be satisfied if laetrile did not produce the effects that consumers expected. But in this case they might be justified only in providing more information, not in banning its sale. Standards used against the sale of laetrile might be that of health, if it could be shown that purchasers suffered in health relative to their situation if they did not purchase it, or truth, if observers believed that consumers should not deceive themselves but should act consistently with established scientific knowledge.

9. If one favors majority rule in this case, he or she is likely to be using majority rule itself as a criterion, or some other criterion that deemphasizes the "large" effects on the minority. If one favors giving weight to the minority because it is affected to a "large extent," then the terms in which this "extent" is measured (possibly benefits, costs, or other measures of welfare) constitute the criterion being used.

10. Five dollars presumably means more to a poor person than a rich person. If the same types of guns are being bought by rich and poor, the tax should be more of a disincentive to poorer purchasers. We must also assume, if this argument is to be used, that the area in which homicide is committed is a reliable indicator of the income of the person committing it. It might be argued that this tax bears more heavily on the poor than on the rich and deters poor people differentially from the legitimate use of guns.

11. Equity requires that people be treated by the justice system in terms of their own acts rather than in terms of probabilities associated with their socioeconomic status. Vertical equity would provide strong arguments against legislating further disadvantages for the poor or for those of low status. Efficiency, however, would require that any information relevant to the prediction of a parolee's committing another crime be considered and used.

12. Criteria of short-run efficiency were evidently used to justify including place of residence in the first place. Longer-run efficiency might extend our view to possible consequences of people's moving out of neighborhoods where they would be considered credit risks. If this led to decreases in production or earning, for example, it might be used as an argument for amending the law. The major arguments for amend-

ment, however, are based on equity; that is, credit worthiness should be based on individual merits, and racial discrimination might result from the existing law.

13. Quality of health services, which is often indexed by measures such as physician's training and technical equipment available, may be inconsistent with increased availability. Quality and quantity refer to different ways of using resources. Equity often refers to wider availibility—to poor and rich on similar terms—and if equity is so understood, this criterion may run counter to quality. Whether maximizing health is equivalent to maximizing quality of services as a criterion depends on the contribution that high-quality services make to health. If other policy variables besides services (e.g., nutrition and work conditions) contribute importantly to health, then using quality as a criterion will lead us to neglect these other variables.

Availability and equity in health services, like quality of health services, are consistent with maximization of health only to the degree that services promote health. Possibly the wider distribution of health services will increase health, if the marginal productivity of a unit of services is greater when that unit is expended on the poor than on the rich. Health itself may be the most difficult of these criteria to measure as a quantitative aggregate for a population.

14. Conceivably the maximization of the quality of life could be used in population policy. This would require, first, that the "quality of life" be defined precisely. If it were, it would probably refer to an average or per capita characteristic of populations, analogous to per capita income. If we could relate a variable of this kind to the productivity (in welfare or quality of life) that resulted from combining people with resources in a given area, we might conceivably estimate the optimum population for that area, given a technology of production.

The difficulties are far greater for defining optimum population in terms of preference satisfaction. Preferences are usually defined as the preferences of those persons who are now alive. They are thus not even defined for persons yet to be born. Judgments about future population are sometimes made by taking into account only the preferences of persons now living, but this approach is likely to be challenged on ethical grounds.

15. If the resolution of conflicts is our criterion, we are paying no attention to the merits of the cases of the parties to the conflict. Conceivably greater general welfare would be produced by the victory of one party and the defeat of the other, rather than the compromise implied in the standard of conflict resolution.

16. These four approaches differ from one another in two ways: First, citizens are asked either their opinions about policy or their judgments about how it affects them personally; second, they may be questioned before or after the policy is put into effect. The before-after distinction does not imply a difference in ethical criteria. Questioning afterward possibly implies that democracy can be guided better by concrete judgments rather than abstract and speculative ones.

The distinction between opinion and effect may correspond to a relatively less selfish and more selfish notion of democracy, insofar as opinions are based on notions of the general interest rather than self-interest. This difference depends, however, on how the surveys are used. If reports of the effects of a program are used like votes or opinions, the result will be an aggregation of selfish preferences. If, however, these reports of effects are combined and reported back to citizens or representatives to inform their opinion, they may provide a means for citizens to judge the general welfare more accurately.

17. Vertical equity, unless specified more clearly, is an imprecise criterion. Maximization of welfare might lead to precise conclusions if welfare could be expressed as a function of income. In the short run this criterion might well lead to complete equalization of incomes, though in the long run differences might be retained as incentives to produce or to invest. Cost-benefit analysis, being based on dollar sums, would dictate no transfer at all if any administrative costs were incurred, and this would probably be the most precise conclusion. Pareto optimality in redistribution might well lead to a precise conclusion as long as the preferences of participants could be ascertained precisely. The first two criteria are likely to imply the greatest transfer of income. We cannot say which will transfer more until they are spelled out further.

18. The criterion of equity may be invoked if the residents were there first and claimed rights based on expectations of clean air. The residents might then claim compensation from the factory. If the factory was there first, the building of houses nearby would create an external effect and a departure from efficiency; but the residents could not claim to have been unexpectedly damaged by it.

19. Even though it is conventional to discount future earnings, an alternative ethical position is that life is of equal value in the future and in the present. If we believed that life in the future was worth progressively less, we should eventually consider the life of some future generations to be essentially worthless. Although these later lives may be worth little in terms of the preferences of persons now living, this judgment might be disputed on ethical grounds. Another standard that has been proposed is that of years of life, added but not necessarily discounted, and weighted if possible to take their quality into account.

20. An isolated person would presumably value the future less as he became older. His discount rate could thus be said to rise over time. If he were utterly selfish, he would have no concern whatever for the welfare of the second person. But if he regarded the second person as similar to himself, he might be justified in weighting the second person's benefits equally with his own. The position you take on this question depends on your own system of values.

CHAPTER 4

1. Many observers of a recently established program continue to consider the alternatives they considered before the program was established. The personnel and clientele of a long-established program ordinarily consider its existence as unquestionable, and other observers come to take it for granted. It is also possible that programs that survive longer, having proved themselves, tend to have some value that is not shared by all new programs.

2. a. Dental decay, the reduction of which may be a means to health or happiness or a source of preference satisfaction; cost, the reduction of which may satisfy preferences or increase happiness.

b. Incentives to work, which may be means to production or efficiency.

c. Registration by the poor, which if increased may increase the equity of both procedures and outcomes of the democratic process; fraud, which may be considered undesirable either in itself, or as a cause of inequity, or (if discovered) as a source of lessening of support for democratic processes.

d. Access to medical services in rural or inner-city areas, which is an expression of the value of equity and may be a means to the health of the populations in these areas.

e. Recidivism or crime, which decreases preference satisfaction or happiness for the victims.

3. An intelligent class can think of a large number of policies, but a systematic classification may help. We first need to distinguish causes of shortage that are local or temporary from those that are widespread or lasting. For widespread and lasting shortages we need to cope with overall relations between supply and demand. Nuclear, solar, geothermal, wind-related, or biological (wood) sources of energy and desalination of water are policies to increase supply. Conservation of energy or water to reduce demand can take numerous forms. One means to conservation is to raise prices.

If shortages are local, then shifts of supply from one area to another may be considered, for example, regional electrical networks or water pipelines from one place to another. If shortages are local and prolonged, migration may be necessary. If they are temporary, larger reservoirs may be used to store water, but such storage seems less available for energy. To a limited degree, consumption of electricity may be shifted from one time period to another. Peak pricing may encourage such shifts.

4. The expected values and residuals for Randolph Road are

	PM	SP	LANG	ACM	ACN	AAPP	SS	SC
Expected	75.25	81.375	74.25	62.625	76.75	70.375	75.625	79.5
Residual	−15.25	+.625	+4.75	−.625	+2.25	+5.625	+3.375	+1.5

Six out of eight residuals are positive, though the largest residual is negative. We cannot treat these as eight independent observations, since one test is likely to be correlated with another. The results appear to give only weak support to Judge McMillan's decision in favor of busing.

5. Most relevant are items a and d, which can be used in calculations of overall costs and benefits of policies. Item a has to be supplemented by some judgment as to the social cost per discarded bottle. Item d relates to costs of production. Items b and c are less directly relevant, as they give only percentages rather than absolute numbers. Item e may represent a temporary cost to Schaefer and its employees. But wherever Schaefer relocated there would be compensating long-run benefits so that the cost to New York would not be a net social cost in the long run.

6. Only model d is relevant, as your criterion is numerical desegregation. The criterion relates to the dependent variable, not the independent variable.

7. If the incidence of colon cancer declines, the screening policy then incurs the same costs per person as before for the screening test but achieves lesser benefits. As a result, we would favor the screening policy less strongly. We do not work out the numerical details because some of the other probabilities would also be different in this new population.

If the cost of surgery were reduced, our support for the screening policy would be strengthened. The net gain from surgery would be greater and the expected costs other than that of surgery would be unaffected.

Advanced Exercise

8. Basic researchers claim that their discoveries are more general and have wider applicability than those of applied research. If this is true and if the findings are of positive value when applied, d would be larger for basic research. The probability p that research will make a difference, however, may be larger for applied research. The $pd > c$ rule cannot resolve the question concerning which type of research is more valuable in general, but it can point to relevant considerations for comparison. We need not consider variation in c here if we ask about the relative value of the two types of research *per unit* of expenditure.

CASE 4–A

1. The total cost would reach its lowest value, for any of the speeds given in the table, at 40 mph and 45 mph. At either of these speeds the total cost would be $.370 per vehicle-mile. The optimum v, in these terms, would be between 40 and 45 mph.

2. Accident costs per vehicle-mile in 1973 were $30,407 million divided by 1308.5 billion vehicle-miles, or $.02324 per vehicle-mile in 1973 dollars. The corresponding 1974 figure in 1973 dollars is

$$\frac{\$30,415 \times 10^6}{1289.6 \times 10^9} \times \frac{133.1}{147.7} = \$.02125$$

a decline of 8.5 percent.

3. Inclusion of any additional cost that increased as the speed limit was lowered would *raise* our estimate of the optimum v. We assume the cost in question is that which is necessary to bring v into a fixed relationship with the posted speed limit.

4. If drivers are less hurried on weekends, a case could be made for lower speed limits on weekends. However, some drivers would object on grounds of inequity if they had urgent travel requirements on weekends. They might claim that the mere willingness of some drivers to go slower is not a reason for reducing the limit. Administrative and educational costs might also be incurred in putting a changing limit into effect.

5. The most direct method of comparing these two values might be to ask drivers how much time saving they would consider to be equivalent in value to a given

change in probability of an accident with specified consequences. Until such questioning is tried systematically, however, we cannot be sure that it would be workable and reliable.

6. We neglected the costs of highway maintenance and air pollution; assumed that v adequately summarized the speed distribution as it affected costs; assumed that costs were proportional to traffic volume; assumed that the price of gasoline exclusive of taxes measured its social cost; neglected the costs and benefits for trucks in our principal calculations; dealt with only one type of road, only in the daytime; ignored the costs of law enforcement; used overall accident-cost figures to estimate changes in these costs with v under high-speed conditions; considered only differences in the value of time, but not in operating or other expenses, for trucks; and made arbitrary assumptions about compliance in order to connect v with the speed limit.

7. For the speeds listed in table 4A–1, total cost would be lowest at 60 mph ($.127 per vehicle-mile).

Advanced Exercise

8. There are no clear examples of demerit goods. But if we could limit our consideration to those drivers who risked only injuring themselves or damaging their own property, then by setting a speed limit we would be declaring faster driving to be a demerit good. We might then be preventing the individual from freely and deliberately making a choice that affected only himself.

CHAPTER 5

1. The new market supply curve will be to the right of the old one, indicating a willingness to supply increased quantities at each possible market price. This new supply curve will intersect the unchanged demand curve at a new equilibrium point, which indicates that quantity will rise and price will fall. The lower market price will bring a greater consumer surplus to demanders. The producer surplus of the established producers can be seen from the original supply curve. Since the market price will have fallen, the established producers will obtain a smaller producer surplus, which indicates the degree to which they dislike the infringement on their market by the new producer. The total producer surplus may either rise or fall after the entry of the new supplier, the answer depending on the slopes of the demand and supply curves.

2. As consumers change their preferences for the two goods, the demand curve for bread shifts to the right and the demand curve for potatoes shifts to the left. The resulting higher bread price is a disappointment to former bread demanders and a gain (in producer surplus) to bread suppliers. The lower price of potatoes provides increased consumer surplus to those continuing to buy that good and reduced producer surplus to potato suppliers. The change in the relative prices of the two products moderates the gains achieved by the consumers whose tastes changed.

3. a. Fellow lettuce farmers in the same valley receive an external benefit in the

form of increased crop yields that the artificial rain produced, benefits they had not paid for.

b. Lettuce farmers from another state will be faced with a lower market price for their product as a result of the increased supply. Their reduced producer surplus is a cost (or loss) to them, one which is internal to the market and similar to the impact on established producers in exercise 1.

c. Salad lovers find that a good they like has gone down in price. The resulting benefit in the form of increased consumer surplus is internal to the market.

d. Steak-restaurant owners will gain internal benefits in the form of higher profits if their lower salad costs are not fully passed on in lower meal prices. They may possibly bear internal "costs" from lower business if diners switch from steak meals to vegetarian meals at other restaurants.

e. Lettuce pickers are internal beneficiaries to the extent that there is increased demand for their services and either wage rates rise or opportunities to work increase (or both).

f. Lettuce-crate makers receive the internal benefit through increased demand for their product.

g. Corn farmers (presumably located in other places) may have an internal cost imposed on them in the form of lower producer surplus if the lower lettuce price causes consumers to switch from corn to salads, thus lowering the demand for corn. It is possible for corn farmers to receive an internal benefit from an increased demand for corn. This could happen if lettuce and corn were complementary goods (lettuce-and-corn salads) or if the purchasing power released by the lower lettuce prices was to some extent used to purchase more corn.

h. The tennis-club owner would bear an external cost in the form of higher maintenance costs for his courts and possibly reduced demand for his club's services.

i. The tennis-club owner in the next town would receive increased demand for court usage as tennis players switch from the rainy to the clear area. His benefit of increased producer surplus is external to the lettuce market and is an offset to the reduced business of the club owner in part h.

4. a. The demand curve in figure 5–1 can be algebraically expressed as $Q_D = 7 - 5_P$ or as $P_D = (7 - Q)/5$. If we integrate the latter, we obtain $1.40Q - .1Q^2$, which evaluated over the first three loaves yields $3.30. This could also be calculated through the geometry of part b.

b. The value of two loaves equals $2.40 and of five loaves equals $4.50.

c. If consumers value five loaves at $4.50 and have to pay $2.00 to purchase them, their consumer surplus is the difference of $2.50.

d. The area under the supply curve, representing the marginal costs of producing three loaves, is $.78. When this amount is subtracted from the revenue of $.96, we obtain a producer surplus of $.18.

e. Similarly, with revenue of $2.00 and marginal costs of $1.50, the producer surplus is $.50. In this part and the previous one, the area under the supply curve could be found with the aid of calculus by integrating the supply curve $P_s = (Q + 5)/25$ to obtain the expression $.02Q^2 + .2Q$, which can then be evaluated over the relevant output range.

5. a.
$$\text{Total Revenue} = P_D Q = \frac{7Q - Q^2}{5}$$

$$\text{Marginal Revenue} = \frac{d(P_d Q)}{dQ} = 1.4 - .4Q$$

The marginal revenue is equal to zero when $Q = 3.5$ loaves.

b.
$$\text{Marginal Revenue} = 1.4 - .4Q$$
$$\text{Marginal Cost} = P_s = .04Q + .2$$

To maximize profits, marginal cost must equal marginal revenue.
$$.04Q + .2 = 1.4 - .4Q$$
$$.44Q = 1.2$$
$$Q = 2.73 \text{ loaves}$$

We have chosen not to find this answer by differentiating a total profits function since we do not know what the fixed cost part of total costs is from examining the supply curve. Because fixed costs are a constant, say K, we could say that total profits equal total revenue minus total costs, or $(7Q - Q^2)/5 - (.02Q^2 + .2Q + K)$. If this is differentiated with respect to Q and set equal to zero, we should get the same answer.

6. a.
(1) c_2
(2) c_1
(3) c_2
(4) none
(5) c_1 and c_2
(6) c_2
(7) c_2
(8) c_2
(9) c_2
(10) c_1

(11) ex
(12) none
(13) lc (perhaps)
(14) c_1
(15) ex
(16) c_2 and (perhaps) m
(17) c_1 and (perhaps) c_2
(18) c_1
(19) m

b.
(1) c_1 and (perhaps) c_2
(2) c_1 and c_2
(3) c_2
(4) c_1
(5) i and (perhaps) dm
(6) dm
(7) eq and (perhaps) m
(8) eq, m, and c_1
(9) ex and (perhaps) dm
(10) eq
(11) eq, dy
(12) c_2

(13) c_1 and c_2
(14) c_2 and (perhaps) c_1
(15) ex
(16) lc and eq
(17) eq
(18) eq
(19) c_2
(20) lc and eq
(21) lc, eq and (perhaps) fp
(22) i
(23) c_2 and (perhaps) eq
(24) dm

CHAPTER 6

1. Formal choice points include at least one relevant committee in each house of the legislature, approval by the two legislative chambers themselves, and approval by the governor. In addition, for any legislation affecting medical practice the position taken by the state medical association is of great importance.

2. After a constitutional amendment is proposed, it must be ratified by legislatures or conventions in three-fourths of the states. For fifty states this corresponds to thirty-eight choice points. In addition, amendments must be initially proposed. The smallest number of choice points by which this may be done is two—the two houses of Congress, each by a two-thirds majority. If we count each chamber as a single choice point, the total number of choice points is forty.

3. If the policy is defined by enactment, then the model of consequences includes all the causal processes that follow enactment, including those that influence the degree and type of implementation (enforcement). If the policy is defined as that which results after implementation, the task of analysis is limited to calculations of the effects of a given speed distribution, such as we carried out in the earlier part of case 4–A. In the latter instance the activities of the state police department and the responses of drivers in altering their speed will have to be considered separately.

4. In a loosely organized community it is more likely that you will have to seek agreement among several groups in order to have the policy enacted. This agreement will require negotiation with such groups, seeking common justifications for the policy or at least a common policy on which the groups can agree. It may also require appealing to the public through the mass media. An example of action in this type of community is given in case 6–A.

    In a highly organized community, unless there is a possibility of overturning the existing leadership, you must persuade the leadership of the merits of your policy or of its value to them. Your persuasion will be centered more narrowly, and you are less likely to go to the public for support.

5. One of the most effective methods for getting information about the carrying out of a federal policy is through inquiries made by congressional representatives, since Congress controls the budget of the implementing agencies. Representatives respond to inquiries from individuals in their districts. But organized groups with potential influence over votes or campaigns are likely to receive more attention.

    Agencies themselves may also release information about their activities, but this information is likely to be favorable to them. Under the Freedom of Information Act citizens may sometimes get additional information, but they need to learn what to request.

    Former members of an agency may supply information about its general activities, to guide inquiries more accurately. Current employees who are disaffected from an agency sometimes reveal critical or negative information to investigative reporters. But they do at risk of their careers, and great skill and precautions are required for gathering information in this way. This approach is not usually available to ordinary citizens unless they have personal acquaintance with such employees. The information given by disaffected employees may also be biased negatively.

Externally financed surveys of clients of an agency or reports by individual clients may provide information about the agency's activities. But systematic studies of this sort are usually difficult to organize without the cooperation of the agency.

6. The typical intentions or goals of an organization are usually estimated by consideration of its material interests and its essence, or internal value system. The material interests of an organization typically lie in maintaining and increasing its budget and personnel; satisfying its clients, especially those who can influence its budget through political relations; or satisfying sponsors such as trustees, donors, or legislative committees that provide its support.

The essence, or internal value system, of an organization is usually closely related to the general conditions for career advancement of persons within the organization. These values do not necessarily correspond to the ostensible societal function of the organization or to the nominal purpose for which it was created.

These typical goals may not correspond to the actual goals of specific organizations or their leaders at particular times. Both the particulars of leaders' personalities and values and possible considerations of the general welfare may modify these initial estimates.

7. Bureaucracies and associations offer different opportunities. In a bureaucracy you have a single superior, through whom you are expected to communicate upward; you are expected to go through channels. There may in actuality be exceptions to this formal rule, if you have informal contacts with persons at higher levels or with persons on the same level in other branches of the organization. But these types of contact are less accepted in bureaucracies than in voluntary associations. In associations you are usually free to join with other members to organize support for candidates or resolutions at meetings and to try to influence the political positions that the association will support. In a large national association your opportunities as a rank-and-file member are likely to be limited, and you may not even know the names of other members. But national leaders can attempt to influence the association.

Your capacity for influence is obviously affected by whether you occupy a higher or lower position in either type of organization or, in general, by whether you have resources for influence.

If the organization is divided into parts that have special functions, such as agencies in a bureaucracy or committees in an association, your influence on a particular policy will be greater if you are a member of the relevant functional subgroup. If you are an acknowledged expert on the question at hand, you are also more likely to be heard.

8. a. Each individual union is a voluntary association in the respect that members pay dues. If members belong to a union shop, membership is less voluntary. The individual unions are federated in a larger association whose members are organizations rather than individuals. In addition, each union as well as the entire organization has a central paid office staff that constitutes a small bureaucracy.

   b. Basically, a voluntary association in which influence flows upward through the nominating conventions. Participation in primary elections, however, involves a very loose definition of membership and no dues. There is a small bureaucratic staff. Officeholders also exert influence by patronage.

   c. A private bureaucracy. At the top there is a loose affiliation of individual bureaucracies. The board of directors and various management committees also depart from a strict bureaucratic structure.

d. A bureaucracy.

e. A voluntary association whose members are local merchants.

f. A voluntary association with a small bureaucratic staff.

g. Neither. It is a "collegial" association of equals on which is superposed a loose system of authority in the form of leaders and committees in each chamber. Membership is by election; but once elected, members act in some ways like members of a voluntary association, as influence flows upward.

h. Within each campus the nonacademic personnel constitute a bureaucracy. Faculty members who have tenure are subject to very limited control from above, although they do have prescribed duties that occupy part of their time. The relation among the campuses is usually one of loose coordination and considerable autonomy.

Advanced Exercise

9. For several decades prior to the mid-1960s the American Medical Association (AMA) took a generally conservative stand in favor of free enterprise. It opposed not only government interference in relations between physician and patient but also government involvement in regulation of many aspects of business enterprise. In an open alliance with business it entered congressional campaigns in favor of conservatives.

During this period the Food and Drug Administration (FDA) was involved with government intervention in the market and cooperated with the medical profession in insuring the quality of drugs that were available by prescription.

The possible conflict between these two values held by physicians—free enterprise and government intervention—did not come to the fore until there was an organized movement in favor of allowing the purchase of a substance prohibited by the FDA. Most of the substances prohibited by the FDA were harmful. Laetrile was prohibited simply because it had not been shown to be helpful, as its sellers often claimed it to be. Moreover, the organized support for laetrile came not from producers but from consumers. An increasing incidence of cancer, an expectation that diseases could be cured, and an inability of medical science to produce a cure for it strengthened this movement.

It is also conceivable that the attitude of the AMA toward government intervention changed after the enactment in 1965 of laws providing for Medicare and Medicaid. Physicians became accustomed to receiving some of their fees through government. This change, together with the fact that consumers of laetrile threatened the authority of the profession, may have led to a lessening of physicians' opposition to "overweening government."

CHAPTER 7

1. When a program director wishes to reduce or avoid a threat from outside evaluation, he may first try to prevent the evaluation by arguing that it is too early to

evaluate, that his own organization is preparing an evaluation, that the outside team is not competent to perform it, or that his program has been unfairly selected for evaluation when others should be examined as well. He may also contend that existing information is sufficient to assure the relevant audiences that the program is functioning well: that clients are satisfied, that administrators and professionals in the program are recognized as technically competent, or that other organizations with which the program interacts are satisfied with its performance.

If he cannot avoid the evaluation, he can still try to affect its course. He can ask that the findings and report be considered confidential until they have been reviewed by him or by reviewers sympathetic with the program; that the evaluation incorporate criterion variables of his choice or exclude variables that he considers irrelevant; that the population or parts of the program studied be approved by him; that the evaluation be of a formative rather than summative kind; or that it be scheduled over a long time period so that its results will not be damaging in the short run.

2. Program evaluation typically begins from the goals of the program and asks whether they are being accomplished. The problem situation that leads to evaluation is likely to concern questions about whether the program is attaining its goals (unless the evaluation was prescribed in advance by a prior decision). The problem situation is thus likely to concern the program as such, rather than the needs or dissatisfactions of the population with their conditions more generally.

Since the criterion is the fulfillment of program goals, it is usually more specific than the criteria we have recommended and less likely to permit comparison of the program in question with others that might be adopted. Examination of fulfillment of program goals usually leads to use of measures of effectiveness, with or without measures of cost. In contrast, sometimes a budgetary review of a program will consider only its cost, without regard to its effectiveness. Policy analysis usually requires consideration of both effectiveness and cost, in comparable terms if possible.

The alternatives typically considered in evaluation are the expansion, maintenance, reduction, or abolition of the program. They may also include modification of the program. But the greater the modifications that are considered, the more these judgments require information other than mere observation of attainment of goals by the program. Prior analysis considers a wider range of alternatives, though usually with information that is less specific.

The model of causation in evaluation is also likely to be more specific to the program in question than a model for prior analysis would be. This may have the advantage of realism and detail, but may also lead the model to have less applicability for other programs elsewhere.

Calculations of feasibility in program evaluation often include the interests of the program itself and of its supporters as a major ingredient. For prior analysis, before the program in question exists, these particular interests do not exist, though previously existing programs' interests may be important to consider.

3. The data normally needed for an evaluation study include information not only on outputs and outcomes but also on processes within the organization. All these data, but especially the internal information if it is frank and accurate, are potentially sensitive for persons in the organization. Sometimes respondents or other persons who give information have to be guaranteed anonymity. Prior analysis, in contrast, is more likely to make use of general scientific models that do not depend on data on individ-

uals. Thus, both the data of evaluation studies and some of their results need to be guarded more carefully in view of the rights and privacy of individuals, over and above possible threats to people in the organization from premature or unjustified release of information.

4. The experience of the 55-mph speed limit provides time series on speed distributions, both nationally and in various localities. In addition, it provides series on accident costs, vehicle- and passenger-miles traveled, and monetary costs of various items that enter into total cost. Data on enforcement may also be available. The most relevant information is that which contributes to the assessment of quantitative relations that tell how policies will affect costs (if costs are our criterion). Some of the relevant information is that which permits us to set aside irrelevant causes of changes in cost, causes not related to the speed distribution. Time series on miles traveled and on traffic volume may be useful for this purpose.

Acton, Jan Paul. *Evaluating Public Programs to Save Lives: The Case of Heart Attacks.* Santa Monica, Calif.: Rand Corporation, 1973.

Allison, Graham T. *Essence of Decision.* Boston: Little, Brown, 1971.

————. "Implementation Analysis: 'The Missing Chapter' in Conventional Analysis. A Teaching Exercise." In *Benefit-Cost and Policy Analysis 1974,* edited by Richard Zeckhauser et al. Chicago: Aldine, 1975.

American Association of State Highway Officials. (AASHO). *Road User Benefit Analysis for Highway Improvements.* Washington, D.C.: AASHO, 1960.

Andersen, Leonall C. "Statistics for Public Financial Policy." In *Statistics: A Guide to the Unknown,* edited by Judith M. Tanur et al. San Francisco: Holden-Day, 1972.

Anderson, Jack, and Les Whitten. " 'Human Error' Labels Guns as Books." Raleigh, N.C., *News and Observer,* 22 July, 1977.

Baerwald, John E., Matthew J. Huber, and Louise E. Kafer, eds. *Transportation and Traffic Engineering Handbook.* Englewood Cliffs, N. J.: Prentice-Hall, 1976.

Banfield, Edward C. *Political Influence.* New York: Free Press, 1961.

Bardach, Eugene. *The Implementation Game.* Cambridge, Mass.: M.I.T. Press, 1977.

Barrett, Rolin F. *Crashes and Costs.* Raleigh, N.C.: North Carolina State University, 1974.

Bartlett, Maurice S. "Epidemics." In *Statistics: A Guide to the Unknown,* edited by Judith M. Tanur et al. San Francisco: Holden-Day, 1972.

Barton, Allen H. *Communities in Disaster.* Garden City, N.Y.: Doubleday, 1969.

Bator, Francis M. "The Anatomy of Market Failure." *American Economic Review* 72(1958): 351–379.

Beach, Philip F. *Public Access to Policymaking in the United States.* Morristown, N.J.: General Learning Press, 1974.

Becker, Gary S. "Crime and Punishment: An Economic Approach." *Journal of Political Economy* 76(1968): 169–217.

Behn, Robert D. "Termination: How the Massachusetts Department of Youth Services Closed the Public Training Schools." Durham, N.C.: Institute of Policy Sciences and Public Affairs, Duke University, 1975.

————, and Martha A. Clark. "Termination II: How the National Park Service Annulled Its 'Commitment' to a Beach Erosion Control Policy at the Cape Hatteras National Seashore." Durham, N.C.: Duke University, Institute of Policy Sciences and Public Affairs, 1976.

Behn, Robert D. "Termination III: Some Hints for the Would-be Policy Terminator." Durham, N.C.: Duke University, Institute of Policy Sciences and Public Affairs, 1977.

Blissett, Marlan, ed. *Environmental Impact Assessment*. New York: Engineering Foundation, 1976.

Braybrooke, David, and Charles E. Lindblom. *A Strategy of Decision*. New York: Free Press, 1963.

Brewer, Gary D., and Ronald D. Brunner, eds. *Political Development and Change: A Policy Approach*. New York: Free Press, 1975.

Brown, B. W., Jr. "Statistics, Scientific Method, and Smoking." In *Statistics: A Guide to the Unknown*, edited by Judith M. Tanur et al. San Francisco: Holden-Day, 1972.

Buchanan, James M. *The Bases for Collective Action*. Morristown, N.J.: General Learning Press, 1971.

———. *The Demand and Supply of Public Goods*. Chicago: Rand McNally, 1968.

Cain, Glen G., ed. *Symposium on the Graduated Work Incentive Experiment. Journal of Human Resources* 9(1974): 156–278, 504–555.

Campbell, Angus, Philip E. Converse, and Willard L. Rodgers. *The Quality of American Life*. New York: Russell Sage Foundation, 1976.

Campbell, Donald T. "Measuring the Effects of Social Innovations by Means of Time Series." In *Statistics: A Guide to the Unknown*, edited by Judith M. Tanur et al. San Francisco: Holden-Day, 1972.

———. "Reforms as Experiments." *American Psychologist* 24(1969): 409–429.

Cesario, Frank J. "Value of Time in Recreation Benefit Studies." *Land Economics* 52(1976): 32–41.

Cleveland, Donald E. *Speed and Speed Control*. In revision of *Traffic Control and Roadway Elements in Their Relationship to Highway Safety*. Washington, D.C.: Highway Users Federation for Safety and Mobility, 1970.

Coase, R. H. "The Problem of Social Cost." *Journal of Law and Economics* 3(1960): 1–44.

Cobb, Roger W., and Charles D. Elder. *Participation in American Politics: The Dynamics of Agenda-Building*. Boston: Allyn and Bacon, 1972.

Coleman, James S. *Community Conflict*. New York: Free Press, 1956.

———. *Policy Research in the Social Sciences*. Morristown, N.J.: General Learning Press, 1972.

———. *Power and the Structure of Society*. New York: Norton, 1974.

———, Ernest Q. Campbell, Carol J. Hobson, James McPartland, Alexander M. Mood, Frederic D. Weinfeld, and Robert L. York. *Equality of Educational Opportunity*. Washington, D.C.: U.S. Govt. Print. Off., 1966.

Coleman, James S., Sara D. Kelly, and John A. Moore. *Trends in School Segregation, 1968–73*. Washington, D.C.: Urban Institute, 1975.

Coplin, William D. "Introduction to the Analysis of Public Policy From a Problem Solving Perspective." Learning Packages in the Policy Sciences PS6. Syracuse, N.Y.: Syracuse University, International Relations Program, 1975.

————, and Michael K. O'Leary. *Everyman's Prince: A Guide to Understanding Political Problems* 2d ed. North Scituate, Mass.: Duxbury, Press, 1976.

Council, Forrest M., Linda Pitts, Michael Sadof, and Olin K. Dart. *An Examination of the Effects of the 55 mph Speed Limit on North Carolina Accidents.* Chapel Hill, N.C.: University of North Carolina, Highway Safety Research Center, 1975.

Davis, Otto A., and Morton I. Kamien. "Externalities, Information and Alternative Collective Action." In *Public Expenditures and Policy Analysis*, edited by Robert H. Haveman and Julius Margolis. Chicago: Rand McNally, 1977.

Dorn, Dean S., and Gary L. Long. "Sociology and the Radical Right." *American Sociologist* 7(1972): 8–9.

Downs, Anthony. *Inside Bureaucracy.* Boston: Little, Brown, 1967.

Dunnett, Charles W. "Drug Screening." In *Statistics: A Guide to the Unknown*, edited by Judith M. Tanur et al. San Francisco: Holden-Day, 1972.

Dye, Thomas R. *Understanding Public Policy.* Englewood Cliffs, N.J.: Prentice-Hall, 1972.

Etzioni, Amitai. *The Active Society.* New York: Free Press, 1968.

————. *Social Problems.* Englewood Cliffs, N.J.: Prentice-Hall, 1976.

Faigin, Barbara Moyer. *1975 Societal Costs of Motor Vehicle Accidents.* Washington, D.C.: National Highway Traffic Safety Administration, 1976.

Fairley, William B. "Accidents on Route 2: Two-Way Structures for Data." In *Statistics and Public Policy*, edited by William B. Fairley and Frederick Mosteller. Reading, Mass.: Addison-Wesley, 1977.

Federal Highway Administration. *Traffic Speed Trends.* Washington, D.C.: U.S. Govt. Print. Off., 1976.

Frankena, William K. *Ethics.* Englewood Cliffs, N.J.: Prentice-Hall, 1963.

Freeman, A. Myrick, III. *The Economics of Pollution Control and Environmental Quality.* Morristown, N.J.: General Learning Press, 1971.

Friedman, Robert S. *Professionalism: Expertise and Policy Making.* Morristown, N.J.: General Learning Press, 1971.

Friedrichs, Robert W. "Dialectical Sociology: Toward a Resolution of the Current 'Crisis' in Sociology." *British Journal of Sociology* 23(1972): 263–274.

Galbraith, John Kenneth. *The New Industrial State.* Boston: Houghton Mifflin, 1967.

Garn, Harvey A., Michael J. Flax, Michael Springer, and Jeremy B. Taylor. *Models for Indicator Development: A Framework for Policy Analysis.* Washington, D.C.: Urban Institute, 1976.

Gellhorn, Walter, Clark Byse, and Paul R. Verkuil, eds. *Problems in Administrative Law*. Chicago: Foundation Press, 1974.

Gell-Mann, Murray. "How Scientists Can Really Help." *Physics Today* 24(1971) 23–25.

Gerth, Hans H., and C. Wright Mills, trans. and eds. *From Max Weber: Essays in Sociology*. New York: Oxford University Press, 1946.

Gilbert, John P., Richard J. Light, and Frederick Mosteller. "Assessing Social Innovations: An Empirical Base for Policy." In *Benefit-Cost and Policy Analysis 1974*, edited by Richard Zeckhauser et al. Chicago: Aldine, 1975.

Goldberger, Arthur S., and Otis Dudley Duncan, eds. *Structural Equation Models in the Social Sciences*. New York: Seminar Press, 1973.

Gramlich, Edward M., and Patricia P. Koshel. *Educational Performance Contracting: An Evaluation of an Experiment*. Washington, D.C.: Brookings, 1975.

Grant, Gerald. "Shaping Social Policy: The Politics of the Coleman Report." *Teachers College Record* 75(1973): 15–54.

Habermas, Jürgen. *Theory and Practice*. Translated by John Viertel. Boston: Beacon, 1973.

Halperin, Morton H. *Bureaucratic Politics and Foreign Policy*. Washington, D.C.: Brookings, 1974.

————. *The Role of the Military in the Formation and Execution of National Security Policy*. Morristown, N.J.: General Learning Press, 1974.

Hargrove, Erwin C. *The Missing Link: The Study of the Implementation of Social Policy*. Washington, D.C.: Urban Institute, 1975.

Haveman, Robert H., and Julius Margolis, eds. *Public Expenditure and Policy Analysis*. 2d ed. Chicago: Rand McNally, 1977.

Haveman, Robert H., and Burton A. Weisbrod. "Defining Benefits of Public Programs: Some Guidance for Policy Analysts." *Policy Analysis* 1(1975): 169–196.

Hawley, Willis D. "Horses Before Carts: Developing Adaptive Schools and the Limits of Innovation." Durham, N.C.: Duke University, Institute of Policy Sciences and Public Affairs, 1976.

————, and David Rogers, eds. *Improving the Quality of Urban Management*. Beverly Hills, Calif.: Sage Publications, 1974.

Heller, Walter W. *Economic Growth and Environmental Quality: Collision or Co-Existence?* Morristown, N.J.: General Learning Press, 1973.

Henshel, Richard L., and Leslie W. Kennedy. "Self-Altering Prophecies: Consequences for the Feasibility of Social Prediction." *General Systems* 18(1973): 119–126.

Herber, Bernard P. *Modern Public Finance*. Homewood, Ill.: Irwin, 1971.

Hewitt, John P., and Peter M. Hall. "Social Problems, Problematic Situations, and Quasi-Theories." *American Sociological Review* 38(1973): 367–374.

Hicks, Donald A., H. Brent McKnight, and Michael Dailey. "The Charlotte-Mecklenburg School Busing Controversy, (1965–71)." Unpublished case study. Chapel Hill, N.C.: University of North Carolina, 1973.

Hicks, John R. "The Rehabilitation of Consumers' Surplus." *Review of Economic Studies* 9(1941): 108–116.

Hilsman, Roger. *To Move a Nation.* Garden City, N.Y.: Doubleday, 1967.

Hirschman, Albert O. *Exit, Voice, and Loyalty.* Cambridge, Mass.: Harvard University Press, 1970.

Hochman, Harold M. "Rule Change and Transitional Equity." In *Redistribution Through Public Choice,* edited by Harold M. Hochman and George E. Peterson. New York: Columbia University Press, 1974.

Holsti, Ole R. "The Baseline Problem in Statistics: Examples from the Study of American Public Policy." *Journal of Politics* 37(1975): 187–201.

Huitt, Ralph K. "Political Feasibility." In *Political Science and Public Policy,* edited by Austin Ranney. Chicago: Markham, 1968.

Janowitz, Morris. "Sociological Models and Social Policy." In *Political Conflict,* by Morris Janowitz. Chicago: Quadrangle Books, 1970.

Jones, Charles O. *An Introduction to the Study of Public Policy.* 2d ed. North Scituate, Mass.: Duxbury Press, 1977.

Kaufman, Herbert. *Administrative Feedback: Monitoring Subordinates' Behavior.* Washington, D.C.: Brookings, 1973.

Kemeny, John G., J. Laurie Snell, and Gerald L. Thompson. *Introduction to Finite Mathematics.* Englewood Cliffs, N.J.: Prentice-Hall, 1957.

Knight, Frank H. "Some Fallacies in the Interpretation of Social Cost." *Quarterly Journal of Economics* 38(1924): 582–606.

Kolko, Joyce, and Gabriel Kolko. *The Limits of Power.* New York: Harper & Row, 1972.

Land, Kenneth C. "Social Indicator Models: An Overview." In *Social Indicator Models,* edited by Kenneth C. Land and Seymour Spilerman. New York: Russell Sage Foundation, 1974.

Landau, Martin. "On the Concept of a Self-Correcting Organization." *Public Administration Review* 33(1973): 533–542.

Lave, Charles A. "Transportation and Energy: Some Current Myths." *Policy Analysis* 4(1978): 297–315.

Lewis, Margaret C. "Evaluating the Effects of Lower Speed Limits on Safety: A Case Study of Route 2." Cambridge, Mass.: Harvard University, John F. Kennedy School of Government, 1973.

Lindblom, Charles E. *The Intelligence of Democracy.* New York: Free Press, 1965.

———. *Politics and Markets.* New York: Basic Books, 1977.

Long, Norton R. "The Local Community as an Ecology of Games." *American Journal of Sociology* 44(1958): 251–261.

McCarthy, John D., and Mayer N. Zald. *The Trend of Social Movements in America: Professionalization and Resource Mobilization.* Morristown, N.J.: General Learning Press, 1973.

MacRae, Duncan, Jr. *The Social Function of Social Science.* New Haven, Conn.: Yale University Press, 1976.

———. "Professions and Social Sciences as Sources of Public Values." *Soundings* 60(1977): 3–21.

Marmor, Theodore R. *The Politics of Medicare.* Rev. ed. Chicago: Aldine, 1973.

Marrow, Alfred J. *The Practical Theorist: The Life and Work of Kurt Lewin.* New York: Basic Books, 1969.

May, Ernest R. *"Lessons" of the Past.* New York: Oxford, 1973.

Mayer, Robert R. *Social Science and Institutional Change.* Washington D.C.: U.S. Department of Health, Education, and Welfare, 1978.

Mazur, Allan. "Disputes Between Experts." *Minerva* 11(1973): 243–262.

Meade, James E. "External Economies and Diseconomies in a Competitive Situation." *Economic Journal* 62(1952): 54–67.

Meltsner, Arnold. "Political Feasibility and Policy Analysis." *Public Administration Review* 32(1972): 859–867.

Merewitz, Leonard, and Stephen H. Sosnick. *The Budget's New Clothes.* Chicago: Markham, 1971.

Mills, Warner E., Jr. "Martial Law in East Texas." Inter-University Case Program 53. Indianapolis: Bobbs-Merrill, 1960.

Mishan, Edward J. *Economics for Social Decisions.* New York: Praeger, 1973.

Moses, Lincoln E., and Frederick Mosteller. "Safety of Anesthetics." In *Statistics: A Guide to the Unknown,* edited by Judith M. Tanur et al.

Mosteller, Frederick, and Daniel P. Moynihan. *On Equality of Educational Opportunity.* New York: Vintage, 1972.

Moynihan, Daniel P. "Income by Right." *New Yorker* 48(1973): I, 13 Jan., 34–57; II, 20 Jan., 60–79; III, 27 Jan., 57–81.

———. *The Politics of a Guaranteed Income.* New York: Random House, 1973.

Musgrave, Richard A., and Peggy B. Musgrave. *Public Finance in Theory and Practice.* New York: McGraw-Hill, 1973.

de Neufville, Judith I. *Social Indicators and Public Policy.* New York: American Elsevier, 1974.

Neuhauser, D., and A. M. Lewicki. "National Health Insurance and the Sixth Stool Guaiac." *Policy Analysis* 2(1976): 175–196.

Niskanen, William A., Jr. *Bureaucracy and Representative Government*. Chicago: Aldine-Atherton, 1971.

Ogburn, William F. *Social Change*. New York: B. W. Huebsch, 1922.

Okun, Arthur M. *Equality and Efficiency: The Big Tradeoff*. Washington, D.C.: Brookings, 1975.

Olson, Mancur, Jr. *The Logic of Collective Action*. Cambridge, Mass.: Harvard University Press, 1965.

————. "The Principle of 'Fiscal Equivalence.' " *American Economic Review* 59(1969): 479–487.

Oppenlander, J. C. "A Theory on Vehicular Speed Regulation." *Highway Research Board Bulletin* 341 (1962): 77–91.

Page, W. Johnson, Alexander French, and Joseph E. Ullman. "Estimated Highway Fuel Savings in 1975." *Federal Highway Administration Bulletin* 18 Nov. 1976.

Parsons, Talcott. "Social Strains in America—1955." In *The Radical Right*, edited by Daniel Bell. Garden City, N.Y.: Doubleday, 1963.

Patton, Carl V. "A Seven-Day Project." *Policy Analysis* 1(1975): 731–753.

Pignataro, Louis J. *Traffic Engineering: Theory and Practice*. Englewood Cliffs, N.J.: Prentice-Hall, 1973.

Plaut, Thomas F. A. "Fluoridation in a New England Town." Report prepared for University of Michigan School of Public Health. Ann Arbor, Mich., about 1965–1970.

Porter, Sylvia. "Maybe Zip Code Kept You from Getting a Loan." Raleigh, N.C., *News and Observer*, 22 Sept. 1977.

Quade, E. S. *Analysis for Public Decisions*. New York: American Elsevier, 1975.

Raiffa, Howard. *Decision Analysis*. Reading, Mass.: Addison-Wesley, 1968.

Rawls, John. *A Theory of Justice*. Cambridge, Mass.: Harvard University Press, 1971.

Riecken, Henry W., and Robert F. Boruch, eds. *Social Experimentation*. New York: Academic Press, 1974.

Riker, William H., and Peter C. Ordeshook. *An Introduction to Positive Political Theory*. Englewood Cliffs, N.J.: Prentice-Hall, 1973.

Riordan, William L. *Plunkitt of Tammany Hall*. 1905. New York: E. P. Dutton & Co., 1963.

Rivlin, Alice M. *Systematic Thinking for Social Action*. Washington, D.C.: Brookings, 1971.

Rogers, David. *110 Livingston Street*. New York: Random House, 1968.

Ross, H. Laurence, Donald T. Campbell, and Gene V. Glass. "Determining the Social Effects of a Legal Reform: The British 'Breathalyser' Crackdown of 1967." *American Behavioral Scientist* 15(1970): 110–113.

Rossi, Peter H., and Walter Williams, eds. *Evaluating Social Programs*. New York: Seminar Press, 1972.

Rubington, Earl, and Martin S. Weinberg, eds. *The Study of Social Problems*. 2d ed. New York: Oxford University Press, 1977.

Salamon, Lester S. "The Time Dimension in Policy Analysis: The Case of the New Deal Land Reform Experiments." Working Paper 8741. Durham, N.C.: Duke University, Institute of Policy Sciences and Public Affairs, 1974.

Salasin, Susan. "Exploring Goal-Free Evaluation: An Interview with Michael Scriven." *Evaluation* 2(1974): 9–16.

Samuelson, Paul A. "The Pure Theory of Public Expenditure." *Review of Economics and Statistics* 36(1954):387–389.

Savas, E. S. "Policy Analysis for Local Government: Public vs. Private Refuse Collection." *Policy Analysis* 3(1977): 49–74.

Schattschneider, Edgar E. *The Semi-Sovereign People*. New York: Holt, Rinehart, and Winston, 1960.

Schmenner, Roger W. "Bus Subsidies: The Case for Route-by-Route Bidding in Connecticut." *Policy Analysis* 2(1976): 409–430.

Schultze, Charles L. *The Politics and Economics of Public Spending*. Washington, D.C.: Brookings, 1968.

Scriven, Michael. "The Methodology of Evaluation." In *Perspectives of Curriculum Evaluation*, edited by Ralph W. Tyler, Robert M. Gagne, and Michael Scriven. Chicago: Rand McNally, 1967.

Shumate, Robert P. *Effect of Increased Patrol on Accidents, Diversion, and Speed*. Evanston, Ill.: Northwestern University Traffic Institute, 1958.

Simon, Julian L. "Interpersonal Welfare Comparisons Can Be Made—and Used for Redistribution Decisions." *Kyklos* 27(1974): 63–98.

———. "Some Principles of Practical Welfare Economics." *Management Science* 13(1967): B-621–B-630.

Smigel, Erwin O., ed. *Handbook on the Study of Social Problems*. Chicago: Rand McNally, 1971.

Solomon, David. *Accidents on Main Rural Highways Related to Speed, Driver, and Vehicle*. U.S. Department of Commerce, Bureau of Public Roads. Washington, D.C.: U.S. Govt. Print. Off., 1964.

Steiner, Gilbert Y. *The Children's Cause*. Washington, D.C.: Brookings, 1976.

Steiner, Peter O. "The Public Sector and the Public Interest." In *Public Expenditures and Policy Analysis*, edited by Robert H. Haveman and Julius Margolis. 2d ed. Chicago: Rand McNally, 1977.

Stockfisch, J. A. *The Political Economy of Bureaucracy*. Morristown, N.J.: General Learning Press, 1972.

Tanur, Judith M., et al., ed. *Statistics: A Guide to the Unknown.* San Francisco: Holden-Day, 1972.

Temporary National Economic Committee. *Petroleum Industry Hearings.* New York: American Petroleum Institute, 1942.

Thompson, Victor A. *Decision Theory, Pure and Applied.* Morristown, N.J.: General Learning Press, 1971.

Titus, Robert E. "Speed Regulations and Other Operational Controls." In *Transportation and Traffic Engineering Handbook,* edited by John E. Baerwald, Matthew J. Huber, and Louise E. Kafer. Englewood Cliffs, N.J.: Prentice-Hall, 1976.

Tolchin, Martin. "O'Neill's Role as Speaker Draws Praise." *New York Times,* 2 Jan. 1978.

Uhlenberg, Peter. "Changing Structure of the Older Population of the USA During the Twentieth Century." *The Gerontologist* 17(1977): 197–202.

United States Bureau of the Census. *Statistical Abstract of the United States: 1976.* Washington, D.C.: U.S. Govt. Print. Off., 1976.

Vaupel, James W. "Early Death: An American Tragedy." *Law and Contemporary Problems* 40(1976): 73–121.

————. "Muddling Through Analytically." In *Improving the Quality of Urban Management,* edited by Willis D. Hawley and David Rogers. Beverly Hills, Calif.: Sage Publications, 1974.

Weiler, Daniel, et al. "A Public School Voucher Demonstration." In *Evaluation Studies Review Annual,* vol. 1, edited by Gene V. Glass. Beverly Hills, Calif.: Sage Publications, 1976.

Weinstein, Milton D., and William B. Stason. "Foundations of Cost-Effectiveness Analysis for Health and Medical Practice." *New England Journal of Medicine* 296(1977): 716–721.

Weiss, Carol H. *Evaluation Research.* Englewood Cliffs, N.J.: Prentice-Hall, 1972.

Wildavsky, Aaron. *Budgeting: A Comparative Theory of Budgetary Processes.* Boston: Little, Brown, 1975.

Williams, Walter. *Social Policy Research and Analysis.* New York: American Elsevier, 1971.

Winfrey, Robley. *Economic Analysis for Highways.* Scranton, Pa.: International Textbook Company, 1969.

World Almanac 1975. New York: Newspaper Enterprise Association, 1974.

Wright, G. O. *A General Procedure for Systems Study.* Wright-Patterson Air Force Base, Ohio, 1960. Reference from *Systems Analysis,* edited by Stanford L. Optner. Harmondsworth, Middlesex, England: Penguin, 1973.

Zeckhauser, Richard, and Donald Shepard. "Where Now for Saving Lives?" *Law and Contemporary Problems* 40(1976): 5–45.

Competition: in education, 278; market, 171, 174–178
Concord Township, Pa., 87
Connecticut: bottle bill, 208; speed limit, 275
Consensus, 191, 228
Constituencies, 227–228, 234; internal/external, 271
Constraints as criteria, 54–55, 177–178, 265
Consumer protection, 172–174, 188, 190
Consumer Protection Agency, proposed, 235–236
Consumer surplus, 164, 167
Continuous alternatives model, 106–110
Contract enforcement, 173
Control groups, random/nonrandom, 266, 267, 274–275, 276
Cost and facility sharing, 176
Cost-benefit analysis, 8–9, 45, 46, 48, 51, 61–64, 66, 68, 111, 120, 189, 273; personal, 49–50, 123–124
Cost curves, 165, 166
Cost-effectiveness ratio, 63
Costs, 165–190 passim; speed limit, 142–145
Crime, 55, 98, 101–102, 190–191
"Crimes without victims," 189
Cross-sectional data, 102, 110, 274
Cuban missile crisis, 3, 21, 24, 103, 231; and blockade, 233–234

Dam construction, 33, 61, 62
Day care, 19
Decision analysis. See Decision trees
Decision-making costs, 170, 189
Decision systems, 220, 226–229; problem of changing, 21–23
Decision trees, 115–119; and medical screening problem, 119–124
Decreasing-cost collective goods, 182–183, 185
Decreasing-cost monopoly, 174–176
Demand and supply curves, 162–168; Texas oil case, 211–213
Democratic process, 225–226
Denver, 84
Dependent variables, 101, 112, 274

Deposit-bottles case, 19, 29–30, 34, 61, 67–68, 201–208, 228, 236
Desegregation, 49, 52, 65, 105, 107–109, 110, 224, 233
Differential pricing, 161
Discounting, 63, 68
Discrimination, economic, 67
District of Columbia, 82
"Do-nothing" option, 34, 61–62, 97, 273
Douglas, William O., 90
Downs, Anthony, 173
"Dynamic" models, 186–187, 274

Economic criteria, 45, 58. See also Cost-benefit analysis; Pareto criterion
Economic growth rate, 186
Economic indicators, 27, 112
Economic power, distribution of, 58
Economies of scale, 174
Economy, stabilization of, 186
Education: as collective good, 183–184; and equity, 65; government policy to promote, 190; Head Start, 231, 269, 270, 271; as "merit good," 188; performance contracting for, 97, 276–277; and policy implementation, 223, 224; statistical models of, 107–108, 110; voucher systems for, 97, 277–278. See also Busing; Desegregation
"Educational" lobbying, and bottle bill, 207, 208
Effectiveness, 112; vs. efficiency, 272
Efficiency, 46; and benefit-cost ratio, 63–64; vs. effectiveness, 272; vs. equity, 64–65, 160–161; and external costs, 178–179; productive, 165, 170
Elder, Charles D., 232
Electricity rates, 175, 185
Employee, role of, 220–221, 226, 268–269
Environmental Protection Agency, 203, 206
Epidemics model, 113–114
Equal Rights Amendment, 68
Equality of Educational Opportunity. See Coleman Report
Equilibrium effects, 61; market, 167, 170, 171; transition states, 186–187
Equilibrium labor price, 168

Political communities, 8–9, 56, 97, 225–226

Political feasibility, 6–7, 9, 10–11, 119; and agenda setting, 232–235; and indirect influence, 235–237; models and social science, 239–240; and optimum speed limit, 150–152; and personal feasibility, 237–238; and policy desirability, 49–51; of policy enactment and implementation, 222–232; and program evaluation, 273; and social roles of analyst, 220–222

Pollution, 178–179, 190

Population: adaptation and reaction of affected, 112–113, 115, 265; intergroup comparisons, 28–29; target, 112, 275

Power structures, 225, 228, 240; making changes in, 25

Predicting model, 224–225

Preference alteration, and government action, 190–191

Preference satisfaction ethic, 57–58, 60, 64; and democratic process, 225; and free market, 160, 168, 172; maximization within constraints, 54–55; vs. "merit goods," 188–189; and program evaluation, 272; and "true preferences," 181

Price signals, 169, 170

Pricing practices, 161, 162–168, 175–176

Prince Georges Co., Md., 85

Prior analysis, 270

Priorities, 230, 232–235

Private collective action, 189

Private goods, and collective goods, 180, 183–186

Probabilities, 104, 105, 117

Problem definition, 7–8; choice of, 33–35; and problem situation, 17–26; and program evaluation, 270–272; and use of statistics, 26–30

Problem redefinition, 30–33, 95

Problem situation, 23–26; and analyst's problem, 17–21; and policy alternatives, 95

Procter & Gamble, 235–236

Producer surplus, 167

Product differentiation, 177

Production costs, 165, 168

Productivity, 164, 165, 170, 176–177

Professionals, 7, 56–57, 222; and evaluative research, 267–268

Profit-maximizing, 164–165, 166, 178

Profit rates, guaranteed, 175–176

Program evaluation, 12, 46, 114, 232, 265, 270–276; data accessibility, 270, 273; formative vs. summative, 269; and professionals, 267–268

Program goals and side effects, 272, 275

Program managers, 266–267, 268–270, 272, 273

Program termination, 273–274

Progressive taxation, 68

Prohibitions, 190

Property rights, 22, 66, 172, 178

Public-interest groups, 221, 226, 227

Public policy, defined, 3

Public services, 161, 276

Public support: mobilization of, 26, 32–33, 221, 225, 233; sources of, 25–26

Public utilities, 174–176, 185

Quarles, John R., Jr., 29–30, 202–203

Quasi-experiments, 266

"Quasi-market policies," 97, 179, 190, 276–279

Ramapo, N.Y., 88

Rand Corporation, 277

Random/nonrandom control, 266, 276

Rawls, John, 68

Regan, Edward V., 205

Regression models, 109–110

Regulatory agencies, 175, 190

Reitze, Arnold W., Jr., 86, 90

Richmond, Frederick, 204

Rivalness/nonrivalness, 180–181, 182, 183, 184, 185

Rouse, James, 86

"Rule of capture," 215–216

"Rules of the game," 226, 237

Salamon, Lester S., 268

Samuelson, Paul A., 180

San Jose, Calif., 83, 277